2 3 / 5

Zombies in the Academy

1) why, if we know and can articulate
this, does it persist? - what to do?

2) the problem with collections is that they are
repetitive - how many times did what is a
zombie have to be dissected?

3) trope!

4) satisfaction survey, tendancy to 'norm' p 222
Reduction of educators to products.

5) Solutions also in zombies are us

6) P 305

Zombies in the Academy
Living Death in Higher Education

Andrew Whelan, Ruth Walker and Christopher Moore

Zombies-book. creative.
Conceptions of teaching, + epistemology - relativism = creative
dualism = non-creative ?
contested, but open minded commitment to a position.

intellect Bristol, UK / Chicago, USA

First published in the UK in 2013 by
Intellect, The Mill, Parnall Road, Fishponds, Bristol, BS16 3JG, UK

First published in the USA in 2013 by
Intellect, The University of Chicago Press, 1427 E. 60th Street,
Chicago, IL 60637, USA

A catalogue record for this book is available from the
British Library.

Cover designer: Ellen Thomas
Copy-editor: MPS Technologies
Production manager: Jelena Stanovnik
Typesetting: Planman Technologies

ISBN: 978-1-84150-714-9

Printed and bound by Hobbs, UK

Contents

Introduction

Andrew Whelan, Ruth Walker and Christopher Moore

This collection brings together scholars and writers from around the world to confront the 'living death' of higher education. The contributors break out of their fortified offices and bunkered lecture halls, and claw their way free of burial mounds of student marking, grant applications and committee minutes, equipped not with shotguns and fire axes, but with a radical metaphor and a critical eye. Alternately, they come shuffling and decrepit towards you out of the shadows, with lifeless expressions, blank hunger and the stench of death surrounding them.

The figure of the zombie here provides an opportunity to express unease and dissent about the state of higher education. Working from a range of disciplines, together we refuse to helplessly succumb, choosing instead to diagnose, rally resistance, produce inoculation and contemplate an antidote. Some voices within this volume speculate that perhaps the zombie apocalypse has already happened in the academy, and that recognizing this might provide us with the best means of understanding and dealing with the conditions under which those who live, work and study in universities operate.

The chapters that follow, then, test the various ways in which universities and their populations, systems, customs, processes and pressures can be understood as undead. They do so with the aim of reanimating – or at least 'undeadening' – the current debates about the future of the sector. As such, the volume is intended as a contribution to the emerging field sometimes referred to as 'critical university studies', which investigates and critiques the massified education system and advocates on behalf of the progressive values and ideals that universities claim to embody (for example, Collini 2012; Donoghue 2008; Evans 2004; Giroux 2011; Newfield 2008; Nussbaum 2010; Readings 1996; Slaughter and Leslie 1997). Cris Shore describes the contemporary scene as follows:

What we have witnessed here is the transformation of the traditional liberal and Enlightenment idea of the university as a place of higher learning into the modern idea of the university as corporate enterprise whose primary concern is with market share, servicing the needs of commerce, maximizing economic return and investment, and gaining competitive advantage in the 'Global Knowledge Economy'. Several factors are driving this process: the cost-cutting fiscal regime of 'economic rationalism' in which government funding for universities has been steadily eroded; the move from 'elite' to 'mass' university education, which has brought many more students with no comparable increase in permanent staff numbers; and the trend towards universities increasingly operating like private businesses, accompanied by the emergence of higher education as a significant export industry. Audits, performance indicators, competitive benchmarking exercises, league tables, management by targets, and punitive research assessment exercises and periodic teaching quality reviews are the technologies that have been used to spread new public management methods into the governance of universities – and all at a time when overall government funding for universities and per student has declined.

(2008: 282)

This reconstitution of the higher education sector has led to increasingly untenable discrepancies between what universities espouse as their stated aims, and how they actually work (or do not work).

The academic labour force is already precarious. In Australia, for example, nearly half of all tertiary teaching is provided by sessional or short-term contracted staff (Blackwell 2012). Half of the current Australian academic workforce is reported to be hoping to leave or retire within the next five years (Rea 2011). The casualization of part-time and fixed-term contractual academics, 'growing at the periphery of the professional core', can also be taken as evidence of the 'deprofessionalization and proletarization' of higher education across all European countries (Enders 2000: 31). According to the OECD, the Asian university sector too has turned to greater levels of casual and fixed-term employment to reduce operating costs (Santiago et al. 2008: 153). Research is increasingly commercialized, bureaucratized and rendered obvious and 'auditable' in the fiercely competitive processes of securing grants. These structurally driven discrepancies are corrosive of academic productivity and intellectual freedom, and thus of the core business of the institution (Boden and Epstein 2011). They involve managerial strategies of 'asset sweating', and as such have deleterious affective consequences for those living through them (Burrows 2012; Sievers 2008).

As soon as we look closely at the university (and particularly its gargantuan *scale*), we find almost immediately that we are looking also at a host of other phenomena at the porous boundaries of the institution: ubiquitous technology and the digitization of print cultures; the labour market and the extent to which universities are (or should be) designed to service it; the expansive bloat of immaterial labour as it grows beyond office time in an always-on culture; student debt and youth unemployment; international migration; social mobility, social closure, and the perpetuation of privilege; the contexts of knowledge production and transfer and the fields of its legitimation; the paywalls of academic publishing for publicly funded research; the nature and commitments of the public sector; new public management and the neo-liberal state; the colonizing ascendance of market fundamentalism (for instance, branding exercises that wilfully evacuate the ethics and ideals of academic culture), and so on. These are some of the sorts of contexts through which higher education institutions are articulated. The overall implication is that the university, despite the nostalgic image of an elitist, inviolate ivory tower, has become a central location in contemporary societies for testing out the relations between the public, the market, and the state, and as such a kind of laboratory of the social.

4

Ulrich Beck famously referred to 'zombie categories', which continue to circulate despite being emptied of meaning in contemporary social and political contexts (Beck 2002: 47; Beck and Beck-Gernsheim 2002: 203). These are not yet abandoned husks of institutional categories, or ways of thinking, that continue to be used despite their increasing irrelevance, and as such can come to distort not only how things are conceptualized or imagined, but also how things are done. The 'ivory tower' model of the university, along with most of the other traditional archetypes of the institution, is just such a category: an undead, lingering ghoul. Given the changes that have radically reconstituted the sector over the last 30 years, these traditional imaginings are indeed dead, and yet bizarrely still alive.

The contributions that follow, however, are not simply pessimistic or cynical accounts of the straitened circumstances under which those who populate universities carry out their peculiar work. They also reflect the creativity, wit, imagination and commitment with which this work is conducted. As the anthropologist of academic culture Eli Thorkelson (2012) says of his research:

> [I]t's too easy to reduce universities to rather stale bureaucratic conceptions, to a boring metanarrative about the state and capital, for instance. So part of the project has to be to confront the gothic element of academic life, its moments of dejection and rejection and abjection, its fantastic, romantic qualities, its dynamics of lunacy and wasted effort, its moments of ignorance and forgetting. The academic world has structures of chaos as well as structures of order; it enchants as much as it disenchants; it's not only about the play of socioeconomic structure, but about the dramatic, poetic, affective play of everyday life.

This collection takes up Thorkelson's call, celebrating and exposing all that is absurd, ridiculous, abject, gratuitous and excessive – the destructive, the perverse, the unhinged, the redundant, the insane, the morbid and the grotesque in twenty-first-century higher education. Coming from a variety of perspectives, these chapters work through the figure of the zombie as a sign of our sense of what it means to occupy the field of contemporary higher education.

As such, the collection also contributes to the study of the zombie in popular culture, drawing on the power and ambiguity of the zombie as a critical metaphor, relevant also to a broader audience beyond the academy. As Comaroff and Comaroff (2002) have compellingly argued, the zombie is uncanny in its astuteness as a political metaphor, through which anxieties about globalization, economic forces, power relations and changing conceptualizations of identity and the body are articulated.

The reader will note recurring references across the collected essays to that primal scene for the zombie as a mode of socio-political critique: George Romero's *The Night of the Living Dead* (1968), where survivors barricade themselves in an isolated farmhouse in the face of a ravenous horde of flesh-eating ghouls. Various authors use this scene to interrogate the state of higher education: the survivors are figured as academics bunkering down in a disintegrating university, with the zombie horde clamouring at the door, cast either as bureaucratic processes or the monstrously transformed student body. Some authors position themselves as the zombies shuffling about outside, deliberately drawing attention to the ossified processes of the academy, and the moribund writing that continues to circulate in many current scholarly publications. Still others might be unknowing and as yet asymptomatic carriers, caught by the contagion that is zombified scholarship but steadfastly classifying themselves as healthy and critically-thinking survivors.

The book is divided into four sections, each addressing the theme of the undead in the academy in distinct contexts. Amongst the essays, shorter ficto-critical and other experimental pieces can be found. These short pieces move beyond and thereby illustrate the limits of traditional (we might say zombified) academic research and writing practices, which are already recurring motifs in the other, more 'orthodox' scholarly contributions. While each chapter pursues and develops its own argument in accordance with the conventions of scholarly logic (in much the same way the zombie genre follows, inflects and pursues the inexorable logic of the zombie outbreak), all warrant a reading attentive to the affect expressed by the authors, and what that might indicate about the attenuated conditions of academic practice.

The first section addresses the corporate nature of the contemporary university. In 'First as tragedy, then as corpse', Andrew Whelan exhumes an early instance of audit culture in the work of the English utilitarian Jeremy Bentham. Following this, Rowena Harper presents a critical analysis of the instrumentalizing policy language with which students are framed and positioned as 'zombie learners', in much the same way that academics are positioned so as to perform excellence and quality. Rowan Wilken and Christian McCrea discuss press coverage of the 'crisis' in higher education as a discourse of lamentation, and link this to the peculiar rhythms that constitute academic life. Drawing on extensive interview data, Holly Randell-Moon, Sue Saltmarsh and Wendy Sutherland-Smith, in their chapter 'The living dead and the dead living', describe the survival strategies academics use. Ann Deslandes and Kristian Adamson then more broadly contextualize the preceding chapters with regard to discrepancies and tensions in the hierarchy of university employment, making a case for a 'zombie solidarity'. The section concludes with David Slattery's 'The journal of Doctor Wallace', a cautionary short story about the university undead.

The second section of the book, 'Moribund content and infectious technologies', looks to the relationships between digital technologies and the university, concentrating on issues of abundance and lack as these are enacted technologically. Christopher Moore proposes two categories of the zombie, 'undead technologies' and 'zombies processes', as a means to critique institutional responses to the moral and legal relationships formed between the education and technology industries. Martin Paul Eve uses the 'botnet', a network comprising 'bots' or enslaved machines, as a theme in a detailed modelling and analysis of the academic publishing paradigm. Jonathan Marshall then examines the mythic similarity of the cyborg and the zombie contained in the Cybermen of the British science-fiction series *Doctor Who*. His critique of the university experience of computers and computer networking finds that the disorder created by the ordering of the machine is the very guarantor of further machine ordering. Nick Pearce and Elaine Tan review the experience of teaching within the 'virtual learning environments' (VLEs) of British universities, discussing parallels between the massification and commodification of universities through VLEs and the 'zombi' and 'bokor' of the Vodou tradition. Mark Graham, Taylor Shelton and Matthew Zook provide an insight into how the zombie is represented in the geoweb, using geographical data to explore, imagine and reconstruct the world through the rendering of geotagged searches for words associated with the zombie apocalypse. The final contribution for this section is Gordon Carlson and Jim Sosnoski's diagnosis of the zombification of 'glossaried' concepts, where they suggest a range of techno-pedagogical responses to the deadening of meaning in communication and media theory.

In the third section of the book, zombie pedagogies and literacies are addressed more directly. Ruth Walker experiments with academic literacies to model how scholarly emphasis on hyper-citation can both reveal and enact the pervasive anxiety and paranoia that both haunts and deanimates scholarly writing practice. Several authors then describe their own pedagogical practices as they teach inside media studies programmes. From the United States, Jesse Stommel reflects on his experience teaching a multidisciplinary course on zombies in film, literature and new media, where students consider the material and immaterial nature of composition as it rots and decays. Shaun Kimber offers a bleaker vision of the state of English media studies in light of recent political pressures, before proposing a 'collaborative necromancy' of both media education in the United Kingdom and the relationship between teachers and students. Sherry Truffin explores the recurring anxieties and fears experienced by teachers and students in her chapter's close reading of two of Joyce Carol Oates' novels, where the campus is represented as both a source and a scene of terror, a kind of Schoolhouse Gothic. Extending the critiques of audit culture and managerialist universities found in section one, David Marshall offers a fresh perspective on normative academic work in his chapter, 'Queer pedagogies in zombie times', applying an analysis of queer metrics and theories of subjectivity to illuminate contemporary Australian pedagogical conditions. Sara Felix presents a disturbing account of English for Academic Purpose (EAP) programmes that, instead of inducting students into higher levels of scholarly practice as promised, are instead invested in pedagogies that work to zombify students' reading, writing and thinking. She proposes critical thinking as the antibody to this zombification. Focusing on more specific academic literacies, Hans Petter Langtangen, Kent-Andre Mardal and Pål Røtnes use mathematics to indicate ways of escaping the zombie holocaust, demonstrating both a serious orientation to the metaphor and the near delirious pleasures of disciplinary immersion.

The final section of the book addresses 'the post-apocalyptic terrain'. Here Sarah Juliet Lauro, already a major contributor to the study of the zombie (Lauro and Embry 2008; Christie and Lauro 2011), presents some findings from her larger zombie walk project, as she investigates the relationship between zombie events and student protests. David Beer considers 'glossy topics' in his chapter, arguing for the critical relevance of these areas of study and research in times when funding only ever diminishes. In his chapter 'Feverish homeless cannibal', the artist George Pfau investigates ambivalent representations of the figure of the zombie, finding evocative moments where the zombie teeters on the brink between life and death, healthy and sick, home and homeless, individual and group, other and self. The concluding chapter is a ficto-critical piece by Howard Gregory and Annie Jeffrey, reporting from the future about a zombie outbreak that decimated the early twenty-first century. In their optimistically speculative chapter, higher education institutions happily provide the environment and the collaborative learning practices that constitute the means to survive the apocalypse.

That such a book can be produced is indicative of the morbid condition of the denizens of the academic underworld, the fanaticism of intellectual inquiry, the spectacular and almost hallucinatory absurdity of university 'dead time'. Many of our contributing authors are asking: 'can you see what is happening here'? In a similar situation, characters in *Invasion of the Body Snatchers* (Siegel 1956) recoil in horror:

> Oh, God!
> You see them?
> This is where they grow them.
> This is where they cultivate them.
> It's enormous.
> What are we gonna do?
> There are so many.
> We've got to figure out a way of stopping them.

SECTION 1

Zombification in the corporate university

First as tragedy, then as corpse

Andrew Whelan

Further uses of the dead to the living

In the South Cloisters corridor at University College London, there is a large, glass-fronted mahogany case, containing the mortal remains of the English philosophical radical, Jeremy Bentham. Essentially a stuffed mannequin containing Bentham's bones, the 'auto-icon', as he called it, is armed with his walking stick (named 'Dapple', after Sancho Panza's mount), and seated at a small writing table. Bentham's remains, importantly, are *not* at repose: even in death, Bentham remains diligently and tirelessly productive – he is never finished being never finished. Instructions regarding the auto-icon are presented in harried style in Bentham's will:

> [T]he whole figure may be seated in a Chair usually occupied by me when living in the attitude in which I am sitting when engaged in thought in the course of the time employed in writing I direct that the body thus prepared shall be transferred to my executor He will cause the skeleton to be clad in one of the suits of black occasionally worn by me The Body so clothed together with the chair and the staff in my later years borne by me he will take charge of And for containing the whole apparatus he will cause to be prepared an appropriate box or case and will cause to be engraved in conspicuous characters on a plate to be affixed thereon and also on the labels on the glass cases in which the preparations of the soft parts of my body shall be contained as for example as in the manner used in the case of wine decanters my name at length with the letters ob. followed by the day of my decease If it should so happen that my personal friends and other Disciples should be disposed to meet together on some day or days of the year for the purpose of commemorating the Founder of the greatest happiness system of morals and legislation my executor will from time to time cause to be conveyed to the room in which they meet the said Box or case with the contents there to be stationed in such part of the room as to the assembled company shall seem meet.
>
> (Marmoy 1958: 80)

Bentham's wishes concerning his 'soft parts' were unfulfilled, and the head now on the body in the case is a wax replacement. Bentham's actual head was for some years stored in his chest cavity; later on it rested at his feet. It has been through a number of unfortunate misadventures, not least of which an only partly successful desiccation process. It is now stored elsewhere in the College, in a locked box requiring four separate keys. Bentham died in 1832. University College London has been in possession of the body for over 160 years. Among the apocrypha that circulate around this bizarre curio is the story (untrue, of course) that the body is presented at College Council meetings, that Bentham desired to be so present, and that when a motion is tied, Bentham usually votes in favour.

This chapter describes the long shadow cast by Bentham's dead hand on the apparently permanent 'crisis' of the university, and with what the location and status of his corpse and corpus can help us to think through.

While the contemporary university evolved alongside and within an overarching Benthamite socio-logic, there have been notable developments since the introduction of 'new public management' in the 1980s (du Gay 2000), and much of the contemporary critical lamentation regarding the university orients to these developments. Extending this orientation, I take zombification here to refer to those processes within the university – and the public sector at large – which, in instrumentalizing action (teaching, research) in the service of pseudo-market principles, decapitate the real ends of that action, while reconstituting the means as a kind of spectral presence of themselves. An undead social space is one in which social activity continues to occur, but as a gruesome and dreary parody of itself, not to meet its own ends but those of its correct and compliant 'recordation'.

I aim to trace here the contours of the origins of the kind of thinking that is now said to have done damage to the university. In doing so, I will describe the peculiar and uncanny consequences that follow from the principles according to which the university is governed, and indicate the senses in which those principles present a deformation of Bentham's already fantastic vision. The main aim of doing so is to show how now allegedly redundant bodies of knowledge constitute, and are articulated through, the very processes that are micromanaging them into the grave.

Grave and elaborate humbug

The impact of Bentham's work across a range of fields is unparalleled. Through his influence over the young John Stuart Mill, who was raised unhappily according to utilitarian principles, Bentham was catalyst to the development of liberal political theory. Mill, who suffered a breakdown at the age of 19 while editing Bentham's five-volume *Rationale of Judicial Evidence*, later remarked that Bentham 'failed in deriving light from other minds' (2003: 64).

Bentham is perhaps most widely encountered today at one remove, through Foucault's account of the Panopticon (1977), originally designed by Bentham with his brother Samuel. In Foucault's treatment, the model prison serves as the disciplinary society's template *par excellence*. For Bentham, this structure is the very material form of transparency, accountability and economy: the fundamental contemporary principles of good governance (Blamires 2008: 314).

Bentham was an early advocate of women's suffrage, animal rights, the abolition of corporal punishment, tolerance for sexual diversity, the separation of church and state, the legalization of trade unions, representative democracy, and a system of welfare. In all of these instances, the principle of utility is the engine of his radicalism. Bentham coined the word 'international'. His contributions to jurisprudence cannot be overstated (Hart 1982; Postema 1986). Robert Peel sought Bentham's advice in the establishment of the police force. Bentham's contributions to the philosophy of language can be evinced by the fact that the 'felicific calculus' underlying utilitarianism is partly derived from his 'theory of fictions', where he proposed that abstract, non-referential moral terms like 'right' or 'wrong' be rearticulated through successfully referential terms like 'pleasure' and 'pain'.

Mack goes so far as to assert that 'Seldom if ever in the history of ideas has a man's thought been so directly and widely translated into action' (1968: 57). Bureaucratic organization as a mode of governance first emerges as a theoretical possibility in Bentham's work (Hume 1981: 8). He made profound contributions to the theory and practice of public administration (Martin 1997), and of accounting (Gallhofer and Haslam 2003). Rational choice, game theory, neoclassical microeconomics, cost-benefit analysis, risk management and SWOT analysis ('strengths, weaknesses, opportunities and threats') are all essentially utilitarian. The principles of new public management find their original expression in Bentham (Bowrey and Smark 2010). It has been suggested that Australia, in particular, is a thoroughly Benthamite state in its culture and organization (Collins 1985), and that state systems of education in both Australia and the United Kingdom developed directly under utilitarian influence (West 1992: 596).

It is unfortunate, therefore, that Bentham's 1815 work on educational reform, *Chrestomathia*, is not more widely read, as it presents a prescient account of the administration and governance of education. Anyone conversant with the contemporary university will recognize the institution run according to

> Principles, having, for their special object, the preservation of *Discipline*: i.e. the effectual and universal performance of the several prescribed *Exercises,* and the exclusion of *disorder:* i.e. of all practices *obstructive* of such performance, or productive of *mischief* in any *other* shape; and, to that end, the correct and complete observance of all *arrangements* and *regulations,* established for either of those purposes …
>
> *Reward economizing* principle.
>
> *Constant and universal Inspection promising* and *securing* principle …
>
> Principles, having, for their special object, the securing the *forthcomingness of Evidence*: viz. in the most correct, complete, durable and easily accessible shape: and thereby the most constant and universal *notoriety* of all *past* matters of *fact,* the knowledge of which can be necessary, or conducive, to the propriety of all *subsequent* proceedings; whether for securing the due performance of *Exercises* … or for the exclusion of *disorder* …
>
> Place-capturing probative exercise employment *maximizing* principle …
>
> *Constantly and universally apposite Scholar-classification securing* principle.

Principles, having, for their special object, the union of the maximum of *despatch* with the maximum of *uniformity*; thereby proportionably *shortening* the *time*, employed in the acquisition of the proposed body of instruction, and *increasing* the *number* of Pupils, made to acquire it, by the *same Teachers*, at the *same time*.
Simplification maximizing, or *Short lesson employing,* principle …
Constantly-uninterrupted-action promising and *effecting* principle.
(Bentham 1843: 29–31, all emphasis in the original unless otherwise indicated)

The list goes on. What, if anything, is amiss with principles such as these?

Sinister interest

The highest art for which training was to be delivered in the Chrestomathia was 'recordation' or bookkeeping: 'the art of securing and perpetuating *Evidence*'. Bentham advocated for education in methods of accounting:

Correct, complete, clear, concise, easy to consult; in case of *error,* so framed as not to *cover* it, but to *afford indication* of it: *appropriate,* i.e. adapted to the particular practical purpose it has in view; the purpose, for the sake of which the labour thus bestowed is expended, in these epithets may be seen the *qualities* desirable in a system of this kind. The new system of instruction, at any rate the original inventor's edition of it, presents to view a perfect specimen of the practice of this art, as applied to those inferior branches of instruction, which it has already taken in hand … In the practice of this most universally useful art, all those Scholars, who, from the lowest up to the highest Stages, in the character of *Teachers, Private Tutors,* or *Monitors,* bear any part in the management of the school, will gradually be initiated, and insensibly perfected: and, in proportion as any *Scholar* appears qualified to take any such part in it, it will be the duty and care of the *Master,* to put the means of so doing into his hands.

(1843: 996)

Such accounting is for Bentham value-neutral, objective and social-scientific. Yet it also has the most to offer in securing collective happiness. Bentham, it must be remembered, campaigned for both the prison and the poorhouse to be converted into places of education – not the other way round (Gallhofer and Haslam 1996: 15). In the science of morals and legislation, assuring accountability, economy, and transparency is a *rational* means of holding the powerful to task. Everyone in the Benthamite universe should be 'empowered' to practice accounting, because it serves as an empirically grounded means of sustained social critique.

Bentham's lifelong assault on the authorities of his day (the law, the church, the government) stemmed, in part, from an indomitable hostility towards the cynical exercise of power, and especially towards the justification of such exercise with reference to tradition, custom and superstition. This is what Bentham referred to as *sinister interest*. One of the functions of accounting and making known the facts so accounted is for Bentham to demystify what social power is and how it operates, and to demonstrate good reasons for doing things differently. Transparency plays a crucial role in this:

> Of the several departments of government, howsoever carved out and distinguished – judicial, financial, military, naval, and so forth – suppose that in all, or any of them, *abuses* exist – abuses, from which the persons, or some of the persons, by whom those departments are respectively filled, derive, each of them, in some shape or other, a sinister advantage. In this state of things, if there be any such thing as an instrument, by the operations of which all such abuses, without distinction, are liable to be exposed *to view*, the tendency of it is thereby to act with hostile effect, against the several sinister interests of all these several public functionaries; whom thereupon, by necessary consequence, it finds engaged, all of them, by a common interest, to oppose themselves with all their means, and all their might, not only to its influence, but to its very existence.
>
> (Bentham 1821: 59)

The art of recordation is just such an instrument. Bentham hopes to demolish those mystifications bolstering belief that the 'institutions of society are infinitely complex and difficult to understand, and that this is an invincible fact of nature, so that long-standing institutions cannot be changed' (Hart 1982: 21). This is underpinned by Bentham's theory of language, and his particular insistence on precision in expression. He found 'obsolete language, technical language undefined, nonsense, fiction', and 'ordinary language perverted' repugnant (Bentham 1827: 288). Such terminology, Bentham maintained, works in the service of the abuse of the greatest happiness by sinister interest.

That Bentham's obsession with accountability should be appropriated, deployed and made worse than useless in service of an obscure and inscrutable lexicon is, therefore, banal, poignant and monstrous by turns. Managerial instrumentalization in the university has its own curiously occult enchantments, working through

> rituals, invocations and incantations; the accumulation of talismanic, fetishistic objects (most of which take electronic form); an occult hierarchy; ritual sacrifices; and a predilection to consult professional occult practitioners. ... words of power, expressions and incantations deriving from the globalized corporate world, are invoked repeatedly, as if frequent repetition will bring into being that which they denote, or will summon up the divinities of the market to work a transformative magic upon the institution. These terms, which possess a talismanic quality, and an almost voodoo-like potency, include 'quality', 'excellence', 'mission', 'premier', 'benchmark', 'strategic', 'top rank', 'world-class', 'flagship', 'team-building', 'innovation' and 'auditing'.
>
> (Wood 2010: 232–233)

This is what pitches us into Bentham's nightmare: he is himself working from beyond the grave for ordinary language perverted, and technical language undefined.

Dialogues of the dead

As the most devout of utilitarians, Bentham had no time for squeamishness or superstition. He dismissed religious taboos around the corpse as useless, the cardinal sin against the principle of utility. Coffins take up space, and decomposing bodies spread disease. Bentham willed that his body be dissected in public, and preserved in the manner in which it is now on display. He did so at a time when the corpse was culturally inviolable to a far greater extent than today (Richardson 1987: 160).

The auto-icon is thus literally the embodiment of Bentham's effort to *transparently* represent himself and his grand vision; not to be mediated by headstones, graves or statues, but instead to engage corporeally with the future and his legacy 'in person'. Through the auto-icon, Bentham aimed to accomplish a secular immortality. He sought to become himself a sign of the radical evacuation of all symbolic meaning from the body (and thus from life itself), to become a sign only of utility in death, to transcend death through utility:

> Subtly, but unmistakably, the auto-icon profanes both the dead and the human body, regarding it in instrumental terms; the eradication of the sacred transforms each of us, including the living, to means rather than ends, even if the greatest happiness of the greatest number ostensibly serves as the ethical end … It thus quite concretely represents how utilitarianism instrumentalizes the world.
>
> (Collings 2009: 127)

Everyone, in short, becomes a thing, and every thing is in the service of the monologic of utility. Utility, of course, presupposes some other principles obliging us to act morally, even where good or right moral action is pared down to the greatest happiness of the greatest number. The issue is not just around the extent to which individual and collective happiness (Bentham's egoistic ethics and his administrative politics, respectively) can be reconciled without some sort of intervention. In attempting to eradicate all other ethical systems and the grounds for their justification (the virtues, the Kingdom of Ends, or what have you), Bentham surreptitiously installs himself as legislative authority, far beyond his avowed aim to be 'the Newton of the moral world' (Sil 1986: 245).

The auto-icon therefore gives the lie to Bentham's visionary, secular fundamentalism. It undercuts the utility of the social order it supposedly represents and advocates; throwing into stark relief the strangely distorted social and moral space it generates. In Bentham's own morbidly jocular accounts of the auto-icon, a fantasy plays out of Bentham as a sort of atavistic totem. This is after all what is meant by *icon*: Bentham's corpse as a venerable fetish in a modern cult of the intellect. He imagines that his followers might like to come on secular pilgrimages, to commune with his body, which could be installed with his works and unpublished manuscripts close by.

In his last writing, *Auto-Icon, or, Farther Uses of the Dead to the Living*, he speculates that the corpses of other famous thinkers might also be so preserved; arranged into tableaux of sorts for edifying educational purposes, and through ventriloquism and manipulation, made to move about and interact as though alive (Bozovic 2004: 250; Collings 2000: 123; Schofield 2006: 339). This undead mannequin is at the core of Bentham's hugely influential legacy, a physical testimony to himself, a corporeal manifestation of a vision of a social world governed by a single principle. The auto-icon is disturbing, grotesque, absurd and frightening *not* because it is spooky – it is *not* a thing that goes bump in the night – but because it corporealizes an impossibly rational and instrumental drive. Bentham perhaps is the first to embody a mode of the *unheimlich* with which we have since become familiar: he 'creates a new version of the uncanny – one shaped not by superstition but by its opposite, not by the ghost but by the radical secularization and instrumentalization of the corpse' (Collings 2000: 99).

The corpse of everything and the value of nothing

Insofar as is practicable, it is worth distinguishing between issues with the principles and presuppositions subtending Bentham's utopia, and the interesting anomalies that have arisen in the course of their contemporary implementation in the university.

The primary and perhaps most significant issue with Benthamite utilitarianism is the under-determined nature of 'happiness'. The problem seems to begin with the *nominalism* of Bentham's theory of language. It is true that Bentham subdivided the pains and pleasures, and held also that they could be measured in terms of their intensity, duration and so on (Bentham 2000: 31–41). Yet there is a tension between this individualistic empiricism and Bentham's nominalism. General moral terms, like 'good', are always abstract for Bentham, and insofar as they refer, that is only in the specific instances in which they refer to phenomena such as 'pleasure' and 'pain'.

This tension has a number of unresolved consequences. The relationship between 'pleasure' and 'happiness' is ambiguous in Bentham's writing; the latter appears as a term, the meaning and definition of which is contextually variable (rather like 'excellence' in university discourse). A consequence of this is that opinion plays some part in determining what happiness is, and Bentham acknowledges this (Steintrager 2004: 117–118). Almost immediately, a fundamental question is raised about how abstract, persistent, collective social systems are to be organized according to, or aggregated out of, individual subjective states (Hume 1981: 8). For, cannot opinion be manipulated? This tends to undercut the entire enterprise, inviting utilitarian legislators to enlighten self-interest (perhaps through 'legitimate' manipulation). Moreover, Bentham grossly overestimated the benevolence of utilitarian legislators. As West demonstrates, in relation to the development of rentier educational managerialism over the course of the nineteenth-century utilitarian experiment in education, 'the Benthamite administrative apparatus appeared to take on a life of its own' (1992: 597).

There is another peculiar aspect of the Benthamite system that reverberates through the critiques of the instrumentalization of the university. It is not just that Bentham has an impoverished, almost Pavlovian notion of human motivation, as Mill points out:

> The sense of honour, and personal dignity – that feeling of personal exaltation and degradation which acts independently of other people's opinion, or even in defiance of it; the love of *beauty*, the passion of the artist…the love of *action*, the thirst for movement and activity, a principle scarcely of less influence in human life than its opposite, the love of ease: – None of these powerful constituents of human nature are thought worthy of a place among the 'Springs of Action'.
>
> (2003: 69)

It is that this notion plays out for Bentham in an extremely specific way in relation to *work*:

> *Aversion* – not *desire* – is the emotion, the only emotion, which *labour*, taken by itself, is qualified to produce. Of any such emotion as *love* or *desire, ease*, which is the *negative* or *absence* of labour, *ease*, not *labour*, is the object. In so far as *labour* is taken in its proper sense, *love of labour* is a contradiction in terms.
>
> (Bentham 1983: 104)

It is a fundamental theorem of the principle of utility, related to its basis in the sensations, that *work cannot cause pleasure*. There is a blind spot here: presumably, Bentham did not reflect on his own engagement with his work in these terms. He is known to have written for eight hours every day. His corpse is arranged as though still at work. Why, then, is work so inherently horrible for Bentham? This curious aspect of Bentham's thought, from which so much follows, can be further unpacked:

> 'Aversion' leads to the division of labour in the first place and then motivates people to keep track of the time spent in various tasks. Although the labour theorists of value seldom dwelt on the quality of exertion expended in production, they nevertheless assumed as axiomatic that everyone strives to counterbalance the affliction of labour by the pleasures of remuneration and consumption. If work were intrinsically pleasurable, economic calculations would be unmotivated, and one would not be able to tell the difference between labour and leisure. The labour theory of value, in short, rested on certain naturalistic assumptions about how our individual sensations, our sensitivity to pain and pleasure, are aggregated into complex economic systems. The labour theory of value in the hands of political economists, therefore, was not a platform for praising labour. To them, labour was important because it was so *unpleasant* a thing that no one would voluntarily undertake it.

(Gallagher 2006: 24)

It is for this sort of reasoning that Marx famously described Bentham as 'that insipid, pedantic, leather-tongued oracle of the ordinary bourgeois intelligence of the nineteenth century' (1959: 609). Ambiguity about the referential status of terms like 'happiness' compounds the incompatibility between Bentham's egoistic ethics and his administrative politics. When this is combined with Bentham's predication of the system on a model in which work cannot cause pleasure, the means of utilitarianism begin to hijack the ends. The system defaults: the greatest happiness of the greatest number is folded back into the administrative techniques and methods by which it must be secured. It does not help that Bentham is robustly 'egalitarian', which is to say, he has no interest in ranking pleasures (pleasures derived from opium, or opera, cannot be said to be more or less valuable than each other), such that there is no *teleos* in the Benthamite universe (Thomas 2011: 16). Mill referred to this as 'swine morality' (2003: 186). Without the benevolent utilitarian legislator, who decides the direction in which the Chrestomathic principles guide us?

Benthamite utilitarianism, we could say then, is an imperfect system. Sadly, it is also imperfectly realized in its application. If Bentham had a grave, he would be spinning in it. Latent problems in his thinking become pathologies in the world. Chief among these are the institutionalization of distrust, and perhaps most gruesomely for Bentham, the misappropriation and deformation of his thought in the service of 'sinister interest'.

It follows logically enough from the natural inclination towards indolence on which Benthamite utilitarianism is based, that worker-scholars cannot be trusted to work, and that they must be incentivized to do so. Actually, as far as Bentham is concerned, *no one can be trusted*: the social world is governed by utility-maximizing self-interest. Really those at the mercy of the administration should rightly be chary of them. The science of morals and legislation is a difficult business, 'a science for legislators who employ it either because they understand it themselves or because they are advised by those who do' (Steintrager 2004: 113). Bentham considered the capacity of the public to grasp the benefits of utilitarianism suspect; although in time and with correct information, he thought, they might eventually come around. Given this ignorance, Bentham's follower Sidgwick proposed a covert utilitarianism:

[T]he Utilitarian conclusion, carefully stated, would seem to be this; that the opinion that secrecy may render an action right which would not otherwise be so should itself be kept comparatively secret; and similarly it seems expedient that the doctrine that esoteric morality is expedient should itself be kept esoteric. Or, if this concealment be difficult to maintain, it may be desirable that Common Sense should repudiate the doctrines which it is expedient to confine to an enlightened few. And thus a Utilitarian may reasonably desire, on Utilitarian principles, that some of his conclusions should be rejected by mankind generally; or even that the vulgar should keep aloof from his system as a whole, in so far as the inevitable indefiniteness and complexity of its calculations render it likely to lead to bad results in their hands.

(2002)

With such grounds for febrile paranoia, anyone with the wit to grasp the principle of utility would be wise to keep a watchful eye on the governing utilitarian regime, lest it be subverted. Bentham foresaw this; hence his interest in transparency, an interest which finds its fullest and most malformed expression in the culture of audit (Strathern 2000).

Having your brains and eating them

The Chrestomathic principles are a particular manifestation of utilitarianism as a universal system. In their distorted new public management guise, they are further corrosive of trust in themselves being decapitated – in imagining themselves as context- and content-indifferent (Yeatman 1990: 9). Managing a university faculty, a psychiatric hospital ward, or a mincemeat production line become identical. Utility maximizing, financially-accountable administrative techniques override the substantive content of any work conducted. Where that content involves disciplinary specialization, or the careful maintenance of networks and relationships (among researchers, with students), it is actually a *threat* to the techniques of administrative control and efficiency.

Both academics and administrative staff are thus divested of professional autonomy and identity. Nothing can be taught that some other (increasingly casualized) 'information-delivery personnel' cannot teach (Donoghue 2008: 87). Any member of administrative staff, similarly, can be rotated into any administrative role. Everyone is expendable, excluding, perhaps, the managerial elite, who maintain a separate and remote corporate identity, estranged from the core business of the institution. In the absence of trust, the incentive to and guarantor of productivity is marketization: 'a philosophy – an anthropology – of human relations that makes competition the organizing principle of society' (Bruno and Newfield 2010). In this way 'excellence' is assured.

Competition implies metrics, as metrics are the means by which system outputs can be ranked. The higher they score, the more excellent they are. It is here that the spectre of Bentham has the most ghoulish aspect: assessment of quality, or the *forthcomingness of Evidence*. Quality, of course, is measured through quantification. Only quantifiable things count, and extraordinary resources are diverted into conducting the counting, second-guessing how the metrics will be deployed, and manipulating the exhaustively assembled data in such a way as to get 'bang for the buck' for the countable objects submitted. Anterior to all of this, quality assessment dictates 'targets'; the numbers of outputs individuals at given locations within the hierarchy are obliged to produce, thereby reshaping research as a process oriented to the regular appearance of these outputs.

All of this is done within arbitrary and confused classification schemes, which are imposed upon the chaotic reality of emergent research conducted in stolen time, which have significant consequences in terms of research funding, and which moreover are subject to continuous revision. Shore and Wright present evidence that this is an undeclared (we might say Sidgwickian) policy: 'to keep systems volatile, slippery and opaque', and thereby preclude the possibility of anyone fully coming to grips with and mastering whatever the latest iteration is (1999: 569). Excellence in this system is entirely tautologous: 'The relationship between the genesis of quality and associated assessment systems becomes mutually constitutive' (Sousa et al. 2010: 1447).

Elaborate institutional mechanisms pitting all against all, however, undercut their ostensible purpose: in their erosion of trust, they undermine 'the very risk-taking and innovation purportedly at the core of the knowledge era' (Vidovich and Currie 2011: 53). Bentham's word made flesh is unnervingly un-utilitarian in its profligacy and inefficiency, as the burgeoning field of 'academonomics' attests (Clarke and Frijters 2010). Competition is enforced, although essentially the sector remains a command economy. Externalities and perversities multiply in such a context. Taxpayer-funded research is placed behind the paywalls of closed journals (edited and peer-reviewed by academics, for nothing); research generated at public expense must therefore be paid for twice (Hall 2009; see also Eve in this collection). There is extraordinary deadweight loss in the competitive grant application process (Graves, Barnett and Clarke 2011). In order to appear 'competitive', academics are required to fill out grant applications for research funding they know they will not receive. This is an especially perverse and morbid kind of busywork, which obliges researchers to contort what they do and make up in advance what they will find out. This is not conducive to trust, but it is chilling to innovation, which involves, presumably, investigating that which is not known in advance.

Where this sort of absurdity is combined with high teaching loads and spiralling staff-student ratios, the routines and rituals of zombification become most evident. The cultures of audit and compliance oblige academics, with their dogmatic faith in research methods and critical inquiry, to participate in processes they know to be ideologically driven and methodologically unsound. Disingenuousness and cynicism are endemic. Gill, for example, discusses 'a change to auditing procedures that ... made it impossible for staff to record the total number of hours worked, if these exceeded those for which they were nominally contracted. In this way, academics' working hours were systematically and quite deliberately rendered invisible' (2009).

Audit, through ranking, drastically collapses the scholarly future into the present in the pursuit of accountability, or more precisely, short-term bureaucratic coherence and control: any long-term project is radically disincentivized where it would not produce the appropriate countable items in the specified time frames. Through the same process, systemic bad faith in the enforcement of audit collapses morale. The Benthamite demand for transparency produces its opposite, a kind of grey twilight, as first-order activities are supplanted by the second-order accounting procedures that are supposed to ensure their quality (Docherty 2011). Academics lurch through a valley of shadows where what they *thought* were their roles, and how those roles are justified or rather *performed* or *fabricated* as justified, become grotesquely discrepant (Ball 2001). The folk mythologies of collegial anarchy and free inquiry are reconstituted by the occult powers of bureaucratic performativity. The consequences are a profound and alienating reification, and a headless, auto-iconic exhibition of this reification. The social world of the university disappears into the constitutive metrics of its own policing. The Chrestomathic university, like Bentham, becomes an undead mannequin, its own doppelgänger.

Palethorp arise

In line with the standard rationalization model derived from Weber (1968), Winter argues that the instrumental or economic rationalism of the academy involves 'a systematic distortion of meaning, an evasion of questions of value, need and ultimate purpose. To acquiesce completely in the commodification of knowledge would thus be, at the very least, a cultural disaster' (1995: 139).

Such an argument is predicated on a sequence of notions: that knowledge can be meaningfully distinguished from information; that knowledge can be rendered in a commodity form (and that such rendering must be corrupting); that universities deal in this knowledge (as opposed to some other 'good'); that their hold on it allows them to correctly determine value, and so on. While it is common, compelling, and likely correct to argue that 'capitalist realism', as Fisher dubs it (2009), does indeed distort and evade such questions, that the university was ever representative of 'undistorted' versions of such notions is quite a distinct assertion. This assertion is grounded in a model of the university as a stable, unitary, and homogeneous social space, which not only houses knowledge, but houses knowledge autonomous from (and to be defended against) market logics. What kind of place is this that houses such knowledge?

A core paradox is exemplified here: the kind of useful knowledge that Bentham advocated for in *Chrestomathia* now customarily excludes knowledge of Bentham. The corporatized university is largely ignorant of and indifferent to the foundations of its own organizational logic, or how the ends of that logic, strange though they may be, have been perverted. One of the concerns trotted out around the corporatization of the university is the decimation not just of a certain kind of liminal social space within which people might be given the time and opportunity to productively understand something of themselves and of the world, but also of a kind of sanctioned social space that allows for certain kinds of understandings of the world *per se*; specifically, those understandings that show the relative, contingent and emergent nature of the world as it is. Where it is increasingly difficult to recall or investigate how things came to be this way and how they might be otherwise, we are radically disempowered from dealing with how things are. We enter into a society without history, a permanent, unchangeable present. Let us imagine for a moment that the university is not in danger of death; it is *undead*. Were the university ever really, as Winter asserts, the place where such activity was housed, it has surely forfeited this role. Over the course of their instrumentalization, as Graham puts it, universities have not 'exhibited that very critical independence which must lie at the heart of their rationale' (2002: 17). Perhaps we could consider the costs of this in the following way:

The holistic planner overlooks the fact that it is easy to centralize power but impossible to centralize all that knowledge which is distributed over many individual minds, and whose centralization would be necessary for the wise wielding of centralized power. But this fact has far-reaching consequences. Unable to ascertain what is in the minds of so many individuals, he must try to simplify his problems by eliminating individual differences: he must try to control and stereotype interests and beliefs by education and propaganda. But this attempt to exercise power over minds must destroy the last possibility of finding out what people really think, for it is clearly incompatible with free thought, especially critical thought. Ultimately, it must destroy knowledge; and the greater the gain in power, the greater will be the loss of knowledge.

(Popper 1957: 88–89)

Bentham's childhood was scarred by tragedy. Five of his siblings died in infancy or early childhood. When he was 11, his mother, Alicia Grove, died. All his life, he suffered from nightmares. As an extremely precocious, imaginative and impressionable child, Bentham was tormented by servants with a figure they said lived under the stairs, a 'horrible phantasm' by the name of Palethorp. When the servants tired of little Jeremy's company, he later recalled, a footman would 'repair to the adjoining subterraneous apartments, invest his shoulders with some strange covering, and, concealing his countenance, stalk in, with a hollow, menacing, and inarticulate tone' (Bentham 2001: 19). Such was the terror into which the figure of Palethorp cast the young Bentham, that he once threw a pair of scissors at the footman, hitting him in the eye. He never forgot the punishment meted out to him for this. Sage, among others, suggests that this story is significant: that when Bentham 'grew up, one of his primary aims was to lay out the rational foundations of knowledge, so that no false beliefs could again be admitted to hamper the course of individual or society' (1988: 162; Ogden 2001: xi–xiv; Schofield 2006: 1–2).

In devising the greatest happiness system of morals and legislation so as to exorcize sinister interest and the language through which false belief in its justification was propagated, Bentham laid out the foundations of contemporary bureaucratic administration, outside, and inside, the university. Perhaps, as Foot suggests, it is now time to exorcize Bentham himself (1985: 196). His extraordinary vision has helped to produce the university as a social system likened after him, but not quite in the way he would have hoped: a corpse forever as at work, with its head in a locked box.

'Being' post-death at Zombie University

Rowena Harper

If the presence of zombies signals the advent of an apocalypse – and in cinema it invariably does – then the recent appearance of zombies in the academy should prompt an anxious survey of our surroundings for signs of imminent collapse. The literature (both academic and governmental) has been increasingly insistent that higher education is in the midst of a dramatic transformation. While it can be argued that this transformation has been informing the sector for some time (in Australia the significant Dawkins reforms, for example, were announced in 1987), a globalized context characterized by 'increasing pace ... economic and social pressures ... and uncertainty over the future' (Nicoll and Fejes 2008: 1) is contributing a fresh degree of anxiety to a scene that feels increasingly beyond our control.

In exposing the academy to a zombie infection, theorists must manage the process with care, for it could come back to bite them in one of three ways. Firstly, in American horror cinema, and that of George A. Romero particularly, zombies act as the sign, the source and also the *symptom* of apocalypse, a horrific embodiment of certain problematic tendencies within society that pre-date the appearance of zombies (Pagano 2008: 75). For higher education, the deployment of the zombie must therefore involve identifying particular features of higher education of which zombies may be symptomatic. This process – of identifying certain people, practices or policies as zombified – requires an ideological judgement, one that proclaims something to be dead from a privileged position of life. The zombie, after all, 'cannot see itself as such, much less claim a zombie identity for itself' (Lauro and Embry 2008: 105). So unable to declare *oneself* as a zombie, identifying zombidity in the university involves a degree of finger pointing that should be performed with caution.

A second issue is that the choice of the zombie as a metaphor yields both opportunities and challenges. On the one hand, as a body that is simultaneously living and dead, the zombie has the capacity to release us from dualistic (either/or) thinking. However, as a theoretical construct, it has perhaps too often been deployed at ideological extremes in the exploration of limits. One example of this can be seen in Lauro and Embry's (2008: 95) 'Zombie Manifesto', which suggests that the subject/object figure of the zombie is a theoretical impossibility that invalidates the idea of the capitalist subject and requires the destruction of the individual. Given the inherent infectiousness of the zombie archetype, this 'posthuman' zombie – when taken to its logical conclusion – spells the end of the individual, the end of capitalism (2008: 106), and the total ascendancy of the zombie. While the zombie is therefore useful in testing the validity of certain intractable concepts (subjectivity, ideology and consciousness), certain applications to the ontology of the subject and the realm of lived experience in higher education are liable to bring about absolute death for the university and all those within it. Again, caution is required where zombie theory is concerned, lest we all end up dead.

A third issue, and possibly the most important, is that identifying zombidity within higher education constructs a *loss* of something fundamental to vitality in the institution. In the archetypal zombie, an unnerving change has occurred. There has been a death, signalled by a rotting corpse, which confronts us with the fact that something we have long held dear – mum, cousin Betsy, or the university – just isn't what she used to be. Those with long enough memories can perhaps be comforted by the thought that they were there in the good old days – before the zombies came. But it is necessary to consider what this might mean for students in the contemporary environment who are being encouraged in increasing numbers to enter a university system that is supposedly in decay. By suggesting that staff within the current system are busy fending off a zombie threat, zombie discourse (if rashly applied) has the potential to position this system – and the students within it – as the enemy, and widening participation agendas as harbingers of a kind of death.

This chapter negotiates the apocalyptic terrain of the contemporary university by suggesting that zombidity has taken hold largely via the discourses that bring people to and position them within higher education. Such neo-liberal discourses function to dehumanize both students and staff and position them as mere parts in an educational machine. Using Kristeva's concept of the *abject*, this chapter suggests that while the zombie is a figure of horror, like many persistent monsters its significance lies in its ambiguity. The zombie is particularly useful for its disturbing similarity to humankind, the horror of which offers opportunities for examining the ontology of the higher education subject. This chapter will illustrate that zombie discourses, and people's reactions *to* them, offer opportunities to better understand how we think our subjectivity, and how we constitute our *being* in a space that many argue is 'dead'. Finally, drawing brief parallels between assertions from the literature and the films of Romero, it suggests that his *Dead* series may well offer a longitudinal imagining of the possible development of both zombies and survivors in a post-apocalyptic landscape that is useful for higher education.

The death of the university?

If much of the academic literature on higher education is to be believed, the university is, sadly, dead, a victim of the infectious creep of neo-liberal discourse. Texts such as *The University in Ruins* (Readings 1996), *Killing Thinking: The Death of the Universities* (Evans 2004) and 'The death of the university, English style' (Couldry and McRobbie 2010) suggest that contemporary processes of governance and accountability have 'deadened' the function of the university and the roles of those within it by stripping it of its social, cultural and political meanings and imbuing it with a predominantly economic function. The claim, which is becoming increasingly widespread, is that universities of old were once provided their *raison d'être* by the nation-state, for which they produced an educated, engaged and critical citizenry (Readings 1996: 3). Societies, however, are becoming ever more global, no longer definable by geographical boundaries alone (Beck 2003), and universities are subsequently being 'colonized' by governments' international economic agendas (Kamola and Meyerhoff 2009: 5). Such agendas privilege 'the rule of the cash-nexus' (Readings 1996: 3) over the idea of the university as a site for developing in students the capacity to be critical of their social conditions and 'constraining relations' (Nicoll and Fejes 2008: 5). Knowledge is thereby becoming progressively more commercialized (Shore 2010: 16) – a process often referred to as the 'McDonaldization' of universities (Ritzer 1998). For many, these shifts mark an end to liberal education and the emergence of 'audit culture' (Shore and Wright 1999). The idea of the university, then, might be thought of as a kind of 'zombie concept' or a living/dead idea that is no longer representative of reality, but still 'haunting people's minds' (Beck 2000: 80).

For students in the contemporary 'massified' environment who are being encouraged in increasing numbers to enter university, assertions that the university is dead have the potential to devalue their experience entirely, instead suggesting that they have arrived on the scene too late and must settle for a decaying version of tertiary education. Taking a step back, however, the pervasiveness of neo-liberal discourse is such that students are possibly already enfolded within its ideology; the same mechanisms that position the university as an 'enterprising institution' (Reid 2009: 337) are likely to simultaneously position the student as a co-conspirator of sorts, who is complicit with, or at least aligned with a zombified model of education. If this is the case, they may not be too upset about enrolling at 'Zombie U'.

While the relationship between neo-liberalism and university staff has been explored quite widely in the literature, the effects of neo-liberalism on students have been the focus of less attention. The main observation is that neo-liberal discourses have a worrying capacity for changing the relationship of the student to the university from one of learner to one of *consumer*, whereby the product that they consume is their own educational transformation (Readings 1996: 27; Evans 2004: 96; Naidoo and Jamieson 2005). This shift in the way learners are positioned is particularly pronounced within narratives of social-inclusion, which have been examined in some detail by Percy (2011). She suggests that narratives of inclusion, while maintaining the 'sentiment of democracy' (131), work to constitute students previously out of reach of higher education 'as an object of government', and that they do so via an ideology of empowerment and freedom (133). They enable in the population greater levels of economic productivity through a set of discourses and practices that encourage individuals to 'consume [their] way out of poverty' by investing in education (Percy 2011: 137). The social difference represented by students targeted by social-inclusion policies is not accommodated by universities, but rather problematized. Consequently, the role of universities and their learning support staff in particular is to 'ameliorate the alienating distance between the students' own cultural background and the cultural practices of the disciplines' (Percy 2011: 135). The outcome of this is that students are ultimately positioned as products of the educational 'machine', emerging as 'skilled and qualified bodies' that can be put to work in the global knowledge economy. Percy (2011: 135) describes these students as a 'set of individuated capacities, dispositions and skills', rather than people *per se*, the product of a kind of governmental control that Freire (1970: 77) has described as 'necrophilic ... [and] nourished by love of death'. Students, then, as objects *upon which* educational processes are enacted, might aptly be described as zombie learners.

The rise of zombifying discourses: the Bradley report

Neo-liberal discourse is perhaps nowhere more evident in an Australian context than in the *Review of Australian Higher Education: Final Report* – commonly known as the 'Bradley Report' – which was released in 2008. Commissioned to establish whether Australia's higher education system was able to 'position [the country] to compete effectively in the new globalized economy' (Bradley, Noonan, Nugent and Scales 2008: xi), its significance for Australian universities is akin to that of the 'White Paper' in Great Britain, or the 'Tertiary Educations Strategy 2007–12' in New Zealand. At the launch of the Bradley Report at Macquarie University in Sydney in early 2009, Professor Denise Bradley (its lead author) mentioned that the higher education sector 'has been in a sense reviewed to death'. While it was an innocent choice of words that referred jokingly to the number of recent reviews conducted in the sector, it succinctly describes the way this review enacts a kind of death on those it addresses. A brief analysis of it here will demonstrate the ways in which its application of neo-liberal discourses to the Australian higher education system creates a linguistic framework that is zombifying in its effects, and particularly so for students.

The report's Executive Summary provides the neo-liberal frame within which the remainder of the report is to be read:

> Australia faces a critical moment in the history of higher education. There is an international consensus that the reach, quality and performance of a nation's higher education system will be key determinants of its economic and social progress. If we are to maintain our high standard of living, underpinned by a robust democracy and a civil and just society, we need an outstanding, internationally competitive higher education system.
>
> (Bradley et al. 2008: xi)

The report gains our attention immediately, echoing portents from the literature that universities are in the midst of an apocalyptic moment. Claiming the existence of an international consensus of which we are unaware, it undermines our national confidence and induces anxiety and fear that we may be left behind the rest of the world. The stakes are largely financial: 'economic and social progress' in the international arena. While it makes reference to traditional principles of higher education, for example, justice, civility and democracy, these are relegated to a subordinate clause, overshadowed by the need to maintain a 'high standard of living' and remain 'internationally competitive'.

The report continues in much the same way, rationalizing principles of social justice and equity within an economic frame. Amongst its highly-publicized recommendations are ambitious targets set for student participation and success by 2020: 20 per cent of higher education undergraduate enrolments should be 'low-SES' (financially disadvantaged) students, and 40 per cent of 25- to 34-year-olds should have attained at least a bachelor degree. It states explicitly that 'we must address the rights of all citizens to share in [higher education's] benefits', and particularly 'those disadvantaged by the circumstances of their birth: Indigenous people, people with low socio-economic status, and those from regional and remote areas' (Bradley et al. 2008: xi). But the report is clear about the *reason* for this imperative: our 'nation will need more well-qualified people if it is to anticipate and meet the demands of a rapidly moving economy' (Bradley et al. 2008: xi). Again, principles of equity and widening participation come to service Australia's economic needs, and as Percy observed, students are invited to join the global knowledge economy so they might consume themselves out of poverty and consume the nation into economic success.

Also evident is a high degree of control exercised on and around students' bodies, which begins long before they even arrive at a university. While the report proposes a 'demand-driven, student-entitlement system' (Bradley et al. 2008: xv), which connotes *choice* on the part of the student, their choice will very much need to be manufactured by the higher education system itself. It is acknowledged, for example, that some areas targeted by the Bradley Report contain 'thin markets' (Bradley et al. 2008: xii), meaning the desire to participate in higher education is simply not strong. The report makes it clear, however, that universities must make it part of their mission to 'ensure that those from disadvantaged backgrounds aspire to' higher education (Bradley et al. 2008: xiv).

What becomes of these students once they enter the university is that they are transformed into the 'skilled and qualified body' mentioned earlier and traded internationally as part of 'Australia's third-largest export industry' (Bradley et al. 2008: xii). Needing more of these bodies to survive, the report urges:

> We must increase the proportion of the population which has attained a higher education qualification. To do this we need to reach agreement on where we need to be; provide sufficient funds to support the numbers we agree should be participating.
>
> (Bradley et al. 2008: xiii)

The language here constructs two distinct groups. One group is the 'we', or the group that speaks the discourse, which is a group that is animated via personalized, collective and exclusive language. The other group is that of the invisible 'numbers', which is de-identified, objectified, dehumanized and disempowered – zombified, if you will.

Rendered passive under the imperatives of the global knowledge economy, these zombie learners appear later when the report emphasizes the need 'to maintain the stock of researchers in the innovation system' (Bradley et al. 2008: xvi). Not unlike factory-farmed cattle here, they are constructed as consumable bodies that can be regenerated when supplies are low. And finally, lifelong learning is defined in the report not as the empowerment of individuals to continually self-educate, but 'the need for skills upgrading over the life cycle' (Bradley et al. 2008: xiv). The report therefore asserts the need for all zombie learners to perpetually return to universities in order to submit to further education.

The Bradley Report thereby represents one example of a linguistic application of neo-liberal discourse to the field of higher education. It promises to provide participation in the benefits of education, offering training in skills and knowledge that will convert the 'lay-body' into the infinitely more tradable 'skilled and qualified' one. Yet the type of education it provides is what Horkheimer and Adorno would call 'hypocritical': 'while individuals as such are vanishing before the apparatus they serve, they are provided for by that apparatus and better than ever before' (2002: xvii). In this way, Marx's proletarian subject comes to be 'a living appendage of the machine' (1959: 484), in this case, the global knowledge economy. Part subject, part object, the student becomes what Lauro and Embry (2008: 87) describe as the 'capitalist drone' zombie.

The possibility of performativity

Thus far, the zombie has been a figure of horror. Representing loss of life, consciousness, self-awareness and agency, it has been depicted as that which should be feared. The zombie is, however, an *abject* figure and as such, its significance stems from its ambiguity (Larsen 2010). The zombie creates within us panic and fear, not because it is Other and distinctly different from us, but because it is eerily similar, an embodiment of Freud's *unheimlich*. As an abject presence, it functions to draw us 'toward an elsewhere as tempting as it is condemned' (Kristeva 1982: 1) and in our responses of revulsion and rejection, abject bodies show us what we 'permanently thrust aside in order to live' (1982: 3). As Kristeva writes, faced with an abject presence, '[there] I am at the border of my condition as a living being. My body extricates itself, as being alive, from that border' (1982: 3). To put it another way, the death and decay of a corpse body 'is itself a way to find the world of the dead among the living, to reintroduce death into society, so as to confirm what life is' (Peake 2010: 66). In short, zombies lurking within the academy could ultimately alert us to what little life remains.

In higher education, the moment of abjection, where *I* pulls back from the *not-I*, is acutely felt when we come into direct contact with zombie discourses, and where they threaten to consume the *I*. This happens most often in moments of 'performance'. Staff, for example, are frequently asked to perform 'quality' or 'excellence' for a range of surveillance mechanisms. This act of performance is frequently accompanied by feelings of uneasiness about the way in which the value systems of the 'quality frameworks' position us as practitioners. Strathern has described this audit context as one in which 'people both deploy, and are sceptical about deploying' a range of discourses (2000: 310). We thereby sit uncomfortably in a position that requires us to embody conflict and make some sense of it. Examining performativity in higher education, Ball (2001: 211) describes the difficulty of the situation:

> [W]e now operate within a baffling array of figures, performance indicators, comparisons and competitions – in such a way that the contentments of stability are increasingly elusive, purposes are contradictory, motivations blurred and self worth slippery.

This brings with it a sense of 'ontological insecurity' (Ball 2001: 211), a profound uncertainty about our ways of being in the university. These multiple recognitions create an internalized 'stammering' (Lather 2006: 45) between the layers of disjunctive ideologies that make up our subjectivity.

That this type of performativity *occurs* – that we must live with this stammering – is sometimes looked upon pessimistically, as if meaning has been drained entirely from our work (Evans 2004: 120). Indeed, such a state can be easily experienced as a dissolution of the *I*, a disintegration of coherence that tempts us to 'collapse into zombie status: mindlessly consume, and/or exile from ourselves the capacity to feel, and thus to be' (Webb and Byrnand 2008: 96). I would argue, however, that Kristeva's theory of abjection demonstrates that it is the very act of recognition of the *not-I* that pulls the body back from death. As unpleasant as it may be that we regularly perform zombie discourses, the *awareness* of one's own performance is the very thing that keeps zombidity at bay.

It is exciting to consider that university staff are not the only higher education subjects that may have access to the possibilities of performativity. Students too experience similarly difficult modes of being in the contemporary university that performativity could be used to describe. In a discussion about 'low-SES' students in Australian higher education, Priest (2009) has examined the literacy and language capacities they bring with them to university. She suggests that not only do low-SES students have 'their own knowledge and skills, and their own literacies and language', but also that 'these have the potential to enrich and ultimately transform the university' (Priest 2009: 71). While Priest may be right, this is not the spirit in which these students have been invited into the institution. As the Bradley report makes clear, it is the students who will be transformed by the institution, and not the other way around. The introduction of alternative discourses threatened by the low-SES student would undermine attempts by neo-liberal discourse to enfold all other sociopolitical discourses within an economic-rationalist framework. In studies of disadvantaged students similar to those discussed by Priest, Bourdieu, Passeron and Saint Martin found that students are likely to experience educational contexts with a sense of 'dualism' (1994: 9), whereby they feel a tangible incongruence between their social realities and those of the academy. While Bourdieu, Passeron and Saint Martin argue that this dualism often results in a 'resigned submission to being excluded' (1994: 9), I would suggest that for those who persist, this reflexive recognition of difference, this struggling on *within* difference, could equally be envisaged as a space in which the performative elements of identity could be recognized and used to develop their capacities for critical scholarship.

Although Bourdieu, Passeron and Saint Martin's insights emerged from working with French students in the 1960s, they have been affirmed more recently by Young (2004) in his examination of black students in America and their relationship with 'White English Vernacular' – the language of instruction in schools. Problematizing the suggestion that the students should become 'bidialectal' and learn how to 'code switch' (2004: 704), he suggests that schools need to move beyond such practices of 'enforced educational schizophrenia' (Young 2004: 705). Young's discussion of positive approaches to literacy learning is beyond the scope of this chapter, but his observations of the student experience confirm that they are often keenly aware of how they are awkwardly positioned within and by competing discourses.

Dwelling within the ruins

To borrow a key phrase from Readings (1996), if the university is indeed dead, then survivors need to find a way to dwell within its ruins. The films of Romero provide a useful narrative here, as he has explored, over five decades, the possibilities and limits of surviving a post-apocalyptic landscape. Perhaps his most significant theme, that is reiterated ever more explicitly through *Night of the Living Dead* (1968), *Dawn of the Dead* (1978), *Day of the Dead* (1985) and *Land of the Dead* (2005), is that survivors of apocalypse should be deeply suspicious of dominant ideologies. Romero frequently creates stark divisions within groups of survivors in order to construct the main source of fear as emerging from other surviving humans rather than the zombies themselves (Bishop 2010a: 120). Typically, human survivors band together and lock themselves into a fortified space that becomes a refuge. It is usually somewhere exceedingly familiar and comfortable, and for that reason it encourages some survivors to stage a response to the apocalypse based on survival of and within the status quo (Bishop 2010a: 104–05). The spaces Romero uses across the four films are a family home, a shopping mall, a military bunker with scientific laboratories, and a cramped metropolis; within these spaces, splinter groups fruitlessly try to rebuild the tattered past, and in doing so recreate old divisions across race, gender and class lines. Their plans do not revolve around annihilating the zombie horde. Rather, labour goes towards the defence and preservation of dominant ideological and social structures (Bishop 2010a: 157). In barricading themselves away in order to revive the past, there is an utter denial of the transformations occurring around them that renders the survivors little more than zombies themselves, waiting out their existence and 'going through the motions of a lost life' (Bishop 2010b: 242). What ultimately distinguishes those who survive beyond the final showdown is an appreciation that 'the world has completely changed' (Romero, cited in Bishop 2010a: 30).

It is perhaps fitting that Readings echoes Romero's message, asserting that dwelling in the ruins means avoiding nostalgia and any preoccupations with 'rebuilding a ghost town'

(Readings 1996: 169). It is vital for the subjects of higher education to think anew about the university and their being within it. This prompts us to embrace the apocalyptic moment as an opportunity to imagine an alternative future.

In a classic scene from Romero's *Dawn of the Dead* (1978), two survivors sit quietly in a shopping mall watching zombies lurch from store to store, the muzak framing them as absurd and comical customers. One survivor asks 'what the hell are they?' The other replies, 'they're us, that's all.' The point I have sought to make in this chapter is that zombies are *not* us, at least not yet. While the Bradley Report, and the broader neo-liberal mechanisms of which it is a part, provide the prevailing discourse that currently brings people to and positions them within higher education, identities are not entirely constructed by these mechanisms. Abject bodies such as that of the zombie threaten the *I*, and *therefore* simultaneously allow us to temporarily reaffirm it. As Larsen (2010: 1) suggests, 'if the zombie is defined by ambiguity, it cannot be reduced to a negative presence. In fact, it could be a friend.' While this may be somewhat optimistic, Larsen's point, and possibly my analysis here, may allow us to live alongside zombie discourses with a little less anxiety.

For Readings, what he saw as the death of the university generated deep feelings of ambivalence, and he wrote his influential text as 'an attempt to think [his] way out of an impasse between militant radicalism and cynical despair' (1994: 5). It is difficult to deny the lurking presence of zombies in the academy, but I am not yet entirely convinced that the university is dead, and neither are a number of other writers. Boyer (2010: 78), for example, asks and answers:

> Can we have reached the end of the project of liberal education, with only a post-liberal anxiety left … ? The very fact that we engage in critical scholarship challenges such pessimism.

While it may seem simplistic to say so, the very act of creating critique such as that represented in this book indicates there is life in here still.

Instead of thinking about the university as dead, we might think of the higher education landscape as perpetually on the verge of apocalypse, which we hold back daily through our resistance to zombifying discourses. The way in which we might do this was glimpsed by Readings himself when he suggested that it may be enough that we are able to gain a degree of critical distance from our positions within the system to *think* about how we are being positioned to speak and act in certain ways (1994: 5). Percy supports this point also, suggesting that if agency is 'embedded in the ethical project of self-formation and critique as we actively engage with the politics of truth about ourselves and the subject/object of our practices' (2011: 131), then we need to 'live with a commitment to thought', where thought is a form of reflexivity that allows us to step back from thought and action, in order to examine their self-evidence and their contingency (Percy 2011: 139).

Indeed, I would suggest that the way in which we exercise our 'being' in this post-death university will emerge from moments of performativity, which provide glimpses into new ways of thinking about ourselves and what it means to exist in higher education. While performativity is often pointed to in the university as a sign of zombidity, in that it is the conduct of an action that seems inauthentic to us, the presence of consciousness problematizes the zombie label, and we free ourselves from zombidity with the *awareness* that we are indeed caught up in a performance. The opportunity inherent in performativity has been observed by a number of other writers too. Gunn and Treat for example suggest that performativity generates 'agential maps that enable us to locate its contradictions and constructedness' (2005: 163). Lather also sees its significance, as it emerges from 'the between space of what seems impossible from the vantage point of our present regimes of meaning, a between space situated as an enabling site for working through ... present practice' (2006: 45). In light of what zombie discourse can offer, as a catalyst of abjection, it is important to reconsider the concept of performativity in higher education as what Lather might describe as a 'stuck place', rather than a 'dead' end.

University life, zombie states and reanimation

Rowan Wilken and Christian McCrea

What about this 'life' at and in university? Is it the way the university is taken up and experienced? Indeed, the question must be posed concretely: how do we here, now, today, take it; how do we live it?

Martin Heidegger (2001: 57)

One prevailing and profoundly pessimistic view of academic life would suggest that we are entering a condition of permanent zombie states. In exploring this view, in this chapter we argue that zombification is a state that is entered into, willingly, coerced, both through external famine and a willing compact to enter the state in exchange for amorphous, ineffable outcomes. We develop this argument in three steps. First, through an analysis of mainstream press reportage, we examine the ways in which a 'culture of pessimism', or 'discourse of lamentation', has pervaded public discussion of academic labour conditions. Second, we develop the insights of literary theorist Rebecca Saunders to argue that this discourse of lamentation has quite distinctive structural features, which can usefully shed light on how this rather bleak perception of university life can and should be open to reinterpretation and reanimation. Finally, we discuss this potential for reanimation via a brief exploration of the particular rhythms that are both characteristic of and can be seen to shape university life. To begin with, however, and in order to frame the textual analysis that follows, we establish some of the key complications and compensations that give form to contemporary university life.

Complications and compensations: university life, audit culture and 'cool'

The 1980s and 1990s witnessed a marked increase in interest in the notion of auditing, and a migration in the practice of audit from the realm of financial accounting into new areas of professional life (du Gay 1994; Hoskin 1996; Munro and Mouritsen 1996; Power 1996; 1997). Most noticeable has been its prominence in the tertiary education sector, where universities are seen increasingly to be governed by an all-pervasive audit culture (Holmwood 2010). As Shore (2008: 292) explains, 'audit is not just a series of technical practices', it is a form of governmentality – that is, it is a 'process, and a set of management techniques'.

Audit culture is not neutral for Shore. Rather, 'it actively transforms the environments into which it is introduced' (2008: 281). This occurs in a university context via discourse – that is, 'the subtle and seductive manner in which managerial concepts and terminologies have become integrated into the everyday language of academia' (283), and at a meta-discursive level, where 'knowledge management ... aspires to be knowledge itself' (Sahasrabudhey 2009: 43). It also occurs via the practices associated with this discourse, and the routinized effects of these as they impact on 'conditions of work and thought and, more importantly, on the way in which individuals construct themselves as professional subjects' (Shore 2008: 58). Giroux (2011: 51) refers to the bureaucratic discourse of audit culture as 'zombie-like language', which works to make 'power invisible' and is 'often deployed by those with social, political, and economic resources that narrow its horizons ... and empty [its] content of any viable substance'. This 'zombie-language' tends to be solely in the service of corporate 'self-interest, exchange values, and profit margins' (54). Academics themselves are complicit in this process, not least because they agree to staff performance-based evaluation matrices articulated to collective agreements and multifaceted 'workload models' (notice the language at work here) that are increasingly difficult to meet, let alone excel at within the nominal 38-hour working week (Shore 2008: 291).

An alternative take on the particularities and ambiguities associated with academic labour as a form of 'knowledge work' is that this work involves certain pleasures on the one hand (or, perhaps, more precisely, certain *compensations*), and certain perils on the other (Liu 2004). For Liu, the former can be aligned with a 'cool' style of work:

[C]ool is the shadow ethos of knowledge work. It is the 'unknowing', or unproductive knowledge, within knowledge work by which those in the pipeline from the academy to the corporation 'gesture' toward an identity recompensing them for work in the age of identity management.

(Liu 2004: 78)

Liu's concept of cool is an evocative capture of the tensions between the widely understood but little acknowledged economies of academic charisma, and the simultaneous mummification of the academic in the trappings of self-promotion. Cool operates in the classroom and in the research community more than ever, with all the tropes of genre, trend, culture and counterculture. The exploitative nature of such knowledge work has frequently been addressed (Gregg 2011; Liu 2004; Ross 2003; Terranova 2004).

Two notions can help articulate these tensions: the *discourse of lamentation*, and the method of *rhythmanalysis*. Lamentation drives media consumption and creation around declining or decrepit sociocultural traditions. In this case, it reacts to the decline of higher education, of the humanities, of cultural studies, of essayists, of opinion, of free thought, and so on. While the pressures and changes are real, lamentation charts the decline and makes from it a ceremony. Like Max Nordau's *Degeneration* (1993) or, less sympathetically, Spengler's *Decline of the West* (1932), the charting of the downfall presupposes a turnabout or revolt to halt the slide. Rhythmanalysis serves here as a sketching tool for that decline. In examining the responsive system around 'news', the epidemiological vectors of lament spread and resonate, allowing the zombification analogy greater latitude.

Pressures exist for postgraduates to emulate the 'living dead' academic, a role which casts the postgraduate research student as equivalent to the vampire fan who dreams of the embrace in the cemetery. Academics in turn are encouraged to zombie behaviour, to seek brains to devour and then add to the combinatory engine of the academy. Academics must now demonstrate their fecundity, vitality and the ability to overwork, to add value outside of and above the audit matrix. At least, this is the ideal model of behaviour from the perspective of the university. From the network of academic colleagues, the ideal is that of rising above the everyday auditing and work cultures, of engaging in activities and research with real value rather than audit value. Both images are of excess, of overflowing time and energy. Both contain spectral traces, not of the dead, but of the living – the ghostly presence as addition rather than remainder.

In light of the above, the pessimistic view would suggest that we are entering a permanent zombie state. The prevailing narrative is that the outlook for universities appears bleak. In Australia, the fiscal position of the tertiary education sector is increasingly volatile. Of necessity, universities rely less and less on government funding and are increasingly dependent on other revenue streams, such as full fee-paying local and international students. What access there is to government funding is distributed via complex research metrics or ever more competitive grant schemes that draw from stagnant or shrinking pools of research monies.

These forces are the conditions of professional zombification in the university. Academics are living in a kind of permanent 'twilight zone', the realm of the undead or living dead. Many fully qualified university staff form a 'reserve army of marginal and casually employed professionals' (DiGiacomo, cited in Shore 2008: 282). They are the insatiable living dead, like the staggering, shopping-mall bound hordes in Romero's *Dawn of the Dead* (1978), seeking whatever temporary and piecemeal sustenance is available from the 'zombie capitalism' of the university system (Giroux 2011). There is also another, quite different kind of living dead within the system, as a specific effect of audit culture has been 'the rise of a regime of bureaucrats, inspectors, commissioners, regulators and experts' (Shore 2008: 282) and agencies (Shore and Wright 2000: 61).

In what follows we interrogate the prevailing pessimism of this perspective, which we term the 'culture of pessimism'. Inspired by the work of Eugene Thacker (2010) and Ben Highmore (2009), we approach life and death in this context as zones of interpretation, or 'passions' in Highmore's terminology. The merit of this approach is that it emphasizes ambivalence and ambiguity. As Highmore explains, 'there is no scholarship without passion' (2009: 19). In general terms, passion 'is about the pull and push of your feelings, the peaks and troughs of your liveliness, the poundings of your creaturely-ness' (3). But passion is very much a polysemic term, as much associated with 'zeal and eagerness' as it is with 'suffering and emotional pain' (xi). So, while one might experience 'passionate enthusiasm' (3) for academic work, one might equally experience this same work as a 'passion of uncertainty and anxiety' (4).

43

These ambiguities and tensions are here worked through in three ways. First, we map the ways in which a culture of pessimism or discourse of lamentation about academic labour has pervaded the popular press over the past decade. Drawing on the insights of literary theorist Rebecca Saunders, we argue that this discourse of lamentation, while intended to be critical, can also be remobilized in ways that open up our understanding of academic labour and its various facets to reinterpretation and reanimation. Our arguments about the potential for reanimation are then developed towards the end of the chapter, through an exploration of the particular rhythms that shape university life.

Crisis reporting

In order to further understand the culture of pessimism and how it is represented, we undertook a study examining mainstream press reportage of the higher education sector in Australia. Using the online Factiva database (primarily because of its comprehensive coverage of the major Australian news dailies), we searched for any articles discussing Australian academic labour conditions for the period 2000–10. An emphasis on the mainstream press provides valuable insight into how academics, with their insider perspectives, are representing their work conditions and circumstances to the public, as well as into how journalists and other commentators writing from the outside seek to understand and report on the sector. Rather than develop a detailed content analysis of this material, the key aim was to identify the major themes. What follows is a summary of these dominant themes. The narrative of crisis is shot through with assumptions and ideological leaps, not the least of which are the preemptive capitulations of academics: we are the teaching/research living dead, serving that other populace of corporate/bureaucratic living dead. The general picture that is painted of the higher education sector in Australia serves as a forceful restatement of the discourse of lamentation described above.

Cultural studies scholar Meaghan Morris sets the tone in a 2000 op-ed piece for *The Australian*, in which she describes with unflinching frankness what she sees as the parlous state of Australian university employment conditions:

> Along with low wages and bad conditions, our brand of managerialism rewards [all academics, but humanities scholars in particular] with the most depressing and abusive professional climate on offer in the Western world ... I can't believe the ill-informed abuse that Australian academics suffer ... the atmosphere in many of our universities is worse than unrewarding. It has become repellent.
>
> (Morris 2000)

Writing for the same newspaper the following year, the Australian National Tertiary Education Union (NTEU) gives a detailed account of the sorts of changes in the sector that lie behind Morris's blunt assessment. These include significant declines in public investment in higher education, increased dependence on private investment, and dramatic rises in higher education cost structures, the outcome of which has been a series of restructures and course and departmental rationalizations (NTEU 2001). Furthermore, they report a rapid growth in and over-dependence on casual labour, which reportedly rose by 18 per cent between 1998 and 2000 to comprise 15 per cent of the university workforce as at 2000, with a commensurate decline in permanent staff numbers, with flow-on effects claimed to include a decline in teaching quality, and increased workloads and stress (NTEU 2001).

Over the 10-year study period, reportage was punctuated by responses to two key events. The first was the radical shake-up of tertiary education funding and staff employment arrangements proposed by the then Coalition Government's education minister Brendan Nelson (McCulloch 2003; Jackson 2002). This was condemned by the then president of the NTEU Carolyn Allport as yet further evidence of that Government's 'rigid ideological obsession' with neo-liberal economic principles (Taylor 2002). The second key event concerned the Bradley Review (Bradley et al. 2008) which was published towards the end of the decade, led by the former vice-chancellor of the University of Adelaide Denise Bradley, and was considered Australia's most significant review of the higher education sector since the Dawkins Review of the late 1980s (Dawkins 1987). This generated a great deal of industry commentary (Gilmore 2009; Sharpe 2009; Matchett 2008).

A series of recurrent themes emerge: a gradual but marked drop in public investment in universities (Trounson 2009; Lindsay 2007), with a growing gulf between operating costs and income (Matchett 2008); 'creeping commercialization' (Moodie 2003); declining educational standards (Matchett 2008; Illing 2002); the impacts of these and other factors on staff morale (Sharpe 2009; Adelaide Advertiser 2002); and, especially, labour force casualization (Illing 2002; Rowbotham 2010; Perkins 2009; Davison 2002; Buckell 2003; cf. Long 2003). In addition to the above, concerns were expressed over inflated student–staff ratios (Perkins 2009); the challenges faced by an aging academic population (Brown 2009), described by one commentator as a 'demographic timebomb' (Floud 2002); and excessive auditing and micro-management of academic staff by university administrators (Dann 2010).

The patterns described above are indicative of zombie capitalism: a 'totalizing market-driven society' (Giroux 2011: 65) that, among other things, involves the fetishization of 'cognitive capitalism' and 'cognitive labour' (Caffentzis and Federici 2009: 128). Within this society, education is in danger of becoming 'a form of commerce and nothing more' (Giroux 2011: 68).

The discourse of lamentation

What has been largely overlooked but is especially interesting about these assessments of the current academic situation is their narrative quality. Characteristic of this reportage and wider industry commentary is a very strong discourse of lamentation. This rehearsed and persistent tumult feeds and creates the crisis, and the idea that we as educators are 'living dead' in the thrall of (or, perhaps better, given the zombie trope, under the spell of) zombie capitalism. The last wave of cuts causes lamentation, which creates readiness for the next. Direct action is rarely considered under the false realism of government cuts, whereby 'we must all tighten our belts' endlessly, without question. The well-examined notion of 'there is no alternative', attributed amongst others to Margaret Thatcher, is emblematic of the futility of resistance. Examining this 'zombie-inspired discourse' (Giroux 2011: 51) is instructive for understanding the terms in which the academic labour market is discussed, and the stakes that are at play in these discussions.

Drawing on three key insights from Rebecca Saunders, we wish to argue that the discourse of lamentation has distinctive structural features and, as such, can be productively translated to the present from its original setting. Saunders' ideas are developed within the context of a re-reading of modernity and modernist literature and cultural production as shaped by, and a reaction to, a series of epistemological crises that are marked by experiences and sensations of loss and lamentation.

First, Saunders argues that many of the key critical accounts of modernity are deeply ambivalent. For instance, in discussing the work of Anthony Giddens (1991), she details the way that modernity is understood by Giddens to produce conditions of 'psychological vulnerability'. This vulnerability is simultaneously denied under conditions of modernity, or more accurately, the mourning and lamentation that result from them are denied by, among other things, being characterized as madness, or sickness (Saunders 2007: 7). Thus the mourning period passes, while the crisis normalizes. At a later point Saunders discusses Marshall Berman's *All That is Solid Melts into Air* (1983), and his contention that modern society, 'although racked with … uncertainty, nevertheless enables men and women to become freer and more creative' (Saunders 2007: 8). Saunders contrasts this perspective with that of Leo Bersani (1990), who 'points out, these two attitudes – celebration and lamentation – are not so much opposed, as related to, even productive of, each other' (cited in Saunders 2007: 8). As Bersani goes on to put it, loss can provide the impetus 'for reinvention of the terms and conditions of human experience'. It is this emphasis on ambivalence that proves important to critically reengaging with and rethinking academic labour in light of press and industry reportage on it.

The second insight concerns Saunders's argument that 'at stake in any historicized analysis of modernism is the degree to which modernist artifacts not only express (or respond to) the circumstances of modernity, but *produce* them': 'lamentation is intended not only to express, but to produce grief' (2007: 10). For Saunders, the 'confusion and disorientation produced by crisis are also often generated by modernist works of art' (2007: 10). Our point is that it pays to be aware that the confusion and disorientation produced by the academic labour market 'crisis' (Deresiewicz 2011) might also be seen as generated by commentary and reportage. To adapt Saunders' words, 'the languages of loss' characteristic of debate on academic labour conditions 'may, to a greater or lesser degree, create the effects they apparently document' (Saunders 2007: 10). This, in effect, is to draw attention to Derrida's deceptively simple (almost self-evident) but nonetheless significant point that news outlets and the media *produce* rather than simply record events (Derrida and Stiegler 2002: 4–7;

Lucy 2004: 4). Reinforcing this point, Saunders cites the work of Eyerman (2001) and Alexander et al. (2004). The former writes that, 'as cultural process, trauma is mediated through various forms of representation' (quoted in Saunders 2007: 15). The latter takes this further, contending, in Saunders' words, 'that trauma is culturally constructed through a claim to some fundamental injury that is then transmitted through influential cultural agents, such as the mass media' (2007: 15).

The last insight relates to Saunders's engagement with Dominick LaCapra's work (2001) and his observations concerning the conversion of 'absence' into 'loss', and the 'frequent leakage between them', as well as the 'necessity of exploring the ideological work done by their indistinction' (Saunders 2007: 11). In the present context, we might characterize this slippage as one where absence (of, for example, anything other than contract positions and casual labour) is translated into loss (of certainty, of clearly defined career pathways, of the protections to free speech that are seen to come with tenure, of identity and of the social capital associated with full-time academic employment and so on). The difficulty with this movement from absence to loss is twofold. On the one hand, LaCapra writes that 'to blur the distinction between, or to conflate, absence and loss ... creates a state of disorientation, agitation, even confusion' (quoted in Saunders 2007: 11). This progression is evident in industry reportage (see Rowbotham 2010; Sharpe 2009; NTEU 2001). On the other, as LaCapra also remarks, 'when absence is converted into loss, one increases the likelihood of misplaced nostalgia or utopian politics' (quoted in Saunders 2007: 11). In this case, that would be the belief that, academically speaking, things were once much better and that we can (indeed *ought* to) return to a pre-absence, pre-loss period, a (pre-zombified) period when career pathways were clearer, more certain, and more strongly articulated to postgraduate study.

If we are to work from the understanding that 'return does not necessarily constitute [nor in fact guarantee] recovery' (Saunders 2007: 17), what, then, are the alternatives? To adapt Saunders' words, 'what kind of recovery is implicitly called for' (16) in descriptions of the academy in crisis, and in accounts of conditions of permanent and total professional zombification?

The traumatic crisis culture described exists in part to renegotiate the status quo. This is because 'what is recognized as traumatic is everywhere implicated in negotiating the borders of normalcy' (25). The significance of this issue in relation to deliberations on academic labour conditions can be expressed as follows:

> How we define 'normal experience' excludes certain kinds of distressing occurrences from being acknowledged as trauma and ... legitimates, lays out the boundaries of, and creates tolerance for, 'acceptable' forms of violence and suffering.
>
> (Saunders 2007: 25)

If this analysis holds true, then it is also possible that the ambivalence and ambiguity creates tolerance for violence not merely from systems onto subjects, but between people, between academics, between staff, between students. If the normal state of affairs constitutes a crisis, then responding to the crisis can justify more and more. What we wish to suggest is that Saunders may well have a point when she writes that 'normal experience' incorporates exclusion and legitimation of suffering and the conditions of lamentation. After all, life, as Thacker points out, is constituted by 'a set of fundamental contradictions', contradictions that are inherent, 'logically coherent, and yet ontologically necessary' (2010: xiii).

The interpreted ones: academic reanimation

The scene of reanimation, of overseer and subject, is our entry point into these contradictions. Reanimation is a multivalent concept well suited to describe the nature of undermined work. Research has its own constituent purpose, but for the people producing it, it is often more important that research produces reputation. This reputation can be managed and appropriated in the service of the life-as-career of the academic, who requires reputation more than ever, not to progress forward, but merely to persist. Research activity demonstrates life; proof that life stirs within the shell after all. This does not account for all the natural pleasures of research, but the ways which life is accounted for: presence in classrooms; activity on abstract registers.

In the process of an actually existing academic career, these overarching questions are abstract. The smaller pressures from the lamentation culture are those that position people through a negative lens. We have just seen that the academic career must be animated, to be seen to move, to possess what Alan Cholodenko called the 'illusion of life', the outward signs of controlled movement that make up the animated subject (2007: 9). The subject has to be reanimated to be seen to be alive, to withstand the threshold of academic death, of research inactivity, of social inactivity, or increasingly of inactivity on social networks. These signs of life are most visible in the steps of animation – the research itself.

So, how is this different than any other job that relies on outcomes? Why does this state of affairs require a special reading? Unlike the much-misunderstood 'real world' of business, which has become the cargo cult of universities rather than a touchstone and partnering structure, efficiency is not the metric of success. For research to be of high quality, it must now simply exist. The old thresholds of quality are gone, some with very good reason. This leaves the academic trained in the production of one kind of work, labouring under an entirely different circumstance where their existence is always in danger. Their status is yet-to-be-confirmed and often on the threshold of inactivity, of being inanimate.

We can look at this in another way, where the very idea of the inanimate is literalized across academic situations: 'The market discourse in essence camouflages the pursuit of higher returns. Reduced employment security is traded for the promise of employees' "active and engaged relationship with the productive machines"' (Saravanamuthu 2002: 80).

How this impacts the kind of work that gets produced is at the centre of the zombification problem. Research becomes consciously and unconsciously contaminated with the culture of crisis and complaint. Pierre Macherey (2006) contends that 'the act of knowing' what goes on in a text (which, in this context, we take to include academic work itself as well as commentary on it) involves the 'articulation of a silence' (6), or what he calls a text's 'unconscious'. Thus, he writes, 'to explain [a] work is to show that ... it is not independent, but bears in its material substance the imprint of a determinate absence, which is also the principle of its identity' (89). Viewed in this way, Storey suggests that

> [t]he task of a fully competent critical practice is not to make a whisper audible, nor to complete what the text leaves unsaid, but to produce a new knowledge of the text: one that explains the ideological necessity of its silences, its absences, its structuring incompleteness – the *staging* of that which it cannot speak.
>
> (2001: 100)

In short, Macherey's contention is that, whenever something is said, something else is left unsaid. 'What is important in the work', he writes, 'is what it does not say' (2006: 97), and, therefore, 'we investigate the silence, for it is the silence that is doing the speaking' (96). In this way, we agree with Storey (2001) that, 'it is the reason(s) for these absences, these silences, within a text which must be interrogated' (101). Little wonder, then, that we see a proliferation since the late 1990s of academic work about academic work (the same graveyard this book is buried in); the resentment of the living by the dead is mirrored by shadowing within the work itself.

Several dimensions of academic reanimation take place at once, then.

- Theory: From within, the academic who teaches springs back into life between semesters and searches for life to ingest; the university system also has lightning rods to provoke movement and life (think of the terminology of Research Inactive or Lapsed Candidate); reanimation techniques surround the academic from the gravest crime of all, inaction.
- Field: That is to say, the breathing of life into disciplines long dead. The product of a degree subject is not to deliver a topic to students but to sacrifice students at the altar of the topic or field. Fields are reanimated with every class that invokes its name, with the limit case of this reanimation being the eager honours student inspired to a funereal thesis in a dead topic. The teaching academic works to continue and disseminate ideas and even fields in an era where vocational pragmatism alerts students to the risks of scholarship. To teach theory in a vocational environment is to propose a kind of death.
- Life: Including, working overnight to mark student work, existing in sleep and disease states in order to persist in the academic realm. Moreover, to give over your presence online and in social networks to the caricature of an engaged academic citizen for whom contemporaneity is a default state of production.

The conceptual framework that anchors and meshes these three dimensions is the Lefebvrean notion of rhythmanalysis. Rhythms have been understood to take many forms and to operate at a variety of scales and durations. For instance, there are complex social rhythms that, as Edensor and Holloway explain, 'can be institutionally inscribed (marked by national festivals, religious occasions, hours of commerce or television schedules), locally organized (via hours of work and local folk customs), or form synchronized collective habits (eating, playing, sleeping and working together)' (2008: 484).

These rhythms are interwoven with cyclical 'natural' rhythms, such as 'days, nights, seasons, the waves and tides of the sea, monthly cycles, etc.' (Lefebvre 2010: 8), and with what Lefebvre designates as 'linear' rhythms which he associates with 'human activity' as embedded in everyday life, especially 'the monotony of actions and of movements' and of 'imposed structures' (8). In addition, rhythms are always 'multiple, complex', sometimes harmonious, 'often dissonant' (Edensor and Holloway 2008: 484), or in Lefebvrean terms, both cyclical and linear, but just as commonly characterized by 'eurhythmia', 'arrhythmia' and 'polyrhythmia' (Lefebvre 2010: 16). Re-examining the zombified academic as a rhythmic problem allows us to comprehend the culture of crisis as one of changed and changeable life patterns. The culture of pessimism creates its narrative through a rhythmic system of despairs – local campus despairs, bad news from Government despairs, funding cycle despairs, and so on.

If we take the thematic concerns that are evident in the press reportage examined earlier and interpret them from a rhythmanalytic perspective, we discover a densely interwoven skein of rhythms which, when considered together, become a concert of despairs. There can never be a happy result, only further decline. Education is over. Education needs to be transformed, reanimated. Efficiency measures are invented to attempt to restart the illusion of life, but serve to only falsely extend life.

To draw a musical analogy, some of the rhythms structuring academic work are dominant, some minor, some serve as a kind of *leitmotif* rippling along the surface, while still others are contrapuntal in character. For instance, there are the rhythms particular to the academic calendar: in many Australian universities, two 12-week semesters, punctuated by short 'non-teaching' periods at the mid-point of each, as well as 'non-semester' time in the middle of and book-ending each calendar year which traditionally are marked by the rather different rhythms of research and the 'conference season'. These are also shaped, in key ways, by established, slower rhythms that include everything from the systematized temporal strictures imposed by 'industrial time', the Gregorian calendar, as well as seasonal cycles, as well as the more intimate biorhythms of each individual worker. Again, this is no different to many other professions and sectors that are slowly being fragmented and overturned by the pressures of communications technology and shifts in work cultures. However, the academic zone is interesting for its responses to these broad changes.

The result is a series of rhythms that are at once structural, processual, organizational, individual, cyclic, and (to invoke de Certeau's pairing) simultaneously strategic and tactical.[1] What is more, these rhythms can be personally and professionally fulfilling and enriching, as well as being more of the order of obligation. Some would seem in harmony while others appear in conflict with one another.[2] Some signal depletion, while others signal various forms of renewal.

These often conflicting 'braided' rhythms are deeply embedded in academic work in a variety of ways, reinforced through the various forms of 'apprenticeship', and thereby internalized. Lamentation offers a kind of seasonal festival for reaction, analysis and self-reflection. A festival of renewal and sacrifice like any other. It forces part of the discussion, and therefore part of the life of the contemporary humanities academic, to be about the abstract changes in their environment. We discuss the decline of the environment to ritualize not the passing of one type of world or another, but also to foster our own resentment and to build resentment in others. This helps form bonds against the injustice characterized; the lamentation serves the purpose of allowing braided rhythms to form in unusual places.

Conclusions

As zombification has become a prevailing image of popular culture, and equally an obsession of academics seeking to explain the popular, it has also become the image of a certain type of academic life. Lurching in reaction to any signs of life, zombie academics rush to devour anything that reminds them of the life they never properly lived. The ideal state belongs to no person; the disappointment of the dream defines the same dream.

The nihilism described in this chapter is never abrupt. Nihilism has always pervaded the humanities academic environment and many of these shifts and changes are products of their time, indicative of the broader changes to social institutions whereby the fantasy of use-value and economic rationalism erased the purposes of those institutions.

However much the individual may have a highly individualized work practice and personal relationship with their craft, the total environmental collapse of the culture of the humanities is a peculiar and perhaps historical moment. The negativity associated with this moment strips away the capability of the individual to respond, and crisis replaces order as the organizing principle of the humanities.

In trying to make sense of academic life, what the discourse of lamentation (or zombie discourse) struggles to come to terms with is the 'banal, messy, complex, contingent' (Milne 2010: 134). This is particularly so as it structures the relationship between what Thacker terms 'life-as-time, life-as-form, and life-as-spirit' (2010: 250). The discourse of lamentation has difficulty accounting for the messiness which comes with the understanding that 'life is always "meat" (the thickness, the facticity of life)', life is '"soul" (the formal principle of the creation of life [and the possibility of its recuperation in the face of destructive forces])', and life is '"pattern" (the intangible plane of organization running throughout life)'. What is left in the middle of these half-states is the shambling shape lurching across fields, arms outstretched, hungering for the symbolic return to a normalcy that has long since been devoured.

Notes

1   A colleague once suggested that the considerable flexibility that comes with academic work (especially concerning the times and places of work) tends to escape organizational measurement and the bureaucratic desire to capture and rectify this apparent lack of accountability is precisely why academics are audited in so many different ways. As Moten and Harney put it, 'this is the weakness of the university, the lapse in its homeland security. It needs labour power for … "enlightenment-type critique", but, somehow, labour always escapes' (2004: 103).

2   With respect to the second of these, the ramped up rhythms of contemporary academic review and publication cycles at times appear to increasingly share the 'just-in-time' metrics of freight logistics and are thus at direct odds to the slower, contemplative rhythms long taken to be seen as 'proper' to considered critical analysis. It is in this sense that Derrida bemoans the fact that, in our time, 'the least acceptable thing on television, on the radio, or in the newspapers today is for intellectuals to take their time or to waste other people's time' (Derrida and Stiegler 2002: 6–7).

The living dead and the dead living: contagion and complicity in contemporary universities

Holly Randell-Moon, Sue Saltmarsh and Wendy Sutherland-Smith

In this chapter, we examine the current state of professional academic freedom and research in terms of what we see as the zombification of the academy. We argue that neo-liberal reforms to the academy have created a research culture that treats academics as non-thinking entities (the living dead), who feel they have limited control over their research and funding amidst a pervasive and contagious audit culture. But whilst these reforms may be experienced by academics as an externally introduced form of control that saps or sucks the 'life' out of research activity, the proliferation of neo-liberal reforms is only enabled through the complicit reproduction of the audit culture by academics themselves. In this sense, academics (as the dead living) contribute, in ambivalent and contradictory ways, to the zombification of the academy.

This chapter and its concern with zombification in academic life emerges out of a 2009–10 study[1] in which we interviewed 31 Australian academics in sixteen different universities across four states[2] about research leadership in practice-based professions such as business and management, teacher education and nursing. Although the project focused specifically on research leadership and mentoring in these fields,[3] what emerged from the study was a palpable and widespread concern expressed by academics about institutional and governmental research assessment and audit exercises. Practice-based professions are experiencing a rapid reorganization of research culture as a result of neo-liberal policy reforms. Those who teach and research in practice-based professions know and understand how complex organizations outside of the academy can be run productively. As such, the responses to research policy examined in this chapter come from academics with considerable business acumen and organizational experience, who are concerned with the sustainability of a competitive and audit-based research culture. These responses also speak to wider concerns about academic labour across the broader higher education sector. In light of these concerns, we apply the trope of 'zombification' to our interview data, to explore how neo-liberal reforms to the academy, which are centred on discourses of productivity and activity, paradoxically create feelings of compliance and passivity.

Participants in our study experienced the impact of a pervasive audit culture on their working lives as largely negative. Reflecting on these experiences, we consider audit cultures and their contagious grip on university work to be exemplified by the zombie trope. In particular, this chapter focuses on three features of zombification: (1) inability to think, (2) loss of individual control, and (3) contagion. These features as applied to academic labour encapsulate the loss of control and autonomy over research experienced by the academics in our study. Nonetheless, academics are neither completely powerless, nor removed from the impost of a seemingly infectious neo-liberal audit culture on the academy. To this end, we draw on a Foucauldian conceptualization of power as diffuse and productive, in order to examine the interplay between contagion and complicity in relation to the spread and reproduction of audit culture. By framing audit culture in simplistic binary terms – as something that individual academics must free themselves from or become fully complicit in – academics permit audit culture a power of oppression and centralized control. It is important to remember, however, that the zombie's role in reproducing zombie contagion simultaneously makes it possible for the zombie to exceed and thwart the control of its zombie masters. We would argue that through engagement with the *productive* aspects of neo-liberal culture, which depends for its operation on *active* rather *passive* subjects, critical scholars are better situated to name and critique our complicity in the production of neo-liberalism in the academy. In channelling this activity, we can begin to reformulate and reanimate academic life and work.

The living dead and the dead living in academic culture

The recent re-emergence of the zombie in popular culture has led critics to argue that we are experiencing a 'zombie renaissance' (Bishop 2009). Indeed, the proliferation of zombies on media screens led one journalist to enthuse, 'zombies are so hot right now' (TvFix 2011). Scientists have recently discovered a new species of fungus in the Amazon 'that turns ants into zombies' (Osborne 2011), universities now offer courses on zombies (*The Telegraph* 2010) and a group of mathematicians hypothesized that the only pandemic capable of wiping out the human race is zombies (Lenon 2009). As the latter events indicate, zombies and their kin have now begun to invade the academy. Felicity Wood describes academics as the zombies of audit culture (2010: 237) who become enchanted by the occult qualities of corporate managerialism 'purported to bestow efficiency, economic prosperity and success' (227). Nick Couldry and Angela McRobbie describe 'the idea' of the university as dead (2010: 1); Henry Giroux claims that it is 'hardly breathing' (2009: 691); and Mary Evans finds that higher education has become infected with a 'horrible psychic reality' (2004: 32) that has produced a 'nightmare world' (34) full of 'dead bodies' (42) with creatures 'from the depths of hell' (46).

The permeation of popular and academic culture with zombie metaphors can be linked to the emergence of a volatile and intensifying neo-liberal economic climate. Chris Harman, for example, writes that 'twenty-first century capitalism as a whole is a zombie system, seemingly dead when it comes to achieving human goals and responding to human feelings, but capable of sudden spurts of activity that cause chaos all around' (2009: 12). If the current neo-liberal order is 'dead' to human desires that are oriented to goals outside of market forces, Richard Sennett argues that it takes a particular kind of human to flourish in this environment. 'A self [that is] oriented to the short term, focused on potential ability, willing to abandon past experience is – to put a kindly face on the matter – an unusual sort of human being' (2006: 5). That the skills required to succeed in this new culture of neo-liberal capitalism seem unusual and strange is reflected in the historical association of zombification with the dehumanizing effects of capitalist economies.

In their study of colonialism, capitalism and the occult, Jean Comaroff and John Comaroff note the zombie's association in rural South African provinces with the 'fear of being reduced to ghost labour' and 'being abducted to feed the fortunes of a depraved stranger' (2002: 789). They argue that the contemporary proliferation of zombie urban legends in South Africa must be understood as a revivification of older zombie motifs, which first made their appearance with the introduction of new colonial forms of labour and social organization in the late nineteenth and early twentieth centuries (794; see also Taussig 1980: 20). Elsewhere, the origin of the zombie trope has been traced to stories and representations of the plight of indentured Haitian labourers in the 1920s (see Dayan 1997; Dendle 2007; Stratton 2011a). Zombies appear to emerge in times of crises generated by shifts in the evolution of capitalism. They function to explain the otherwise sudden and mysterious appearance of a select few who control the means to wealth and the alienation felt by those whose lives become subject to the inexorable demands of labour (Comaroff and Comaroff 2002: 782–783).

In a western academic context, zombification aptly describes the embodied, dehumanizing effects of business and consumption models as applied to the administration, teaching and research work undertaken by academic staff. The alignment of higher education 'with corporate power and market values' (Giroux 2009: 670) has been justified on the basis that such models enable greater transparency of the research conducted in universities (ensuring that public funds are well spent) and that students (repositioned as consumers of knowledge) will have greater choice and flexibility in their learning (Schmidtlein 2004: 264). Under the auspices of economic accountability, neo-liberal governments have adopted benchmarking or auditing exercises to collate and evaluate the research produced in publicly funded universities. For example, the Research Assessment Exercise (RAE) in the United Kingdom and the Excellence in Research for Australia (ERA) initiative both involve the collation and ranking of publication data and research produced by professional academics. Government funding is then allocated to public universities on the basis of these rankings.

Whilst these policies purport to boost research productivity and quality, most participants in our study took a different view. Interviews with academics in professional practice-based fields such as teacher education, nursing, business and management included a range of participants – early career academics, department heads, members of university support units, professors and senior faculty executives. Despite considerable diversity across interviewees' positions and tertiary locations, there was a common concern at the loss of autonomy and control over research brought about by institutional demands for increased output and productivity. These responses to neo-liberal reforms and the economic management of academic labour are exemplified by the zombie trope in terms of the inability to think, loss of individual control, and contagion. The first two features are consistent with scholarly treatments of neo-liberal capitalism as a proliferating force that reduces workers to the living dead, unable to think or exhibit autonomy over their working conditions – something felt acutely by professional academics whose role is predicated on the ability to think critically.

corruption on us

The third feature of the zombie trope, contagion, is reflected in the ambivalent and contradictory ways in which academics acquiesce to neo-liberal reforms, further reproducing and spreading audit culture throughout the higher education sector. Whilst audit culture produces zombiism insomuch as it transforms academics into the living dead, the living dead also function to comment on the dead living. By dead living, we refer to those aspects of everyday life, work and relationships that are lifeless or meaningless; a form of living that is 'dead' to creativity, risk, challenge or change. This might involve 'playing it safe' by developing curricula within widely accepted paradigms, or producing research solely for the purposes of achieving a high ERA ranking. Dead living is the inverse of zombiism, as living is reduced to a series of monotonous tasks which hold little significance or meaning for individuals – they are intellectually and emotionally 'dead' already – but it is also the precursor to zombiism. Zombies typically go unnoticed at first, because they simply blend into an environment that is already mundane and tedious. What aspects of academic life were already host to the dead living before the plague of audit culture set in? In order to answer this question, we will firstly provide a fuller account of how academics become the living dead.

Sucking the life out of academic freedom

As discussed above, higher education reforms have changed the ways research funding and activity are accounted for, typically involving auditing and quality control mechanisms designed to assess and ensure 'research excellence'. However, as Schmidtlein notes, 'there is a tension between governments' legitimate interests in institutional accountability and quality and the values represented by institutional autonomy that have been described by many scholars and practitioners' (2004: 264). For instance, scholars have argued that government initiatives such as the ERA rely on arbitrary and vague notions of 'quality' and 'excellence' (Shore 2008), emphasize process over the substance and long-term effect of research (Cooper and Poletti 2011; Redden 2008) and increase bureaucratic and administrative academic labour whilst reducing the time available for research and teaching (Evans 2004; Giroux 2009; Sparkes 2007). It is here that we find the first two features of the zombie trope in academic culture: (1) inability to think, and (2) loss of individual control.

Most participants in our study took the view that assessment and benchmarking exercises value conformity and subservience to university policy over critical scholarship. For example, one interviewee argued that auditing measures produce 'an over-emphasis on the unimportance of ratings and counting' and a 'culture of compliance and counting'

(Leila, Senior Lecturer, Business/Management). As these policies are often underpinned by vague terms like 'quality' and 'excellence', it can be difficult to keep track of institutional requirements; as one interviewee noted, 'it's a bizarre game' (Sylvia, Senior Lecturer, Business/Management). These sentiments bear out Stephen Ball's observation that 'we now operate within a baffling array of figures, performance indicators, comparisons and competitions – in such a way that the contentments of stability are increasingly elusive, purposes are contradictory, motivations blurred and self worth slippery' (2001: 212). In order to reconcile the seemingly disparate incentives to accomplish institutional audit requirements whilst maintaining a critical research culture, Ball suggests 'we tell ourselves "necessary fictions" which rationalize our own intensification or legitimate our involvements in the rituals of [audit] performance' (2001: 216). For Leila and Sylvia, reducing the significance of audit exercises to 'counting' and imagining them as a 'game' constitutes one way of resolving the split between the performance of audit tasks and the capacity to exercise criticism.

But while Ball contends that fabrications and fictions are necessary to cope with the cognitive gap between neo-liberal policy imperatives and traditional understandings of academic scholarship, the expansion and intensification of audit exercises may simply evacuate the critical and creative capacity for action. For instance, one academic spoke of researchers being unable to act due to the increasing complexity and confusion of institutional policies:

> I see people being paralysed ... by all [the] demands on them [such] that they don't actually act, even if, however much encouragement and sticks ... [are] waved at them, how much resources seem to be there.
>
> (Penny, Senior Lecturer, Business/Management)

As Penny observes, even when resources are available, often accessing (or attempting to access) this support simply creates more layers of bureaucracy for staff to negotiate, ultimately detracting from research work. Paralysis is the logical response to bureaucratic reforms that transform 'educators into dispensable labour with little or no power over the basic decisions that structure academic work' (Giroux 2009: 683). Compliance with bureaucratic reforms and external impositions all too often reduce academic labour to mindless busywork, despite the fact that these reforms are intended to bring about increased productivity and activity.

Another area in which academics experience a devaluing of their critical thinking skills and a loss of autonomy over their research is the institutional organization of research into strategic or priority areas. This aspect of research management was particularly galling to interviewees who considered that their own research interests and plans were being defined for them. As one interviewee noted:

> [B]ecause the whole system is geared towards getting university support it's much easier to gain university support when the person can point to the fact that it's a research priority

in that university … if you happen to be a person whose area is smiled upon, well you're very lucky; if you're not, then you're unlucky.

(Tim, Professor, Teacher Education)

This method of research management and organization is often coercive. For example, one interviewee was told by her Head of School that it would be advantageous if staff shifted to discipline-based research in terms of internal and external funding opportunities. She concluded:

[Y]ou're in this constant struggle [where] I won't be bothered doing anything then, I'm too busy anyway.

(Penny, Senior Lecturer, Business/Management)

These responses attest to an overwhelming view that little that could be done to claw back the individual autonomy, both within and beyond the workplace, seen as necessary to intellectual life. One participant, for example, described how his Dean of Research suggested that academics write 'papers at midnight on a Saturday night' (James, Lecturer, Business/ Management) in order to meet the research demands placed on them by the university. Another researcher felt that there was an expectation that 'you've almost got to approach research as if it's your hobby because it will … it inevitably impinges on life beyond the university campus and so I think that you don't get to switch research off' (Amy, Research Director, Teacher Education). The notion that research is a 'hobby' is one of the necessary fictions both research managers and academic staff tell themselves so that production of work outside normal university hours is not understood as the excess of labour that it is. Many of the early career researchers interviewed in our study lamented the idea that a 24/7 academic lifestyle was required for success in academia. One early career researcher expressed his disappointment that 'a lot of people who have made it, who are supposed to be the ones who could mentor me, they're a 24/7 academic – and it's as if that academic identity has taken over' as the norm for academic work (Gary, Lecturer, Teacher Education). Such expectations imply that academic labour necessarily extends beyond a working week and unproblematically dominates life outside the university.

That it has become almost *de rigueur* for academics to research outside of normal university working hours is a consequence of neo-liberal reforms to the academy which attempt to maximize productivity. The association of zombiism with capitalist labour is centred on the loss of autonomy and control over production, but the association also draws attention to the dehumanizing effects of the long hours required to sustain an increasing production rate. In order to increase productivity within capital relations, workers are reduced 'to separate, marketable commodities in the form of their body parts' (Wood 2010: 238). When applied to academic labour and the production of knowledge, the alienated body part is the brain. The zombie trope then is a fitting explication of the exploitation and control over that research-producing organ by university managers.

Contagion and complicity in contemporary universities

We have been discussing the zombification of the academy so far in terms of the increasing bureaucratization of academic life and neo-liberal imperatives to maximize research productivity. Both of these features of academic life lead to an inability to think and loss of control over research production, exemplified in the zombie figure as mindless and lacking autonomy. Given 'the speed and enthusiasm with which the corporatization of many universities has taken place, both locally and internationally' (Wood 2010: 231), the means through which academics are reduced to zombies also bears a resemblance to the virus or plague that spreads zombiism. At the same time, however, it is important to note that in popular culture, zombie contagion often exceeds the control of the authorities or the scientists who are initially responsible for creating the zombie virus. As with films such as *Night of the Living Dead* (Romero 2004) and *28 Days Later* (Boyle 2002), zombies themselves are responsible for spreading and increasing zombification. Thus, whilst neo-liberal university reforms may be experienced by academics as an externally introduced form of control that saps or sucks the 'life' out of research activity, the proliferation of neo-liberal reforms is only enabled through the complicit reproduction of an audit culture by academics themselves. Although our study indicated there is considerable anxiety and negativity about the ways in which neo-liberal reforms have been implemented by research leaders and managers in Australian universities, many participants also expressed an ambivalent acquiescence to these reforms. As one professor in the field of education reflected:

> Having limped through the changes in the VET sector in the 90s and the changes in the senior secondary schooling areas, what I see this institution and other institutions doing is exactly the same thing. Canberra cracks the whip and every institution has to turn around and fall in line. So the bureaucratization it's moved ... I just see it that it's, bureaucratization and forms of self-surveillance that have been brought in that we're all complicit in, aren't we?
>
> (Belle, Professor, Teacher Education)

While recent reforms to the academy have had pervasive and negative effects on the ability of scholars to think critically and maintain autonomy over their research, Belle's comments illustrate that these reforms are not so much 'new' as they are an extension of earlier forms of bureaucratization whose success hinged on institutional and academic complicity. In pointing to this earlier complicity, it is useful to think through the ways the zombification of the academy has fed off the dead living or lifeless aspects already permeating academia such as: the privileging of publications over the experience of developing research, a focus on student results rather than learning, and career progression through individual achievement, which obfuscates the collegial nature of scholarship. Typically in zombie films, it is the seemingly lifeless and mundane aspects of a society or city that enables the proliferation of zombiism to initially go unnoticed. In *Shaun of the Dead* (Wright 2004), the parallel between zombiism and the mundane is used to humorous effect. In an early scene from that film, Shaun (played by the film's cowriter Simon Pegg) and Ed (Nick Frost) are leaving their local pub late at night, singing the Grandmaster Melle Mel song 'White Lines'. Their singing is interrupted by the moans of an approaching zombie. Shaun and Ed, however, mistake the zombie for someone who is extremely inebriated and incorporate his moans into the bass-line of the song. In focusing on the association between zombiism and the dead living, we want to argue that apathy, complicity and competitiveness play a role in reproducing a zombie academic culture and exemplify the third feature of the zombie trope: contagion.

In our study, compliance, and in some cases strategic complicity in the form of 'playing the game', were often described as necessary in order to secure competitive funding and to ensure job security. For example, one interviewee commented, 'the whole thing is just game theory as far as I'm concerned' (Sylvia, Senior Lecturer, Business/Management). Acquiescence to research reforms, whilst still maintaining a critical position in relation to them, is one way that academics endeavour to negotiate a research culture that requires compliance. However, such complicity is also a form of contagion because it reduces research or teaching to a form of passive instrumentalism. Acquiescence can also lead to intense competition and the abandonment of collegiality. One senior research manager described negatively the type of scholar who is able to succeed in contemporary academia:

> The other interesting phenomenon we've noted is that rather unpleasant comment the other day called the selfish researcher. So they're saying right, okay my promotional prospects and reward systems in here depend on what I'm doing in research. Great, then I'll do what I'm required to do in teaching, so if you want me to front that class but you know I'll do the minimum I can get away with. If you want me to serve on that committee, no sorry, can't actually fit that one in. Can I come to meetings or school meetings or research meetings, nah, you want people to put their hands up and ... and they become dedication [sic] to furthering their research career which in one sense it's about output and then they'll be snapped up and they will leave.
>
> (Daryl, Dean of Research, Business/Management)

This notion of a 'selfish' researcher embodies a sort of contagion that disregards collegiality and the value of research beyond an individual academic's interests, and further reinforces the asymmetries of academic labour. But whilst academics may emphasize the importance of transformational and democratic scholarship in the face of neo-liberal reforms (see Giroux 2005; Molesworth et al. 2009) – a characterization of academic research with which we are aligned – we note nonetheless that the competitive and hierarchical nature of the academy has been in play for some time. Evans argues that it is precisely these negative aspects of academic culture that have created an enduring public perception of the academy as elitist and esoteric in its research (2004: 33). Although scholars are right to contest this image and the instrumentalization of research under neo-liberal reforms, the cynical pursuit of knowledge or 'playing the game' exemplify a kind of dead living that lays the groundwork for the induction and proliferation of the living dead into the academy.

Drawing on Foucauldian conceptions of disciplinary power, we would argue that academics are the pivotal point at which these neo-liberal policies are enacted and embodied. For Foucault, power is never simply an oppressive force, but rather a system of self-directed control and discipline whose very effectiveness lies in its ability to encourage individual subjects to reproduce technologies of control and rule (1977: 26). This self-directed control eliminates the need for external physical or institutional coercion, since subjects carry out this coercion on themselves. For this reason, Foucault does not treat power as a repressive or oppressive force but as constitutive and productive:

> Power functions. Power is exercised through networks, and individuals do not simply circulate in those networks; they are in a position to both submit to and exercise this power. They are never the inert or consenting targets of power; they are always its relays. In other words, power passes through individuals. It is not applied to them.
>
> (2003: 29)

If we consider this Foucauldian conception of power in relation to the zombification of the academy, it is possible to see the complex ways academics work to perpetuate audit culture even as they are simultaneously concerned about its effects. As Ball notes, neo-liberal models of job performance and efficiency encourage academics 'to think about themselves as individuals who calculate about themselves, "add value" to themselves, improve their productivity, live an existence of calculation' (2001: 223). Whilst academics may *feel* disempowered and at a loss to counter neo-liberal reforms to the academy, they nevertheless participate in and perpetuate these reforms and their dehumanizing effects. By internalizing, adopting and enacting the competitive pressures and demands of a neo-liberal culture, academics only make themselves more attractive as victims to the zombification of research culture. As such, when academics acquiesce to neo-liberal reforms, they enact the very technologies of control to which they are opposed.

If we follow the zombie trope to its logical conclusion, it is evident that 'the phantasm of the zombie ... does nothing but attest to the fulfilment of a system that moves the victim to internalize his condition' (Dayan 1997: 33). The zombie has been misread as a passive rather than active agent. In other words, it is the zombie's role in reproducing zombie contagion that simultaneously makes it possible for the zombie to exceed and thwart the control of its zombie masters. The problem with conceiving the zombification of the academy as a system of management which oppresses academics is that audit culture is then framed in simplistic binary terms as something that individual academics must free themselves from or become fully complicit in. This permits audit culture a power of oppression and central control that overlooks the role of academics in reproducing this system. Audit culture is credited with too much power and academics with too little. One of the effects of disciplinary power, Foucault argues, is that the 'mastery and awareness of one's own body' required to carry out self-discipline can also produce 'a counter-attack in that same body', in the form of resistance to disciplinary regimes (1980: 56). Following Foucault, we would argue that through engagement with the *productive* aspects of neo-liberal culture, which depends for its operation on *active* rather than *passive* subjects, critical scholars are better situated to name and critique our complicity in the reproduction of neo-liberalism in the academy. In channelling this activity, we can begin to reformulate and reanimate academic life and work.

Reanimating academic life

Zombies seem to emerge when life itself, hinging as it does on the importance of human relations, thinking and freedom, is threatened by the loss of that which constitutes us as humans. In this chapter, we have argued that three features of zombification – inability to think, loss of individual control and contagion – characterize the experiences recounted by most participants in our study of research leadership and research culture in Australian universities. For these academics, neo-liberal reforms that emphasize slavish compliance to audit cultures are experienced as dehumanizing processes that erode, rather than cultivate, the kinds of innovation, productivity and interdisciplinary problem solving claimed as policy goals and outcomes. Zombie cultures emerge as both new and experienced academics alike struggle with limited time and even less institutional support, to find themselves shuffling through increasingly meaningless bureaucratized terrain that was, for many, once the vibrant ground of intellectual rigour and collegial endeavour.

The proliferation of zombie myths and stories in a newly colonized and industrialized culture makes sense when the bodies and creative capacity of indigenous workers are exploited and then discarded. Yet here we would ask by what strange turn of events do highly paid professional workers in a privileged institutional setting such as a university find themselves in such peril that they resort to the language of magic to explain their predicament? If we follow Ball's thesis that zombiism is a necessary fiction created by academics to explain how an otherwise incompatible audit culture operates alongside critical scholarship, we could see this representational abstraction as an extension of the 'complex set of ... strategies and practical tactics which underpin the fabrication of performance' in contemporary neo-liberal universities (2001: 221). In the current academic climate, 'we make fantasies of ourselves, aestheticize ourselves' to meet institutional requirements (221). Importantly though, once performance is embedded in audit culture, 'we also have everyday opportunities to refuse these ways of accounting for ourselves' (223). In this sense, we would call for a consideration of the ways in which zombification remains in many respects an active, agentive process, in which autonomy is in part relinquished rather than taken by force in every circumstance.

Despite the havoc wrought by zombie contagion, zombification ultimately presents as the fate of those who fail to recognize its dangers, refuse to exercise agency in resisting its power, or endeavour to manipulate it to their own ends. In *Zombieland* (Fleischer 2009), the United States has become infected with a zombie plague. A surviving quartet travel to Los Angeles, where they discover that Hollywood actor Bill Murray has managed to stave off infection by dressing as a zombie. The quartet is initially impressed with Murray's survival strategies. That is, until one of their members fatally shoots him, having mistaken Murray for an actual zombie. After this incident, the quartet learns that it is essential to operate as a team and avoid acquiescence to zombification, even through subterfuge.

Our research findings demonstrate that these potential perils are being played out in the academy today – some treat zombie culture as a game to be played, others give up in resignation, and others capitalize on the zombification of colleagues in order to gain power and privilege for themselves. As academics we are not controlled by power, we exercise (differing levels of) power. This power can be used for inclusivity, in terms of distributed leadership models that encourage the exchange of ideas and input from staff, so that they have some ownership over research management. Other forms of inclusiveness involve maintaining contact among teaching teams so that staff are not 'a legion of lost souls' struggling in the 'valley of the shadow of death' without contact or support, and treating knowledge as a living entity that requires new ideas and insights, in course content and research, to survive. Cross-disciplinary collaboration in teaching and research also reanimates thinking, discussion and action. The development of partnerships between seemingly distinct disciplines, such as cultural studies and education, can challenge the externally imposed and institutionally organized research 'hubs' or 'strengths' that limit creative collegial research relationships. By refusing to succumb to neo-liberal constructs of research, intellectual life can be reclaimed. It is the power of thinking and sharing ideas that stops contagion in its tracks. In our view, the reanimation of academic life relies in no small part on individual and collective commitment to and insistence upon recognizing, naming and actively resisting the dehumanizing effects of neo-liberal reforms on scholarship and collegiality.

Notes

1   The interview excerpts used in this chapter are drawn from a 2009–10 Gippsland Small Grant Research Support Scheme (SGRSS), Monash University, which is acknowledged with thanks. The authors also extend their thanks to the interviewees for their generous time and personal contributions to the study.

2   The number of universities in each of the states from which we interviewed participants were as follows: New South Wales (five universities), Victoria (four), Queensland (five) and Western Australia (two).

3   See Saltmarsh, Sutherland-Smith and Randell-Moon (2011a, 2011b) and Sutherland-Smith, Saltmarsh and Randell-Moon (2011).

Zombie solidarity

Ann Deslandes and Kristian Adamson

Resisting corporatism on campus

As the chapters in this collection testify, the system of higher education in the Anglosphere is presently overdetermined by the imposition of scarcity via corporatization and neo-liberalization. These phenomena are characterized, respectively, by excessive regulation of academic practice and deregulation of capital circulation in the sector. However, far from symbolizing the downfall of higher education as a public good, the zombie can offer a model of collective resistance to this state of affairs. The cinematic zombie, we note, possesses a *radical disinterest* in participating in this deadening culture as well as a palpable – indeed deeply threatening – lack of desire for the goods this culture produces and the differentiated class status it compels us to pursue. By radical disinterest, we don't simply mean the state of a 'disinterested observer', or of having a 'lack of interest', but rather a conscious refusal of the very terms in which one can be 'interested'. As in the scenes of everyday capitalist life in zombie films, on the scene of higher education we propose that a 'zombie solidarity' offers the most chance of resistance to the exhausted world that many of us writing in this collection are experiencing on and around the campuses we are attached to.

However, in the rampant majority of cases, the zombie appears as a negative figure, with the epitext for this book being no exception. In Gora and Whelan's op-ed introducing the book in *The Australian,* the zombie characterizes the life-sucking practices of institutional bureaucracy and management and the stupefied undergraduate, as well as the vacated ambience of university campuses (2010). As they put it, 'the deadly hand of corporatism has drained all life from campus', affecting all who set foot upon it. Tenured academics have become 'incapable of responding meaningfully' to the encroaching virus, whilst sessional staff wander as 'a legion of lost souls', supplying 'the raw material for University Inc'. As for students, they 'occupy a joyless twilight world that, superficially at least, resembles a university, although in reality they are vocational charnel houses'. Further afield, the global economic system governing this parlous state has been characterized by John Quiggin as 'zombie economics', whereby – despite a global financial crisis – the 'dead ideas' underpinned by market liberalism 'still walk among us', threatening mass contagion (2010; see also Peck 2010). For Henry Giroux, 'zombie politics' dominates the public sphere (2011).

Taken together, these critiques for which the zombie is the vehicle are targeted at neo-liberalism – the economic ideology that places the agency of the free market at centrestage and reduces the responsibility of states (as collective expressions of social governance) to provide the conditions for 'the good life'– including higher education, which instead becomes corporatized and standardized. As with other contemporary critiques of neo-liberalism, these writings present us with the imposition of scarcity onto such agencies of the good life, regulated through deadening systems of accounting such as the Research Assessment Exercise in Britain and the Research Quality Framework in Australia. As a loosely convergent worldview, these critiques of neo-liberalism articulate with many sophisticated analyses of, and strident campaigns against, the enculturated marketization of the higher education sector in the Anglosphere over the past decade (see e.g. Gregg 2009, National Tertiary Education Union 2009, Gill 2009, Ross 2008). They are marked, we suggest, by a profound attachment to a particular kind of good life. This is the good life of critical debate and democratic liberties, buttressed by a middle-class standard of living and characterized by financial stability and opportunities for self-actualization.

In this chapter, we consider the dominant critique of corporatization-as-zombification alongside a closer-up picture of those who co-labour on university campuses: not only salaried academics, union organizers and student activists but also cleaners, caterers, casual research assistants, casual tutors and lecturers, retail staff, undergraduate students, postgraduate students, administration managers, administration assistants and governors. We ask: what is it like to be together on campus under conditions of apparent zombification? Who, exactly, *are* the zombies? What are those of us in the humanities who critique current higher education cultures, and models of policy and funding, compelled to resist? And most importantly, how might we resist? What kind of solidarity is called for? We begin our exploration with the cinematic (primarily Romero) zombie as our touch point.

Resisting corporatism in the mall

Where can we find solidarity in zombie lore? Is it with the frightened survivors boarding themselves up inside a farmhouse, as in *Night of the Living Dead* (Romero 1968)? No: driven by fear, paranoia and a little racism, the living ultimately cause as much grief to themselves as the walking dead do. Is it in between the citizenry and the military as their nations are swamped by undead invaders, as in *28 Days Later* (Boyle 2002) and *Day of the Dead* (Romero 1985)? Again, no. The brutality of the military over the civilians ultimately jeopardizes the survival of both. In *Land of the Dead* (Romero 2005) and *Resident Evil* (Anderson 2002), it is greedy and corrupt corporate entities who destroy the cities. Consistently, we find that it is the living, not the dead, that are the true danger in most cinematic representations of the zombie. Indeed, the zombie operates merely as background to a distinctly human – or, more precisely, living – drama. When this human drama becomes too much, the doors begin to rattle and the moaning hordes shuffle out of the darkness. As such, the experience of the zombie is rarely central to the narrative. Besides occasional identifiable vestiges of their former lives, the zombies are as anonymous as they are many. The genre then tends to be more about us, as living; rather than about them, as dead. Indeed, Romero's zombie quartet has always been recognizable as social commentary, dealing with Cold War paranoia and racism (*Night of the Living Dead*), consumer culture (*Dawn of the Dead*) militarism (*Day of the Dead*) and class (*Land of the Dead*).

Take the opening credits of *Zombieland* (Fleischer 2009). Two men are fleeing a casino, zombies in close pursuit. One of the men is clutching wads of cash, the other his mug of beer, taking care not to spill too much. Neither is willing to let go of these material icons of consumer culture. For the two men, not even the walking dead can disrupt the value of consumption. Likewise, in Romero's cinema the living continue to operate within the discourses of the old world – consumption, competition, consumerism, and so on – trying to rebuild their place in the world. The zombie is a disruption to this – a force that keeps interfering with the attempts of the living to reconstitute the world that was. To be sure, this is usually by eating the living: but if we take a second look at the zombie inside the iconic mall of *Dawn of the Dead* (Romero 1978), we find that eating the living is not all that zombies 'do'.

The standard interpretation of *Dawn of the Dead* is that it is a commentary on the mindlessness of consumer culture (e.g. Paffenroth 2006: 45–69). The zombie/consumer moves about the mall unable to critically engage with their environment in pursuit of the commodity. Though this interpretation was clearly the intention of Romero, the consumer-as-zombie and zombie-as-consumer equivalence may be broken by the observation that the zombies are obviously not consuming anything within the mall at all – at least, not until the living turn up. This break between consumption and place-of-consumption is significant in our rethinking of the zombie.

The shopping mall is a particular kind of built environment, specifically designed to attract and facilitate the consumption of goods and services. The centre itself regulates these demands, both by formal (security guards ensuring teenagers aren't loitering, restrictions on dress) and informal means (pricing to attract different demographics, physical layout), and also by broader social and cultural habits: rules of interpersonal interactions, acknowledgement of private property, consumer culture, etc. (Voyce 2006). In *Dawn of the Dead*, many of these regulations are broken down: security guards are long gone; price no longer has meaning. Nonetheless, the survivors that begin to build a new life within the otherwise abandoned mall are still enthralled by the commodities the mall offers. In other words, the *habitus* that the mall demands remains within their relation to the mall and continues on the terms that were originally laid out, symbolically and physically. The survivor's attraction to the resources of the mall goes beyond what is needed to survive. With food and shelter secured they indulge in the luxury items around them and go 'shopping' for expensive clothing, fancy watches and so on.

The zombies in the mall, however, are marked by an absolute disinterest in these luxuries and habits. The undead treat the mall as any other space, and the demands of consumption it makes and signifies are refused and go unrecognized. Everything from the pleasures of luxury commodities to the safe operation of escalators is not only foreign to the zombie but a matter of complete disinterest. So, far from being the ideal consumer subject, the zombie is a nightmarish subject that fails to be interpellated by the economic discourses of consumer spaces. This does not result in the loss of desire. The zombie does not need to give up something in this mode of resistance, but rather the resistance of the zombie comes about because of the kinds of desires it has. It emerges as a subject defined by a disinterested refusal of the privilege, pleasure and leisure the corporate world permits.

This refusal is transformative in that it interrupts the consumerist cycle of desire and consumption that the mall both caters to and encourages. Through their lack of engagement with the mall as consumer space, the undead dissolve the consumerist imperative the mall fulfils – it becomes just another concrete building. In more militaristic terms, their refusal of the *habitus* of consumer culture liberates the mall from its social and economic regulations. In such a way, the zombie can provide us with a cultural resource for imagining resistance to the corporatized campus, based on autonomous and collective refusal. We suggest that this disinterested refusal might be a means to disrupt the *habitus* of the present-day campus, just as we have suggested it was within the consumer space of the shopping mall. So, rather than being something to avoid, zombies in the academy may be precisely what is required.

Campus co-labourers

Last year Tara Brabazon, a media studies professor at the University of Brighton, wrote her regular column in the prominent *Times Higher Education* (2011) in the form of a bilious take-down of a metaphoric member of the administrative staff at her workplace. The staff member, she suggested, was pathologically unable to communicate appropriately and had a particularly problematic use of e-mail; using it too frequently and without due consideration of the busy and important schedules of the academics she was employed to serve. Running through the article is a clear distinction between the academic and the administrator – not only the tasks performed and the status of those tasks but also their respective class positions. Brabazon paints herself as extraordinarily busy and important and the administration staff member as a major impediment to this performance. Particularly troubling to Brabazon is the administrator's 'personal' use of e-mail – its use for soliciting expressions of interest in '[renting her] sister's flat in Maidstone' or adopting 'one of [her] mother's kittens' – as well as the form or style of e-mails ('please stop using caps lock'), and the presumed personal deficiencies of the administrator ('You think that if you send enough Ccs to random citizens in the UK, you will be invited to Kate and William's wedding', e-mails 'sent after 3 pm on Fridays appear to be the result of a rather long and lubricated lunch', 'no, I do not watch *Neighbours*').

Underpinning these issues, for Brabazon, was the imperative of busy staff '[needing] to think carefully about their correspondence in difficult times'. These 'difficult times' are the very times that are the subject of this collection and for which the zombie is being used, largely, to communicate the depth of the crisis in university life and labour. In Brabazon's words:

We are moving into desperate times for a deeply underfunded higher education system. Time is our most precious resource. Research for most academics will be unfunded, with time for reading and writing pinched from family responsibilities. Teaching will be crowd control. Keeping lectures and tutorials at a level of quality – and even humanity – remains a stark challenge.

The distinction between academics and other university workers is driven home by Brabazon when she explains what an academic is and is not responsible for:

> I am a university academic. I am not responsible for computer systems, the printer, the photocopier, the car park, the environmental consequences of a university maintaining a car park, the woman who left the lights on her Ford Fiesta this morning, the stationery cupboard, your inability to find a pen in the stationery cupboard, or the central heating and its relationship to Al Gore's *An Inconvenient Truth*.

Doubtless intentionally, Brabazon's article generated strong responses with comments appearing (at least ostensibly) from academic and administration staff (including, again at least ostensibly, from her own university workplace). In many cases, deep offence was registered by university administration staff who felt they were interpellated, on a number of levels, as inherently inferior. In other cases, comments praised Brabazon's highlighting of breakdowns in university communication systems, which are considered symptomatic of the funding and identity crises particular to the neo-liberalized institution and represented by the apparent incompetence of administration staff.

Comments also debated the relative valuation of time and work produced between academia and its administration, with some comments variously disputing the percentage of income earned, time spent on work and distribution of risk and opportunity between academic and administrative staff. By way of example:

> Given that Tara is a professor, it's certain that the person she's attacking is on half her salary or less, and quite possibly a third of it or even a quarter of it (average professorial salary: nearly £70k in 2007–08, according to THES [Times Higher Education Supplement]; junior administrator: anywhere between £18-24k). Tara might feel bullied and harassed in her role, but to take that out publically [sic] on someone who's literally earning half of what she earns or significantly less … wow.

The question of collective resistance to deleterious conditions in higher education was therefore raised, such as by 'JohnH':

> In the institution where I work I spend a lot of time socializing with academic staff – I count many as friends (and yes, they count me as one too). I am not ignorant of or unsympathetic to the pressures they have. But I won't stand in solidarity with them if the supposed solution is to demean, insult and chastise those other workers who are at the lowest ranks, who wield the least power, who have the least say of all.

Indeed, the prospect of the 'go-slow' trade union tactic is raised in a number of comments, as Brabazon is felt to have clearly refused solidarity with her colleagues in administration during difficult times in the university sector. 'Brighton administrator' warns Brabazon of the following:

> Congratulations on ensuring your future career is full of misery. You have, with one simple and effective letter, guaranteed that no administrator you work with will ever put themselves out for you again. Prepare yourself for meetings scheduled in the downstairs out-of-order toilet, the constant disappearance of your mail, and never again receiving a message on time.

As Brabazon's piece and its comment thread implies, the current state of higher education in the Anglosphere cannot be understood as a lived experience without accounting for the diversity and inequality of status, roles, resources and rewards on campus, as a physical as well as a virtual space. Zombie solidarity, as we have termed it, subsists within this experience. In a system that is collapsing under the weight of imposed scarcity, we propose that the signification of the zombie may itself collapse across the system's stakeholders. Thus, the question of solidarity goes beyond the designation of 'intelligent life' as bulwark against 'zombification' (Gora and Whelan 2010), and it becomes difficult to determine who the zombies are and who needs to protect themselves from zombification. This chapter is concerned with the prospects for collectivity where there is entrenched inequality, and the role that people like us, writing in this collection – students, scholars and teachers – might play. We argue this not in spite of the university's privileged place in access to the good life – which we take as read in the fight for higher education as a public good – but because of it. Indeed, the prospect of collectivity where there is inequality is a founding question for most studies of solidarity within and beyond campus, and one that remains a serious preoccupation in our efforts as scholars to bring a humanities pedagogy to life. We turn here (as Stratton has done recently, 2011b) to the zombie as a figure of resistant collectivity: against its signification as necessarily threatening to the good life, loosely and collectively conceived.

In observing 'the functional dimension that its abjectness seems to lend to it', aesthetic theorist Lars Bang Larsen asks, 'why does it [the zombie] lend itself so easily as a metaphor for alienation, rolling readily off our tongues?' (2010, see also Lauro and Embry 2008). Larsen puts the zombie to work in the mode of solidarity, suggesting that '[what] is useful about the monster is that it is immediately recognizable as estrangement, and in this respect is non-alienating'. Larsen's zombie is also amenable to the university context, being a figure of immaterial labour. As he puts it, 'the zombie's intellectual capacity may be brought to bear on the terms "intellectual labour" and "cognitive capitalism", used to denote brain-dead – and highly regulated – industries such as advertising and mass media', and indeed higher education (Neilson 2010). The zombie thus 'can help us meditate on alienation in our era of an immaterial capitalism that has turned life into cash'. It also marks the possibility of a space beyond cash-converted existence: 'the zombie represents the degree to which we are incapable of reimagining the future.' That being the case, the zombie never finally settles, and always falls apart. 'What is left', declares Larsen, 'are material traces to be picked up anew.'

So what, then, might be a material analysis of an apparently zombified campus? How are the labourers we listed above differentiated? In this view, perhaps the first mark of distinction operates between university workers by income and its associated class location. University campuses reflect the inequality of income present in Australian society as well as the unequal distribution of other forms of capital such as cultural and social capital. In such a way we can observe the mutability and undecidability of the zombie. Consider for example the extremes of the income gap at the University of Sydney, as a representative example of Australian 'Group of Eight' universities. At Sydney, outsourced cleaning staff can expect to earn about 44 per cent of the wage of entry-level full-time academic staff, just 20 per cent of the wage of professorial staff and 4 per cent of the Vice-Chancellor's wage. To put this in some perspective, the Vice-Chancellor will earn the cleaner's yearly income in about two weeks; a professor will do the same in a little over two months. These figures do not take account of the other benefits enjoyed by academic staff, such as social capital, job security, the privilege of working a job of relative choice rather than a job of necessity and so on. Likewise, the income gap between general and academic staff sees general staff earning about 60 per cent of the wages of their academic colleagues, depending on the stage of their career. As a nexus of the social, university campuses also contain inequalities such as those associated with gender, sexuality, race and ability. To turn from staff to students: we note that higher education participation rates for Indigenous people (DEEWR 2011), women (AVCC 2006) and migrants from non-Anglo countries (with the exception of China, see Hugo 2007) continue to remain markedly lower than those of white, able-bodied men (see also Mason 2010).

This is the scene on which claims are made about the flight of capital from the university sector, the audit culture that stunts intellectual inquiry and the economic insecurity faced by graduates and entry-level academics. That is, it is a scene that reflects the inequalities of liberal capitalist democratic society and yet, as demonstrated by the primary connotations of a 'zombified academy', critics of these inequalities tend only to account for certain effects or instances in the name of a universal public good. Brabazon will speak of desperate times for the humanity of higher education whilst writing off an entire class of university workers as always-already incompetent; politically progressive academics will hire casuals for teaching or research relief but do not take responsibility for their adequate contracting and payment (see Jonas 2009). In this view, we suggest that those who are living lives that are not reportably affected by the neo-liberalization of the university – the gamut from cleaners to caterers, admin to adjunct whose labour counts for nothing on research quality indexes – are actually the most likely candidates for refusing zombification. To be sure, as Brabazon sneers, they may be more interested in other pursuits entirely.

Zombie solidarity

This is how we come to the zombie horde as a response to the political problem faced by university workers and their place in neo-liberalized culture and society. The more prominent modes of resistance are made visible by salaried academics – those with the cultural and material resources that give rise to strike action and op-ed columns in prominent media outlets. The negligible participation of casual academics and other lower-paid university workers in these activities suggests their lack of relevance to a project that may seem to be aimed at wresting some purchase back on the life-goods that an academic career once promised. Little wonder then that prevention of the zombie apocalypse is more visibly sought by the relatively privileged. For if humanity (as the 'good' opposite to the 'bad' zombie) is to have a future, then the existing world of inequality and class hierarchy has a future. The alternative picture is one of those who are privileged by the system (and can therefore access the requisite resources to advocate for its reform) using their privilege to make conditions better for workers across the system (among other ideological goals). This has been the basis of many solidarity campaigns through modern history. In view of such a commitment, the limitations on traditional organized labour and public intellectualism are made particularly clear. The small pool of participants in each quickly exhaust themselves, as neither strategy redistributes the burden of labour nor the goods of abundance. The 'siege mentality' cited by Andrew Ross (2008) and exemplified by the survivors holed up in the mall remains: the minority clinging to the scarce resources they have managed to hold onto, though goods lie all around for the taking.

Zombie solidarity, we are arguing, is a latent force on the unequal scene of campus life. Hence, it manifests here as *making liminal space habitable* – before a future that is already dead ('he's telling me he's futureless,' says an unflinching Major Henry West of an infected subject in *28 Days Later*). This is a future in which hopes for tenure or tenability might seem to have evaporated; but also a future in which 'racism, capitalism, sexism, militarism' (Larsen 2010) may not survive. We note that zombies are not interested in each other, but they are not interested in turning on each other either. At the same time, their experience is uncontainable – in fact it replicates itself by definition – except through the most brutal and militarized practices. The force of this latency, we suggest, can be mobilized in the interstices of the campus zombie drama as zombie solidarity.

A key aspect of zombie solidarity on the scene of higher education – and one represented in this volume – is the 'communities who already exist and are reproduced within the university', as David Harvie puts it (2004). As he notes, there is a distinction between 'a lecturer on a short, fixed-term contract, with a heavy teaching load, for example' and those in an academic department with a comparatively higher 'degree of job security and access to resources'. In this spirit, we propose that those who are in possession of this comparatively higher level of security and access to resources might engage in redistributing these resources to their colleagues and those they are responsible for employing. In general, those with access to resources may commit to sharing them with those in their immediate vicinity who do not have this access. Such resources might include: library subscriptions, electronic logins, books, academic discounts on books and other resources, laptops, office space, meeting space, time flexibility, expertise and prestige for wielding influence, travel funds, vehicles, financially secure and spacious homes, student and staff cards providing access to buildings and other resources including print accounts, discounted public transport, academic freedom as a defence for activities, access to governance processes, access to the media, access to publishing, first aid and security on campus, and tea and coffee and snacks.

Possibilities might be as follows:

- Salaried academics who hire casuals might commit to ensuring that they are contracted and paid properly and that their conditions are monitored even where that, as it often seems to, involves frustrating and/or lengthy interactions with the appropriate people in financial or human resources administration on campus. It is an exercise of institutional privilege to employ a tutor, or lab assistant, and leave them struggling against the bureaucracy, with no pay cheque and the fear of causing a fuss and ruining the opportunity.
- Senior, tenured and/or salaried academics could contribute to a fighting fund that would pay the wages of casuals for a day or a week of mass strike action. Under current conditions it is not widely considered as realistic for casual staff to join a union, and it is not realistic for them to participate in strike action. However, a mass strike of casual staff would doubtless have an effect, given that they now perform 50 per cent of university teaching (Jonas 2009; see also Bexley et al. 2011).
- 'Zombifying' audit measures might be refused as a measure of academic productivity and value. Sympathetic consortia of academics might decide to cease reporting audit points or decide among themselves which journals they believe are worth publishing in for the reporting of research and promulgation of ideas.
- Staff might opt to do their own cleaning and catering on occasion – by way of providing relief to precarious and low-paid workers, or to demonstrate the refusal of a class designation whereby such work is not considered to be appropriate for a person at that level of the social hierarchy. Similarly, at the behest of leaders in departments and schools, 'administrative' and 'academic' tasks and skills could be shared more equitably. Collaborative management of this kind is particularly apt given the number of so called 'general staff' who hold academic qualifications. Such a program may also assist in making visible the widely reported shortfall across the system of funds required for effectively administering universities. Tasks performed across the system would be itemized and delegated in a more shared context rather than the hierarchical context exemplified by Brabazon.

Implicit in such strategies is a refusal of the competition that is currently endemic to the system – the apparent setting of departments, disciplines and docents against each other in a scramble for the meagre resources produced by the imposition of scarcity under the guise of ensuring 'quality'. A systematic pooling of resources is not necessarily doing the corporate state's dirty work of rationalization for them. At any rate, this is already taking place through the supplication to atomized competition. This vision seeks to open the question of what constitutes work in the university, and by extension, who is working (and can contribute) towards the public good of knowledge and education. Further, it asks us to consider the desires we bring to an academic life. The zombie does not give up desire, but rather comes onto the scene as an embodiment of different desire, one that disrupts the means by which other desires are regulated and reproduced. In such a way, the zombie academic may be in league with the zombie cleaner, zombie casual, zombie general staffer in the undead ivory towers.

The zombies that roamed Romero's shopping mall achieved two things that the living couldn't: they managed to refrain from turning on each other and they resisted, through disinterest, the privileges and comforts of the mall. This combination of collectivity and resistance is what we have termed zombie solidarity. In contrast to the frequent figuring of the zombie as a negative category, we have sought to present it as a role model for collective action. In the university, then, the figure of the zombie is not necessarily the duped student, the half-living casual tutor or the academic forced through the drudgery of bureaucratic and corporate process. It may instead be the diversity of students, the mass-striking casuals, the consortia who refuse to report journal quality points, those who refuse to turn on each other, refuse to take the flesh of their colleagues, those that disrupt and refuse the benefits of a world they find ... distasteful.

The Journal of Doctor Wallace

David Slattery

Dying is pointless. You have to know how to disappear.

Jean Baudrillard

When I stepped off the train in the Irish university town of M_____ a rat scurried out from under the empty wooden ticket booth and bit me on my hand as I lowered my suitcase onto the platform. Examining the skin, which seemed transparent, I saw twin jagged holes running deep into the flesh, but there was no blood. Just in case I tied a handkerchief around the wound and walked to the taxi rank carrying my heavy bag in my unbitten hand. I asked the man in the only taxi that was waiting to take me to the old campus. While I stood outside his window, he seemed to study me, slowly moving his gaze from my sweating face down to my bandaged hand, before starting his engine and driving off without me.

I shrugged and trudged on through the slush. Turning a corner, I saw ornamental gates at the end of a short street, which I assumed was the entrance to the university. I already felt so exhausted that I decided to make the journey in short stages, stopping every few yards to catch my breath. A wind blew down the empty street and into my face. The stench of rotting flesh in the air filled my nostrils making me gag. I imagined the smell was coming from the direction of the university.

Just beyond the gates, the old stone buildings rose straight up like a prison out of the snow that covered the finer points of the stonework and made the gargoyles look ridiculous in their temporary white night caps. Towers framed the building at the end of each flat stretch of wall. A single set of footprints in the snow led away from the direction of the anthropology department indicated on a fingerboard. Following the steps in their opposite direction I came to a small gothic door placed low in the stone wall with The Department of Anthropology painted on to it in white letters.

I stood in the cold in front of the door in a daze, struggling to remember how I had gotten here. The effort brought sweat out on my forehead, and the bite on my hand began to throb. Just then the door opened. A large figure inside shouted, 'Ah there you are. Good man. It's splendid of you to help out with our little emergency at such short notice. As I told you on the phone, I have lost yet another member of staff just last week. Everyone in this wretched place keeps disappearing on me. Terrible thing but I will tell you about that some other time. I know you said that you had no time to prepare, but I need to put someone in front of our students as soon as possible or there could be a riot. The show must go on,' he laughed. He wrapped a protective arm around my shoulder and continued in a quieter tone. 'But seriously, the students should feel privileged to be exposed to your practical knowledge if only till the end of term when I can recruit some permanent replacements. Permanent – that's what I want. You will have a captive, young, and impressionable audience, so it will not be all misery.' Then suddenly he released my shoulder and shouted, 'Let's get you settled in to your office upstairs. Give me that bag. You look like shit. Come on. Follow me and don't go disappearing like the rest of them. I'm the only one around here with stamina.' He laughed again as I followed him inside. 'I think I am coming down with the flu,' I said. 'I might have caught something or something might have caught me,' I tried to feebly joke, embarrassed to tell him that a rat had bitten me on my arrival. 'Nothing wrong with you that a few stiff drinks won't cure,' he said, slapping me on the back. As I climbed the stairs behind him, he told me that he had organized a welcome drink in the local bar if I were still alive around 8 o'clock. We arrived at an office door that still had the name Doctor Wallace on it. 'Here you are. Your new home.' He caught sight of a few students further along the dark corridor. He shouted for them to wait up, and laughing, he strode off fast in their direction.

Looking into my cell-like office, I felt so tired that I wanted to lie on the floor in the hallway and fade away quietly. Summoning what was left of my willpower, I got to the chair at the desk and began to unpack my laptop, the dozen books I considered essential reading that accompanied me everywhere, and my pile of notebooks. My hand throbbed, and my fingers had swollen, which made holding my books difficult. I decided to put my notes away and go to my hotel for a rest before the pub.

A noise woke me causing me to jerk my head back from where it had nodded onto my chest as I slept at the desk. The office door stood wide open against the bookshelves that lined the walls. The door swung halfway closed with a loud groan. I stood up and walked out into the hallway and looked up and down the dark passage. There was no one there. Going back inside, as I closed the door, I saw that there was no key in the lock, and the receiver for the latch was broken so that the door wouldn't close. Splinters of wood were missing from the frame. The door had been broken open with force.

The bookshelves that lined the entire room were bare except for a small collection taking up less than half a shelf in the far corner. A brush and an overflowing black plastic bag beside them were indications that whoever was assigned to clean the room seemed to have lost interest in this corner. I sorted through the books with mild curiosity because this small collection was the only evidence of my predecessor. There was a pile of marked essays held together by an elastic band and a folder containing photocopied articles. These I threw in the plastic bag. Also on the shelf was a series of outdated student handbooks. Amongst these, I saw a thin brown spine, distinguishable from its neighbours in that it was the only one that was free of any lettering. I picked out the leather-bound book and opened it. Inside the cover was a date and the name Pauline Wallace. The notebook contained unlined pages, which were covered with handwriting. It was my predecessor's journal. I took it back to the desk.

I opened a page at random and read:

I can't get my students interested in reading. I thought the problem was the moderns, so I changed the reading list to include contemporary writers. Even fiction doesn't engage them. Maybe I am just a dinosaur. Steven down the hallway tells me that this is normal student behaviour, and I will adapt to it soon. Better still, he advises me, to forget that I have any ambitions to teach them anything. He patronizingly told me that he wished he was still as naïve as me. Cynical bastard! Didn't I know that what I was experiencing was just the standard passive behaviour of utilitarian students in the context of the contemporary massification of education? No, I didn't. Thanks for that tutorial Steven! Didactic bastard! He says that if I tell them what will be on the exam they will leave me alone. Try to get them actually to learn anything and I would soon be in trouble. Supposedly, the students 'love' him because he tells them what will be on their exam papers. The management also love him because he gets outstanding student feedback. Besides, he has his own research to concern him. He told me to go on sabbatical as often as possible – that's what they are for. I asked him what is the point in a job where you are only happy when you are not doing it. He laughed and told me that there was a department drinking session down the pub to forget our troubles and that I should meet him there.

I read another excerpt from a few pages on.

Despite the on-going collegial advice from Steven, today I talked to the second years for forty minutes nonstop about Lévi-Strauss. I felt embarrassed when I finally stopped because my passion caused me to go red while I was speaking. Also, I talk too fast when I get excited about something. I must remember to slow down. I probably got carried away. But isn't that what I should do? When I finally asked if there were any questions someone asked if this stuff would be on the exam. 'In future, can we have a break in the middle?', someone else asked. A Goth in the front row asked if I could talk slower because she couldn't understand what I was saying. I should be careful, or I will get poor results on the student feedback forms.

Flicking through the pages, I saw that the journal recounted several weeks of similar pedantic self-examination and frustrated attempts to make her subject matter and herself more appealing to the students. Further on, I read another entry where it seemed as if a new author had taken over because the handwriting had become agitated.

My nerves are so tightly strung that I jump at every sound. The students know this, if nothing else, and appear suddenly at my door making strange noises. A student from second year is here every day to check up on me. Maybe Steven is right. I am trying too hard, but I think there is something wrong with these students, especially the second-year group. If it weren't for the fact that they seem to move so fast, I would say they were drugged. Hah! Listen to me. I am worrying that the students are on drugs!

I read a note from a week later in an even shakier hand:

> Today I found a group of students standing in the hallway outside my office. When I asked if they needed anything they stared blankly at me and moved off without saying a word. If they are on drugs, it is a drug that I have never come across.
>
> Last night I heard barking from the Quad below my window and when I looked out I could see students standing around in groups. No one seems to go anywhere alone. They are always in packs. They looked up at my window as if they could feel that I was just then looking down at them. This place gives me the creeps.

While reading this, I became anxious. I slowly made my way to the broken door. Feeling both frightened and stupid I placed a chair against it to keep it closed. I went back to the desk and the journal. I must have a fever, I thought. I have had fevers before, and they have often made me paranoid. I flipped through the pages skipping detailed self-critical assessments on how the content of various lectures had been appreciated by the students. As I searched for more detail on my predecessor's breakdown, I read:

> Should proven interest in the subject be an entry requirement for a course? When I asked this question in the staff canteen, someone from admissions told me to grow up. Didn't I know the pressure they were under to achieve national targets for participation in third level? Didn't I know that competition between colleges is so intense? We have to do everything we can to attract and – more importantly – to keep students. But you are admitting zombies into the university I screamed causing a sudden silence in the room. I got up and left. I am too embarrassed ever to go back.

Further on the handwriting became even more erratic. I turned the pages.

> They all stare blankly at me during lectures. I mentioned Foucault last week in class and someone shouted 'fuck you too' from the back of the room. At least it was the first evidence in weeks that someone is listening to me.
>
> This afternoon I was asked if the class could end early because it was getting dark. I joked that night was the time for students to be active, but they just stared at me in silence.

I read on another page where the writing was getting bigger:

> The Head called to see me today to let me know that he was starting to worry about me. He heard rumours that I might be under mental strain. I lost my temper and started screaming at him that it wasn't me that he should be worrying about. It was his students. I should be embarrassed, but I don't care. I don't like him. He is always in the corridors sneaking around and laughing with the students. He thinks they can do no wrong. When

I complained about their lack of interest, he told me that I am living in the past. No one, especially him, wants to know what I had to go through as a student. Apparently, I am terminally old-fashioned: I am trapped in redundant sixties ideals. When I calmed down he advised me to join him and the rest of my colleagues later in the pub for a drink: it would do me good. What does that bastard want from me, coming in here telling me how concerned he is about me? Why does he care?

I slowly walked over to the lead-framed rectangles of glass in the window and looked down at students standing in groups below. Some sensed my presence and stared up at me, and exchanged some words amongst each other before turning away.

Back at the desk, I read:

There was an incident today in my office when a couple of students called to see me and stood together in the corner with their backs to the wall just staring at me and licking their lips and snarling like dogs. I asked them why they were here since they have no interest in anything I have to tell them. One said he wanted to get a job. I asked how being there was going to help him get a job. He didn't know, and they left together. I shouted after him that he was a zombie and that I knew what he was doing. I heard them stop outside the door and hesitate as he muttered something about coming back. For the first time, I felt terrified. I heard growling. One snarled 'leave it', and they left me alone.

In extremely shaky handwriting:

I think my students might be the living dead: zombies. Either that or I am having a nervous breakdown. But they move so fast they seem to relocate without actually moving and are agitated all the time. They move so fast compared to me: they have so much energy. I truly need to take a sabbatical. I need to get away from here for a while. I am so cold that my hands are numb all the time, but I can't stop sweating. I can't even remember how I came here in the first place. I wonder if one of the bastards has poisoned me! I wonder if one of them has bitten me.

Another entry read:

Students stand in the hallway as I pass and stare at me. I can hear some of them growling behind my back. They stare at me in class. Most have purple bruises around the whites of their eyes, which are always bloodshot. They don't stop staring at me. But I stare back at them. I don't care. I was so frustrated that I told them that I knew that they were the living dead. I knew that they were trying to kill me. There was such an embarrassed silence that I walked out of the lecture. I was stupid to warn them that I knew they were zombies.

I am extremely frightened now because the students have stopped pretending that they are not real zombies. One held her arm up in front of my face. 'See if you can feel a pulse?' she snarled. She took my fingers in her claw and pressed them into her wrist. I could feel nothing. Her companions growled their satisfaction and laughing all walked off together holding their arms straight out in front of them chanting 'zombie, zombie, zombie'. She turned back and hissed at me 'We're coming for you tonight'.

The final entry read:

I can't go on. I don't trust him, but I have to tell the Head of Department what I know. I have to tell him that the students are the living dead. I wonder if he is in it with them. I don't care any more. I just have to tell him everything I know.

I closed the journal and felt embarrassed that I was reading the intimate details of a stranger's mental collapse. The throbbing in my arm and the ringing in my ears had both ceased. For the first time since arriving on campus, I felt normal. Now I knew why this post had come up so suddenly. The Head would probably want to keep the details quiet.

It seemed likely that the over-wrought imagination of a social theorist had finally lost its tenuous links to reality. Doctor Wallace had found plenty of evidence that her students might be zombies in their glazed expressions, their failure to show interest in social and political issues, their general indifference to the way in which the college treated them, and a preference for nocturnal existence. I was convinced that these suspicions created a theory in her mind that only differed from her other theories in that it eventually undermined her sanity. The drama had ended with a well-needed rest in the local asylum. Sitting at that desk in that dark office, I believed that it could even happen to me. I realized that I needed to look after my own mental health in a place like this.

The chair moved on the linoleum floor when someone pushed against the door from outside. Embarrassed, I stood up to move it, but before I could reach the door, I heard a growling noise from the hallway as the handle was violently rattled. The throbbing began again in my arm. I took a deep breath and held it while I moved the chair and opened the door. The Head of Department stood outside staring intently at me. 'The lock is broken,' I said feebly indicating the chair. 'Maybe it's this office, maybe it's unlucky,' he said. He didn't laugh. He wasn't even smiling. He poked a talon-like finger into my chest to punctuate the words that emerged from between his gritted yellow teeth. 'Between you and me, we had to bust in here and get the previous occupant out for her own sake. I don't want anyone else getting worked up in this office. Go home and lie down and we will talk this evening.'

I woke suddenly on my hotel bed with a feeling of panic from a disturbing dream that I couldn't recall. I instantly remembered that I had left the journal in full view on my desk. It was dark outside. I was suddenly horrified that a student would find what I had been reading. My arm was completely numb, and my clothes clung to my body with sweat. It took me nearly an hour to get to my office less than a mile from the hotel. Standing in the broken doorway, I could see the diary open on the desk inside. As I stepped into the room, the cold light of the moon that hung outside with the strength of a 40-watt bulb illuminated a figure in the far corner. I saw deeply veined eyes framed by black rings in a snow-white face and vivid red lips that failed to hide a set of pointed teeth. The mass of matted dreadlocks and the descriptions in the journal convinced me that this was a student. He wore a white T-shirt with the message ~~God is Dead (Nietzsche 1882)~~ Man is Dead (Google 2012) emblazoned on the chest. Immediately, without introduction, he began to speak in a slow snarl.

I feel sorry for you. Your kind has been overthrown in a great revolution, and you don't even know it. You are no longer the gatekeeper of knowledge because technology has destroyed your power. If you were a great thinker, you would just be silent. But you are no great thinker. You will not just shut up because you constantly need to analyse the situation. You are dead, but you don't know it. You just won't lie down.

He stepped closer to where I stood frozen in the doorway. My nostrils filled with the stench of decaying flesh. 'That is not true,' I stammered. 'There will always be a need for teachers. Academia will always have an appropriate narrative response to radical changes in the world. You are not the first person in the last two thousand years to make that argument, and I guarantee you that you won't be the last.' I wasn't sure whether I was actually speaking words or just thinking them. Whether he heard my words or discerned my thoughts in reply, he just threw back his head and howled. Struggling not to vomit from the stench I turned away and staggered along the hallway, down the stairs and through the door at the bottom.

As the air outside revived me, I started walking towards the railway station as fast as I could move my swollen legs. The white-faced student had emerged from the gothic door and was steadily following 10 yards behind me. I saw several other dark forms joining him to converge on my route. Beyond the gates, a car slowed beside me. 'Get in,' said the Head of Department. 'It's too cold to be walking anywhere. Where are you going? I will give you a lift.' 'I am going to the railway station to collect a bag,' I lied. To get away from the students who were gathering behind, I got into the car. We had travelled in embarrassed silence before he said, 'I have a confession to make. I am really worried about you. Because you seem so stressed, I asked some of our students to look in on you. They are good guys really. They actually care about their lecturers. They kept an eye on Wallace for me. They are out there in the snow now freezing their asses off for you.' 'I am fine,' I lied again. 'I just need to pick up my bag.' When we arrived at the railway station that was now dark and empty, he told me that he would wait and bring me back to my hotel. Going inside I stood on the platform and looked up and down the track willing any train to appear. There was nothing as far as I could see through the gloom in both directions along the track. I felt something in my mouth and spat a bloody tooth onto the platform. I stepped across the tracks and into an open field beyond. I ran across the open ground to a small stand of trees. I sat down heavily in the snow, resting my back against a tree trunk as my lungs heaved for air and my limbs lost all their power. My brain seemed to rattle inside my skull. I couldn't remember where I was or what I was doing there. I held my hands close in front of my eyes and saw that they were black and blue with strips of rotting skin hanging down over my nails. The sleeve of my suit along with my arm inside it came away at my shoulder and dropped to the ground beside me. The voices of the students who were frantically calling my name faded in the direction of the city lights on the horizon.

SECTION 2

Moribund content and infectious technologies

Zombie processes and undead technologies

Christopher Moore

And it came to pass in the third year of the Desert War that Paul-Muad'Dib lay alone in the Cave of Birds beneath the kiswa hangings of an inner cell. And he lay as one dead, caught up in the revelation of the Water of Life, his being translated beyond the boundaries of time by the poison that gives life. Thus was the prophecy made true that the Lisan al-Gaib might be both dead and alive.

'Collected Legends of Arrakis' by the Princess Irulan, *Dune* (Herbert 1965: 285)

It's the night of the living dead,
all these bodies moving round.
When Hell is full the dead will walk the Earth.
Run. Run right now if you have the chance.

'Night of the Living Dead', Conversations with Enemies (2009)

The zombie is a figure of horror and comedy, of unrelenting consumption, its post-life a reductive and twisted parody of Darwinian logic. As a metaphorical critique, the zombie dramatically reveals a desubjectification of political will, a condition of simultaneous undeath and non-life, rendering all questions of the social infeasible. The zombie consumes the body, animating its victim as a vector for the continued transmission and transportation of further infection. The zombie has no self to be dangerous to, producing more of its kind as it feeds, never able to satisfy the urgent and constant hunger. The doom of its own kind is inevitable as the zombie's food source is converted and consumed into extinction.

Zombie metaphors are at once a new and ancient terror, found in myth, religion and popular culture, from the Tibetan Ro-Langs – reanimated corpses possessed by Gdon spirits (Wylie 1964) – to the figure of Christ and the resurrection reinterpreted in terms of both zombie and zombie hunter (Pippin 2010), and the 'Renaissance' of apocalyptic, dystopian zombie nightmares in modern horror games, comics, movies, television that began with Boyle's *28 Days Later* in 2002 (Bishop 2009). Appropriating the zombie's available set of archetypes, narratives and power relations, the undead becomes a means for communicating a critique of new patterns and articulations of power that are hauntingly similar to older ghoulish forms, carrying on long after their effective deaths.

The zombie provides multiple frames and timelines from which to examine a complex topic like higher education. This chapter takes two elements of the living dead as markers of the occupation of the socio-technical relationship between education and technology in the corporate university and higher education setting. First is the 'zombie process', a function that cannot be killed without a specific, and often brutal, act; as the TV news anchorman in *Shaun of the Dead* recommends 'by removing the head or destroying the brain' (Wright 2004). Unix programmers first employed the term to describe a defunct operation, one that has completed its task but still continues to occupy the resources allocated to it. Many zombie processes can occupy a system, gradually reducing its effective operation as they accumulate, continuing to register beyond their lifecycle, such that a specialized 'script' is required to decapitate the zombie and put an end to the afterlife of consumption.

The second marker of zombiedom's occupation of the university is the presence of undead technologies, ensnaring instances of software and hardware that plague our living, working and learning lives with senseless, repetitive, bureaucratic or toxic conditions: PowerPoint, plagiarism software, Digital Rights Management (DRM), e-mail, Learning Management Systems (LMS), committee structures, student and staff surveys, manual and automated systems for student and staff administration and management. Undead technologies hide the extent of their purpose and operations from their users, bunkered within black-boxed software, hardware or user policies. The risks of iPads, Kindles, and other mobile devices and social media platforms, especially when functioning as pedagogical tools, are the obfuscation of their dangers, their potential capacity for informing on our correspondence, location, online browsing and reading habits, and their removal of access without recourse to material purchased or created. In *Fido* (Currie 2006), the zombie is domesticated and controlled through an electrical collar, with the slightest failure resulting in disaster. As with Shaun and Ed at the conclusion of *Shaun of the Dead* (Wright 2004) occupying the garden shed and chained in position, the zombie Ed is convenient for Shaun, his video game playing is a mimicry of a former existence, reminding us that labour enslaved by technologies, however proficiently bound, is still (un)dead and never without risk.

Undead technologies disconnect the user from the benefits of their labour, but not the devices' effects on the environment, the body or the self. They distance control while silently directing and channeling us from behind code, policy or linguistic strategy. Perhaps once carrying revolutionary potential, these devices, designed for obsolescence, continue to be utilized and normalized. In Hertz and Parikka's *Zombie Media* project (2011) undead technologies are revealed to have an even darker side to their horror exposing their planned obsolescence and afterlife. The *Zombie Media* project draws attention to the toxic nature of phones, computers, screens and other devices as they are cast out, collecting in landfill and the DIY recycling slums of techno-shanty towns like Agbogbloshie in Ghana, one of the world's largest electronic waste dumps. An interventionist media art practice, the *Zombie Media* project is an opposition to the idea of any media being 'dead'. The appliance designated 'no longer useful' finds new life in its refusal to go away, its undead and abject presence contaminating the lives and lifecycles of the communities whose geographies are turned over to technologies that require decontamination to rejuvenate.

Higher education is replete with zombie processes and beset with undead technologies employed to treat the symptoms of massification (increased student numbers, longer working hours, uncertain futures, etc., the litany is familiar). Together they signal the powers of bureaucratization, corporate managerialism, centralization, outsourcing, marketing and jingoism that have colonized the vital operations and capacities of universities. The goal here is not to inoculate higher education or criticize those survivors who have adapted to the zombie's *habitus*, but to recognize the malefic phenomena most prominent in the technologies and practices that we are all responsible for conducting and implementing. The challenge of the zombie is to assess to what degree its ambiguity and abjection offers post-apocalyptic resistance or damnation.

The availability of the zombie as a critical metaphor is usually taken from Hollywood's first appropriation of the Vodoun mythology in Halperin's *White Zombie* (1932). Following the psychocultural enslavement of the Haitian 'zombi', the zombie was reinvented in the shambling horror of Romero's cannibalistic hordes, and has further mutated into the hyper-undead nightmare monsters of the *Resident Evil* (Mikami 2002) multi-format franchise. The zombie invasion respects no boundaries or borders, and with each wave the zombie reiterates and expands the ideological and semiotic register of the metaphor. Each reworking expatiates the zombie's ambiguity and its signifiers multiply; the zombie becomes a threat at once familiar and raw, carrying narratives of the body, death and an afterlife that is forever 'gesturing to alterity, racism, alienation, speciesism, the inescapable and the immutable' (Webb and Byrnand 2008: 83).

The tension between the different representations of the undead is categorical to the ambiguity of the zombie as the monstrous abject. The unique availability of the zombie metaphor as a heuristic device is in debt to the abjection that results from the liminality of the monster as neither truly living nor dead. In Kristeva's (1982) terms, the zombie as abject is a perpetual and unstable threat of disruption to the social order, and a violation of the cultural categories of existence that must be cast out. The discrete ontological entity of the monstrous locates in its ambiguity in both violent revulsion and perpetual revolution.

Lauro and Embry consider the zombie's origins in the Haitian zombi as indicative of an insufficiency in the subject/object dialectical model. As both slave and slave rebellion, the metaphor of the zombie is an 'ontic' and 'hauntic' figure, encoding the 'inferior' and unable to function as a liberating position (Lauro and Embry 2008: 87). Caught between life and death, the zombie is an anti-subject, claiming the body and debilitating the consciousness, leaving only a betrayal of the self:

What underlies this symbolic duality, however is that the zombie, neither mortal nor conscious, is a boundary figure. Its threat to stable subject and object positions, through the simultaneous occupation of a body that is both living and dead, creates a dilemma for power relations and risks destroying social dynamics that have remained – although widely questioned, critiqued, and debated – largely unchallenged in the current economic superstructure.

(Lauro and Embry 2008: 90)

The culturally constructed divisions of mind and body break down upon contact with the zombie: neither totalizing nor liberating, the zombie is undead and unalive, an 'uncontrolled ambiguity' (Bang Larsen 2010). The zombie thus defined by ambiguity cannot simply be reduced to a negative presence, as it is entirely without morality (Bang Larsen 2010). Even if only a symptom of a larger malady, the zombie functioning as allegory expands its metaphorical capacity, dramatizing the 'strangeness of what has become real' (Bang Larsen 2010).

The zombie's infection of popular culture follows a predictable cycle of the monster turned antihero, in games like *Stubbs the Zombie* (Seropian, 2006), the TV series *Woke Up Dead* (Fasano 2009) and films such as *Fido* (Currie 2006) and *American Zombie* (Lee 2007). Unlike the 'defanged' vampire or werewolf (Clements 2011), the zombie's status as an ambiguous figure (neither hero or villain, friend or foe, but occasionally both) suggests its redemption is impossible beyond a dangerous tolerance; its abject nature is only ever fractionally and momentarily permitted, at the thin line between imminent narrative and subjective collapse.

Resistance, immateriality and abject strategies: passing as zombie

Any number of zombie tropes and metaphors might be applicable to an analysis of higher education; we might label each new cohort of students as yet another mindless horde, or frame academics as ghasts resurrecting themselves each semester. In light of Lauro and Embry's ontic/hauntic model, we understand that becoming or claiming others as zombie is not a tactic of liberation, but admit to the occasional proximity to the zombie that is necessary for survival, as a perilous and sometimes legitimate zombie strategy.

In the online multiplayer zombie 'shooter' series *Left4Dead* (Valve 2008) not all the zombies can be defeated in a straightforward gunfight. To survive an encounter with the finger-bladed mutant zombie, dubbed the 'Witch' by the game's characters, the players can attempt to sneak stealthily past the monster, moving as close as they can without disturbing it or alternatively risk closing in directly, creeping around behind the figure to administer a lethal shotgun blow to the back of the head. In *Shaun of the Dead* (Wright 2004), the survivors affect a zombie stance to pass as undead and move amongst them undetected. This logic is taken to its extreme in the comic and TV version of *The Walking Dead* (Darabont 2010): characters cover themselves in the viscera of destroyed zombies in order to mask the smell of the living and move between the 'walkers' unmolested.

To do battle with the zombie directly is more dangerous, to face them head on is to antagonize the horde and risk infection, a tactic that announces the anointment of the hero or the martyr (Moretti 1982). Moretti considers monsters like zombies and vampires to be powerful metaphors that serve to embody the antagonisms and horrors evidenced within everyday life and a society outside of itself. To stand out and oppose the monster is a parlous endeavour, suggests Moretti, as it means to be anointed as representative of the species, to become the monster if only to defeat it. Even in metaphor this is an abject strategy, to become the monster is to accept the unknown, to sacrifice the self and become a figure forever threatening to destroy and destabilize. To do both, to oppose the monster, while becoming the monster is to deliberately risk zombiedom, a strategy that is neither liberating nor damning but an act of survival in a social landscape permanently in a state of crisis.

The epigraph, from Frank Herbet's *Dune*, describes the outcome of Paul Muad'Dib's ascension to godhood, when he gains the ability to see the future: to maintain his humanity, that humanity must be sacrificed, and he must become the monster of the self in order to defeat the monster that is his own future self. When the autonomy of the subject/object is perpetually in question, becoming a zombie is still an abject strategy, something not quite alive or dead, crossing the social boundaries physically and symbolically, never entirely part of the system's nature or its social order. Activities like Zombie Walks exhibit this kind of biopolitical irony inverted, a body with organs exposed and adorned, taking the tactics seen in *The Walking Dead* in celebration of the futility and the horror of fitting in, becoming one of the horde in order to stand out.

For the university, the abject is never entirely expunged, and so the rituals of lectures and tutorials, semesters and assessments, student surveys and graduation ceremonies are emptied of all but their symbolic power in order to maintain the boundaries and functional instances of 'Higher Education' as zombie processes. As open systems of learning, alternative modes of research and publication and new paradigms of knowledge emerge, threatening to destabilize the institution, the university appropriates from governmental, bureaucratic, and corporate models to reinforce privileged distinctions and categories of knowledge work – this is most obvious in its approach to the management and enforcement of regimes of intellectual property. The zombie then provides a new lexicon, one to interrogate what it means to be human and participate in a system at odds with its own ambiguities.

Zombie processes and undead technologies extend Beck's 'zombie categories', historical social groupings turned inaccurate descriptors that are 'dead' but still spoken of as being 'alive' (Beck and Beck-Gernsheim 2002). These include family, class, sexuality and secularism, among many others that no longer apply in a global, networked and 'cosmopolitan society' and thus need to be 'beheaded' (Possami 2007: 238). Zombie categories exist within the bureaucracy, but are not connected to actual lived social conditions; they are historical remnants infecting newer conditions with old inequalities. The family is a zombie category, one that implies stability, while in reality it fluctuates dramatically and is composed almost entirely through subjective perspectives set against complex and dynamic social relationships.

Capitalism is a definitive zombie category (Beck and Beck-Gernsheim 2002: 203–04), a descriptor offering an illusion of consistency that belies massive fluctuation and inequality as it oscillates wildly in conjunction with the drives of the market and other chaotic contributors. The persistence of the idea of the nation state and the constraining revenants of categories of class continue to lurch onwards, despite the structural and technological transformations within the institutions that shape them. Beck considers the adaptations that occur in response to these categories as capable of altering biographical and social patterns to produce an 'individualization' of society, but the human refugees from the Deleuzian 'societies of control', with their mutated forms of capitalism, cannot escape the monetizing of their data and access to forms of identity, community and other networks: like the Facebook zombie, created by abandoned accounts, misplaced passwords and deceased users, haunting our digital lives as rank combinations of zombie processes and undead technologies.

Frankel offers a critique similar to that of Beck, applying the zombie metaphor to a legacy of Australian politics that lags behind actual lived experiences: 'Zombies are also practitioners of political and cultural ideologies that are highly rigid and based on outdated and unrestorable social relations and institutional practices' (Frankel 2004: 23). Frankel uses the zombie to criticize and communicate a view of the political, cultural or social landscape that defines 'zombie politics' as obscured by long dead ideas, with perspectives belonging to the past. Frankel is critical of the zombie processes of the Australian political duopoly, split between Labor and Liberal, left and right: 'They are politically and culturally the walking dead' (2004: 24).

Not all old ideas and political perspectives are zombified, but those responding to new political, economic and cultural practices with unreflective, knee-jerk reactions reveal key symptoms. The telltale zombie characteristics are frozen patterns of political behaviour and the deployment of cultural stereotypes: 'zombies ... continue to intellectually and emotionally deny the overwhelming contemporary sociopolitical realities that prevent the realization of the unfulfilled hopes and dreams' (Frankel 2004: 24). Higher education is not a zombie category and universities are not undead technologies, but they are in danger of being caught in their freezing patterns and their lurking presence.

The modern zombie, suggest Deleuze and Guattari in *Anti-Oedipus* (1972 [2004]: 355), is war myth, the body brought back to work against reason, a living dead casualty of consumption without conscience. The metaphor of the undead plays an important role in the theoretical lens of the autonomist Marxists' take on Marx's 'general intellect', which Dyer-Witheford uses to examine the metamorphosis of universities in the era of advanced 'cognitive capitalism' (2005: 71). He argues that the cognitive capitalism of universities depends on the immaterial labour and biopower involved in the commercial absorption of universities, 'pacifying and restructuring academia':

> Universities are now frankly conceived and funded by policy elites as research facilities and training grounds for the creation of the new intellectual properties and technocultural subjectivities necessary to a post-Fordist accumulation regime.
>
> (Dyer-Witherford 2005: 71)

Universities, argues Dyer-Witherford, are the sites of immaterial labour in a doubled sense:

> Along with other educational institutions, they are the locales where future 'immaterial labourers' are trained and taught. And this training and teaching is itself an immaterial

labour, in which the information and communication is used to shape the emergent commodity – the student – that will result from the academic process.

(2005: 71)

With the homogenizing of sites of mass immaterial labour, networked or physical, come some advantages, as continental campuses (to stretch Becks' categories) and university-based staff and students are more diverse in age, gender, sexuality and ethnicity than any previous generation (Dyer-Witherford 2005: 80). This suits the zombie; it does not discriminate.

The zombie's 'pedigree of social critique' of alienation is extensive (Larsen 2010). Marx characterized the alienation of capital as the vampire feeding on life, sucking labour from the living in an endless cycle: life sustaining the ability to feed but no more. Vampire-capital, argues Shaviro can only survive on the extraction of surplus 'by organizing its legions of zombie-labour' (2002: 282). Shaviro describes a particularly common zombie process, expansion by constant accumulation, a transformation of living labour into dead labour through the realization of its value at the cost of life. The zombification of the work force, however, is incomplete without the undead technologies and zombie processes of administration, communication and control.

Marx's comparison of capital to that of 'dead labour' energized vampirically in a parasitic cycle of growth that devours the lives of workers, also serves in the critique of globalized consumerism signified by the zombie. Proximity to the zombie is an abject strategy, risking complete alienation, most especially in the digital and online environment where it is almost impossible to escape undead technologies. The hordes of software, hardware and networks feeding on user input, transforming the consumer to consumed are as ubiquitous as they are massive and global; Apple, Microsoft, Google, Facebook, Twitter and the technologies, services and tools that regulate our access to information and dominate our social, work and creative networks, harvest any input as intellectual and immaterial labour. The exchange of personal information for access and use value is, to services like Google, the main business, transforming each word search into a commodity exchange, an intellectual property dependent on the value output of the search to be outweighed by the value of information inputted by the user. Further, this input represents an improvement to the technology, increasing its effectiveness and assisting its owners in refining its payload of targeted advertising, enabling the auction of the results of those word searches to be delivered to the highest bidder.

The zombie is without the explicit sexual politics of the vampire, and it expands the individual threat of the Frankenstein monster to that of the horde. Capable of limited physical and intellectual labour, the zombie is motivated by the most rudimentary instincts and desires. These old ideas find new forms in the combinations of zombie processes and undead technologies to produce automation, deskilling and the alienation of the immaterial labourer. Such technologies are not always devices or software and include institutional cultures, everyday ways of doing and operating. The most potent example is intellectual property laws, which are not only zombie categories, but operate as both zombie processes and undead technologies dedicated to harnessing the intangible lifeblood of cognitive capitalism:

> Enabled by changes in intellectual property laws to exercise ownership rights over patents [and copyright] resulting from government funded grants, universities become active players in the merchandising of research results.
>
> (Dyer-Witherford 2005: 75)

The zombifying elements of industrial labour are digitized for the era of immaterial labour, occupying the efforts of both the body and the brain. As Bang-Larsen (2010) argues, the zombie's ambiguity to subjectivity, consciousness and life itself is a representation of the paradigm of immaterial labour: the zombie is that 'which must be thought' (Shaviro 2002: 288).

The zombie wars

Plenty of opportunities to see the combined effects of zombie processes and undead technologies present themselves in the university, but few are as obvious as the 'plagiarism war' (Tabarrok cited in Murphy 2011). The institutional response to the perceived dangers of plagiarism in higher education, however, is one battle in a much larger campaign, which Cory Doctorow calls the 'war on general computing' (2011). Plagiarism, copyright and privacy conflicts have unfolded in parallel, serving as the 'beta versions' and weapon testing sites for the zombie processes (laws, user policies, media responses) and undead technologies (DRM, malware, surveillance) to be used in the crackdown on computation.

One of the latest attempts to provide new powers for established zombie processes emerged in the form of the Stop Online Piracy Act (SOPA) and the Protect Intellectual Property Act (PIPA) in 2011, under the direction of the major US intellectual property rights lobby groups, most notably the Recording Industry Association of America (RIAA), the Motion Picture Association of America (MPAA) and the Pharmaceutical Research and Manufacturers of America (PhRMA). These laws were only narrowly postponed as the television, radio and print media voraciously fed on the outpouring of concern and contention from a global community of internet users showing clear signs of life via Twitter, Reddit and Facebook, described as a 'digital tsunami that swept over the Capitol' (Sherman 2012). These skirmishes continue, through the secretly negotiated US multilateral deal, the *Anti-Counterfeiting Trade Agreement* (ACTA) and the vaguely-worded scope of the Internet bill *Protecting Children from Internet Pornographers Act of 2011*. The MPAA responded to Anti-SOPA protests by promoting Daniel Castro's (2011) report, which emphasizes the effectiveness of DNS filtering, the technology used by nations with explicit censorship regimes including China, Iran, Syria and Saudi Arabia.

The war on general computing is not only a matter of maximized rights protection and enforcement, the accompanying arms race involves the doubling of technologies of enforcement as a means for the conversion of immaterial labour of the user into other manageable forms of intellectual property. This involves every appliance, device and object with an onboard computer (however simple) being chipped and crippled by DRM, informing on our habits, movements and choices, but allowed only to perform its functions when, how and where its makers decide (Doctorow 2011). These undead technologies whose brains are zombified convert the immaterial labour of everyday life into intellectual property removed from the user's control. These devices can only be stopped with the drastic act of 'severing the head and removing the brain', often called 'jailbreaking', which replaces the device's operating system; a practice actively discouraged and protected against by zombie processes including click-through user-license agreements and the anti-circumvention provisions of the Digital Millennium Copyright Act (1998). Developers like Apple and Nintendo have no hesitation in protecting their undead technologies from tampering, by 'bricking' their devices at the first sign of potential user interference.

The predictable results of these zombie wars will be similar to the wars on drugs and terrorism: militarized police, increased prohibitions, privatized jail systems, security and enforcement agencies, and increased surveillance from spyware, Digital Rights Management and other versions of malware. The introduction of new undead technologies perpetuates and spreads already festering zombie processes, encouraging new ones, and producing explicit zombifying effects, including automation, deskilling, black-boxing, alienation and dispossession, with each victim adding to the power of the horde. The response of universities to the issues of plagiarism, outright cheating and collusion has been to bureaucratize and corporatize the problem, rendering itself inert through policy, quasi-jurisdictional and committee formations, relying on the few pedagogical advantages of text-matching anti-plagiarism software affords as a positive justification. The most successful arms dealer in the plagiarism war is iParadigms, a company that provides institutional subscriptions for its web-based application Turnitin. The software works by comparing the students' work against a morbid collection of brains, which it amasses by taking a copy of each article it screens and incorporating that work within the company's database, providing an 'originality' report in return. The company also provides subscriptions to those wanting to check their work against iParadigms database outside of the universities' monitoring. More accurately described as a 'plagiarism software' company, iParadigms is 'arming both sides of the war' (Murphy 2011), a strategy equivalent to handing the shotguns over to the walking dead.

Turnitin and other plagiarism software packages do offer some beneficial pedagogical advantages. Students can use Turnitin like a 'spell-checker' to assist in isolating problematic instances of referencing, paraphrase and citing, but like any such tool it cannot be relied on to perform the job of the student or the teacher. The software cannot stop serious cheating or motivated students from tricking or even hacking the system:

It cannot detect cleverly paraphrased passages, or copied text that has been vastly altered by the student's use of a thesaurus. It is also ineffective for detecting works that have been written by another student, person or a 'ghost writer', unless more than one student submits the paper. Turnitin cannot distinguish between text that has been properly quoted and cited and text that has not. Subsequently, it returns an inaccurate originality report. Turnitin often returns a report of unoriginality for paper headers, and bibliographies. Therefore, the initial plagiarism percentage rating cannot be used as a trustworthy indication of the degree of plagiarism.

(Bishop 2006)

Despite these limitations, Turnitin expands with every student assessment submitted, and while students have been placated through various box-ticking options when submitting their work to instruct iParadigms to remove their work from the collection, it is not clear how thoroughly this is implemented. The company has successfully defended lawsuits against students claiming infringement of their intellectual property rights, protected by its click-through licenses and other zombie processes. Reversing the traditional copyright model – which protects individual expression, but not the ideas contained in the work – iParadigms disavows claims to ownership of student submissions, arguing no right to the intellectual content or ideas contained in the work, but remains at liberty to use, manipulate and profit from their expression regardless.

One of the more powerful arguments in favour of Turnitin is its advantage as a labour saving device, emphasizing its undead nature, particularly when use is mandatory or automates the marking of assessments. Such implementation deskills both students and the legions of sessional tutors and casualized academics who are responsible for the majority of university teaching. Any increase in student numbers increases the marking and administration load, to which Turnitin offers a false panacea, especially when there are many non-zombified responses to plagiarism active in higher education. The most common is the front line discretionary tactics of the teacher. While self-checking via Turnitin helps students know if their work has 'originality' concerns, it does not aid the student in overcoming the types of problems associated with research, writing, and citation that lead to the majority of the instances of plagiarism. MS Word does not teach students how to write, Photoshop cannot teach us graphic design, and Excel will not balance our budgets for us, and while EndNote produces excellent lists it does not teach core referencing skills. Mandatory uses of Turnitin are particularly destructive, removing discretion, and relying on the frustrating and often ritualistically humiliating experience of higher education plagiarism grievance procedures to shame and discourage further transgressions.

The irony, of course, is that Turnitin is much less effective at detecting plagiarism than Google. The difference is that Google provides the evidence but requires the human eye to determine instances of direct copying, while Turnitin provides an automated and much less accurate service. Without teachers willing to tackle instances of plagiarism one-on-one with the student, greater dependency on plagiarism software could greatly encourage further plagiarism (Harrington 2011). The resulting escalating cases of plagiarism is inevitable, as students turn to circumvention measures, commercial essay writing services and other methods to cheat, as the treatment in this case is significantly worse than the cure.

Conclusion

The zombie wars in higher education and intellectual property are not only battles for the minds of students and the brains of academics, many of whom thrive under the conditions of zombiedom, but also for the brains of our computational devices, which can be disconnected and occupied beyond our control in the institutional setting. Bruno Latour frames such a death, a disconnection between the body and learning:

> [T]o have a body is to learn to be affected, meaning 'effectuated', moved, put into motion by other entities, humans or nonhumans. If you are not engaged in this learning, you become insensitive, dumb, you drop dead.
>
> (2004: 205)

To employ a technology for the extraction of labour from the body (however digital) is to enforce a disaffected state, disconnected from learning: an abject strategy. Similarly, casting out the core principles at the centre of intellectual property protection and professional integrity, failing to acknowledge those who come before and those on whose shoulders we stand, is central to the concerns of plagiarism, yet the technologies employed to police this activity fail to acknowledge, let alone compensate, those who are forced to submit their work and whose contribution improves the system.

This logic is reflected in Giroux's (2010) use of the undead metaphor to critique the 'casino capitalist zombie politics' that devour human and physical resources without discrimination. This is a politics rendered graphically in Robert Kirkman's *Marvel Zombies* (2006), where Earth's superheros are infected with an undeath curse, and must devour each other to retain their strengths and powers, stuffing partly digested morsels of former allies back into their digestive tracts to re-digest, over and over, without real sustenance. Proximity to zombie processes as a strategy risks alienation, automation, deskilling, abjection and disaffection, but it is increasingly difficult to avoid undead technologies. The hordes of software, hardware and networks gathering to feed from user input and transform the consumer to consumed grow tirelessly.

Universities should be at the centre of the 'depunctualization' now required to promote public hacking and understanding of 'black box' systems of hardware and software, to reduce the 'unsupportable death drive' of consumption, and encourage the reuse and remix of technology (Hertz and Parikka 2011), but they have so far shied away from this challenge. Google, Turnitin, Facebook, and the other tools and devices we permit to dominate our information production and regulation and our socializing exchange their use value for the user's intellectual and immaterial contribution. If nothing else, we must be aware that each time we enter a search term or update our status we shuffle zombie-footed a little further towards the Winchester, which as it turned out for Shaun and his friends, was not the greatest place to wait out the apocalypse.

The botnet: webs of hegemony/zombies who publish

Martin Paul Eve

With apologies to Mark Twain: rumours of life beyond death have been greatly under-exaggerated online. Every day, amateurs (dangerous for their lack of experience) use pre-weaponized exploits to install covert FTP servers on home and high-bandwidth machines for the distribution of pirated software, films and music – 'pubstros' and the 'FXP' scene (Braithwaite 2003) – while corporate spammers (dangerous for their malice and fiscal motivation) employ sophisticated technicians to illicitly gather machines for their vast relay mechanisms. In each case, the physical owner of the computer is, if the intruder is successful, entirely unaware that their machine has been cracked; to all intents and purposes it still functions, but in reality it is walking dead, working against them. Both of these models of intrusion have been referred to as botnets. The less widely utilized terminology, which resurrects the notion of the undead internet, describes the individually compromised machines that constitute this network not as 'bots', but rather 'zombies' (Cooke et al. 2005).

As the subscription-based academic publishing model is dragged into the twenty-first century, almost all aspects of the existing system are facing changes, arising from technological developments and ideological initiatives such as open access and the CopyLeft movement. They are also, however, under threat of self-subversion. In this chapter, I propose the 'zombies' of the author, the library and the publisher in higher education publishing as sharing much in parallel with the information security inflexion of this same term: a being not only dead and colonizing, but also exhibiting superficial autonomy while covertly acting under foreign influence against its own living purpose. The area in which this concept can most easily be elaborated is in the underlying political tensions in various library-publisher-researcher relations.

This interrogation takes a tripartite structure. The first examines the motivations for a researcher's choice of publication venue when considered as a semiautonomous agent, within a prevalent audit culture, alongside the current *modus operandi* of libraries and publishers. This takes account of the pressures brought to bear from such elements as 'Impact Factor', the economic interactions between each of these actors, and the coming of age of open access. The second brings focus to the interrelations of power between actors within this network and the constraints that compel them to behave in a self-subverting fashion, which in the botnet typology correlates to the command and control component. The final section examines the means by which such a network could be dismantled, the zombies reconsigned to their rightful resting places, and the repercussions this action would have upon a revitalized, once-again living, academic landscape.

'Another fine mess you've gotten me into': why is academic publishing as it is?

In order to understand the interrelations between the various stakeholders, or factions, within the academic publishing world, it is necessary to examine the motivations that drive researchers to publish and the roles played by each of these factions. While in several instances it will be clear that actors are competing against one another in this system, it is the ways in which such competitive behaviour becomes self-destructive that is primarily of interest here.

To begin at the point where material enters the publishing cycle, the motivations for researchers to publish are well covered by Glenn McGuigan and Robert Russell, who split the drivers into two categories: 'the norms of the profession' which 'encourage faculty members to participate in the generation and dissemination of new knowledge based on research', and 'the academic process of promotion and tenure and the role of credentialism in determining faculty advancement' (2008). The latter includes the monograph as standard tenure-track or career progression material in many arts disciplines, a format under huge threat at present (Thompson 2005). While one might conclude from this breakdown that academia has been irredeemably lost to a Weberian framework of quantified economic determination, in omitting the more altruistic, or perhaps egotistic, psychological desires – to be read and to be valued by peers – we are actually led towards a different aspect of Weber. It was common knowledge long before Maslow that this vocational humanism is subordinate to the need to eat, but at the tangible level the motivation is to hold an academic position in order to obviate the work-life dichotomy: to truly answer one's calling.

Already one can begin to see how choice of research publication is hardly autonomous or altruistic, but rather automatic, coerced and self-centred. While pragmatic encroachments upon ideals are expected in all walks of life, in this case, if researchers wish to find themselves employed, they must select the publication outlet of the longest standing, with the highest 'impact', the most citations; this is zombie-like in its no-brainer logic. Under such a value-system, in which the economic – be that financial, or in the supply-and-demand scarcity principle of impact – is given a high level of precedence, one would expect the academic library to be highly empowered. The academic publishing economy is a market, after all, and through acquisition budgets, the library is the customer. Interestingly, however, this is not the case.

The library is actually disempowered because it acts under the direction of the researcher. By the same criteria of their output, researchers must also have read the highest-valued material, necessitating a purchase of these materials by the library. Thus, the library finds itself doubly constrained, firstly by researcher activity when it functions as material provider, and secondly by publisher prices (and lengthy contracts, so called 'big deals') when it purchases material. This double-bind does a disservice to researchers; the very system they are using and which they believe they control actually negatively impacts upon their own practice and the zombification demonstrates its first aspects of contagion as it cascades down the chain. This is because the same valorization criteria bestowed upon journals drives the prices of those journals up, thus making it impossible for libraries to afford them. The model of esteem conferred by a researcher upon a publisher within this culture implies the right to charge a higher premium for a title, which then restricts – owing to contracting library budgets – this same researcher's access to material.

To understand how these constraints became so effective and binding, the economic situation of libraries and the emerging models designed to counter this problem must be considered. In recent times, the traditional publishing model has faced its biggest threat to date: open access. In much the same way that the entertainment sector has had to adapt to a digital medium, publishers are increasingly finding, perhaps rightly, that their mode of distribution is being challenged. On a purely ideological plane, nationalistic interests put aside, there can be little disputing that publicly-funded research should be published under an open access mandate; for citizens to pay a private company to obtain research for which they have already paid through their own taxes would be logically inconsistent. Indeed, in the largest survey on open access to date, 90 per cent of researchers felt that open access was valuable to their discipline, with availability of publicly funded research ranking as the most agreed-upon factor among the 36,507 respondents (Dallmeier-Tiessen et al. 2011: 6), while a separate substantial market research exercise described how 75 per cent of their 'participants said they think it is "very important" or "important" to be able to offer their work free online' (InTech 2011: 7).

In response to this ideological drive, the term 'open access' was put forward in 2002 by the Budapest Open Access Initiative to describe a system under which peer reviewed articles would be available free of charge to the reader, with Green and Gold mechanisms proposed for author self-archiving and pure open access journals respectively (Chan et al. 2002). Furthermore, subsequent thinking on this terminology has sought to distinguish the removal of price barriers from permission barriers as independent components: gratis (instead of purchased) and libre (instead of restricted in terms of reproduction) (Suber 2008). It would be disingenuous, however, to solely credit this provision to a utopian hope. One of the main motivations has been the aforementioned pressure upon university library budgets, alongside ever-increasing journal subscription costs. This is aptly illustrated by William Walters, whose 2007 study of the economics of open access publishing estimated an aggregate annual saving in US higher education library expenditure of almost ninety-eight million dollars in the event of institutions switching to a PLoS or 'Public Library of Science' model (2007: 8) with similarly-scaled predictions repeated in a UK study (Houghton 2011).

Superficially, this all sounds fantastic: research that could be free in both of Richard Stallman's well-known senses: beer and speech (Free Software Foundation 2010). However, regardless of whether funded publicly or privately, institutions are committed for the foreseeable future to reduction of central expenditure while, conversely, the efforts involved in the various stages of open access publication – from server hosting through to copy editing – are not zero cost. To make matters more complicated, competitive frameworks for research assessment such as the upcoming United Kingdom Research Excellence Framework are, despite much criticism, reliant on quantitative metrics to determine the impact weighting of a journal: the Impact Factor, calculated 'by dividing the number of current year citations to the source items published in that journal during the previous two years' (Garfield 1994). Evaluating the Impact Factor of open access journals is a difficult task, but the best estimate at present, based on the 2008 IF, is a 39.43 per cent share in the top fifty (0–50) percentiles, although open access journals counted, respectively, for only 5.38 per cent in the sciences, and 1.52 per cent in the social sciences *Journal Citation Reports* (Giglia 2010: 34). With this in mind, it becomes possible to fully consider the pressures borne by the library.

Libraries: the locus of subversion

Academic libraries are not the culprits responsible for a self-sabotaging researcher paradigm; they did not build the botnet. They are, however, the focal point of all relations as they currently stand, and the black box that renders these interrelations opaque. Were the costs exposed directly to the researcher, rather than through the non-transparent medium of the library, it would be possible for competition on price to play an active role in researcher selection of publication outlet. This considered, could elimination of the library as a gateway, or custodian, constitute a viable means of identifying the Trojan malware in the system? Could open access provide this?

When speaking of economic savings, there is always a free-market flip-side for the provider: loss of revenue. It is clear that on the topic of library budgets, the movement towards open access systems benefits the library at the expense of the publisher. Likewise, on first inspection, the positives for the researcher, over the publisher, appear clear: instant gratis access. From this appraisal, it seems that the researcher and the library both stand to benefit while the publisher must wholesale lose out. This assumption, however, is shortsighted.

Traditionally the custodians of material, the library needs to rapidly rethink its status in a world where there are no physical guardians beyond fail-safe archives. Instead, it is redefining itself as a provider of 'research tools' whose purpose is to educate users on new technologies and assist with the sifting of vast quantities of metadata (Bosc and Harnad 2005). The problem here is that this encroaches upon the role of IT Services who may well argue that they, or perhaps an external contractor such as Google, are better placed to undertake this role. Also less frequently considered are the implications for the power relations that sit atop this financial substructure. As Walters puts it: 'Open access pricing is likely to shift journal costs from libraries to other parts of the university, thereby shifting authority from those who make decisions about particular journals (chiefly librarians) to those who evaluate the apparent value of particular research projects (chiefly departmental faculty and funding agencies)' (2007: 12). Certainly, in this cession to external budget pressure through an embrace of open access, it is clear that the library both disempowers itself financially, and begins to erode its rationale for existence, as with all compromised zombies within a botnet.

It could be argued, however, that within an institutionally devolved funding model, the library performs a mediating role vital for academic freedom. This is because, in order to maintain profitability in open access, publishers are implementing a system of author payment for each article. In this case, the academic wishing to publish in an outlet will have their work peer reviewed and is then expected to pay the journal the publication fee. Should central management hold these funds, it could be posited that a conflict of interest arises between marketeers and academics. On the other hand, allowing departments unlimited sovereignty in their spending removes many of the aspects of accountability of funds that open access is supposed to mitigate. The library as the centre of funding allocation for publishing could function as a go-between, a mechanism of accountability towards management, but also as a guarantor of academic freedom. The rationale for this being a library, rather than a funding committee, is that this mediation process would require longer term interaction and understanding of a researcher's project than a snap-decision funding committee could hope to achieve. The library can, perhaps, make a case for its existence in this way.

Publishers: an evil? A necessary evil?

On the other side of the debate there has been, in light of open access developments, much discussion as to whether there is a continuing need for academic publishers. As is common knowledge, much of the editorial process for publishers – peer review, copy-editing and authorship – is performed by academics free of charge to the publisher, as an expected part of their employment at the university. A materialistic view of the current situation would see, in this, that the publisher contributes little more than a transcription of academic work into physical format and then sells it, with extremely small financial return for the author. For an ideally self-critical institution, it seems that an absolute extreme of alienation and commodity fetishism is inscribed directly within the academy; a disconnect between surface motivation and underlying action exists in the compromised zombie.

This, of course, in no way encapsulates the full scope of the academic publishing environment. As has already been touched upon, publishers are the gatekeepers of reputation, the self-admitted key to academic success, in terms of both tenure and audit. In many ways, then, researchers are directly responsible for their own circumstance here. However, publishers have obtained this position only by the now-shifting sands of tradition upon which they are founded; their head start will not last forever. Secondly, again, the activities are not zero-cost. However, a transition to open access brings these costs down to a level which could almost certainly be managed institutionally. Furthermore, at this crucial stage where open access is only beginning to emerge, particularly in the humanities, it is unlikely that early career researchers would be able to secure institutional funding for the up-front costs publishers are demanding. In short, the current model of publishing is unsustainable from the library's (and therefore, the researcher's) perspective, while the move to open access is financially untenable, or at least uncertain, for publishers. As a final hurdle, attempting to make this profitable through up-front payment renders it impossible for some of the keenest advocates of open access, the early-career researchers, to publish. Indeed, it is this subset who realize, more than any other that, as Thomas HP Gould puts it: 'Print academic research journals are dead' (2009: 232–35).

In this mode, then, the publisher is pitched against the library. In their bid to stick to traditional publication methods and make themselves financially viable, publishers weaken the library in the view of the researcher, who becomes frustrated at the lack of available material. This is a far more appealing prospect for publishers than the upfront charges of open access that impact directly upon the researcher. If the publisher can use the library as a shield to mask the financial transactions underpinning the economics of academic publishing, then it appears to be in their interest to do so. On the flip-side, though, libraries are increasingly 'declaring war' on publishers over the unaffordable and unsustainable rates of subscription costs and big-deal lock-ins, while also attempting to make this relation perspicuous to researchers (Shubber 2011). It is here, then, that publishers begin to exhibit self-subversive behaviour. As they are manipulated by financial motivations and the incompatibility of researcher demands with a for-profit schema, they are pushing for a strategy that can only jeopardize the library acquisition-budget and could lead to their own extinction. When this has been achieved, who will pay the subscription costs if not the institutions? Is it a repetition of the Cree proverb: 'Only when the last tree has died, the last river has been poisoned and the last fish has been caught, will we realize that we cannot eat money'?

Finally for this section, then: what do academic publishers actually add? Stephen Mooney, in a barefaced attempt to identify the threats to publishers' traditional models of marketing and offer countermeasures, suggests that the three saving graces of the industry are marketing, editorial and reputational (2001). Mooney posits that the role of the publisher is self-marketing, so that they are identified as the provider of reputable information, distinct from the 'bad information' on the web. This is fallacious and dangerous; it is the role of education to develop the knowledge and critical faculties to independently evaluate material, regardless of its source. Relying on source of publication as evidence of quality is not the way forward, regardless of whether this provides an easy solution for publishers and researchers. Secondly, Mooney lambasts the peer-review system on the grounds of its inability to select content that will sell; hardly a criterion that should be the foremost aspect of selection, over academic merit. Mooney suggests that editorial direction is actually a form of marketing, and is about understanding what will sell, rather than what is well received by peers: 'Only you can provide … review *targeted toward your market,* he declares (2001: 27, emphasis in original). The final of this triad, reputation, is clearly predicated upon the former two. If the marketing machine of the academic publisher promotes itself as absolute quality and the better arbiter of what material should be published, then of course, were this to be accepted, it would be the ultimate accolade to have one's work published there, heralded as The Truth. Clearly, these recommendations will do little to endear academics to publishers, particularly when couched in this vein; we will return to what can be done about it later.

From the picture painted here, the self-subverting nature of all three parties can be clearly canvassed. Researchers, in their blindness to the processes driving acquisition, limit their own access to material by the very criteria of prestige to which they cling. Libraries, in pushing for the open access solutions to their budgetary woes, put themselves at the mercy of a reconfigured power structure within the institution, threatening their own existence. Publishers, in their nostalgia for an impossible future, either hide financial relations behind libraries, resulting in the extinction of their own customers, or alienate early-career researchers by locking them out of the publishing cycle, deferring the problem until a later date. Attempting to trace back from this situation to an origin seems to yield no clear result. Any one of these parties could be held responsible for the current situation, the fine mess into which we have been led.

Command and control

Botnets, such as Conficker and Storm, with their millions of zombie machines, sit idle most of the time, awaiting a request for action through their respective communication channels. These channels are known as command and control systems, for obvious reasons. There is only one fundamental requirement of these systems: that they are resilient. This is achieved through a variety of methods: by obscurity (making it difficult for information security researchers to find, understand and thereby disrupt); re-use of existing infrastructures (for instance, running the mechanism through Twitter or Internet Relay Chat so that disabling this will also disable its legitimate uses, a sort of 'Betamax court case' ruling for malware); and distribution (making it harder to bring down the mechanism by distributing it across the network). Academic publishing has managed to build, autosubversively, a resilient command and control mechanism to relay and amplify the destructive signals from each zombie to the other. It is to the parallels with this typology that I will now turn.

Obscurity: as has been noted, the library creates a blind spot in the network. For-profit publishers' prices are translated, through the library, into a straightforward negative imperative: 'access denied'. It appears, to the researcher, that the message originated from the library and blame is thus incorrectly apportioned to this corner. Conversely, the supposed free-market competition that should feed back from researchers' demand to publishers' supply can be masked by limited library budgets. This competition is evaluated on the basis of usage metrics. However, it is clear that the metrics currently deployed – most of which are citation-side – do not adequately capture a usage picture of inter-library loans. It would only be possible to get a true picture of demand were price to be totally removed from the scenario so that researchers were not limited in their access to material. Of course, this would negate the need to measure such use.

Infrastructure: there is a clear parallel with the use of public channels for command and control relay at work here. This is because the problematic features of the system are inherently structural: it has appeared, for a long time, that it would be impossible to remove the autosubversive aspects without also losing the research output. For researchers, open access provides the solution to this dilemma but, clearly, from the logic already outlined, the other actors have strong motivations to keep this from emerging.

Distribution: in many ways attributable to the previous points, there are always two demands made upon any actor within the network, but usually with their own actions as a root cause. Researchers experience twofold pressure from libraries (in terms of access) and publishers (in terms of submission prestige). Libraries are pressured for access to material by researchers and placed under financial strain by publisher prices. Publishers face a commercial pressure from customers (libraries) and suppliers (researchers) while also having to maintain reputation in the eyes of the latter. This constant pressure from multiple angles renders the system resilient, in library-publisher relations, to a single point of failure. For instance, the inability of libraries to pay will not mean the demise of publishers so long as researchers continue to value the journals; it will merely result in already financially strained institutions having to find the money demanded, most likely through human resource cuts. Again, the inability of libraries to supply material to researchers will not impact the entire system; it will merely result in an exodus of academics into the institutions that can meet demand – the dreaded brain drain.

However, the system is not fault-tolerant in respect of the researcher. Should researchers, en masse, decide to trash the currently accepted metrics and journal valuation system, publishers' business models would collapse but – with open access software packages now widely available – research publication would not cease. There are, of course, strong mechanisms in place to check this and it is unlikely that the required unity could be mustered. From funding mandates down to personal egotism, the prestige barrier is a factor that can only be eroded by time, not obliterated in the present, by which time the system could well have adapted to preserve its commoditized nature in unforeseeable ways.

Dismantling the network

So what, then, can be done? The procedure for dismantling a botnet varies as technologies shift but, at present, there are several successful tactics. The first is technological in nature. It consists of analysing the behaviour of the malware, reverse engineering the command and control protocol, crafting a client that emulates the behaviour of a current zombie (but is actually autonomous) and then using this client to disrupt the command and control channel. Likewise, developing effective antivirus signatures for the malware in question can help, although more cleverly crafted botnet entities function at the lowest level, called rootkits, and are thus extremely hard to detect. The next generation of malware will likely employ hypervisor virtualization (for instance, Rutkowska 2006 and King et al. 2006), wherein the entire operating system runs as a guest within the malignant entity and is therefore almost completely at the mercy of its invisible hand. The other recourse for dismantling botnets is an appeal to legal authority. If one can firmly ascertain the identity of the botmaster, arresting this individual or group under computer misuse provisions will result in the shutdown of the network. If it were desirable to eliminate zombie entities from the academy's publishing cycle, might not these models also have their analogies within this typology?

Technological: many researchers do not consider it important to query the mechanisms of dissemination for their work. When this is the case, these researchers have been virtualized, in the sense of one operating system on a computer running inside and under the authority of another, as with rootkits. They are zombies, whose ostensible autonomy is hosted by the botnet and predicated upon their blindness to the controlling concepts sitting beyond their grasp. In this sense, they have already reached the level of a hypervisor rootkit; a system of malware that fools all software running beneath it into believing that it has been given direct access to the hardware, while in reality all channels in and out are monitored and can, at will, be controlled by the rootkit. Such researchers are as unlikely to accept knowledge of their constricted agency in academic publishing as Plato's cave-dwellers: the system seems to serve their interests; it is the reality of academia. As is clear, however, it is also shadow-like.

It seems, therefore, that as with the technological solution of the antivirus, beyond a certain level of 'complicity', or depth of malware, this method will be of limited efficacy. Instead, it becomes necessary to adopt the more extreme approach of 'emulate and subvert'; the very technique that a rootkit would use. This is, essentially, the phased transition approach whereby established researchers who understand the high stakes at play commit to publishing a certain percentage of their work in open access journals. This could even be extended a step further to the suggestion of publishing this quota in specifically non-commercial open access outlets: university presses. In such a system the researcher appears to be continuing along traditional lines, while concurrently tipping the balance in favour of open access.

Legal: writing computer viruses and gaining unauthorized access to computer systems are criminal activities in most jurisdictions. The most effective means of bringing down a botnet is to physically apprehend the individual or group responsible; the gatekeeper who can be compelled to divulge the encryption keys and passwords for the network. Could this find a parallel in the world of academic publishing, in the simple ousting of one party or more?

Would it be possible and desirable to remove publishers from the system? This is certainly a theoretical possibility. When analyses such as that of Stephen Mooney make it clear that publishers are seeking profit first and foremost, rather than providing material to the scholarly community, perhaps it is naïve to hope that business practices could be predicated upon such altruism. On the other hand, researchers have the power to substantially erode these profits should they so choose. If an entire upcoming generation of scholars is aware of this, publishers must – if they wish to survive in this brave new world – re-conceive and re-present the value they bring as existing for the other.

It must also be considered that such a removal would have a huge knock-on effect on libraries for, as has already been explored, what would their role be? This can perhaps finally be answered through another question: do academics have the technical skills and time to embark on publishing enterprises of their own? I would suggest not. It might, in the end, be that knocking publishers off the top spot will result in a simple slide in which their place is taken, in the new open access world, by the library-as-publisher.

Repercussions

Even as open access holds out this possibility, there are strong incentives for publishers to ensure that they are not wiped off the map, and libraries also are not keen on their change of role. Indeed, to coin an unfortunate acronym, the library becomes the Research Output Team. The potential mass decentralization of publication will of course also impact upon researcher activity. For too long, research has been valued for its location rather than its content. The advent of easily available technical solutions should lead to a proliferation of increasingly niche e-journals to the point where location is chosen less on prestige, but rather that the publication is of relevance to the work. This is not to suggest that peer review and quality control should be abandoned, but rather that ranking journals according to their rejection rate is elitist nonsense that does not help researchers find and evaluate scholarly material from their field. Publishers must not be allowed to keep their place merely because of conservatism in the academy and it is certainly not the role of universities to prop up an outmoded business model.

While measures of assessment, such as the United Kingdom's Research Excellence Framework, are designed to perpetuate the botnet by linking funding to a researcher's performance within that very system, such metrics are merely the second edge of a Damoclean sword. If the system is allowed to continue as it stands, researchers will no longer be able to afford access to material as the library heads to extinction; they will no longer be able to carry out their work. If researchers buck the trend and fare poorly in the assessment frameworks they will, likewise, find themselves unable to work as their funding will be slashed. It is perhaps only fitting to conclude by noting that this practice of autosubversion is clearly not unique to publishing, as evidenced in this final example of assessment metrics, but rather seems to pervade the whole academy. Researchers must become aware of the constraints placed upon them by external systems with which they are complicit and work to stem the tide of colonization. Soon it should be possible to banish to history the days when researchers could feign ignorance of the impact their choices make. As the American novelist Thomas Pynchon put it, although not in reference to his later zombie-like beings the Thanatoids: 'we do know what's going on, and we let it go on' (1995: 713). We must all work to know better the mechanisms through which we disseminate our research, so as to break free of the botnet, so as to not act against our own interests, to not let it go on, so as to not be, in this typology of technology, infection and auto-destruction, zombies spun within a hegemonic web.

The intranet of the living dead: software and universities

Jonathan Paul Marshall

VAUGHN: I should of course be angry with you. You've thwarted my elaborate security precautions twice. I'd like to know why.
DOCTOR: Oh, that's quite simple. I hate computers and refuse to be bullied by them.
(*Doctor Who*; *Invasion*, Camfield 1968)[1]

M yths and stories sometimes give us information we prefer not to observe consciously. This chapter argues for a mythic similarity between cyborgs and zombies by considering the Cybermen from the long-running British TV programme *Doctor Who*, and comparing them to zombies. This frames a discussion of people's experience of computing and computer networking, of being on the university's internal administrative network (or intranet). It seems that in the university the cyborg-zombie hybrid rules in a haze of electronic cannibalism, incorporation, deadening routine, computerized disruption, administrative politics and surveillance. The secondary theme is that cyborgs are ordering devices which create disorder by being overly inclusive and suppressing their unseen, thus creating a cyborg unconscious.

While cyborgs generally make optimistic theory and people proudly announce that they are cyborgs (e.g. Warwick 2004), few make similar claims about being zombies. However, popular zombie and cyborg mythologies have multiple parallels, which point to similar dynamics and anxieties. Cyborg myths encapsulate some aspects of reality better than cyborg theory, and help explain why people might embrace zombification in the university.

Myth

In this chapter myths are taken to be recurrent narratives: 'imaginative patterns, networks of powerful symbols that suggest particular ways of interpreting the world' (Midgley 2003: 2). While some myths may be 'true', they can also be contradictory, so that one myth may create, or reinforce, social commonplaces and truths, while another (or even the same one) may express anxieties or denied 'realities'.

Malinowski argues that myths act as charters of behaviour and realities as lived (1926: 18–19, 29, 89). Despite a more elaborate semiotic apparatus, similar assumptions underlie Barthes' writings on mythology: 'myth … makes us understand something and it imposes it on us' (1988: 147), and 'myth has the task of giving an historical intention a natural justification, and making contingency appear eternal' (142). Barthes implies there can be no critical myths. In his view myth is depoliticized (143–44), and 'revolutionary language proper cannot be mythical' (146). This reduces popular myths to sterility. They are seen simply as ideology reinforcing stability and power structures.

Jung adds ambiguity and tension to myth by seeing in it the potential play of unconscious processes. For him myth has a life of its own, it is not completely in the control of the ego or of conscious social forces. Myths and other symbols can compensate for, and challenge, the one-sided inclinations of common ego structures and ideals. For example, alchemy, in the West, acted as a compensation for Christianity's inability to deal with matter, the feminine, and evil. This implies that myths can potentially undermine each other, and partially reveal what is hidden by another myth or theory. Myths may be the way that implicit knowledge or tacit worries gain a dramatic and hence conceivable form. In eras of social change a new compensatory myth may arise from a person's unconscious, perhaps as art, but has to be taken up by others to have social currency and effect. Myths can also be dangerous; too strong an identification with a myth can lead to 'inflation', to a lack of realistic limits, and thus to self-destructive actions. Inflation can occur collectively, and a 'possessed' group can lead others, perhaps voluntarily, to their destruction.[2]

Finally, as Spitzer points out (2011), myth is the ambiguous, denied undercurrent of philosophy, such that *mythos* is basic to philosophy (*logos*) while concurrently disrupting it and being created by it. Plato, as the usually declared founder of philosophy as *logos* and thus remote from sophistry or mythical poetry, has dialogues which are necessarily full of myths, parables and stories, while denying that these are important for what he intends to do. Again myth is dynamic, intertwined with, and disruptive of, conscious intentions and theory.

In what follows, I play out cyberman and zombie myth as the compensation for cyborg theory or philosophy, so as to increase understanding of daily life in the computerized university. I begin by comparing some general features of zombie and cyborg myths, before moving on to consider *Doctor Who*'s Cybermen in more detail.

Zombies and cyborgs

The earliest mentions of zombies imply they are spirits or ghosts: 'the title whereby he [a Brazilian chief] was called, is the name for the Deity, in the Angolan tongue. NZambi is the word for Deity' (Southey 1819: 24). Schele de Vere reports that the word 'Zombi, a phantom or a ghost, [is] not unfrequently heard in the Southern States in nurseries and among the servants … [It] is a Creole corruption of the Spanish *sombra* [shade, shadow] which at times has the same meaning' (1872: 138). Lafcadio Hearn portrays the zombie as a ghost/spirit: something that stands out as unusual and threatening, a breaker of normal boundaries and categories. A woman he interviewed says:

It is the zombis who make all those noises at night one cannot understand … Or, again, if I were to see a dog that high (she holds her hand about five feet above the floor) coming into our house at night, I would scream 'Mi Zombi' …

You pass along the high-road at night, and you see a great fire, and the more you walk to get to it the more it moves away: it is the zombi makes that … Or a horse with only three legs passes you: that is a zombi.

(1890: 187ff)

The first 'non-fiction' account of zombies in the modern sense is usually said to appear in 1929, in William Seabrook's *Magic Island* (Bishop 2010a: 48):

[W]hile the *zombie* came from the grave, it was neither a ghost nor yet a person who had been raised like Lazarus from the dead. The *zombie* they say, is a soulless human corpse, still dead but taken from the grave and endowed by sorcery with a mechanical semblance of life.

(1929: 94)

The use of 'mechanical' is significant with its cyborg resonance. Here the zombies are forced to work on plantations, their pay and life appropriated by their masters. In Seabrook's first tale, they are associated with the Haitian-American Sugar Company: 'an immense factory plant dominated by a huge chimney, with clanging machinery, steam whistles, [and] freight cars' (1929: 95), although the zombies work in the fields as emotionless appendages to the factory. Seabrook tells of meeting some such workers, and of how disorienting this was: 'I had a sickening and almost panicky lapse in which I thought or rather felt, "Great God maybe this stuff is really true, and if it is true … it upsets everything"' (101). These zombies, like those mentioned by Hearn, threaten our conceptions and categories.

The next stage in zombie mythology comes with Romero's *Night of the Living Dead* (1968), which shows the dead as ravenously cannibalistic, converting those they do not destroy into other zombies, who continue the spread. Although the term 'zombie' is not used in the original movie, it is used in the subsequent films, and begins the common myth of the zombie as destructive plague (Tudor 1989: 101). As Bishop indicates, 'almost single-handedly Romero reinvented the sub-genre [of zombie films] … no short fiction, novels or films featuring hordes of flesh eating zombies predate 1968' (2010a: 94). Zombies might appear as slaves, particularly in the early narratives, but they always have potential to open disaster, and as the myth develops they become more and more out of control until, in the so-called 'zombie apocalypse', humans stand against the overwhelming force of the incorporating living dead.

There are five sources of unease with zombies: firstly, they are ambiguous (alive but dead); secondly, you can become one yourself against your will; thirdly, the zombie master may lose control; fourthly, they cannot be stopped by discussion or moderate force; and finally, that zombies will eat you.[3]

While computers and cyborgs rarely literarily eat people, mythically they frequently are ambiguous, convert people, taking their flesh away, get out of control, and cannot be reasoned with or otherwise stopped. Likewise, they become an overwhelming force that threatens to take over the world. Thus, for example, computers and cyborgs are ambivalent, bordering life, death and spirit, and it is sometimes suggested that people's 'souls' can be 'downloaded' into the machine, sometimes to wander the internet as literal 'ghosts in the machine'.

In the *Doctor Who* story *Moonbase* (Barry, 1967a), Jamie thinks the Cyberman he has seen is a ghost foretelling his death ('The McCrimmon Piper!'). In William Gibson's 'sprawl series', the internet/matrix is haunted by loas, or voodoo gods, which can possess users; implying the zombie again. Donna Haraway writes that 'cyborgs are ether, quintessence', they are above mere flesh, 'light and clean because they are nothing but signals' (1991a: 153). Like vampires, the Cybermen on their first appearance (*The Tenth Planet,* Martinus 1966), with their planet, Mondas, suck energy out of people. Early in the story, Bluey remarks: 'It's like something's sucked out all the power out of my body' and 'Cyberman 1' later says: 'The energy of Mondas is nearly exhausted and now we turn to its twin and will gather energy from Earth … until it is all gone.' Exhaustion and drainage is one response to being near cyborg-spirits, and is a commonly reported symptom of the computerized workplace.

The mythology of computers, as represented in popular culture, is well known. At a particular point, their masters lose control and they rise up and attempt to take over the world, as does WOTAN in *Doctor Who's War Machines* (Ferguson 1966). WOTAN converts people into its mindless zombie-like slaves. The *Terminator* movies also feature computerized war machines turning against their human 'masters'. Cybermen lose their emotions and capacity for joy, becoming focused on their mission and devoted to imposing technological order on the disorderly flesh and cosmos. They become a living dead, and such cyborgs, like modern zombies, change others to make more of themselves. Not respecting boundaries or distinctions, they must extend and conquer. Cyborgs see this as inevitable: 'Resistance is useless,' say the Cybermen. 'To struggle is futile,' says the Cyberleader in *Tomb of the Cybermen* (Barry 1967b). In the Big Finish audio play, *Spare Parts* (Russel 2002), not only do the early Cybermen reiterate 'we are the future' with the fervour of cyber-theorists, but their creator comes to realize that 'I created an army of animated corpses'. This metaphor of conquest and inevitability expresses people's experience that the computer programme carries out its plan with regard neither for those caught within it or for changing circumstance.

Mythically, it appears that computers and computer networks are intelligent but non-creative zombie-makers; they occupy the space of the mind in the same way that mundane zombies occupy the space of the flesh. They spread, often claiming necessity or inevitability, deadening life, spontaneity and invention, while remaking the world in their image. The myth implies that every day we risk becoming part of a machine with purposes alien to our own. The cyborg, although ambivalent (like the zombie), also represents conversion, restraint and unarguable force. Metaphorically, it devours all it encounters.

Doctor Who and the Cybermen

The prime cyborg myth addressed here is the one portrayed over many years in the BBC television series *Doctor Who*. There are of course other cyborg creatures in science fiction, such as *Star Trek*'s 'Borg',[4] but *Doctor Who* is noteworthy because as a series involving time and space travel it is not limited to a set of locations or times. Additionally, it has run through much of the late twentieth and early twenty-first centuries, and during this time computers and cyborgs have been a recurrent theme. The first programme was transmitted in the United Kingdom in November 1963, with the final programme of its first incarnation being broadcast in December 1989. This was followed by an in-continuity TV movie in 1996 and a new, also in-continuity, series beginning in March 2005 and currently (2011) still on air. Continuity has been enabled by the main character of the Doctor (an alien 'Time Lord'), being allowed to 'regenerate' his whole body and thus be played by a range of actors. There has also been a vast series of novelizations, independent novels from different publishers, comic book stories, radio plays, web plays, CD-based 'audio adventures' featuring the actors from the series, fan scholarship and general merchandizing. Much of this material took off in the years the TV program was in hiatus, but has continued since the inception of the new series.[5]

The Cybermen, as one of the shows recurrent villains, have faced all but one of the eleven actors who have played the Doctor, and have frequently faced that Doctor more than once. Thus, there is a wide set of examples over a long period of time from which to show the Cyberman myth. The word 'cyborg' was invented in 1960 (Gray 1995: 3, 29ff), and Cybermen first appeared in the *Tenth Planet*, broadcast in the United Kingdom in October 1966, and last appeared in *Closing Time* in 2011. There are 13 official television stories in which the Cybermen are the main antagonists (and several more in which they appear), and at least 10 audio adventures feature them.

The Cybermen were invented when Gerry Davis, the story editor for *Doctor Who*, consulted with Kit Pedler, a medical researcher working at London University. According to Davis, he threw some plot ideas at Pedler, who amongst other things came up with the Cybermen in response (Davis in Banks 1986: 7). Pedler wrote:

> At the time I was obsessed as a scientist by the difference and similarities between the human brain and advanced computing machines ... And so the Cybermen appeared. They were an ancient race on a dying planet who had made themselves immortal by gradually replacing their worn out organs with cybernetic spare parts. They had become strong in the process and always behaved logically, but lost their feelings and humanity as they become more and more machine driven.
>
> (Pedler 1979: np).

Pedler also stated that he was discussing 'spare part surgery' with his wife, also a doctor and they 'conceived the idea of someone with so many mechanical replacements that he didn't know whether he was human or machine' (Banks 1986: 25). As Britton points out, 'from their inception the Cybermen were creatures embodying a range of ambiguities … they sought conquest not out of hatred for other species or desire for dominance but out of logical necessity' (Britton 2011: 76). Although, as Britton argues, later on in the series the Cybermen were sometimes portrayed as yet another series of alien invaders, they were still rational about conquests and their cyborg imperatives.

In the original series, Cybermen initially arose from an attempt to impose order on their flesh and survive on their planet of Mondas, their actions causing them to become homeless outsiders. In the post-2005 series, the new Cybermen also arise internally, on an alternate Earth, through an attempt to conquer the disorders of disease and aging. In the Big Finish audio drama *Cyberman* (Briggs 2006), uncovered Cyberman technology is used to produce order on Earth and victory in war; it then takes over. The myth of Cybermen warns of using technology to order life, and in so doing losing something that was precious and disorderly.

Cyborgs and Cybermen: theory versus myth

Let us further compare Cyborg theory with the Cybermen myth implicit in these *Doctor Who* stories. Obviously in a small space I cannot do justice to cyborg thinkers or *Doctor Who* scriptwriters, but hope that the comparison will help explicate the connection between university life and zombies.

Haraway's 'Cyborg Manifesto' is the beginning of cyborg theory. In fairness to Haraway, her essay was written as a critique of 1970s and 1980s back-to-nature, goddess feminist socialism. However, once introduced, myths have their own life and take other directions. Perhaps as a result, Haraway has discarded the metaphor to start thinking about, and with, 'companion species' instead (Haraway 2003: 4–5). In the original manifesto, Haraway argued that there is nothing 'natural' in human nature, that we have always been tool users, and a feminist socialism based on these misconceptions is not empowering. This idea is undoubtedly useful, but the essay gained a cyborg life itself (replicating independently of authorial intentions) and spread a number of misconceptions of its own. Although Haraway recognized 'cyborg colonization work' and that 'modern war is a cyborg orgy', these ambivalences are largely abandoned for the cyborg's 'fruitful couplings' (1991a: 150). Sean Redmond, for example, distinguishes between the 'humanistic cyborg' 'driven by the logic of machine aesthetic [longing] for the human emotion and human attachment that will add existential meaning to its fragile outer shell', and the 'pathological cyborg', which 'wants to melt away its human simulacra … [wanting] nothing more than the complete genocide of the human race'. However, while there is apparently no 'bad' side to the 'humanistic cyborg', he lessens the pathology of the 'pathological' cyborg by praising its questioning of borders and its transgression (2004: 156–57). But are borders always bad? Sometimes borders may protect or grant independence. Is hybridity always good? Are the living-dead better than the living or the dead? Redmond's convenient binary separates so as to downplay the 'pathology', yet the 'humanist' and 'pathological' may reside together in the cyborg, just as *mythos* and *logos* are intertwined in philosophy and disrupt each other. Cyborgs both enable and restrict.

Often ambivalence is dropped altogether. Negri and Hardt, for example claim the 'cyborg fable, which resides at the ambiguous boundary between human, animal, and machine, introduces us today, much more effectively than deconstruction, to … new terrains of [revolutionary] possibility' (2000:218). Again, the cyborg provides a metaphor for challenging borders, without a pause to wonder if borders could ever be appropriate. Ambiguities may need to be emphasized rather than submerged by praise of hybridity, or accusations that ambivalence is technophobia or conservatism (as in Ryan and Kellner 2004).

Haraway begins the Manifesto with a totalizing assertion: 'we are all chimeras, theorized and fabricated hybrids of machine and organism; in short, we are cyborgs' (Haraway 1991a: 150). The idea we are already cyborgs depends upon blurring tool use with the processing of humans. That there is a continuum does not mean the end points are identical, or that all technology is equally innocent or voluntary. When tool use involves computers, then indeed we must use them, we must use the software that is provided, we must master the upgrades, and upgrades are compulsory, irrespective of whether they are improvements for us or not. We all must become part of the network, and open to the compulsions of that network. There is no space for anything else. This may not be the case for a hammer. Cyborg theory routinely suppresses types of criticism, blurs useful distinctions, and supports incorporation.

'The relation between organism and machine has been a border war. The stakes in the border war have been the territories of production, reproduction, and imagination' (Haraway 1991a: 150). If there is a 'border war', then perhaps that war has already been won through the cyborgs being largely voluntarily incorporated into the network which acts as a mode of ordering as well as enablement? There is no escape; the cyborg is enabled to be on call at all times, to work at all times. The cyborg becomes cyborg to survive and to spread.

In the *Tenth Planet*, 'Cyberman 1' explains the logic of conversion: 'We were exactly like you once, but our cybernetic scientists realized that our race was getting weak … Our life span was getting shorter, so our scientists and doctors devised spare parts for our bodies until we could be almost completely replaced.' Elsewhere, he says, 'We have freedom from disease, protection against heat and cold, true mastery. Do you prefer to die in misery?' Most of the people who involve themselves with the Cybermen admire their power and freedom and aim to control it for themselves, but are usually more ambivalent about becoming Cybermen than in having others changed for them. Managers who can keep secretaries to be their cyborgs know the losses as well. The original Cybermen replaced all their weak fleshy parts as their planet plunged into space (*Spare Parts*). They did what they had to, to survive.

In the *Rise of the Cybermen* (Harper 2006a), a new race of Cybermen is invented on an alternate earth, because John Lumic, a powerful businessman, aims to survive his terminal illness and is happy to spread the benefits around. Indeed, human upgrading is soon required and those unsuitable are to be deleted. Becoming cyborg seems beneficial, pragmatic, inevitable or compulsory, even morally necessary. The Big Finish story *Cyberman* posits that Earth's leaders would be willing to sacrifice themselves and others to become Cybermen, in return for dedicated purpose, superior firepower and victory in a war defending what it is to be human. Visions of order, efficiency and victory are seductive, and cyborgs can be implemented as a mode of extending power, or providing apparent benefit. Sometimes, though, people can ask the vital question of those who intend such order:

CALLUM: What do you two hope to gain from [waking the cybermen]?
KLIEG: That does not concern you.
KAFTAN: Oh, they might as well know, Eric. We are going to build a better world.
CALLUM: Better? Well, who for?

(*Tomb of the Cybermen*)

Organisms that cannot be converted are to be eliminated if they pose a threat, like the Cryons in *Attack of the Cybermen* (Robinson 1985), or the incompatible humans in *Rise of the Cybermen* (Harper 2006a); cyborgs cannot have any part of their organization that is not part of the network. No one is outside cyborg order. This is just cyborg-logic; there is no reason for anyone to rebel against improvement, and rebelling marks the rebel as a threat, or Luddite, who must be eliminated lest they disturb the system. Like a zombie, once the cyborg is given power and an instruction, or a rationale, it keeps on, and keeps on converting or incorporating others.

Haraway states that cyborgs are 'not afraid of their joint kinship with animals and machines, not afraid of permanently partial identities and contradictory standpoints' (1991a: 155), but this is not reflected in our experiential mythic knowledge. The myth implies that once cyborgs exist, there can be no standpoint outside of their order. For example, transhumanist James Hughes argues that cyborgization must be extended to dolphins and apes to end 'human racism'. The compulsory nature of this extension is implied rather than stated (2004: 261). Becoming cyborg allows cyborgs to see the natural world as subservient to them and as part of their intranet. Cyborg theorist Ollivier Dyens writes 'nature cannot exist apart from technologies any more' (2001: 11), not that we need nature in order to live. In *Revenge of the Cybermen* (Briant 1975), the Cyberleader maintains that extension occurs because of their efficiency and superiority: 'Cybermen function more efficiently than animal organisms. That is why we will rule the galaxy.' In *Doomsday* (Harper 2006c), the Cyberleader says:

This broadcast is for humankind. Cybermen now occupy every landmass on this planet. But you need not fear. Cybermen will remove fear. Cybermen will remove sex and class and colour and creed. You will become identical, you will become like us.

As this implies, Cybermen may be 'creature[s] in a post-gender world' (Haraway 1991a: 150), but become so by eliminating all difference. Without biological reproduction they

128

need no women. Being female is classed as messy, weak and eliminable. The cyborg is not 'resolutely committed to partiality, irony, intimacy, and perversity' as Haraway claims (1991a: 151), but to uniformity, efficiency and power: at best, to ease of programming.

Haraway admits, her cyborg does not have much disruptive unconscious, so as to avoid the totalizing ('cannibalizing') nature of psychoanalysis (1991b: 9–10), but this implies that there is nothing outside the machine. Cyborgs think they see all; that disorder is external and everything is orderable by conscious will. 'It is quite useless to resist us. We are stronger and more efficient than your Earth people. We must be obeyed' (*Tenth Planet*). 'Everything we decide is carried out. There are no mistakes' (*Tomb of the Cybermen*). What cyborgs are unconscious of is denied, repressed and depoliticized. Dyens suggests we should fear the bomb and pollutants (2001: 14), not those with their fingers on the buttons or who benefit from pollution. Similarly, he suggests climate change results from unchecked culture (18), as cyborg culture is a unity, with no fractures, politics or oppositions.

Differences in power are vague, and Haraway says, 'it is not clear who makes and who is made in the relation between human and machine' (1991a: 177). With no demarcation between human, machine and network, there is nothing to rebel against. Cyborg power is always elsewhere, but locating oneself in the 'belly of the monster', as Haraway recommends (1991b: 6) is a good way to be digested or incorporated.

One of Haraway's more illuminating insights is that 'our machines are disturbingly lively, and we ourselves frighteningly inert' (1991a: 152), although she quickly moves on. In cyborg worlds, machines have the active role in our lives. We have to respond to them. Without them we are lonely and unconnected. With them we are part of the capital machine, evaluated according to the categories of that machine, which becomes our environment. Cyborgs do not allow lifelike category ambivalence or vagueness. In such an environment, practical wisdom is not aimed towards others or towards the intention of the work (say doing research or teaching), but towards the work as defined by the machine (getting the most points and rewards). We manipulate the rules given by the machine, and ignore the possibly different rules of other people. As the Doctor points out when facing the computer Xoanon, who is trying to eliminate him for contradicting its reality, we face the power/stupidity nexus:

> You know, the very powerful and the very stupid have one thing in common. They don't alter their views to fit the facts. They alter the facts to fit their views, which can be uncomfortable if you happen to be one of the facts that needs altering.[6]
>
> (*Face of Evil*, Roberts 1977)

Dyens makes adaptation to (rather than modification of) this electronic environment an evolutionary imperative: 'every living being also attempts to draw his niche in toward him. A complete fusion with the environment (in such a way as to become perfectly adapted to it) is everyone's (and everything's) main objective' (2001: 7). Perfect cyborg fusion is to be aimed for, and it is evolutionarily 'natural' to adapt to techno-extension. Resistance vanishes again. Hence cyborgs are to be admired as perfect replicators (2001: 16), forgetting that biological evolution depends on a degree of imperfect replication. Creatures evolve precisely because of their lack of 'fit' with the environment, and the creatures inhabiting the environment change it. Creative disorder is suppressed by cyborg order. Dyens adds that 'through technologies the environment becomes a human friendly ecosystem', leaving open the question of why, if we aim to merge, it is not 'friendly' already. He assumes a match of intentions, design and outcomes, ignoring the possibility that technology can be crystallized stupidity or authoritarianism.

While the 'ubiquity and invisibility' of machines, as they make the environment, could be liberating (Haraway 1991a: 153), it also implies the environment is designed by the powerful and that power is inescapable. Our love for electronic gadgets lets Vaughn spread cyber-control over the whole planet in *Invasion*, so that humans all become zombies with only his will.

> DOCTOR: The micro-monolithic circuits are an artificial nervous system. Once activated they will produce the Cyber-hypnotic force that controls human beings.
> TURNER: There are hundreds and thousands of these circuits in IE equipment all over the world.
> WATKINS: Exactly.

At the same time, ubiquity means that power is distributed and located nowhere with responsibility. Cyborg governance is impersonal and without blame for those who benefit from it. Supposedly cyborgs have no dependency (Haraway 189:151), yet inherently cyborgs depend on machines and servicing, even while these machines may be elsewhere or under the control of others. When Mondas breaks up in the *Tenth Planet* the Cybermen start drooping and collapsing:

> BEN: What's happened to them?
> BARCLAY: They've disintegrated!
> DYSON: They must have been entirely dependent on power from Mondas!

Distribution means that Cybermen are not 'structured by the polarity of public and private' (Haraway 1991a: 151). For the cyborg there is no privacy and no independent or disruptive self (that is not public or potentially public) can be allowed.

Cybermen, like zombies, are largely interchangeable. What is personal is to be eliminated. The cyborg is a 'disassembled and reassembled, postmodern collective and personal self' (Haraway 1991a: 163), which suppresses the bits that are painful or get in the way of work. Similarly, Cybermen do 'not dream of community on the model of the organic family' (Haraway 1991a: 151), because they have no family, or emotional ties. Cyborgs replace what we try and point to with the word 'community' by simply being together in terms of a project, with no sense of loss.[7] They reproduce, not by sex or genetic engineering, but by conversion of those born organically, again like zombies. They ignore the organic except as raw material.

Like zombies, cyborgs do not have to see the irrelevant, although they have *defined* it as irrelevant and taken that as real. 'Irrationality', the non-conceptual, chaos, and emotions are a weakness, yet this creates their unconscious. In *Invasion*, the wealthy electronics and computer expert Vaughn states: 'I'm convinced, Packer, that emotion could be used to destroy them', and his experiments show that inducing feeling drives them mad. In the new series, Cybermen have a device to suppress their emotions installed, and if this is disabled then they are crippled by distress. Cyber-zombies require that people just work or act as raw materials; if they *feel* where they are, collapse is imminent.

Cyborg behaviour is logical, if we accept both the arguments of Hume (1888), that ethics is based upon sympathy towards others, and the neo-Darwinian view that ethics function to help group survival and reproduction (Dawkins 2006). Without any means of identifying with others, the Cybermen support each other, eliminate threats, and enforce the benefits of conversion to remove the threat from others.

BENOIT: Why are you here?
CYBERMAN 1: To eliminate all dangers.
HOBSON: But you'll kill every single thing on the Earth!
CYBERMAN 1: Yes. All dangers will be eliminated.
BENOIT: Have you no mercy?
CYBERMAN 1: It is unnecessary.

(*Moonbase*)

There can be no respecting the rights of others not to convert, as that leaves dangers and potential disorder. Other models of ethical behaviour towards others are valueless: 'Promises to aliens have no validity. When the Tower is in our hands, he will be destroyed' (*Five Doctors*, Moffatt 1983). This leaves an unpitying duty to order, to render others like them, as when John Lumic after his conversion states: 'I will bring peace to the world. Everlasting peace, and unity and uniformity' (*Age of Steel*, Harper 2006b). Elsewhere a Cyberman says: 'You have fear. We will eliminate fear from your brain' (*Tomb of the Cybermen*).

To cyborgs, repression of emotional pain and disorder is always good and produces order. We either have emotions, or we have strength. Sympathy and pity are inefficient.

LEADER: I see that Time Lords have emotional feelings.
DOCTOR: Of sorts.
LEADER: Surely a great weakness in one so powerful?
DOCTOR: Emotions have their uses.
LEADER: They restrict and curtail the intellect and logic of the mind.
DOCTOR: They also enhance life! When did you last have the pleasure of smelling a flower, watching a sunset, eating a well-prepared meal?

LEADER: These things are irrelevant.
DOCTOR: For some people, small, beautiful events is what life is all about!…
DOCTOR: This isn't necessary. Let them go.
LEADER: And deny them the feeling of fear, the ultimate in emotional response?
DOCTOR: You've already proved your point quite adequately.

(Earthshock, Grimwade 1982)

The myth implies that people become cyborgs to avoid pain or irritation, because of the quest for power and efficiency, because they are compelled, or as a side effect of our good intentions.[8] In *Tomb of the Cybermen*, the Cybermen are woken up by our intelligence as much as by some people wanting power. In any case cyborgs are directed and do not perceive things that trouble them.

It appears that cyborg theory misdirects: central questions avoided by cyborg theory are raised by Cyberman myth. If you keep adding machinery and subtracting flesh from human beings, at what point do we stop being human, and become not superhuman but subhuman; a cyber-zombie? In what zone of decision does technology stop enabling life and start to destroy it? Similarly, within the cyborg framing it is impossible to ask whether work/technology is inhuman or unnatural, because the borders that would allow the question to be asked do not exist. Cybermen enable this question to be asked. Now we can proceed to ask these questions of the computerized and networked university.

Cybermen at university

FENNER: Tell me, would you let a small band of semi-savages stand in the way of progress?
DOCTOR: Well, progress is a very flexible word. It can mean just about anything you want it to mean.

(Power of Kroll, Stewart 1978)

As part of a project investigating software and its relationship to social orders and disorders, a number of interviews were conducted in various Australian universities with both administrative and academic staff, which illustrate a few of the points under discussion. Everyone interviewed was, as we might expect, embedded in software and electronic networks at home and at work. Without this embedding it would be impossible for them to survive, communicate or do things important to them: 'basically everything we do, and everything I do at work, is based on computer software'. When one person said that 'sometimes real life got in the way of computing', this was not because of something beyond the network, but because, 'I don't have a proper internet connection at home.' There was almost no space outside the network. This involvement does not increase a sense of autonomy: 'everything I do is tied in with the system and software in some way. Because we use so much software I don't feel like I have that much autonomy anyway.'

'Okay well you do this and this and this and ... it's a bit robotic I think.' 'You get so familiar with some software, it's deskilling, you're almost useless at anything else.' You become cyborg.

Rather than enabling dispersion or autonomy, software and the internal network enables centralization. While in the past administrative staff could be affiliated with a department, now they are generally centralized as administration only, and not only lose familiarity with departmental work but, in the spirit of Parkinson's (1958) laws, create work and underlings. They transfer labour to the academic staff, who end up having to do their own administration, while remaining unaware of what the real administrators do. Academics, for instance, now have to organize their own classes, which used to be done by administrators, but everything is affected:

> We used to just pass our work receipts to Accounts who then paid us. Now we have to use a highly detailed program, which took several hours of training to explain ... Given I use it once or twice a year, by the time I'll use it next I've forgotten how and it'll take hours to do something that probably took them minutes.

The separation is naturalized by the cyborg dependence upon people elsewhere: 'we're the core of the operation and it shouldn't be based on what some group in Melbourne wants, it should be what we want.' 'My computer now has all its files shifted onto the network. Previously when the network was down I could work on the computer, but not anymore.' Project managers, while outsourcing overseas, also complained about the difficulties such outsourcing brought, but that was the way it was done. Even if contracts were made locally, they ended up working with people elsewhere.

One person pointed to the computer friendly rules and categories of evaluation of academics as creating administration: 'we used to have just a dean, now we have this many layers [gestures] and its all about making sure we manipulate the rules to get the best ranking.' A member of one university's administration said, 'Although I am not supposed to say, the university now spends as much on administration as on academics, and it's growing.' The numbers, he admitted, seemed to take off after the introduction of ubiquitous computing. This allowed more order creation, as well as helping to check up on that order more efficiently. Another person commented: 'Oddly the questionnaires and work-plans we have to fill in [as academics], never have any space for [the category of] pointless administration'; the administration never recognizes the work it creates. Work is demanded but invisible. Form filling is cyborg caring: 'they want evidence on file that when you collapse through overwork they did due diligence to foresee and inhibit you.'

Upgrades occur randomly and without consultation.

> I wanted to continue to use Netscape for mail as it had a good search and was easy to sort mail offline ... The technician screamed at me, he was fed up of people wanting

something different. It had to be 'XX', that was the way it was ... Later I found out IT wasn't keen on using the new program either.

Real cyborgs know that upgrading and new software is always good. 'You put the thing in and then if you have problems then you throw money at it and try and fix it that way, not putting any thought into it first.' People usually reported that before a new programme structuring their work was implemented, no planners actually asked what they did, or there were a few desultory e-mails, with only some questions. 'Nobody in my particular area was really quizzed about what they did.' But, if the management is aiming for some extra efficiency, getting extra work out of people, or restructuring, then there is no need to find out what is done, as that is, by cyborg definition, wrong. They know what is right and it must be extended. So it should be no surprise when software does not work, or does not work helpfully and people have to work around it. 'The programmers are just focused on their result, not on what we need.'

Cyborg categories are made firm, irrespective of whether they are useful.

The new software works by defining people's roles ... We have to fit in a box ... The problem is that it does not recognize the roles we have ... XX, who has to know everything ended up not being able to access anything.

'It's like we have to change what we call things, and do with things, because that's what the software does, which seems really bizarre.' One academic complained that 'Labour Economics is lumped with Management. This means that all the journals [labour economists] publish in are dismissed by the majority of "their" group who never look at them.' Consequently they 'score' badly, but the authority of management is retained.

Expressing the cyborg imperative, the aim of software is control and removal of disorder. Software is not neutral. Politics, imperialism and disruption are inherent within software, and software is affected by the incompatible demands of different departments and people, structures of power and management, temporary victories, allocation of blame and the failures of communication in a hierarchy and across borders. IT departments are caught in this factional war of software extension, and attempt to save themselves as much as get the job done. People in IT complained that other people kept changing the goalposts of what they were supposed to do, and that they were blamed for impossible decisions made elsewhere. There is no real distinction between processes which are wholly computer based, and those administrative or bureaucratic processes which happen to be administered by computer, as the two are intertwined and require each other. That may be the Cybermen's message: there is no conscious place outside of the totalizing hybrid system.

Berg and Timmermans suggest that order and disorder are mutually implicated: 'these orders do not emerge out of (and thereby replace) a pre-existing disorder. Rather, with the production of an order, a corresponding disorder comes into being' (2000: 36). Modes of ordering can produce 'the very disorders they attempt to eradicate. They identify the enemy that they seek to conquer – yet this identification process is not a selection of a pregiven problem, but a process wherein the specific problem is produced' (2000: 45). Software generates disordering panic processes precisely because it enhances the possibilities of universalizing and extending protocols, practices and ideas of efficiency without exploration of the *specific* needs of people and situations. It happily breaks useful boundaries, such as that between work and not-work. It sees disorder as eliminable by using generalized schemas of order and it sees disorder as arising from that which escapes its order, and which by definition needs incorporating into its order, thus creating more problems for itself. Software is easily assimilated to an ongoing attempt to conquer disorder and extend order. The cyborg implies and creates the zombie chaos, which then provides the rationale for its further extension.

Conclusion

Computerization and intranet usage helps spread zombification (mindless, confused and pointless labour) throughout the university. Often it spreads because it appears to solve problems. When people have to work in the network they become extensions of the machine, and hence cyborgs or zombies. Unlike the zombies of film and myth, the cyborg-zombie hybrid is not a product of 'secrets man was not meant to know', bringing forth chaos as a direct attack on order. The cyborg-zombie is a creature produced by a desire for pure order, which creates chaos by its failure to regard disorder as essential. It arises in an attempt to extend power, and to remove unpredictability and the possibility of escape. It thus aims to remove liveliness and life. The cyborg-zombie must spread, with no borders and no mercy. The system is all-devouring as it creates what the system will recognize. That which the system cannot recognize must be destroyed, yet the denied still exists and still has effects. The cyborg-zombie denies the existence of the chaos it creates, lurching away to infect those that it masters with the blame for its own failure. It is born of a desire both to control and to shift responsibility elsewhere. Its remedy for its failure is to apply itself more intensely: as if some cyborgification is good, then more must be better. By enabling 'better' management and administration, it enslaves everywhere and confuses everyone. The academic respectability of the cyborg, with its attack on boundaries, and its covert desire for unity, may make people even more vulnerable to this form of life in death. There is a dearth of appealing theory with which to challenge the extension.

There may be hope. The myth of the cyborg implies that because of their love of order cyborgs lack creativity, and appear to have fixed and inflexible hierarchies and routines. The Doctor says, 'the best thing about a machine that makes sense, you can very easily make it turn out nonsense' (*Tomb of the Cybermen*, Barry 1967b), and 'logic ... merely enables one to be wrong with authority' (*Wheel in Space*, DeVere 1968). The Cybermen are weaker than they appear: 'You've no home planet, no influence, nothing. You're just a pathetic bunch of tin soldiers skulking about the galaxy in an ancient spaceship' (*Revenge of the Cybermen*). Cyborgs disorder and confuse themselves in a vain attempt at total order.

As Zoe says of herself, they are created 'for some false kind of existence where only known kinds of emergencies are catered for' (*Wheel in Space*). In the *Tenth Planet*, the Cybermen's world absorbs so much energy from Earth that it burns up. That the ordering system creates disorder is a certainty, as is the continual creep of the disorder, and the increasingly impossible form of the work the subjects allegedly resisted doing in the first place. Hence humans can win, whatever the apparent odds, and perhaps this myth holds some truth. In which case, as well as being a site for the extension and embrace of the cyborg-zombie, the university is automatically also a site of resistance.

Notes

1   All episode titles referred to are from *Doctor Who* unless otherwise noted.
2   Jung is a digressive writer, and it is impossible to point to one place where all this is said coherently. Walker (1995) is a good introduction, but misses Jung's point about alchemy. See also Marshall (2009).
3   American visitor to Haiti, Henry Austin, although not using the term zombie, writes of a drug which renders people apparently dead, adding: 'Afterwards, the victim was resuscitated for the sacrifice [usually involving cannibalism], since the Voodoo rites require a living, conscious offering' (1912: 175). In this case, the zombie feared being eaten.
4   It seems customary to regard Cameron's *Terminator* and *Star Trek: Next Generation*'s Data as cyborgs, but they are android robots and thus have a somewhat different dynamic.
5   There is no definitive academic history of *Doctor Who*, but there are a large number of popular histories which cover various eras of the program and its spin offs. For a general account with particular focus on the inception, see Robb (2009).
6   Interestingly, while the Doctor eventually repairs the computer, we learn that at some unknown time in the past he had tried to improve its programming and that caused its breakdown.
7   There is a cultural difference between *Star Trek*'s Borg and *Doctor Who*'s Cybermen, in that Borg inflict unease because a person's individuality is threatened and lost in the hive 'community', while Cybermen raise alarm by losing the capacity for relationship altogether.
8   In contrast, androids like the Terminator and Data become more human the more they gain emotion and capacity to relate. The myths suggest that machines can move towards becoming human, and humans can move towards becoming machines.

Virtual learning environments and the zombification of learning and teaching in British universities

Nick Pearce and Elaine Tan

There has been a radical transformation in British higher education in recent years. Three converging trends have led to a dramatic change in the sector: a rapid expansion in student numbers, the introduction of student fees where provision was previously free, and the wholesale adoption of virtual learning environments (VLEs, also known as Learning Management Systems or LMSs) across the sector. This chapter will focus on the British experience, although similar trends are observable across the globe, and the lessons learnt will be applicable transnationally.

In the United Kingdom, it is generally recognized that the large numbers of student-consumers who have overrun higher education have placed a strain on the outmoded institutional structures. Technology can only partially alleviate this strain, and a reliance on it to support the learning and teaching of these students has had a profound effect on the nature of their education.

We apply the zombie metaphor on two levels in order to critically examine this transformation. Firstly, through an analysis of the embedded pedagogic culture of the VLEs, we examine how learning and teaching has been reduced to creating undead students. We explore how these new technologies threaten to replicate the industrial social relations of the factory, commodifying and alienating students in preparation for their future as a brain-dead wage slave.

Secondly, we explore how the functional role of zombies and zombification in Voodoo culture helps us to interrogate the functions that VLEs contribute to zombification in British universities. Here the zombie metaphor takes us beyond a narrative based on alienation and commodification and allows us to focus our attention on power and control. Within Voodoo culture, zombies were created and controlled by a sorcerer (a 'bokor') and then exploited for profit in the plantations and sugar mills. But who is the bokor in higher education? For whose benefit has the technology been used to zombify students?

Massification, commodification and the virtual learning environment

The university sector in the United Kingdom has undergone a process that has been termed massification (Scott 1998). The numbers of UK students graduating with a degree have risen from 50,000 to over 400,000 between 1967 and the present day, and this growth has led to an expansion in the number and diversity of higher education institutions (HEIs). Graduating with a university degree has gone from being a privilege for an elite few to an expectation for many, with 46% of 17- 30-year olds in higher education (BIS 2011b).

For a long time in Britain, going to university was funded entirely by the state and was free for individual students. However, devolution across the United Kingdom complicated this access, as higher education policy developed differently in England, Wales, Scotland and Northern Ireland.

In 1998, the system in England changed so that students were expected to make a contribution towards the cost of their degree, a 'top up fee' of initially £1,000 per year. This fee was generally paid through a state subsidized loan that was repaid upon employment above a certain salary threshold. The level of top up fee initially grew to reach £3,290 in 2010/11. Following the recommendations of the Browne Review (2010), the public sector has withdrawn its direct funding of university teaching altogether, with students now expected to pay the full cost of their degree. Whilst the fee level is still a matter of some debate it looks set to be around £9,000, similarly funded through a loan system, albeit one that is less subsidized than before.

As the degree becomes increasingly commoditized and understood through its exchange-value rather than use-value, the social relations inherent in its production – such as between the teacher and the student – are forgotten. Instead of being about the personal and intellectual transformation of the individual, higher education has become an investment in human capital, so that the degree is now simply a tradable token of cultural capital. As a result, universities are becoming factories for the mass production of graduates.

When Marx wrote about the commodification of labour in factories he often used the gothic imagery of capitalists as vampires and gravediggers, where capital owns and extracts profits from the proletariat (Baldick 1987). The living labour of the proletariat is contrasted with the undead labour of capital, with the latter parasitically extracting profit from the former. Similarly, when students become pure consumers of a commodity (rather than learners *per se*) they are no longer the subjects of academic production but the objects of academic consumption. However, the student as consumer has little autonomy over their own learning let alone the teaching of their degree, and is oriented towards becoming purely a commodity in the employment market.

The massification and commodification of higher education has meant that face-to-face 'live' interactions between faculty and students have out of necessity become increasingly scarce, providing a limited number of traditional seminars, larger groups and a greater focus on developing autonomous learners.

In order to facilitate the development of this desired efficiency and autonomy, the last 15 years has witnessed the widespread adoption of VLEs across the higher education sector (Weller 2007; Browne et al. 2006; Jenkins et al. 2001). The live interaction and essential humanity of the seminar discussion (if it ever existed) has, in many cases, been supplanted by the stunted interactions of online discussion boards. Lectures have been reduced to PowerPoint slides and assessments of learning reduced to performance within the parameters of multiple-choice quizzes. Whilst it is possible to use these new technologies in ways which encourage deep learning, this is not the default option. Bad teaching is easier in this environment than good.

In each case, the technologies of the VLE – which were implemented with the best of intentions as a modern alternative for traditional teaching and learning activities – have worked to strip the emotion and intelligence from pedagogic interactions, resulting often in a mechanized, lifeless learning environment. With the focus on content delivery, mindless consumption and regurgitation of information has been encouraged. Methods of assessment within this environment favour automated tasks such as online multiple choice questions, tests and quizzes, requiring no input from the teacher, and leaving the student to stumble their way through mediated learning rituals.

The zombie: metaphor and reality

The zombie metaphor has been appropriated by US popular culture – and, increasingly, international popular cultures – from a complex position within Haitian Voodoo culture, and thereby stripped of its contextual rationale. Haitian Voodoo was an amalgam of West African religions, brought together through slavery, and formed through particular socioeconomic and cultural pressures (Ackermann and Gauthier 1991). The successful slave rebellions meant that Voodoo, and the zombie, could be out in the open, but also led to a long period of political and social upheaval (James and Walvin 2001).

The American occupation of Haiti, which began in 1915, was well underway when Seabrook's *The Magic Island* (1929), one of the first accounts of Voodoo culture, became a bestseller and opened the way for the first zombie film in 1932, *White Zombie* (Russell 2005). The zombie was cannibalized from one culture to another as part of a wider process of cultural imperialism, and as such underwent a transformation, from a powerful symbol of slavery, to one distanced from its localized meaning and able to take on multiple contextualized meanings.

The zombie metaphor has been most prevalent in film where it has been used to critically assess consumer capitalism in *Dawn of the Dead* (Romero 1978; Snyder 2004), communism in *Invasion of the Body Snatchers* (Siegal 1956; Kaufman 1978) and the threat of viral pandemics in *28 Days Later* (Boyle 2002). That many of these films have been remade and franchised through sequels speaks not only of their popularity in the public consciousness, but also of the film industry's inherently cannibalistic nature, feeding off the carcasses of successful films.

The zombie was thus stripped of its early counter-imperialist meaning and became a lifeless metaphor which could be used to articulate multiple, and sometimes incommensurate, messages. Lauro and Embry (2008) make this distinction clear by differentiating the 'zombi' rooted in Haitian politics and folklore and the 'zombie' as the American import. The Romero zombie from the *Night of the Living Dead* quintet has completely triumphed in popular cultural consciousness, such that cannibalism and a lack of overall control have become synonymous with zombies, despite these not being key characteristics of the Voodoo variant of the zombie, or indeed any account before 1968 (Twohy 2008; Weed 2009).

In this chapter, we re-reanimate the corpse of the zombie, using the functionalist ethnographic accounts of Wade Davis (1988) and others who present the zombie as a key element of Haitian society, a product not just of individual sorcerers but of the culture which sanctions it. This is important, as it places as much emphasis on the structural processes which led to the creation of zombies as the zombies themselves. Taking this approach allows us to critically assess the zombification of learning and teaching in higher education.

Voodoo culture is an amalgam of various African cultures, brought together in Haiti by the importation of huge numbers of slaves by the French for cane production (Davis 1988; Ackermann and Gauthier 1991). The confused etymological origins and nomenclature reflect the murky and undocumented origins of this religion and this confusion continues with the zombi(e) itself. Broadly speaking, within Voodoo the human soul has two components, the *Gros bon ange* and the *Ti bon ange*, with the latter governing thoughts, memories and sentiments: crucially these parts of the soul can leave the body and can be captured, traded and sold (Ackermann and Gauthier 1991). The *Ti bon ange* can be captured in jars or pots – these jars feature prominently in the film *The Serpent and the Rainbow* (Craven 1988), which was based on Davis' book.

Strictly speaking, both the element of spirit in a jar and the body without its full soul is a zombie, although the latter has dominated discourse and will be the focus of our discussion. This zombie of the body has been called *zombi cadavre* (Davis 1998), but for simplicity we shall call it a zombie, whilst acknowledging the other possibilities. What is important here is that the zombie is real in two senses. The zombie is real in that there are documented cases of zombies: whether as drugged individuals or misdiagnosed schizophrenics, there have been individuals who occupy the category 'zombie', who believe themselves, in as much as they are capable, and are believed by others, to be zombies. The zombie is real in another sense, in that within Voodoo culture the existence of zombies is unquestioned, and the belief in the zombificatory powers of the sorcerers is a powerful tool for social control.

VLEs, zombie pedagogies and social control

Despite some individual pockets of resistance, the adoption of VLEs at an institutional level was recently reported to be at 100% by Browne et al. (2010). According to this study, a VLE is a 'learning management system that synthesizes the functionality of computer-mediated communications and on-line methods of delivering course materials'. It is space for online learning to take place, to support the face-to-face learning more commonly associated with education. In the United Kingdom, they have become increasingly common at both primary and secondary schools, colleges as well as higher education institutions. Whilst there are instances of multiple VLE implementation, it is more generally the norm to have a single VLE for an entire institution (Britain and Liber 2004). These VLEs use technology to intermediate staff–student interactions. As students have become consumers of university services, the VLE has become the e-commerce provision, with increasing expectations of superficial 'product' (PowerPoint slides) over service (face-to-face interaction with faculty staff).

Dominant VLE providers such as Blackboard, Moodle and Sakai are global organizations. Blackboard has recently been bought by a private equity firm for $1.64bn (Lachapelle and Kucera 2011). Moodle and Sakai are both open-source alternatives, created through the open contributions of developers from across the sector, and therefore not directly created for profit, but each organization is intent on expanding its market share.

Just because the VLE exists in an institution, it does not follow that it is being consistently used. Within institutions there will be some faculty who use the full functionality (online submission of assessments, discussion boards, blogs, wikis) and many who use the minimum (uploading slides and handouts). Whilst individual universities have e-learning strategies, there is as yet little in the way of compulsion to use the full range of services that a VLE offers, although it is generally an unspoken assumption that they will be used for at least the minimum.

We can see the introduction of the VLE as part of a wider process which reduces the student to consumer, deemphasizing that element of the university experience which has the capacity to be a transformative experience. The question is, can this transformative change be achieved by mindlessly clicking boxes and downloading files? Or does the VLE experience impact on a student's sense of individuality, leaving them with only part of their soul, as what we might term 'zombie learners'?

Many of the current crop of VLEs encapsulate a pedagogic culture which commodifies the learning experience, an example being the buying and selling of standalone e-learning units by companies designed to deliver content in isolation, reducing it to online interactions with machines, memorization and surface learning, rather than supporting the deep learning that is the supposed goal of quality learning (Biggs and Tang 2007; Levy 2007).

Who is the bokor?

Thus far we have discussed how the technology has been used to monitor and alienate students from their learning. We have used the metaphor of the zombie to explore this process, but this metaphor allows us to ask further questions about power and agency. In essence we can ask: who benefits from the adoption and promotion of virtual learning environments in this manner?

A number of candidates therefore present themselves as potential bokors, amongst them the learning technologists, senior management and even the students themselves. Let us turn our attention first to the learning technologists. This is an emerging profession, still defining its remit within the university as it is charged with championing and supporting the uptake, adoption and innovation of practice using technology to enhance learning and teaching. Learning technologists are individuals who control, design and administer the VLE and act as evangelists extolling the virtues and benefits of technological solutions:

> Clearly, designers and developers *control the very essence of the systems they build*. In this respect the developers of any learning technology will have significant levels of *power* and *control* over the forms it takes and thereby how it can be used.
>
> (Ellaway et al. 2006: 76; italics added)

In this sense, the zombification that we have outlined is the *essence* of the system, and is a result of the power and control of the VLE which the learning technologists exert. Their influence extends to all levels of the institution, from administrators to managers and policy makers. They develop systems to perform increasing efficiencies, such as self-assessment, and facilitate the use of the VLE as a repository for content delivery. However, one can view the learning technologists' role as simply fulfilling a need, and in most instances challenging the existing out-of-date practices so as to bring the focus back to individuals and thereby moderate the increased application of technology. In this sense the learning technologist can be seen as protecting students and staff from the threat of zombification.

If the learning technologist is not the bokor, then perhaps it is the senior manager, whose priorities are the support and enhancement of research practice, and who see teaching as a secondary activity. For them, any means of freeing up staff time to undertake higher priority activities is uncritically embraced and mandated as recommended practice (Boyer 1990; Pearce et al. 2011). Departmental policies and priorities dictate a lack of freedom for teachers when they create their courses and teaching activities. Students are seen as sources of funding for research and thus an unwitting workforce to keep the cogs grinding in the research machine.

Perhaps, finally, the students themselves are culpable? Their patterns of behaviour, interactions and expectations are set from an early stage from previous experiences of education in secondary school. If students fail to liberate themselves from the process of zombification, could their failure be because they are their own bokor? Perhaps not. To draw from Paulo Freire's (1970) analysis of liberation and oppression: one cannot hold the dual role of liberator and oppressor, so the oppressed must be able to envisage another way of being and imagine an alternative reality in order to have a focus for which to strive. The normal aspirations of the oppressed are not to become liberated but to assume the mantle of the oppressor: 'their ideal is to be men; but for them, to be men is to be oppressors. This is their model of humanity' (Freire 1970: 45).

Conclusion: possibilities for hope

Now that we have briefly examined the possible candidates for bokors, let us turn our attention to the potential for liberation and the existence of an antidote to zombification and the power of the bokor.

Within Voodoo mysticism the antidote for the zombie spell is salt, and the bokor maintains his control by ensuring the diet of the zombie lacks salt. Zombie tales often conclude with the accidental ingestion of salt, whereupon they regain awareness and free will, and then seek out and kill their bokor (Davis 1088). *White Zombie* (Halperin 1932), *I Walked with a Zombie* (Tourneur 1943) and *Plague of Zombies* (Gilling 1966) all end similarly, with the bokor overpowered and killed by his zombies. It is striking that modern zombie films do not feature a clear bokor or target for attack (except the hordes of zombies themselves); a consequent feature of these modern films is the lack of hope or clear happy ending.

Technology is the tool which has created this enslavement but could this also be the basis for a cure? An uprising as described by Freire will be dependent upon the vision of liberation and the ability to imagine an alternative reality. Technology has the potential to provide visibility of this alternative, where interactions are not monitored and content is not the basis of education, but rather, autonomy, independence and freedom are the basis of this emancipatory pedagogy.

Increasingly open-access resources provide alternative perspectives on not only academic subjects, but content and delivery mechanisms: examples of this are MIT's open courseware and Open University's Open Learn. These are VLEs that allow access to all, and as such undermine institutional control and promote interaction with others beyond the private segregated community of the university. In their environments, the observation and tracking of an individual's learning is made increasingly difficult. Learning activities, including discussions and sharing of content, are taking place in student-controlled environments, for instance the interactions on Facebook and other social media platforms which are beyond the scope of institutional control (Cameron 2007; Pearce and Tan 2011). It should be noted, however, that these spaces are not completely free and are at least nominally under other institutions' control. But the formation of informal self-established learning communities on social networking sites removes the monitoring and teacher-centric bokor, and replaces it with an equitable exchange of ideas and student-directed learning.

As the new technological developments have created the conditions for commodification and control, they also offer the potential for freedom and individualized learning. The impetus for this reversal can only come from the zombie-students themselves. As they find themselves reduced to consumers, and exploited by the various stakeholders, they may regain their *Ti bon ange*, begin to develop class (zombie?) consciousness, and use the tools of oppression for the purposes of revolution.

Mapping zombies: a guide for digital pre-apocalyptic analysis and post-apocalyptic survival

Mark Graham, Taylor Shelton and Matthew Zook

Z ombies exist, though perhaps not in an entirely literal sense. But the existence, even the outright prevalence, of zombies in the collective social imaginary gives them a 'realness', even though a zombie apocalypse has yet to happen. The zombie trope exists as a means through which society can playfully, if somewhat grimly and gruesomely, discover the intricacies of humanity's relationship with nature and the socially constructed world that emerges from it.

In this chapter, we present an analysis of the prevalence of zombies and zombie-related terminology within the geographically grounded parts of cyberspace, known as the geoweb (see also Haklay et al. 2008 and Graham 2010). Just as zombies provide a means to explore, imagine and reconstruct the world around us, so too do the socio-technical practices of the geoweb provide a means for better understanding human society (Shelton et al. forthcoming; Graham and Zook 2011; Zook et al. 2010; Zook and Graham 2007). In short, looking for and mapping geo-coded references to zombies on the web provides insight on the memes, mechanisms and the macabre of the modern world. Using a series of maps that visualize the virtual geographies of zombies, this chapter seeks to comprehend the ways in which both zombies and the geoweb are simultaneously reflective of and employed in producing new understandings of our world.

Undead cyberscapes as a means of understanding living culture

Although it may not need restating, the importance of zombies in contemporary society is primarily metaphorical. As literature scholar Andrea Wood argues, the zombie metaphor is incredibly flexible and adaptable in producing different understandings of society, as its history in popular culture is considerably shorter than other monsters (Wood, quoted in Gross 2009). Indeed, in recent years, zombies have been used by researchers to explore and critique our collective understandings of everything from the importance of life, death and resurrection in Christianity (Blake 2010), to teaching about epidemiology and disaster preparedness (Khan 2011; Schlozman 2011), to learning how to survive graduate school (Meyers 2011). More academic approaches have used zombies to understand theories of international relations (Drezner 2011), processes of urbanization (May 2010), how essentialized notions of culture and 'backwardness' is used to justify colonialism

(Potter 2009), and the role of neo-liberalism in bringing about the global economic crisis and possible avenues for resisting hegemonic social structures (Harman 2009; Giroux 2010). Even the edited volume of which this chapter is a part represents the use of zombies as a means to understand structural changes in higher education. One potential avenue that has yet to be taken, however, is the utilitzation of zombies to explore the spatialities of the global information society.

While virtual rather than metaphorical, the wealth of user-generated internet content geotagged to a particular location on the Earth's surface, known as the 'geoweb', provides a similarly flexible way of understanding the world around us.[1] Because this content can be created by anyone connected to the internet, the geoweb is theoretically open to a myriad of representations of the world, creating palimpsests of hybrid material/ virtual spaces that can be studied, mapped and analysed (Graham 2010).[2] Due to the mutual constitution of the material and virtual spaces in the geoweb, termed cyberscapes (Crutcher and Zook 2009; Graham and Zook 2011), these virtual representations are often reflective of elements from our material lived realities, albeit frequently in highly distorted ways. This opens up new avenues for research, for instance, allowing insights into how the geography of religion is represented within the geoweb (Zook and Graham 2010; Shelton et al. forthcoming) or how non-experts create and use geographic information in response to disasters (Zook et al. 2010; Goodchild and Glennon 2010). Because a significant amount of research on religion and disaster relief is already available, it is possible to compare how technologies and technologically mediated practices are productive of new socio-spatial relationships. Although the virtual reflections and representations and their material subjects are often more or less commensurable, there remain significant variations in the two, owing to differences in language, power dynamics between groups or a general lack of available content, as is often the case in peripheral parts of the world.

To better illuminate the relationships between the material and virtual, this chapter uses the trope of the zombie as an entry point into debates about the Internet, the spatial diffusion of culture and the hybridization of online and offline spaces. The undead offer a powerful lens for understanding the spatialities of the information age without the gory details of their material manifestations. Using a software program designed by the authors to query geographic information indexed by Google, the number of references to a variety of zombie-related keywords were collected in March 2011 (for a more thorough explanation of this methodology see Graham and Zook 2011). By mapping the virtual geographies, or 'cyberscapes', of zombies we are able to understand not only the digital and geographic contours of a hugely popular trope, but also the ways that those digital mappings of zombies can be reflective of cultural augmentations encoded onto lived, material spaces. In addition, the cyberscapes emerging from the zombie trope itself offer a useful device for understanding the ways in which the publics of the Internet produce and reproduce objects of attention and bias and differentially augment lived realities (see also Graham et al. 2012; Graham and Zook 2013).

Mapping the virtually undead

ED: Are there any zombies out there?
SHAUN: Don't say that!
ED: What?
SHAUN: That.
ED: What?
SHAUN: That. The 'Z' word. Don't say it.
ED: Why not?
SHAUN: Because it's ridiculous!
ED: All right. Are there any out there, though?
SHAUN: Can't see any.

(Shaun of the Dead, Wright 2004)

In order to measure the prevalence of zombies on the Web, we first map references to the keyword 'zombies' to geographically visualize zombie content in the geoweb. Second, we map references to a series of material artifacts closely associated with the zombie trope; that is, the weapons used to kill them. Finally, we map the prevalence of zombies in pop culture by using references to the titles of some of George Romero's *Living Dead* film series. These vignettes allow us to better understand how the zombie trope is differentially mobilized across space. After all, knowing where the zombies are is really the most fundamental question we should be asking.

Mapping zombies

Using a keyword search for 'zombies', the following map (Figure 1.) visualizes concentrations of references to the keyword within geo-coded content indexed by Google Maps. The size of each circle indicates the total amount of zombie references in that place. The map reveals two important spatial patterns worth consideration. First, much of the world lacks any content mentioning 'zombies' whatsoever. Second, and related, the highest concentrations of zombies in the geoweb are located in the Anglophone world, especially in the largest cities.

The lack of online information about zombies can likely be explained, at least in part, by the fact that the searches for the word zombie were conducted only in English and Latin characters, thus ignoring all references in other languages and scripts. Many non-English speaking countries nonetheless have *some* references to zombies. For example, Japan is the only non-English speaking country in the world outside of North America and Europe with more than 100 references at a given point. Several non-English speaking countries in Europe (e.g. Germany and France) similarly have relatively higher concentrations of references. It is therefore apparent that the lack of references to zombies around the world is not solely caused by differences in language.

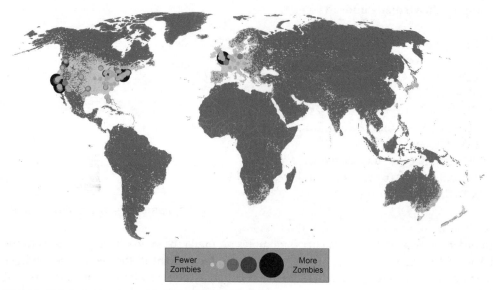

Figure 1: Global references to zombies in the Google Maps database.

Previous research indicates that socioeconomic factors like income and internet access play a significant role in explaining the contribution of online content (e.g. Crampton 2009; Graham 2011a; Graham 2011b; Crutcher and Zook 2009). This ultimately means that much of the world is left out of processes and practices of information sharing and generation, and that content is concentrated in a relatively small number of places rather than ubiquitously distributed across space. Even within Europe and North America (i.e., the parts of the world containing the most zombie-related content), there is a significant concentration of content in just a handful of cities. New York, Los Angeles, San Francisco and London, for instance, contain the greatest number of online references to zombies, a fact that reflects their status as important nodes in the world's information ecosystems. Information, much like zombies, is attracted to existing centres of activity as part of the historical process of urban agglomeration. But there is inequality even within these top-tier cities; the highest concentration of references to 'zombies' is in Jamaica, Queens in New York City, where there are 1,509 references, nearly twice the number of references at the next greatest concentration in La Puente, CA, in the greater Los Angeles area, which has 805 references. However, the Los Angeles area also has the point with the fifth highest concentration, displaying a smaller absolute concentration, but with greater parity across the region.

While connections between zombies and large cities are apparent, the mere concentration of content does not reveal what exactly is being annotated over these places. Each mention of 'zombies' could be positive or negative, earnest or facetious. References to zombies could refer to the location of annual 'zombie walks', place to buy a zombie costume for Halloween, or even perceived sightings of the undead. It is thus worth considering how the specific entrails of the zombie trope differ over space.

The geographies of zombie elimination artifacts

Beyond the simple mapping of references to 'zombies', references to other zombie-related keywords can be particularly revealing. Whether they be medically related, such as Brooks' (2003) fictitious 'solanum' virus, or even a comparison between the relative presence of the zombie food source 'brains', as compared to what we presume to be the inverse, 'salad'. While these selections are certainly amusing, they provide little insight on the connection between the zombie metaphor in the geoweb and the lived realities of different peoples.[3] A potentially better line of exploration lies in mapping references to various material artifacts related to zombies, in this case the weapons used to kill zombies in literature and cinema. After all, upon finding out where exactly the zombies are, the next task usually involves getting rid of them.

Using the following keywords – 'machete', 'shotgun', 'crowbar' and 'AK-47' – we mapped the relative prevalence of each term across Europe. In Figure 2, each shaded dot signifies a point at which there are more references to that keyword than any of the other three weapons. Although this does not take into account the absolute number of hits associated with each keyword, it highlights the dominance of references to any particular weapon and its concomitant cultural implications in a particular place.

There are three noticeable spatial patterns visible in Figure 2. First, a cluster of references to AK-47s exists in the former Eastern bloc countries. Given the weapon's origin within the Soviet Union, the prevalence of references in Eastern Europe is unsurprising. Second, the dominance of references to shotgun in Great Britain is the most noticeable pattern, especially because it broadly conforms to the boundaries of the island. Third is the fact that most locations within Europe have no references to any of these keywords, a fact that indicates that their usage on the Web, like that of zombies, is concentrated in very particular places.

The references to weapons in Figure 2 have the effect of mirroring distinct sociocultural traits in offline, material practices. Although it is not included here, a map of references to weapons in the United States would appear (much like England) blanketed with references to shotguns. This, compared with the dearth of references to any of these weapons throughout much of Europe, is indicative of a greater degree of the embeddedness of the artifact of the shotgun in the cultural practices, and by extension the virtual representations, of some parts of the world. While not resolving the debate of whether 'guns kill people' or 'people kill people', this analysis makes evident that in the event of a zombie horde, shotguns would likely be killing zombies in the British Isles and the United States. On the other hand, continental Europe would draw upon a mélange of machetes, crowbars, Kalashnikovs and perhaps the occasional flamethrower.

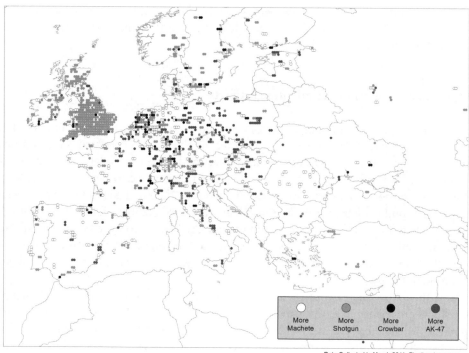

Data Collected in March 2011. Floatingsheep.org

Figure 2: European references to weapons.

Mapping zombies in cinema

It is also helpful to return more directly to one of the cultural sources of zombies by mapping references to some of the most important and seminal zombie films: George Romero's *Living Dead* series. Doing so allows us to again observe the spatial patterns associated with their mentions online. One of the most noticeable elements on the map of references to the films (see Figure 3) is that there are many more references to *Day of the Dead* than any of the other film titles. While also the third film in Romero's series, *Day of the Dead* is much more notable as a Mexican holiday to commemorate the deceased (Dia de los Muertos). The geography of references to *Day of the Dead*, which is largely clustered in the heavily Hispanic areas of the US southwest and northeast, strongly suggests that most references are to the holiday rather than the film. Here again, we observe the ways that online representations mirror material socio-spatial practices, including the religious and spiritual practices of Mexican immigrants in the United States, even if it was not necessarily intended as the object of focus.

The second discernible spatial pattern is the clustering of references to *Dawn of the Dead*, with some mentions to the other film titles, in Pennsylvania. This is unsurprising given Romero's connections to the state and the fact that the film was set and filmed there. This connection

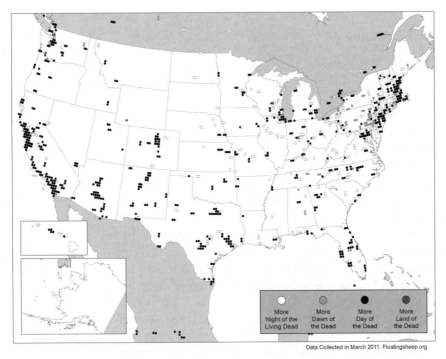

Data Collected in March 2011. Floatingsheep.org

Figure 3: US references to Romero's *Living Dead* films.

(like that of AK-47 references in Eastern Europe) is a useful way of illustrating how cultural artifacts and practices are intimately tied to material places, not just physically, but also in digital reflections of material places. And in this specific case, forming a virtual 'zyberscape' of undead references splattering and spotting the cartographic representation of reality.

A guide for digital post-apocalyptic survival

This chapter has highlighted the metaphor of the zombie as a way of understanding links between material practices and digital representations. By collecting and visualizing geotagged internet data, we have argued that just as the zombie trope is tied to broader social processes, the geoweb is similarly reflective of society and offers an opportunity for understanding the connections between online reflections and material places. For instance, large parts of the world likely contain no references to any zombie-related activity, not because there is any reason for there to be significantly less activity in those places, but because online content only ever tends to be written about relatively small amounts of the planet.

However, the patterns, presences and absences in the maps above can also be employed for an alternate reading of the virtual geographies of content. Some of the clustering of both quantity of content and the subject of content can undoubtedly be explained by technological, social, political and economic positionalities at the sites of production and representation. However, it is also evident that common themes within online digital content (e.g. lolcats, skateboarding videos and indeed zombies) are produced and reproduced because of powerful path-dependencies in and about objects of attention. In other words, within the geoweb we can discern an effect similar to the hording displayed by Kirkman's 'roamers' in the *Walking Dead* series. In Kirkman's post-apocalyptic world, loud noises or other human activity attracts groups of the undead. Roaming zombies then latch onto those hordes as they move in a focused direction (for reasons that have been long forgotten due to the inability of zombies to access any long-term memory).

A similar sort of hording, or path-dependency, is also observable amongst the living (e.g. on the Internet). In a process reminiscent of urban agglomeration, the greater visibility that zombies, shotguns, lolcats, goatse.cx and Wikipedia articles about Germany have as compared to other internet memes, clusters of content, and places can be traced to a range of path-dependencies in which economies of scope, metanarratives, recursive humour and a range of other factors amplify the crowd's focus. The path-dependency of online content and objects of attention therefore ultimately illustrates the danger of using user-generated geo-referenced content to draw conclusions about the material offline world. Uneven communication geographies and the practice of zombie-like hording, for now-forgotten reasons, exhibited by online contributors means that whilst online content is a potentially useful indicator, it often also only serves to reproduce our own objects of focused direction and bias.

Mapping representations of zombies, or anything else for that matter, ultimately allows us to analyse the contours of digital augmentations, and presents a method for usefully tracking important cultural memes. But zombies themselves are additionally useful because the metaphor provides a way to think through often mindless emulation (e.g. 'liking', retweeting, reblogging and reposting content), which can influence many important blendings of the material and the virtual. In any crisis situation, including the zombie apocalypse, one of the most important questions for both survivors and first-responders is 'where'? This chapter demonstrates that while online content may provide broad clues as to the location of important material events and patterns (i.e. the locations of the undead), we ultimately have to rely on more traditional methods of information gathering and dispatch – ranging from critical reflection to crowbars – for both pre- and post-apocalypse survival.

Notes

1   Geotags are metadata used to position information onto distinct parts of the Earth's surface.
2   Depending on the specific platform used, it is possible for multiple types of content (e.g. text, audio, graphics, video etc.) to be created by multiple people about any part of the world.
3   Detailed maps of these comparisons are, however, available at www.floatingsheep.org.

Infectious textbooks

Gordon S. Carlson and James J. Sosnoski

I n this chapter we propose two dominant zombie narratives that parallel patterns in institutions of higher learning. The first suggests that, just as the 'bokor' of the Voudou tradition is said to control their victims, some textbook authors poison students by feeding them dead concepts, burying them in out-of-date contexts, and then digging them up to test whether their deadened minds can hold the infectious definitions. The second proposed parallel finds that textbooks can work like viruses, infecting students with the notion of 'right answers' to memorize, without any obligation to actually understand. This is evident in the mini-glossaries within chapters that identify key concepts, page designs that aim at memorizing concepts, and the tasks at the end of chapters, where concept retention is privileged over analysis or re-conceptualization. These classic textbook components deaden student minds by encouraging rote memorization instead of critical reflection.

Whether students become zombies because of a textbook bokor's instructions, or because of some kind of text-spread viral infection, the net effect, ironically, is that their victims are often rewarded with high grades, because in this system it is easier to be a zombie. Student minds are first deadened, then given a pseudo-life of discipleship with no mind/will of their own, much like the zombies in so many horror films.

Faculty and textbook-publishing bokors use the power of their positions to ensure that students research in 'acceptable' ways. Mindless memorization thus spreads from one group of students to the next, contaminating graduate and postgraduate study, and eventually infecting faculty. Students who believe there is a 'right' answer to every question spread this zombie virus (which we will term the 'Z virus') to other students, thus limiting their expectations as critical thinkers. Humans stop to wonder, inquire or reflect; zombies just keep going.

How student zombification occurs

The principal instruments of zombification in higher education are the textbooks that turn students into automata. The patterns of this process involve two institutional relationships: (1) teachers to textbooks, and (2) textbooks to students. In the first relationship, teachers write textbooks and use them to broker learning, thereby acting as variants of the Vodou practitioner, or 'bokor', as they work to capture their students' spirits. In the second pattern, from textbooks to students, the spread of text-bound viruses is unleashed to infect students.

Bokors take control of their victims by reanimating them as mindless zombies, capable of following simple commands and performing limited tasks. Some textbook authors control students this way by feeding them dead concepts. We refer to these concepts as 'glossaried'. For example, the concepts presented in the glossaries of introductory Communication Studies textbooks are often vacuous. Having been taken out of their contexts, the concepts are given to students in a vacuum. Concepts out of context are (un)dead because they are essentially meaningless.

Consider the definition: '*Configuring* – the identification with a figure in a configuration'. This is actually a viable statement. However, it is meaningless to someone who is unfamiliar with the technical uses of the terms 'identification', 'figure' or 'configuration'. If we supply a context, for example a film such as *Night of the Living Dead* (Romero 1968), the reader can begin to parse out what the definition means: Ben is the main *figure* in the film. If you *identify* with him, then the film can be considered a *configuration* (con = with), thus, the film configures you. Without such contextualization, the standalone definition is vacuous.

For many linguists, it is not possible to grasp the meaning of a concept outside of its context of use. David Lee offers a clear example of this problem in *Cognitive Linguistics: An Introduction*:

> If one were asked to explain the meaning of the word *wicket,* it would be natural to say not only what a wicket is but also something about its overall role in the game. For example, one might explain that one person (known as the 'bowler') tries to knock the wicket down by throwing a ball at it in a special way, while another person (known as the 'batsman') stands in front of the wicket and tries to prevent the ball from hitting it by using a wooden instrument known as a 'bat'. This could be the beginning of quite a long explanation. In other words, a good understanding of the word *wicket* requires a significant amount of knowledge *that extends well beyond the dictionary definition*. We refer to this background knowledge as the 'frame'.
>
> (2001: 8; italics added)

Vacuous, decontextualized concepts are meaninglessness, and thus produce the kind of mindlessness that then incites apocalyptic concerns about the zombification of students.

Tracing a path from bokor to students

In zombie films, the survivors often attempt to trace the origins of the zombie outbreak. Following suit, we trace one vector of a zombie outbreak back to a 'concept bokor' in the discipline of Communication Studies. If our sample is representative, a remarkable number of definitions in introductory communication textbooks are out of date.

The 'concept bokor' in our sample is the author Joseph A. DeVito, who has published an extraordinary 84 textbooks in communication over the course of 31 years, averaging 2.7

textbooks per year. Our principal data is derived from an analysis of one of his textbooks, *Human Communication: The Basic Course*, published in 11 editions across four decades, from 1978 to 2009. Many of the terms in the glossaries of this textbook closely match the glossaries of the other four major textbooks that the author has published.

In the first edition of *Human Communication*, DeVito presents a modified version of Shannon and Weaver's 1949 model of communication. This modification is actually drawn from an essay written by Schramm in 1954, and included in an earlier collection edited by DeVito, *Communication: Concepts and Processes* (1971). The key concepts in the model are found in Figure 1. Notice that these key concepts are repeated in all 11 editions of *Human Communication* with very similar (and in some cases identical) definitions.

Even though any single one of these glossary entries would prove to be outmoded well before 2009, we will focus our examination on the sample concept 'noise'. Although Schramm himself dropped this 1954 concept from his model of communication presented in *Communication: Concepts and Processes* (1971), DeVito chose to revive it in his first 1978 edition of the *Human Communication* textbook, which was entitled *Communicology*. The list below presents DeVito's subsequent definitions for the concept 'noise' across his 11 editions of the same textbook:

1978 — Noise: Anything that distorts the message intended by the source. Noise may be viewed as anything that interferes with the receiver's receiving the message as the source intended the message to be received. Noise is present in a communication system to the extent that the message received is not the message sent. Noise may originate in any of the components of

1978	1st edition	encoder decoder	context		message	noise	decoder encoder	effects
1982	2nd edition	"	"		"	"	"	"
1985	3rd edition	"	"		" + feedback	"	"	"
1988	4th edition	"	"	channel	" + feedforward	"	"	"
1991	5th edition	"	"	"	"	"	"	"
1994	6th edition	"	"	"	"	"	"	"
1997	7th edition	"	"	"	"	"	"	"
2000	8th edition	"	"	"	"	"	"	"
2003	9th edition	"	"	"	"	"	"	"
2006	10th edition	"	"	"	"	"	"	"
2009	11th edition	"	"	"	"	"	"	"

Figure 1: Changes in concepts over 11 editions of a single textbook.

the communication act, for example, in the source as a lisp, in the channel as static, in the receiver as a hearing loss, in written communication as blurred type. Noise is always present in any communication system and its effects may be reduced (but never eliminated completely) by increasing the strength of the signal or the amount of redundancy, for example.

1982   Identical definition.

1985   Identical definition.

1988   Noise: Anything that distorts or interferes with the message in the communication system. Noise is present in communication to the extent that the message sent differs from the message received. Physical noise interferes with the physical transmission of the signal or message-for example, the static in radio transmission. Psychological noise refers to distortions created by such psychological processes as prejudice and biases. Semantic noise refers to distortions created by a failure to understand each other's words.

1991   Identical definition.

1994   Identical definition.*

1997   Adds 'Combat the effects of physical, semantic, and psychological noise by eliminating or lessening the sources of physical noise, securing agreement on meanings, and interacting with an open mind in order increase communication accuracy' at the end.

2000   Identical definition.

2003   Omits 'Physical noise interferes with the physical transmission of the signal or message-for example, the static in radio transmission. Psychological noise refers to distortions created by such psychological processes as prejudice and biases. Semantic noise refers to distortions created by a failure to understand each other's words' but retains the passage added in the 1997 edition.

2006   Omits the passage added in the 1997 edition.

2009   Identical definition to the 2006 edition.

*Also identical to a definition from a similar introductory textbook by DeVito, *The Interpersonal Communication Book*, published a year later in 1995.

In the 4th edition of his textbook, DeVito introduced a broader interpretation of noise, adding psychological and semantic conditions to the physical source presented in Shannon and Weaver's model. The semantic condition is presented as a 'failure to understand each other's words', which can be combated by 'securing agreement on meaning' and open-mindedness, suggesting that 'noise' in this context is equivalent to 'miscommunication'. The same can be said of prejudice and bias as psychological conditions – although in DeVito's 11th edition, these conditions are omitted. DeVito presumably intends his definition of 'noise' to be consistent with the originating concept of 1949. But for students to grasp the concept of 'semantic noise', they have to construe prejudice as belonging to the category of noise – a rather specialized use of that word. Ironically, this understanding would be captured in DeVito's separate concept category for 'semantic noise'.

Similarly, the concept of a 'signal-to-noise ratio' was defined by DeVito in the 1st, 2nd and 3rd editions, omitted from the 4th to the 7th editions, and reactivated from the 8th to the 11th editions. A separate text-boxed explanation of the concept was introduced in the 9th edition (in 2003), and is retained in the later editions. This reads:

> A useful way of looking at information is in terms of its signal-to-noise ratio. Signal in this context refers to information that is useful to you, information that you want. Noise, on the other hand, is what you find useless; it's what you do not want. So, for example, if a mailing list or newsgroup contained lots of useful information, it would be high on signal and low on noise; if it contained lots of useless information, it would be high on noise and low on signal. Spam is high on noise and low on signal, as is static that interferes with radio, television, or telephone transmission.
>
> (11th ed. 2009: 399)

We find it remarkable that a signal in any context can refer to 'information that is useful to you, information that you want', while noise refers to 'what you find useless; it's what you do not want'. Applied to teaching, this would hardly be a viable pedagogical position, as it suggests that whatever students do not actually want need not concern them.

Other definitions repeated in the latest editions of DeVito's textbooks – including the terms 'message', 'encode', 'decode' and 'communication context' – were, in our view, obsolete well before 2009. For example, restricting signification to encoding and decoding hardly evokes the views of contemporary linguists on language use. Constructivist, functional, and cognitive linguists have moved away from the computational model of linguistics since DeVito received his doctorate in 1964. However, the model of communication that DeVito persists in presenting to contemporary students in his textbooks is more representative of the 1960s than of 2009, the publication date of the 11th edition. His stagnant commitment to a computational view of language restricts students' abilities to engage advances in their field.

How the bokor creates zombies

How does an out-of-date concept induce mindlessness? DeVito's definition severs the term from any context of use. Imagine asking communication researchers or students in the domains of media, globalization or political discourse to study 'any signal or combination of signals transmitted to a receiver' (DeVito's definition of a 'message'). Confronted with the futility of using the definition in any meaningful way, students would, and presumably do, find themselves 'without a clue', and are therefore risking mindlessness. This primal scene is acted out in countless horror films, with zombie hordes banging their heads on doors or barricades because they smell humans on the other side. Their mindlessness precludes them from problem-solving around the obstacle by turning a doorknob, throwing a rock, or employing any number of skills a still-human person would think to use. In the case of bokored texts, students end up banging their heads against the wall trying to employ a single, de-contextualized definition where a still-lively mind would re-conceptualize the term to more usefully apply it to a research or learning context.

It can be argued that the definitions in a glossary are not as important as the explanations of the concepts in the text. Let us look at DeVito's text explicating noise.

> Noise is anything that interferes with your receiving a message. At one extreme, noise may prevent a message from getting from source to receiver. A roaring noise or line static can easily prevent entire messages from getting through to your receiver. At the other extreme, *with virtually no noise interference, the message of the source and the message received are almost identical.* Most often, however, noise distorts some portion of the message a source sends as it travels to a receiver. Like messages that may be auditory or visual, noise comes in both auditory and visual forms. Four types of noise are especially relevant: physical, physiological, psychological, and semantic.
>
> (11th ed. 2009: 16; italics added)

This passage does not clarify the glossary definition, and it reflects a very outdated notion of semantics with the remark that 'with virtually no noise interference, the message of the source and the message received are almost identical'. The expanded versions of the four types of noise that follow this passage do not add much to the glossary definition of 'noise' and, in the case of 'semantic noise', identifying 'jargon' as noise suggests that technical jargon is to be avoided in the study of communication. But the whole notion of field-specific definitions of terms (which DeVito is teaching in his textbooks) depends on the use of precisely this 'noisy' jargon.

The role of DeVito's glossaried concepts is made quite clear at the end of his chapters in several ways: summarizing, memorizing, and vocabulary testing. DeVito's 'summary' of the chapter on 'the components of communication' contains brief notes on the chapter. Evidently, his students do not even have to take their own notes. They are then given relevant terms to *memorize*. This becomes explicit in the list of key terms, prefaced by DeVito's remark that 'flash card' activities of the terms in the glossary and practice tests are available online. Figure 2 shows a representation of a quiz published online at www.mycommunicationkit. com in connection with DeVito's *Interpersonal Communication*, the text of which closely parallels that of *Human Communication*:

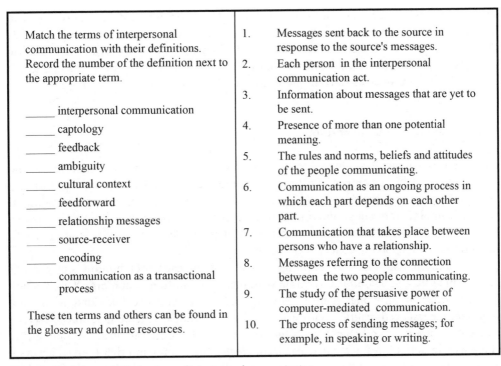

| Match the terms of interpersonal communication with their definitions. Record the number of the definition next to the appropriate term.

_____ interpersonal communication
_____ captology
_____ feedback
_____ ambiguity
_____ cultural context
_____ feedforward
_____ relationship messages
_____ source-receiver
_____ encoding
_____ communication as a transactional process

These ten terms and others can be found in the glossary and online resources. | 1. Messages sent back to the source in response to the source's messages.
2. Each person in the interpersonal communication act.
3. Information about messages that are yet to be sent.
4. Presence of more than one potential meaning.
5. The rules and norms, beliefs and attitudes of the people communicating.
6. Communication as an ongoing process in which each part depends on each other part.
7. Communication that takes place between persons who have a relationship.
8. Messages referring to the connection between the two people communicating.
9. The study of the persuasive power of computer-mediated communication.
10. The process of sending messages; for example, in speaking or writing. |

Figure 2: Vocabulary quiz: the language of interpersonal communication.

It is not surprising that DeVito published an essay arguing that teachers are 'behavioural engineers' (1968). Textbook authors like DeVito are bokors of students when the texts they produce deaden through memorization. Devoid of context, these textbooks spread the Z virus. This vacuous information allows bokor textbook authors to maintain their stranglehold on students' learning by the banal processes of testing that accompany them and produce meaningless grade rewards.

Contagion in the classroom

The second parallel pattern we observe between zombie narratives and textbooks involves the institutionalized relationship between textbooks and students; it is correlative to the first. When students believe in a set of 'right answers', which can be remembered without any obligation to understand, they allow themselves to be infected by the Z virus transmitted by glossaried concepts. Mini-glossaries within chapters, flash cards, quizzes and so forth all contain such contagious viruses capable of infecting students and rendering them mindless. With instructors as 'behavioural engineers', pliant students are *conditioned* to recognize semantic noise – jargon such as 'overly complex terms', 'overly abstract terms' – and to become *conception-phobic*. Student minds are first deadened, and then given a pseudo-life of discipleship, which instils a 'follow-the-leader' disciplinarity. Where faculty staff 'publish or perish', students 'memorize and metastasize'. In the tradition of slogans like 'D gets a Degree', bokored textbooks warrant the slogan 'it's EZ to be a Zombie'.

Conceptual logistics as an antidote

How can this plague be combated? In the pursuit of alternative approaches to research and education, we have advanced the term 'conceptual logistics'. Conceptual logistics is a pedagogical approach that treats students as lively-minded researchers rather than mindless vessels. It employs interactive and multimodal alternatives to passive textbooks. Conceptual logistics is a disposition to engage research problems by learning how to conceptualize, them rather than applying concepts developed in past projects.

The traditional approach to teaching, with roots that reach back hundreds of years, is centred in *terms* and *definitions*. Terms have numerous definitions, but more often than not, students are given only one. The problem with this approach is two-fold. First, it does not represent the nuanced realities of using conceptions to address specific situations. Research conceptions are fluid and change with the contexts in which they are used. Second, giving students one definition for a particular term creates the impression that there is always a single, correct way to conceptualize a problem, neither changing over time nor adjusted for different contexts.

Instead of the pedagogical practice of matching a term to one of its possible definitions, we propose teaching *concepts* in relation to the various *conceptions* they have occasioned in their contexts of use. For example, a common exercise we use in the classroom is to ask students to picture what the concept 'chair' refers to. Next, we ask them to draw a picture or write a description of what they imagined. Although our students share the same concept or 'conceptual schema' (Langacker 2002: 132–38) of a chair as having legs and a seat, their conceptions of a chair differ. Some describe the chair they occupy during the exercise, some a bar stool, others a reclining lounge chair. None of these are wrong (they are all chairs). However, while the same term 'chair' can be applied to them all, they are not the same thing, or are not conceived in the same way.

As the *Stanford Encyclopaedia of Philosophy* notes, 'Instead of these symptoms of the philosopher's "craving for generality", [Wittgenstein] points to "family resemblance" as the more suitable analogy for the means of connecting particular uses of the same word' (Biletzki and Matar 2011). A conceptual logistics approach recognizes not only that multiple conceptions exist, but also that in many research contexts multiple conceptions are welcome.

Take, for example, the concept 'frame', which has a long and storied history in the field of communication. In a study of discipline-specific communication literature spanning nearly

70 years, we have tracked 18 unique uses of this concept. Although the various uses of the word differ, they frequently overlap. The concept of 'frame' is an example of the fluid nature of terms in academic research as their specific conceptions evolve across new contexts. For instance, Robert Entman advanced the now-canonical use of the concept 'frame' in 1993:

> To frame is to select some aspects of a perceived reality and make them more salient in a communicating text, in such a way as to promote a particular problem definition, causal interpretation, moral evaluation, and/or treatment recommendation for the item described.
>
> (51)

Many authors have relied on this conception of framing; however, like many other concepts, this one has changed from context to context, and across time. In fact, Entman himself uses a different conception of framing in 2003:

> Framing entails selecting and highlighting some facets of events or issues, and making connections among them so as to promote a particular interpretation, evaluation, and/ or solution … They use words and images highly salient in the culture, which is to say noticeable, understandable, memorable, and emotionally charged. Magnitude taps the prominence and repetition of the framing words and images.
>
> (415)

Among other changes, Entman replaces 'aspect of perceived reality' (1993) with 'facets of events or issues' (2003), a change that reduces the subjective element in selecting. Substituting 'events or issues' makes the selection one of 'objects' in public (verifiable) view. This is not a trivial tweaking. He made another change in 2004:

> Selecting and highlighting some facets of events or issues, and making connections among them so as to promote a particular interpretation, evaluation, and/ or solution.
>
> (5)

Though it may seem a minor change to replace 'entails selecting' (2003) with 'selecting', omitting the term 'entails' (2004) has considerable import. The lexical database WordNet assigns to 'entail' the meaning: to 'have as a logical consequence', or 'imply as a necessary accompaniment or result'.[1] Removing 'entails' from the definition of framing therefore suggests that selecting may not be a necessary condition of framing.

A popular communication textbook, *A First Look at Communication Theory*, by Em Griffin, covers the concept of framing. However, even in editions of this textbook released after Entman substantially changed his conception of 'framing', the definition remains static. For instance, Griffin's 2006 textbook still cites only Entman's 1993 definition. If a student is taught that only this definition of framing is 'correct', that student is prevented from understanding the reasons for Entman's changes. Knowing these reasons would give students access to a rich and useful example of the re-conceptualization of a concept across different contexts of use. This could provide students with a glimpse of significant methodological and theoretical issues. Students who are taught that there is a one-to-one relationship between terms and definitions are likely to dismiss other definitions of terms as 'wrong' because they do not align with the definitions in their textbook.

Is there a cure for zombification?

Is there a cure for the Z virus? Consider the symptoms of this infection: believing that terms have only one definition. Is it possible to change this belief? The evidence for polysemy is vast and certainly accessible. We can show students that terms are word-forms for concepts and that their underlying conceptions change in different contexts of use. It is a straightforward matter to track these changes. The conceptions underlying terms evolve as they are used in research publications. Tracking their evolution can be accomplished by logistical discourse analysis. This type of analysis is common in studies of the corpus of influential theorists, for example, Wittgenstein. It would be unscholarly *not* to point out, for instance, that the conception of language found in Wittgenstein's *Tractatus* (2001) differs from that in the posthumously published *Philosophical Investigations* (2009).

Acquainting students with the development of the concepts in their chosen field is one cure for zombification. Conceptual logistics, grounded in the work of cognitive and functional linguists, is one such technique for analysing conceptual changes. For instance, the logistical analyses of Entman's conceptions of the term 'frame', outlined above, briefly illustrates one of the analytic techniques used in conceptual logistics.

The subject matter of conceptual logistics is *the relationship between cognition (conceptualization) and the situated use of language in the conduct of research*. It studies the ways a particular research project is conceptualized by describing the language used to conduct it. A species of discourse analysis, conceptual logistics tracks changes over a period of time in the language used to describe research projects. As Schiffrin et al. (2003) testify, there are numerous types of discourse analysis, largely owing to the variety of discourse types. For the most part, they describe the ways texts 'instruct' their readers to construe meanings from linguistic structures embedded in them. Conceptual logistics differs from other types of discourse analysis because it is primarily concerned with changes in conceptions, and with matching problematics to descriptions of problems across fields. Research projects typically address problems related to particular situations by formulating concepts that describe them. These concepts are planned, implemented, and adjusted to fit specific situations. The multiplicity of conceptions attributed to the same term is labyrinthine if and only if the expectation is that research concepts are definitive, that they should fit all the situations in a particular problem category. But we do not believe they ought to be.

From a pedagogical perspective, the difficulty of embracing conceptual change can seem daunting; however, there are already tools out there to help. Online tools such as WordNet make it easier to find multiple *uses* of a concept. The University of California at Berkeley is home to FrameNet, a 'lexicon-building effort for contemporary English' with the goal to 'provide information in ways that are easily interpreted by human users and in a form that is usable by various kinds of computational processes'.[2]

In a broad sense, this kind of work has been and is being done on the social web. Some organizations use social networking services to work collaboratively without having to write their own software. E-mail listservs have for years served as ad hoc conceptual logistic workspaces, where researchers and students ask one another for help tracking conceptions. Graduate student journals and online publication systems now allow faculty and students more latitude and discretion in their work, moving away from notions of definitive statements. It is possible that as the semantic web grows technologically and conceptually, the goals of the World Wide Web Consortium might provide logistical information about evolving conceptions. At present, however, the semantic web works to standardize terminology. With this development in mind, the architects of the semantic web will likely tend towards the categorization of information types, and thus limit competing conceptions of ideas.

Controlling the Z-virus contagion

Undergraduates generally do not have the writing skills necessary to produce quality academic research. But they have plenty of brainpower. Rather than allow textbooks to infect these lively minds, we suggest actively helping students experiment with conceptions. This means moving away from the emphasis on memorization in current tests. For example, in the authors' teaching experience, during exams in upper-division courses in Mass Media and Team Building, our students were first asked to identify five concepts or inventions they viewed as most significant to Communication Studies. Next, they were asked to illustrate how those five items related to one another and to illustrate those relationships as creatively as possible either by verbalizing or visualizing them. To represent the relationship among the printing press, iPod, Media Effects Theory, electricity and democratic government, one student wrote music that represented the significance he applied to various communication concepts. Another student created a timeline of communication and placed his five items, along with others, in order, with lines connecting items not only temporally but also conceptually. A third student created a map of the world, because she saw the geographical locations of her five items as demonstrating the global significance of communication studies.

In another semester, our students worked on individual projects in which they explicated a concept in communication research. They were asked to explain how researchers have conceptualized the idea, and then to explicate their own conception of the idea. Students were not asked to write papers, instead they were invited to create educational artefacts employing a medium and approach that related to the concept they were explicating. Students created podcasts, television shows, comics and paintings. As cognitive psychologists have shown, learning involves both verbalization and visualization. In doing the above assignment, students were developing cognitive skills and building strong mental connections between concepts in communication and other fields, using both their semantic and epistemic memory systems. Grading this work posed interesting challenges for the instructors, since objective measurement tools did not directly apply. However, difficulties in objective assessment were significantly outweighed by the successes in learning demonstrated by students, who were demonstrably using the abstract concepts idiomatically in class discussions in the subject.

Graduate students, especially those who seek future careers in higher education, need to learn independent research skills, but all too often end up being zombie-like disciples of their professors and committees. The zombie effect seems to play out in graduate programs through the styles of instruction, the selection of reading materials, and the need for students to conform to traditions of print-oriented academic culture. This guarantees that the status quo will be duplicated and creativity and *new* contributions to the field (the traits supposedly demanded of 'original research') stifled, for the sake of showing that students blend in with the horde of existing zombies.

A world without zombies

What will a post-apocalyptic world look like? We hope to see faculty working with graduate students using tools like conceptual logistics to help students explore and experiment, leading the more experienced students to develop original research. Textbook authors can bring together visualizations, collaborations, multimedia tools, and knowledge bases in 'living' workbooks. However, there has not yet been a concerted effort to provide dynamic content in online formats. Some publishers offer digitized copies of printed texts, and others offer superficial customization in the ability to combine selected chapters from comprehensive texts. Apple's development of iBooks has not changed the approach to learning we have criticized, merely the approach to buying books. Textbook authors should produce more focused, insightful or logistical analyses of concepts. They could cover several conceptions of a term rather than just one.

Current zombies can be cured and future ones prevented. Living books that talk, show and interact (in place of dead books that are frozen in print) are on the horizon. For the technologically inclined, tools exist to help faculty create these pedagogical text-tools that treat terms with the complexity their histories demand. For instance, the Society for Conceptual Logistics in Communication Research (SCLCR) has developed a *Concept Toolkit* that helps researchers and students alike keep their minds and ideas lively. Drawing from successful elements of the social web, collaborative learners share academically rigorous conceptions of research in specific contexts. In the effort to halt the spread of the Z virus, the *Concept Database* therefore provides useful insights into the many ways research concepts

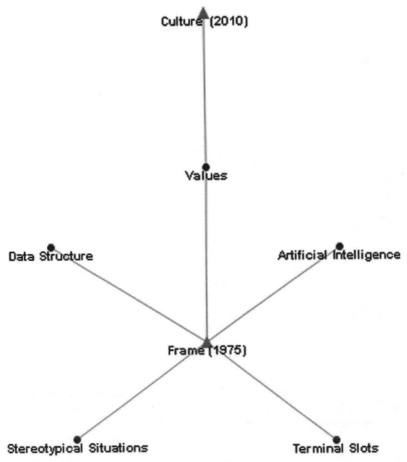

Figure 3: Concept map for Minsky's 1975 use of 'frame' from SCLCR toolkit.

have been conceptualized. It counters simplistic definitions by powering visualizations such as concept maps, timelines, and word clouds. For instance, SCLCR's concept maps in Figure 3 model the term 'frame' as used in 1975:

Concept maps like these allow visitors to interactively visualize how various conceptions of related ideas interact, inform one another, and work against the isolation of terminologies, one of the by-products of zombification. The image depicted in Figure 4 models the term 'framing', but from a 1993 usage:

This kind of tool, along with others being produced by learners and teachers around the world, can be used in the struggle against zombification. Conceptual logistics is just one pedagogical approach that can counter the zombification process of infectious textbooks.

Zombies are created by bokors. Identify these bokors, and resist them.

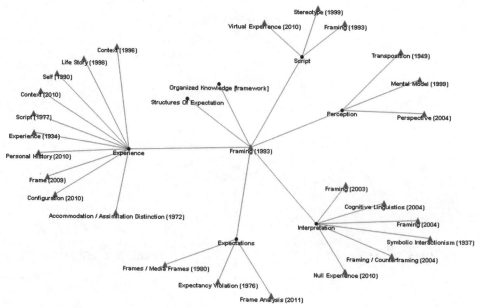

Figure 4: Concept map for Tannen's 1993 use of 'frame' from SCLCR toolkit.

Notes

1   Wordnet is a lexical database for English with a more sophisticated network of lexical concepts than a traditional dictionary, and is available at http://wordnet.princeton.edu/.

2   FrameNet is available at: http://framenet.icsi.berkeley.edu/.

SECTION 3

Zombie literacies and pedagogies

Undead universities,[1] the plagiarism[2] 'plague'[3,4], paranoia[5] and hypercitation[6,7]

Ruth Walker

1. See Bill Readings' *The University in Ruins* (1996) for a vision of the university as a decomposing institution, animated only by the bureaucratized processes that surround the administration of noxious metrics of 'excellence'. The death of higher education has been announced – at least, the death of the ideal traditional university, which was already 'a monstrous body stitched together from Bologna, Cambridge, Berlin, and Baltimore' (Kochhar-Lindgren 2009: 7). In the contemporary reconfiguration of higher education, universities are populated by a corps(e) of teachers and students who are increasingly perceived as 'strangely headless, estranged and disconnected' (Royle 2003: 54) and haunted by questions concerning the future of teaching and learning. Higher education is actively engaged in disembodying itself: teachers and students spend increasing amounts of time in non-corporeal spaces as internet research, distance education, and the online administration and content delivery of subjects take the place of live physical interaction and exchange. However, a pervasive romantic notion of academic conditions and activities still haunts our expectations of research and writing practices. Plagiarism threatens this, as an illegitimate textual practice that weakens the educational integrity of institutions that have simultaneously been reanimated and made vulnerable by the recent and rapid expansion of online research capacities (Eisner and Vicinus 2008). The hunger for a solution to the perceived student plagiarism epidemic (Marsh 2007: 123) has resulted in an appetite for quick antidotes, such as plagiarism detection software and increasingly stringent academic integrity policies and procedures. However, the academy's almost compulsive emphasis on 'hypercitation' (Lunsford and West 1996: 397, see ftn 5 below) paradoxically seems to cultivate hollowed-out or zombie-like citation practices, and often results in technically well-referenced student writing that nevertheless is lifeless and devoid of an animating critical voice. Of course, academic writers are also exposed, particularly those who are under pressure to publish in the current audit culture of higher education and are driven to self-plagiarize (Bretag and Mahmud 2009), to disinter and recirculate their older research papers and projects.

2. For more on plagiarism as a primarily scholarly and textual concern, see Gilmore (2008), Pecorari (2008) and Howard and Robillard (2008). Although not actually illegal, plagiarism is considered to be 'fraudulent academic practice' (Deller-Evans et al. 2003) that lends itself to hyperbole: it has been variously described as the academic death penalty (Howard 1995), a dangerous disease (Marsh 2007), 'literary suicide' (Mallon 2001: 120), a 'cancer that erodes the rich legacy of scholarship' (Zangrando 1991: 60),

and 'intellectual leprosy' (Librero 2011: 1). Some argue that it is a murky offence, 'best understood not as a sharply defined operation, like beheading, but as a whole range of activities, more like cooking' (Kincaid, cited in Widdicombe 2012: 54). However, most common is the rhetoric of revulsion that seems to be inextricably linked to metaphors of death.

This pervasive revulsion is curious in the face of Roland Barthes' essay 'The Death of the author', where he complicated understandings of originality, authenticity and ownership, pointing out that a text is never truly original but always 'a tissue of quotations' (1988: 146). Similarly, Mikhail Bakhtin (1984, cited in Purdy 2005) has stressed that all utterances – including texts – are influenced by those words that an author has previously encountered, as well as future utterances that the author anticipates. From Barthes and Bakhtin it would seem that repetition in future texts of language from previously read texts is inevitable. However, as Paul Mann (1995) contends, plagiarism 'negates the romance of the death of the author by provoking our possessiveness about the corpse'. Plagiarism is therefore still considered a powerful 'taboo' in academic circles (Pecorari 2008: 55). Marcus Boon (2010) draws on Bataille's theories of taboo – as related to both death and the fear of the contagiousness of death – to argue that dead bodies already have some of the qualities attributed to copies, in the sense that they are degraded versions of originals (99). Boon points out that, reduced to skeletons, most humans look the same, and goes on to contend that the taboo-like atmosphere surrounding copying and copies derives from a feeling of discomfort, even horror, with dead bodies.

Intriguingly, there has always been a close connection with plagiarism and abject bodies: Barnhart (1988, cited in Park 2003: 471) traces the etymology of the word 'plagiarism' from the earlier English 'plagiary' (one who wrongfully takes another's words or ideas), from the Latin 'plagarius' (kidnapper, seducer, plunderer, literary thief), and which in turn is from 'plagium' (kidnapping). Denunciations of plagiarism often decry its violation of a text's physical integrity as it transgresses, or even rapes (Howard 2000), the original body of work. In one of the earliest attempts to articulate an inchoate conception of plagiarism, although he never used the term directly, the English poet John Donne draws on an extraordinarily visceral metaphor to describe the misappropriation of his writing:

> And they who write, because all write, have still
> That excuse for writing, and writing ill.
> But hee is worst, who (beggarly) doth chaw
> Others wits fruits, and in his ravenous maw
> Rankly digested, doth those things out-spue,
> As his owne things; and they are his owne, 'tis true,
> For if one eate my meate, though it be knowne
> The meate was mine, th'excrement is his owne.
>
> (Donne, *Satyre II*, c. 1593–1600)

The plagiarist's text is shit and the plagiarizer, who rankly digests and then spews out Donne's 'meate' as 'his owne things', is singularly abject in this invocation of cannibalistic writing practices (for more on this, see Cook 2012: 112).

Judith Butler draws an implicit link between plagiarism and abject authors who attempt to 'pass' as subjects in *Bodies That Matter* (1993). In the practice of 'citation', those who can cite regulatory social norms will become subjects, and those who fail to cite properly become abject. Butler reverses the scholarly celebration of overt citation, so that the abject's discourse is marked as derivative, while the subject appears to be most original and authoritative when the sources remain hidden in order to 'pass'. If the sources that have been cited appear clearly to the reader, the failure to dissimulate reveals the abject. Haviland (1997) points out that Butler mentions in a footnote (1993: 277, ftn 19) that it was Barbara Christian who first suggested the connection between 'passing' and plagiarism, but Haviland notes that this connection is not developed. She found it curious, given Butler's argument about citation as well as the point being made about plagiarism, that this 'citation' of a comment is not acknowledged in the body of the paper where the connection is mentioned, but is instead 'bracketed' in the peculiarly academic form of the footnote, 'that prophylactic against plagiarism' (Haviland 1997: 277, ftn 11). Just as Haviland says in her footnote about Butler's footnote, this is 'where we – you and I – are right now'.

3. See Bowman (2004) and McCabe and Stephens (2006) for more on perceptions of plagiarism as a problem that has reached 'epidemic proportions', and needs to be 'cured' (Marsh 2007). It is persistently described as a 'plague' that has been exacerbated by the expanded cutting and pasting capacities of the internet (for instance, see Campbell 2009; Eisner and Vicinus 2008).

Students are represented as the primary source of contamination for plagiarism. Already, the student writer figures in much educational literature 'as the author's opposite: the error-maker, the plagiarist, the remedial, the Great Unwashed, the enemy' (Grobman 2009: 178). The increasing massification of higher education has led to a parallel increase in anxiety about threat of encroaching hordes of students, particularly international students, who threaten to overwhelm the academy. While anxieties about crowds or mobs are familiar features of zombie movies and literature, even in the early literature crowds have been described as acting 'like those microbes which hasten the dissolution of enfeebled or dead bodies' (see Gustave Le Bon *The Psychology of the Crowd* 1895: 19). The association of plagiarism with particular cohorts of plagiarizing students is similarly perceived to threaten the integrity of the university. Brian Martin (1994), however, argues that blame is often disproportionately focused on students: current conceptions of plagiarism ignore what he calls 'institutionalized plagiarism', which includes bureaucratic ghost-writing, honorary authorship and supervisors coauthoring their postgraduate students' work. For Martin this institutionalized plagiarism is both worryingly pervasive and more objectionable than students' often inadvertent plagiarism, as it reinforces existing problematic and often exploitative power structures (1994: 40–42). Following

Pierre Bourdieu, Kitalong (1998, cited in Purdy 2005: 288) conceptualizes plagiarism as 'symbolic violence' because it involves the perpetrator appropriating someone else's linguistic capital, which may in turn lead to social and/or cultural capital. However, as Bourdieu and Passeron established in *Reproduction in Education, Society and Culture* (1977), because education insists on the imposition of a cultural arbitrary by an arbitrary power, all pedagogical action is a kind of symbolic violence.

Boluk and Lenz (2010) point out that there is already a close relationship between plague and textuality: in *Orality and Literacy* (1982) Walter Ong noted that 'one of the most startling paradoxes inherent in writing is its close association with death' (1983, cited in Boluk and Lenz 2010: 134). That is, the text is deadened in its removal from the 'living' world although paradoxically its rigid visual fixity 'ensures its endurance and potential for being resurrected into limitless contexts by a potentially infinite number of living readers' (134). As it is read by live readers, writing becomes a kind of reanimated corpse, and plagiarism is therefore the apocalyptic pestilence that infects its scholarly writing hosts. Intriguingly, the rhetoric about plague acts much like the plague does, as textual articulations of anxiety regarding biological infection that are almost as prevalent as the disease itself. The plague spreads by copying itself (Gomel, cited in Boluk and Lenz 2010: 139): 'it is governed by the logic of repetition. The chain of death grows by addition of more and more identical links.'

4. Quotation itself has a sinister edge, as the practice of quoting requires words and phrases to be ripped out of their original context and reconstituted in unfamiliar bodies of text. Walter Benjamin, who famously remarked that all writing consists largely of quotations, draws attention to the way that any use (not just the misuse) of quotations is essentially negative or violent, arguing that a quotation is torn from its text, interrupting or breaking into the original context and stealing its authority. He claimed that 'quotations in my works are like robbers by the roadside who make an armed attack and relieve an idler of his convictions' (1928: 81). Susan Stewart (1993: 19) takes this further to suggest that 'the quotation appears as a severed head, a voice whose authority is grounded in itself, and therein lies its power and its limit'. Although the quotation speaks with a voice of authority, it has been severed from the original context that gave it authenticity. Fundamental to academic writing and research practices, therefore, is a violent and somewhat cannibalistic breaching of the integrity of academic authorities and their bodies of writing.

    As Stewart (1993) points out, the 'marks' of the quotation lend it both integrity and limits as they draw attention to the quotation as a foreign fragment imported into the body of a text. In 'Outpatient clinic', one of the short textual fragments that make up 'One Way Street', Benjamin describes his own writing and editing practice as a kind of surgical intervention:

    The author lays the thought on the marble-topped café table … Then he slowly unpacks his instruments: fountain pen, pencil and pipe. The crowd of patrons, disposed in curved rows are his clinical audience. Coffee, carefully poured and as carefully drunk, puts the thought under chloroform … an incision is made in the scrupulous liniments of the handwriting, the surgeon, moving inside, shifts points of emphasis, burns off growths of verbiage, and inserts, as a silver rib, a word borrowed from a foreign language. Finally, punctuation sews the whole thing up for him with fine stitches and he pays the waiter, his assistant, in cash.

(Benjamin 1928: 96–97)

Quotation marks help stitch together the frankensteined body of Benjamin's essay. Elsewhere, Benjamin (1917: 85) mused that 'marks' in works of art or literary creation tend to be a warning sign, as they indicate either guilt (for instance, blushing) or innocence (Christ's stigmata). In academic writing, where citation is highly valued, many quotation marks can be seen paradoxically as a sign of weakness, guilt or anxiety about academic forbears by scholars who self-consciously 'stand in the shadow of giants' (Howard 1999, and see ftn 6 below). Given this, it is unsurprising that Derrida begins the essay 'Le Parjure/The Lie' (2002: 161), a reflection on the uncomfortable revelations about another scholar's corrupted writing practices, with the line 'let us begin with a quotation'

5. Paranoia was one of the names given at the beginning of the twentieth century to the type of psychosis in which a patient develops a delusional system of beliefs centred around the certainty that he or she is a person of great importance, and on that account subject to surveillance and persecution (Freeman and Garety 2004). In the throes of paranoid disorder, the subject systematically constructs an internally consistent narrative that centralizes him or herself, becoming the focus of attention in a reorganization of authentic or fabricated events. This mirrors the plagiarist's claims that they are the original source and authority for their written text. Both paranoia and plagiarism have in common 'an instability in the recognition of and respect for the boundaries between the self and the other' (Haviland 1997: 295).

Freud developed his theory of paranoia in the case study about Justice Schreber (1913). This oft-cited case study is particularly fascinating for its insights into Freud's own critical writing practices, as he anxiously reflects on his own authorial identity, his lack of formal attachment to a medical teaching institution, and his fear of being accused of plagiarism. The focus of the case study was the son of a famous educationalist and social reformer who had introduced physical education into the school curriculum – Schreber himself became a successful judge, even as he was plagued by anxieties and suspicions that led to the development of a complex theory of persecution that was also riddled with the suspicion that the people were continually taking notes about him, writing down and later cross-referencing everything he said and did. Ironically, to this day the Schreber case is one of the most cited studies of paranoia in psychological literature. Schreber was never actually a patient of Freud's but published his own book *Memoirs of My Nervous Illness* (1903) that became a best-selling sensation, and which Freud relied on for his diagnosis in the case study. As Freud notes in his introduction to the case study, paranoiacs like Schreber were not only likely to produce written texts, but were also inclined to reflect on their pathology, with a lucid grasp of their own symptoms and a capability of defending their delusion with wit and intelligence (xi). This scholarly inclination is evident in another contemporaneous paranoia case, that of Ernst Wagner, the school teacher and mass murderer who competed with Schreber in the early psychoanalytic literature, and who himself produced a three-volume memoir. Robert Graupp, who made Wagner his star patient at the time, concluded rather alarmingly that schoolteachers and governesses were particularly vulnerable to the disease 'because their profession provides a milieu in which their genuine mental superiority gives rise to suppressed mental arrogance' (1914: 130–31). Trotter points out that this explicit linking of the pedagogue to paranoia in the early literature underlines the point that 'recognition' is a particular problem, sometimes leading to madness, 'for those who depend on their expertise, and on the symbolic capital it at once accumulates and relies upon for its furtherance, to make a living' (2001: 43). Clearly, the pressure to pass as an expert at the same time as negotiating an underlying 'anxiety of influence' (Bloom 1973) of other academic authorities parallels the paranoid turn.

Freud himself was quite evidently anxious about his critical control of the source material, and spends much of the case study asserting his own interpretive mastery over Schreber, taking pains to correct, extend and out-footnote Schreber's own scholarly references to Goethe, Milton and Byron. More worrying for Freud was the realization that other scholars were publishing simultaneously on Schreber; Freud is careful in a footnoted postscript to distinguish his approach from Carl Jung's, whose article unexpectedly appeared in the same journal. But Freud had also borrowed heavily enough from Schreber's own memoir to feel the need to add a note that semi-jokingly defends himself against charges of plagiarism, complete with an offer to produce testimonials to his own originality:

> I can call on my friend and fellow-specialist to witness that I had developed my theory of paranoia before I became acquainted with the contents of Schreber's book. It remains for the future to decide whether there is more delusion in my theory than I should like to admit, or whether there is more truth in Schreber's delusion than other people are as yet prepared to believe.
>
> (Freud 1913: xx)

Freud had effectively reproduced Schreber's own intense anxiety about the originality of his own thoughts: while Schreber was concerned that he was being scrutinized and directed by a force outside of himself, Freud was anxious to defend himself against an accusation that he had plagiarized from a delusional patient. In this way, the case study explicitly links paranoia with unstable citation practices, even as it prepared the ground for both the practice of psychoanalysis and critical inquiry.

See Hertz (1985) and Meltzer (1994) for more on Freud's sensitivity to accusations of plagiarism. Paul Roazen (1969, cited in Haviland 1997: 317, ftn 9) wrote: 'The theme of plagiarism can be found almost everywhere one turns in Freud's career. Since Freud's ambition was world fame, he was bound to worry lest a discovery of his own be snatched away by someone else.' Reportedly, anxieties about accusations of plagiarism provoked Freud to violence: Haviland (1997) cites Swales' essay 'Freud, Fliess and Fratricide' (1982) as evidence that the rupture between Freud and his one-time writing partner Wilhelm Fliess was precipitated by a dispute about who originated the theory of bisexuality. In 1906, Fliess not only claimed that Freud plagiarized him but that he had planned to kill him by pushing him off a mountain path in the Alps at their last meeting.

As Paul Mann (1995) has argued, the impulse to plagiarize has some of the hallmarks of one of Freud's myths for the founding of culture, the father's murder by the primal horde: 'plagiarism is the return of the repressed of literary authority'.

6. Our nearly compulsive scholarly and teacherly attention to citation and mind numbingly endless listing of sources has led to what Andrea Lunsford has called a compulsion to 'hyper-citation' (1996: 397, see ftn 1 above), which she argues is a manifestation of the academic need to possess and to possess exclusively, taking out the 'little dross of intellectual property and turning it into gold for advancement'. Elsewhere, Derrida develops an important theory of citationality and language, but it is intriguing to note his own considerable unease with conventional acknowledgement practices, of quoting and being quoted:

> I would like to spare you the tedium, the waste of time, and the subservience that always accompany the classic pedagogical procedures of forging links, referring back to past premises or arguments, justifying one's own trajectory, method, system, and more or less skilful transitions, reestablishing continuity, and so on. These are but some of the imperatives of classical pedagogy with which, to be sure, one can never break once and for all. Yet, if you were to submit to them rigorously, they would very soon reduce you to silence, tautology and tiresome repetition.
>
> (Derrida, 1982: 247)

This weariness with a procedural hyper-focus on the acknowledgement of referencing conventions underlines Derrida's unease with the self-protecting, self-promoting and self-justifying practices that serve to bolster pedagogical tradition and yet that can actually inhibit the experience of teaching and learning, as well as silencing the authorial voice. Rebecca Howard (1998) has pointed out that, paradoxically, many scholars and academics are careful not to over-rely on quotations and citations, as they can effectively destabilize their writerly authority. The educational response to plagiarism, then, with its insistence on students' rigorous and full citation practice, serves to underline the message that students are not themselves authors: Howard says, 'thus not only the act of plagiarism but also the act of citation affirms the student's lowly authorial status and accomplishes the student's exclusion from academic subject-hood.'

With the emphasis on hyper-citation comes a hyper-vigilance. The rhetoric about plagiarism is most often couched in terms of violence and struggle: Purdy (2005: 277) notes that the work of the teacher is often framed as hunting, chasing down, catching, combating and fighting. 'Weapons' specifically designed to 'parry' plagiarism are online text-matching software programmes like Turnitin, often perceived as a 'silver bullet' in the 'gunfight' on an otherwise 'lawless online frontier' (Shaw, 2012). These software solutions respond to the violence of plagiarism with yet more violence, according to Kitalong, by working 'to quickly, invisibly, and oppressively identify and punish suspected plagiarizers' in a way that 'reinforces polarized student/teacher relationships that cast teachers as uncoverers and punishers' (1998, cited in Purdy 2005: 288).

A strange suspecting culture has built up around plagiarism, an epistemology underpinned by the affective category of fear (see Sylvan Tomkins for more on fear, shame and paranoia, 1963). The emphasis on deterrents and penalties leads to anxious and attentive students, but it also has negative affects for academics, who are constantly alert to evidence of the plagiarism plague (see ftns 2 and 5 above). The rhetoric of suspicion and disease in discussions of plagiarism maps easily onto Michel Foucault's theorization of surveillance culture. In *Discipline and Punish: The Birth of the Prison* (1975), Foucault utilizes a description of a seventeenth-century village, quarantined as a result of a plague, whose inhabitants are 'arrested' into their own houses so as not to spread disease (195–228). Foucault describes the process of a mobile surveillance team, amassing huge dossiers and documentation as they assessed individual healthy citizens and sentenced to death those who left their homes or otherwise communicated with the potentially contagious. To circumvent the escalating bureaucratization that this system of plague-management produced, an all-seeing tower, or panopticon, was built at the centre of town, which functioned as a tool to discipline the community using active surveillance by an anonymous 'supervisor'. The sinister beauty of the panopticon is that there does not even have to be a viewer present in order for it to work: in theory, the mere possibility that an authority figure or technological tool could be observing is enough to generate fear, suspicion and, in turn, obedience. Turnitin was hoped to work as just such a panopticon to regulate plagiaristic behaviours in educational communities. What has resulted is instead a state of terrible alertness.

7. Footnotes are a good place to bury information; they act as an open grave for the body of the text. Shari Benstock asserts that the discourse of the footnote is 'inherently marginal' (1983: 204), that they are considered secondary to the action happening above on the page. Benjamin, on the other hand, as an obsessive researcher and compiler, thought that books were gradually becoming less important than the annotation and citation work of the scholars who write and read them:

> [T]oday the book is already, as the present mode of scholarly production demonstrates, an outdated mediation between two different filing systems. For everything that matters is to be found in the card box of the researcher who wrote it, and the scholar studying it assimilates it into his own card index.
>
> (Benjamin 1928: 66)

In another aside, Benjamin coyly lists correlations between books and harlots: amongst other similarities, he notes that you can take both to bed, and that 'footnotes in one are as banknotes in the stockings of another' (1928: 73). A footnote adds value, or cultural capital, to a text, which Benjamin presents in sexualized terms, drawing attention to its vulnerability to transmissible disease (see ftn 2 for a discussion of the footnoted citation as a 'prophylactic' against plagiarism). Footnotes here are understood in anatomical terms, like the index, another supporting text to academic publications, which shares its etymological roots with the first finger of the hand. Both act as textual prostheses: Dworkin (2005: 16) strikingly describes footnotes as amputated on the bottom of the page like 'stacks of artificial limbs: legs with feet that note ... and arms with fingers pointing stiffly into space'.

As feet to the body of the text, annotations are trodden down the page to their footer, abject addenda that promise an opportunity to browse through the vigilantly acknowledged research sources, but are basically just interruptions that lurch across the bottom of the page like zombie 'walkers' milling hungrily in the outlying territory of the margins. Unlike the flâneur, who 'embodies the spatial practices of walking as writing, writing as walking' (Reynolds 2006: 70), these zombie annotations have bound feet. In the essay 'This is not an oral footnote', Derrida announces that 'all annotations are destined to be bad' (1991: 200). Here he is referring to the researcher who, when selecting a quotation from another source, and thereby attempting to interpret and transmit its meaning, comes across a 'prescriptive double bind':

> When someone looks at a text, they have to come to terms with it saying: 'Be quiet, all has been said, you have nothing to say, obey in silence', while at the same time it implores, it cries out, it says, 'Read me and respond: if you want to read me and hear me, you must understand me, know me, interpret me, translate me, and hence, in responding to me and speaking to me, you must begin to speak in my place, to enter into rivalry with me'.
>
> (1991: 202)

The selected citation acts as an injunction, as it compels the potential citer to read, respond and reanimate the original text by creating relations between it and their own work or interpretive system, in order to digest and possess it. At the same time the annotation acts as an interdiction, as it demands that the potential citer be silent and humble before all that has been said before. Caught in this double bind, even the quoter who seeks to avoid the plagiarist's perverse hollowing out of their own authorship is trapped in a state of suspended animation – and silenced.

References

Barthes, R. (1988), 'The death of the author', *Image, Music, Text*, London: Fontana Press, pp. 142–148.

Bataille, G. (1957), *Erotism: Death and Sensuality*, trans. M. Dalwood, San Fransisco: City Lights Books.

Benjamin, W. (1917/1996), 'On paintings, signs and marks' in M. Bullock and M. Jennings (eds) *Walter Benjamin: Selected Writings: Volume 1, 1913–1926*, Cambridge, MA: Harvard University Press, pp. 83–86.

———— (1928/2008), 'One way street', in *One Way Street and Other Writings*, trans. J.A. Underwood, London: Penguin, pp. 46–115.

Benstock, S. (1983), 'At the margins of discourse: footnotes in the fictional text', *PMLA*, 98: 2, pp. 204–25.

Bloom, H. (1973), *The Anxiety of Influence: A Theory of Poetry*, New York and Oxford: Oxford University Press.

Boluk, S. and Lenz, W. (2010), 'Infection, media, and capitalism: from early modern plagues to postmodern zombies', *The Journal For Early Modern Cultural Studies*, 10: 2, pp. 126–147.

Boon, M. (2010), *In Praise of Copying: Concerning Contemporary Cultures of the Copy*, Boston, MA: Harvard University Press.

Bourdieu, P. and Passeron J.C. (1977), *Reproductions in Education, Society and Culture*, trans. R. Nice, London: Sage.

Bowman V. (ed.) (2004), *The Plagiarism Plague: A Resource Guide and CD-ROM Tutorial for Educators and Librarians*, New York: Neal-Schuman Publishers.

Bretag, T. and Mahmud, S. (2009), 'Self-plagiarism or appropriate textual re-use?', *Journal of Academic Ethics*, 7: 1, pp. 93–205.

Butler, J. (1993), *Bodies That Matter: On the Discursive Limits of Sex*, New York: Routledge.

Campbell, D. (2009), 'The plagiarism plague: in the internet era, cheating has become an epidemic on college campuses', *Crosstalk: The National Centre For Public Policy And Higher Education*, http://www.highereducation.org/crosstalk/ct0106/news0106-plagiarism.shtml. Accessed January 12, 2012.

Cook, T. (2012), 'The meate was mine': Donne's *Satyre II* and the prehistory of proprietary Authorship', *Studies in Philology*, 109: 1, pp. 103–131.

Deller-Evans, K., Evans, S., and Gannaway, D. (2003). 'Collaborative efforts to resist fraudulent educational practice', paper presented at the *Educational Integrity: Plagiarism and Other Perplexities Conference*, Adelaide, South Australia, 21–22 November.

Derrida, J. (1982), *The Ear of the Other: Otobiography, Text, Transference*, New York: Shocken Books.

———— (1991), 'This is not an oral footnote', in S. Barney (ed.), *Annotation and its Texts*, New York and Oxford: Oxford University Press, pp. 192–205.

—— (2002), 'Le Parjure: perhaps, storytelling and lying', in P. Kamuf (ed.), *Without Alibi*, Stanford: Stanford University Press, pp. 161–201.

Donne, J. (1593-1600/1967), *Satyre II*, in *John Donne: The Satires, Epigrams and Verse Letters*, Oxford: Oxford University Press.

Dworkin, C. (2005), 'Textual prostheses', *Comparative Literature*, 57: 1, pp. 1–24.

Eisner, C. and Vicinus, M. (2008), *Originality, Imitation and Plagiarism: Teaching Writing in the Digital Age*, Ann Arbor: University of Michigan.

Foucault, M. (1975), *Discipline and Punish: The Birth of the Prison*, trans. A. Sheridan. London: Penguin Books.

Freeman, D. and Garety, P. (2004), *Paranoia: The Psychology of Persecutory Delusions*, Hove: Psychology Press.

Freud, S. (1913), 'The case of Schreber', *The Standard Edition of the Complete Psychological Works of Sigmund Freud: Volume XII*, trans. and ed. J. Strachey et al., London: Hogarth Press, pp. 9–80.

Garber, M. (2003), *Quotation Marks*, London and New York: Routledge.

Gilmore, B. (2008), *Plagiarism: Why It Happens and How to Prevent It*, Portsmouth, NH: Heinemann.

Graupp, R. (1914), 'The scientific significance of the case of Ernst Wagner', in S. Hirsch and M. Shepherd (eds), *Themes and Variations in European Psychiatry*, Charlottesville: University of Virginia Press, pp. 121–133.

Grobman L. (2009), 'The student scholar: (re)negotiating authorship and authority', *College Composition and Communication*, 61: 1, pp. 175–196.

Haviland, B. (1997), 'Passing from paranoia to plagiarism: the abject authorship of Nella Larsen', *Modern Fiction Studies*, 43: 2, pp. 295–318.

Hertz, N. (1985), *The End of the Line: Essays on Psychoanalysis and the Sublime*, New York: Columbia University Press.

Howard, R. (1995), 'Plagiarisms, authorship, and the academic death penalty', *College English*, 57: 7, pp. 788–806.

—— (1998), 'The literary production of power: citation practices among students and authors' *Technorhetoric*, www.technorhetoric.net/3.1/coverweb/ipc/practcite.htm. Accessed January 12, 2012.

—— (1999), *Standing in the Shadow of Giants: Plagiarists, Authors, Collaborators*, Stamford, CT: Ablex.

—— (2000), 'Sexuality, textuality: the cultural work of plagiarism.' *College English*, 62: 4, pp. 473–491.

Howard, R. and Robillard A. (eds.) (2008), *Pluralising Plagiarism: Identities, Contexts, Pedagogies*, Portsmith, NH: Boynton/Cook.

Kitalong, K. (1998), 'A web of symbolic violence', *Computers and Composition*, 15: 2, pp. 253–264.

Kochhar-Lindgren, G. (2009), 'The haunting of the university: phantomenology and the house of learning', *Pedagogy: Critical Approaches to Teaching Literature, Language, Composition, and Culture*, 9: 1, pp. 3–12.

Le Bon, G. (1896/1901), *The Crowd*, London: T. Fisher Unwin.

Librero, L. (2011), 'Plagiarism: an intellectual leprosy', paper from the *11th Talakayan Series for Environment and Development* (TSED) conference, January 13, 2011, www.upou.edu.ph/papers/flibrero2011/PlagiarismFL.pdf. Accessed February 23, 2012.

Lunsford, A. and West, S. (1996), 'Intellectual property and composition studies', *College Composition and Communication*, 47: 3, pp. 383–411.

Mallon, T. (2001), *Stolen Words: The Classic Book on Plagiarism*, Bristol: Marina Books.

Mann, P. (1995), 'Stupid undergrounds', *Postmodern Culture*, 5: 3, http://pmc.iath.virginia.edu/text-only/issue.595/mann.595. Accessed January 12, 2011.

Marsh, B (2007), *Plagiarism: Alchemy and Remedy in Higher Education*, Albany: SUNY Press.

Martin, B. (1994), 'Plagiarism: a misplaced emphasis', *Journal of Information Ethics*, 3: 2, pp. 36–47.

McCabe, D. and Stephens, J. (2006), 'Epidemic as opportunity: internet plagiarism as a lever for cultural change', *Teachers College Record*, http://www.tcrecord.org/content.asp?contentid=12860. Accessed December 12, 2011.

Meltzer, F. (1994), *Hot Property: The Stakes and Claims of Literary Originality*. Chicago: University of Chicago Press.

Ngain, S. (2005), *Ugly Feelings,* Cambridge, MA: Harvard University Press.

Park, C. (2003), 'In other (people's) words: plagiarism by university students, literature and lessons', *Assessment and Evaluation in Higher Education*, 28: 5, pp. 471–488.

Pecorari, D. (2008), *Academic Writing and Plagiarism: A Linguistic Analysis*, London and New York: Continuum.

Purdy, J. (2005), 'Calling off the hounds: technology and the visibility of plagiarism', *Pedagogy*, 5: 2, pp. 275–296.

Readings, B. (1996), *The University in Ruins*, Cambridge, MA: Harvard University Press.

Reynolds, N. (2006) *Geographies of Writing: Inhabiting Places and Encountering Difference.* Carbondale, IL: Southern Illinois University Press.

Roazen, P. (1969), *Brother Animal: The Story of Freud and Tausk*. New York: New York University Press.

Royle, N. (2003), *The Uncanny*, New York: Routledge.

Shaw, R. (2012), 'Use of Turnitin software does not deter cheating, study finds', Times Higher Education, January 19, http://www.timeshighereducation.co.uk/story.asp?sectioncode=26andstorycode=418740. Accessed February 2, 2012.

Stewart, S. (1991) *Crime of Writing: Problems in the Containment of Representation,* New York and Toronto: Oxford University Press.

——— (1993), *On Longing: Narratives Of The Miniature, The Gigantic, The Souvenir, The Collection*, Durham and London: Duke University Press.

Tomkins, S. (1963), *Affect. Imagery. Consciousness: Volume 2*, New York: Springer Publishing Co.

Trotter, D. (2001), *Paranoid Modernism: Literary Experiment, Psychosis, And The Professionalization Of English Society*, New York: Oxford University Press.

Widdicombe, L. (2012), 'The plagiarist's tale', *The New Yorker*, February 13–20, pp. 52–59.

Zangrando, R. (1991), 'Historians' procedures for handling plagiarism', *Publishing Research Quarterly*, 7: 4, pp. 57–64.

EAP programmes feeding the living dead of academia: critical thinking as a global antibody

Sara Felix

For many international students, English for Academic Purposes (EAP) programmes are a gateway into the academy. Students from outside the United Kingdom, the United States, Australia and the European Union enter these programmes as a means of bridging the gap between their home educations and the requirements of Anglo-American universities (a term coined by Vandermensbrugghe, 2004). According to the British Association of Lecturers of English for Academic Purposes (BALEAP), the purpose of EAP is to prepare students linguistically, academically, socially and psychologically to study at British universities (BALEAP 2011). This is also the purpose of similar programmes at Australian and American universities that prepare a cohort of new university students in transition to a world of intellectual labour.

There are high expectations for this precursor to academic study, as can be seen in BALEAP's Competency Framework for Teachers of EAP (2008). BALEAP outlines how students are expected to learn academic literacies that include the critical thinking that will encourage them to question, to consider, to evaluate and to create. In tandem, they would learn to use high-level English language. This would allow them to articulate their newly developed critical opinions, both orally and in writing. In theory, EAP guarantees the transition into the academy of a cohort of animated and study-ready students. A common perception, however, is that EAP actually produces a horde of dead-weight students who are trained to rote-learn and who threaten academic standards. The EAP programmes are intended to bolster the mind, encourage critical thought, and demand the independent thinking that should, in turn, lead to protection against potential hazards that lie in wait for the uninitiated or unskilled student as they progress to their desired higher education institution. The underlying purpose of the EAP is therefore to cultivate and inoculate transitioning student minds against the very thing that they are often accused of being. In other words, it is in EAP that many international students experience their first taste of their forthcoming role in higher education: as either intellectual warriors equipped with critical thinking, or as zombies mindlessly lurching through their degrees.

The BALEAP, which was founded in 1989, now focuses on critical thinking and academic literacies. However, historically EAP has been anything but academic. The field continues the traditions of its dead past by actively preventing critical reflection and encouraging student compliance. The approach of EAP now threatens to infect the universities with the zombification of higher education. Hope is not lost: just as current practices infect students' brains and risk the standardization of inadequate teaching and learning, so too can more thoughtful pedagogies at key points in students' academic careers build immunity against infection. EAP has the potential to be both the place of initial infection and the place to develop the antibody against it. This antibody is formulated through the fostering of *conscientização*, a critical consciousness formed by reflective thought that then informs action (Freire 1970; hooks 1994). It offers students a defence against zombification.

Zombies in the age of global capitalism

David Sirota (2009) comments on a notable trend in popular culture when he asks: 'What's with all the zombies lately?' Even family-friendly movie franchises like *Pirates of the Caribbean* have gone zombie with the recent film *On Stranger Tides* (2011). Brad Pitt, cast in the forthcoming *World War Z* (2012), has joined Johnny Depp to star in a zombie themed film, confirming that the genre – along with their spoofs such as *Shaun of the Dead* (2004) – has gone mainstream. However, the zombie trend has not just infected Hollywood, as economists, political theorists and sociologists have also harnessed the zombie trope. There has been a spate of recent non-fiction publications, including *Zombie Capitalism and the Relevance of Marx* (Harman 2009), *Theories of International Politics and Zombies* (Drezner 2011), and *Zombie Politics and Culture in the Age of Casino Capitalism* (Giroux 2011). This book too appropriates the zombie theme in relation to the perceived crisis in higher education. So, what *is* up with all the zombies lately?

A zombie is someone who has died and whose body has been reanimated. Notably, zombies are effectively brain-dead, so that anything that made them individual – memories, language, aspirations, sense of identity and independent thought – is cancelled out. They do not recognize loved ones and they cannot reason. They are no longer human. Films often portray the process of zombification as follows: first an individual is bitten, scratched or otherwise directly infected by a zombie. This eventually leads to the individual getting sick and dying. Once dead, the body reanimates while the brain maintains only basic functions and is driven by a need to feed on other individuals.

Early films depicted the zombie being formed through voodoo, for example *White Zombie* (1932), where Murder Legendre uses voodoo to create the zombies that work at his sugar cane mill. More contemporary iterations depict zombification through infection with an artificial virus, for example the designer 'T virus' in the *Resident Evil* franchise (2002, 2004, 2007, 2010, 2012). Intriguingly, even in early popular cultural representations, business interests exploit the zombie infection. This might offer an explanation for the continued relevance of the zombie trope to an increasingly globalized and corporatized world.

In the *Resident Evil* movies, the T virus did not mutate naturally. Rather, it is a biological weapon developed by the Umbrella Corporation, which, as we are informed at the beginning of the first film, is 'the largest commercial entity in the United States. Nine out of every ten homes contain its products. Its political and financial influence is felt everywhere' (*Resident Evil* 2002). The Umbrella Corporation is presented as the zenith of free-market capitalism, and the T virus was manufactured for profit and exploited to give the company a competitive edge. It was devised for sale to the military: it reanimates dead cells (except for dead brain cells), and could also be used to create self-generating soldiers who would heal on the battlefield. By the third film, because the refined T virus kills the brain but maintains complete body functions, the Umbrella Corporation sees the potential of using zombies as a 'docile workforce'.

The zombifying T virus is represented in *Resident Evil* as a means for large, multinational corporations to create and control a cheap labour force, who are left without the power to question or organize against their subjection to corporate interests. Effectively, this movie franchise uses the zombie metaphor to parallel the economic and political processes of global capitalism. The search for a cheap but highly productive and malleable labour force is driven by the capitalist need for profits: maximum profits require a labour force that is skilled, but relatively mindless. The zombie process represented in these films reflects what is happening to individuals in this age of globalized capitalism.

However, while the subtext of *Resident Evil* is a dark message about how corporations process their worker's bodies and impact more broadly on society, there is a recurring glimmer of hope, which in many cases leads infected individuals to wait too long before killing themselves (thereby putting their friends at risk). This is the promise of an antivirus. The movies set up a clear methodology for the zombie process; with blue injections representing infection, and green syringes representing not just inoculation against the virus, but an instant cure. With this inoculation comes the possibility that individuals can survive zombification by developing artificial antibodies against the virus (more cynically, this also leaves the door open for future sequels). The message seems to be that there are possible resistances to the globalized capitalist reliance on the production of thoughtless labouring bodies, in the form of an elusive antivirus.

Zombie antibody: critical thinking through critical theory

Extending the *Resident Evil* zombification process to form a commentary on the evils of corporatization to the current situation of EAP programmes and higher education is a short stretch. The key question for this line of argument is: if the blue syringe represents infection, which manufactures a technically skilled but unquestioning labour force, what does the green syringe produce? I would argue that that the antivirus it represents is critical thinking.

Critical thinking does not just mean cognitive processes. Both the 'intelligent use of all available evidence for the solution of a problem' (McPeck 1981: 12) and argumentation (Ennis 1991) are vital skills, but they are not quite enough to protect individuals in these zombie times. The current global pressures that emphasize market imperatives require

193

more. McPeck and Ennis's definitions do not offer enough to begin to question the very structures of this system. Critical thinking therefore needs to be informed by critical theory to encourage students to question logically, but also to consider broader social, historical, political and economical contexts and contingencies.

Critical theory questions 'hidden assumptions' (Bronner 2011: 1). While being 'deeply sceptical of tradition and absolute claims', it is concerned 'not merely with how things are, but how they might be and should be' (2). In other words, critical theory constantly questions tacit structures while attempting to understand and critique dominant power. It is a radical questioning. Horkheimer introduced the term in a 1937 essay when he wrote 'every part of the theory presupposed the critique of the existing order and the struggle against it along the lines determined by the theory itself' (1972: 229). This means that to be effective, critical thinking needs to consider the social, economic and political contexts in which the individual lives. Otherwise it becomes, as Habermas argues, the capitalization of an individual's personal life as part of 'the colonization of the lifeworld' (1987: 53). For students to avoid becoming corporate and capitalist zombie followers, they must develop critical thinking skills and question the processes they are submitting to even while envisioning alternatives.

Paulo Freire (1970) offers a definition of critical thinking informed by critical theory for education. He describes a process called *conscientização*, a consciousness through which an individual achieves an understanding of the world, perceiving and exposing the social and political contradictions that surround them, in order to then transform their world by taking action against those oppressive elements. In other words, thinking becomes awareness while considering action. Zombies do not have the ability to communicate anything beyond repetitive groans because they cannot consider and question; once zombified they cannot devise alternatives to the realities in which they currently find themselves. While they may form mobs, zombies have no notions of self and therefore cannot work together to take action for improvement of their situation. Following Freire's prescription, it is by ensuring that individuals are exposed and encouraged to consider, reflect, question and then express alternative realities for their social contexts, that antibodies are produced that can help prevent them from becoming zombies.

Kincheloe (2000, 2008) and Brookfield (2010) extend the work of Freire to develop a critical understanding of critical thinking. Kincheloe (2000) argues that through critical thinking, students become aware of how current political and economic situations are shaping their assumption on the world. He builds on this by proposing a critically complex epistemology (Kincheloe 2008), acknowledging the importance of first understanding the context of the knowledge and power being questioned and then understanding the complexity of that context. Both context and complexity must be considered. Brookfield takes this further:

Critical thinking in this vein is the educational implementation of ideology critique, the deliberate attempt to penetrate the ideological obfuscation that ensures that massive social inequity is acceptable by the majority as the natural state of affairs ... Critical thinking framed by critical theory is not just a cognitive process. It is a developmental project, inevitably bound up with helping people realize common interests, reject the privatized, competitive ethic of capitalism, and prevent the emergence of inherited privilege.

(2010: 58–59)

Critical thinking would be a way of questioning a history of zombie capitalism and hegemony and offering an alternative view. Individuals could reflect on their own social and political contexts while acknowledging their vulnerability to the powers and corporate interests that threaten to consume them. In the case of many international students, the context they would be questioning would not only be the programme of EAP in which they find themselves, but also the larger context of the higher education industry.

Zombification of international higher education

Higher education is not only increasingly internationalized, it is also increasingly influenced by global corporate free-market capitalism. UNESCO's *World Conference on Higher Education* (Altbach, Reisber and Rumbley 2009) and the OECD's *Assessment of Higher Education Learning Outcomes Project* (Nusche 2008) both use the language of capitalism in their reports: institutions of higher education should compete for 'consumers', while higher education should primarily be concerned with the development of professional competencies. The underlying assumption is that universities are creating a workforce ready to enter the job market. Indeed, the World Bank explicitly states that institutes of higher education 'produce the variety of skilled workers and employees sought by the labour-market' (Salmi 2009: 20). It could of course be argued that zombification is not the inevitable result of higher education's focus on advanced jobs training for the labour market, given that another key characteristic of higher education involves students engaging and questioning different ideas. However, I would argue that the increasing emphasis on creating a labour force is matched by a decreasing encouragement of independent thought.

Bernstein's (2003) theory of code curricula makes it clear that zombification is occurring in higher education. Bernstein was convinced that the transmission and reproduction of social class occurs in the classroom, as he examined the difference between the education received by working and middle class families. He argued that different pedagogical practices create a system that ensures that the working class remain in their economic range due to two types of curricula: collection code curricula and integrated code curricula. In collection code curricula, knowledge is rigidly separated, and students are only taught their specific subjects, so that they are not encouraged to use the knowledge acquisition in one subject to question or inform the knowledge base of another. Their thinking is limited.

195

This collection code curricula is used, according to Bernstein, for the education of the working classes and most significantly is directed towards jobs skills. On the other hand, in 'integrated' code curricula, knowledge is integrated more loosely; fields are related to each other and students are introduced to a variety of subjects while encouraged to think about each subject in light of the other. This is the model of education for the middle and wealthier classes.

While Bernstein's analysis was focused on the differences in the transmission of education among classes within the United Kingdom, his conclusions have more recently been found to be applicable across the internationalized student cohort and curricula. Brown et al. (2011) looked at the different modes of education on a global scale and found that Bernstein's original findings remain valid. They noted that curricula were remarkably similar for the lower classes and for international students arriving from outside the United Kingdom, the European Union, Australia or the United States; that is, curricula are clearly focused on job skills and modular education, even at the university level. They also found that the education directed towards the wealthiest 10% in the United Kingdom and the United States was much more integrated and interdisciplinary. In other words, education mirrors the uneven social inequities of the capitalized society, where the elite continue to enjoy more advantageous educational opportunities while future employees are subject to trends in market demands and employability. Higher education for the vast majority, or the future labour force, is significantly different from higher education for the power-elite.

Universities are not hopelessly zombified simply because higher education is generally moving towards skills-based learning and modular education. But this does explain the decreasing emphasis on critical thinking. This chapter draws attention to the impact of corporatized trends and the impossibility of critical thinking in the current design of one of the most rapidly expanding fields in internationalized higher education: EAP. These programmes now perform a key role for many universities, as they act as a processing gateway for increasing numbers of full-fee paying international students. However, EAP has a genealogy that is strikingly different to that of universities. It is in looking at EAP's history that questions arise: did EAP ever specifically focused on critical thought, and is EAP more likely to create zombies rather than inoculate against them?

Zombies from inception: a brief history of EAP

In order to understand why an entire academic field would consist of zombified teaching and learning practices, it is useful to look at the origins of English Academic Programmes. The early EAPs originated in the United Kingdom and were encouraged as they helped maintain British dominance overseas following the disintegration of its colonies. Britain hoped to maintain economic interests and political power in these newly independent states post-WWII. This was most effectively done through the exercise of 'soft power', which ensured that citizens of those states were dependent on Britain for desirable cultural commodities, such as higher education. This was partially accomplished by ensuring that English as a common language of consumption was maintained in trade and business relationships.

Phillipson (1992) chronicles the mission of the British Council, one of the governing bodies of EAP programmes as well as other English as a Foreign Language (EFL) institutions. He describes how under the Drogheda Report (1954), the British Council took on a new directive to build relationships overseas to prevent the spread of communism as well as to bolster Britain's international influence. The British Council began offering language courses and directing English programmes across the world, not only to promote English as the lingua franca, but also as a means of ensuring that participating countries would be invested in maintaining their alliance with the United Kingdom. The publication of a report by the Official Committee on Teaching of English Overseas (1956) reinforced the understanding that there were expanding opportunities for using language teaching as a stepping stone to international influence (cited in Phillipson 1992). The English language and academically aspirational programmes of EAP were therefore perfectly placed to promote colonial, hegemonic and soon corporate interests.

Benesch (2002) unveils some surprising facts about the historical context of a field driven by 'getting the job done with no critical analysis of the consequences for the various parties' (130). What she discovered was an academic field heavily influenced by oil companies. Rather than setting out to develop independently thinking students, these programmes were primarily designed to mould future employees. As her quoted observation suggests, the individual students' interests were considered less important than what was best for the participating companies' business interests. Just as for *Resident Evil's* Umbrella Corporation, it was clearly in these corporations' interests to foster an environment that would create a 'docile workforce', or a domesticated crop of zombies, instead of investing in a pedagogy directed by thoughtful action and intensive critique.

According to Benesch (2002), the first English-medium universities in the Middle East in the 1970s served the purpose of creating local engineers and employees for oil fields drilled by American companies. Education conferences, such as the *Conference on Adult English for National Development* held at the American University of Beirut in 1971 and attended by the Arabian American Oil Company (ARAMCO), implicitly focused on the industry's desire for these early universities to create employees that would best suit the companies' needs. For example, Johnson, ARAMCO's English Curriculum Specialist, argued in 1971 that:

English is the language of oil technology and of the people who work in oil … I think we must say that the principal reason for English training is to enable the Saudi to get the technical training that is required by the oil industry and to be able to read the job manuals and other printed materials relevant to oil production.

(cited in Benesch 2002: 24)

In other words, English language training and EAP programmes at English language universities in the Middle East existed for the sole purpose of preparing Saudi Arabian engineers to work for American petroleum companies. These corporations hoped for more than proficiency in academic literacies and English language; they wanted programmes that would also assimilate students into their company's work culture and institutional practices.

It was not only ARAMCO that promoted this use of EAP. Strevens (1971, cited in Benesch 2002), a scholar in applied linguistics, presented a paper at that same Beirut conference, also arguing that EAP programmes and English medium universities exist for the sole purpose of preparing students for future employers – that is, the oil industry. Corporations were looking for a specific dehumanized product that could be easily controlled while working for their needs. These programmes therefore needed to dedicate their teaching towards the needs of their clients for the purposes of increasing what they termed the 'professionalization' of students (Benesch 2002: 29). The needs of these American corporations were clearly central to the discussion of EAP.

Johnson and Strevens' early endorsements of the EAP programmes at the 1971 conference in Beirut show how EAP fell into Bernstein's (2003) framework for a collection code curricula that reinforced inequitable power dynamics, as well as Brown et al.'s (2011) challenge to the notion that more education will lead to greater individual and national prosperity for developing economies. Instead EAP students at the participating universities would gain knowledge or competencies in job-specific skills, ensuring that their learning was not linked to more ambitious academic or intellectual endeavours. Graduating students would be narrowly educated and therefore unlikely to work outside their designated fields. This created a horde of graduates only trained in specific tasks to be repeated throughout their employment in the industry. Pedagogical synthesis across disciplinary fields to create a wider understanding was not encouraged as it was not viewed as necessary by the prospective employers. Today it is striking that even the proceedings from the conference, held at an accredited university, were so blatantly unconcerned by a consideration of academic standards. Participants were clearly more invested in collaborating with industry in the creation of future working zombies than in developing a programme of academic study that was invested in independent critical thinking.

From the beginning, EAP programmes were considered as vehicles for cultural, political, and economic influence. For the oil industry, the programmes were clearly conceived of as job specific, insisting on competency in English language as a way of ensuring that students/employees would integrate well in the capitalist corporations that were spreading their global reach. This is evident through the strong influence that ARAMCO had on the pivotal 1971 conference that was hugely influential for the newly developing field of EAP. This built on the foundations laid for EAP in the United Kingdom, where it was conceived of as a political and economic opportunity to cultivate a sleeper horde that would be indoctrinated to desire and promote British interests over competing international ideologies. The term 'academic' at the centre of the EAP acronym was clearly an empty rhetorical spin intended to grant legitimacy to the creation of a living dead programme.

Zombies continued: current practices in EAP

While EAP as a field may have been born of hegemonic and corporate self-interest, it has grown beyond that role. In Britain almost every major university has an EAP programme, including the University of Cambridge and University College London. BALEAP was officially founded in 1989 and has emerged as the second governing body for EAP, joining the British Council. Outside of the United Kingdom, Australia and the United States have also added EAP programmes to their education pathways for international students to gain entry to their desired university degree. While the EAP field may have originated as a way of producing job-ready bodies, it does not necessarily mean that it has remained a zombie factory. At first glance, it seems to have grown past its non-academic inception to occupy a key foundational role for universities and tertiary education.

However, zombie-training practices are still pervasive. Three recent studies have, in different ways, analysed the EAP reading and writing curricula (Moore and Morton 2005; Miller 2011; Vandermensbrugghe 2004). They have all found that critical thinking is missing, and that this is not only a key attribute that universities want their students to master, but that it is what keeps EAP from being truly 'academic'. Because of the increase in EAP's role as a gateway to universities, universities are then inundated by a horde of students who have not been inoculated against zombified learning practices and who threaten to infect their peers or even, in a doomsday scenario, to lower academic standards more generally. While there is already much discussion of the danger of universities professionalizing their degrees in response to market demand, and thereby diminishing the intellectual vigour of the disciplines, the three studies caution that EAP is particularly weak in promoting independent critical thought in its students.

Moore and Morton (2005) conducted research on writing expectations at British universities compared to the writing competencies students are assessed in at the end of their EAP programme of study. They found that British universities focused on testing students' ability to write coherent thoughts on specific content: to analyse, reflect and evaluate said content in order to show deep understanding of the subject. However, students exiting EAP programmes are trained to respond to generic assessment tasks, for instance where students are asked to write an essay in exam conditions on topics they have never studied. These tasks require only a general understanding of content and are assessed only for stylistic and linguistic competencies. In this way critical and independent thinking are not rewarded in formulaic assessment tasks: so formulaic in fact that the programmes encourage students to answer all essays in four to five paragraph formats. Needless to say, one can imagine the confusion ex-EAP students face trying to apply such a structure to research essays when they arrive at university. According to Moore and Morton (2005), EAP programmes fail to encourage thinking in writing. Instead, the writing components of the programme foster zombified student literacies, as they are encouraged to respond to empty, generic questions with empty, formulaic responses.

Miller (2011) found similar results when he compared reading in EAP programmes against the reading expected at universities in the United States. Students in EAP programmes focus on reading newspaper articles and other easily processed non-scholarly pieces, whereas university-level texts tend to be more clearly academic in nature. On the surface, this does not seem to be connected with the development of critical thinking capacities; however, academic texts do require quite a high order of cognitive processes in order to be successfully digested, evaluated and analysed. Miller found that students entering university from EAP programmes have problems critically engaging with the content of their readings and linking the ideas to previous texts. This was because (1) students are not assessed on their ability to critically engage with the texts, and (2) the EAP prescribed readings do not build on each other. EAP once again misses the opportunity to encourage critical thinking by its graduates.

Vandermensbrugghe's (2004) study more explicitly examines the issue of critical thinking. She found that students entering Australian universities from EAP programmes were lacking the critical thinking skills to successfully engage in their courses. She defines critical thinking in a similar way to this chapter's earlier consideration of Freire's notion of *conscientização,* or critical consciousness. She presents it as 'the ability to develop a capacity to reason logically and cohesively' as well as 'the ability to question and challenge existing knowledge and the social order' (419). She goes on to develop this definition based on theories of criticality as well as on explanations provided by the Australian university teachers she surveyed. This survey also identified the number one factor teachers described EAP students as lacking: critical thinking. They characterized these EAP graduates as poorly equipped to undertake their university studies, and particularly lacking in their ability to analyse or think through the content they were presented with. Effectively, the EAP programmes had produced a horde of unthinking students infected by their experience of zombified learning processes.

So, in three different contexts – the United Kingdom, the United States and Australia – critical thinking has been found to be a key deficit in graduates of EAP. The students are ill-equipped in the three interrelated areas of writing, reading and cognition, and it is clear that students have not been encouraged to think critically. Following on from its colonizing and corporatized roots, EAP continues to produce zombified students and risks creating a pandemic in higher education as international student numbers increase. To give a small glimpse of the pandemic, in the 2008/2009 academic year, the number of international students in the United States rose 3 per cent to 690,923, of which 54,803 were enrolled in an EAP programme (Institute of International Education 2010). For these 54,803 EAP students, the gateway programmes to their university of choice most likely failed to provide them with the skills necessary to survive academically, let alone inoculate them with the antivirus that would cure them of their zombie-like characteristics. EAP has the potential to deliver that antivirus – the ability to think critically – but so far has instead focused on its original imperative to process a horde of unthinking but job-ready bodies.

Critical EAP: future action for widespread antibody creation

Benesch (2002, 2009) is the first of the few scholars who directly consider critical theory in relation to the field of EAP. She adds a new twist to the argument that critical thinking needs to consider and question dominant power dynamics and capitalistic economics by pointing out that the teaching of content is particularly important for the EAP context. Currently, many EAP programmes insist on teaching general English, and do not focus on content from any specific academic field. While this creates the illusion of being inter- or cross-disciplinary, it leaves students without an opportunity to critically engage with any one subject. By focusing on specific academic content (and not job-specific content as suggested during the 1971 ARAMCO conference), students are able to question and critically engage with dominant ideas in and across particular fields of study, to apply and test a variety of perspectives, and potentially to experiment with theory and methodology while performing their assessment tasks and academic expectations.

Aside from Benesch's work, there are only six other teacher-research studies that consider what is becoming known as 'critical EAP' (Kiely 2004; Dantas-Whitney 2002; Wharton 2010; Park 2011; Granville and Dison 2005; Lo 2010). A small group of survivor/practitioners have felt the frustration of disconnecting language and thought while recognizing the implicit reinforcement of dominant cultural codes within the EAP field. Zombies are being created through a practice of thoughtless decontextualization derived from a historical attempt to control these students by future employers, while ex-colonial powers attempt to maintain influence overseas. Within EAP's zombified programmes, these practitioners have taken some control by introducing students to the possibility of critical thought with small, targeted tasks. However, these tasks are not enough to do more than crack open the door. To push students (and teachers) through that opening, EAP programmes would have to begin explicitly fostering criticality across their courses.

Once critical thinking has been added as a key learning outcome, the following must happen. First, argumentation must be explicitly taught. The theorization of critical thinking by Horkheimer (1937) and Habermas (1987) does not invalidate the ideas of McPeck (1981) and Ennis (1987, 1991), who insist that argumentation and evaluation of evidence are central to the ability to think critically. The types of essays promoted by current EAP courses focus on writing five-paragraph essays framed around simple binaries like pros/cons or compare/contrast and are in consequence heavily criticized by Moore and Morton (2005). Instead, critical EAP would insist that students develop coherent arguments where ideas from texts are synthesized and evaluated in support of a particular position. Thinking would now be activated; essays would no longer be formulaic screeds that regurgitate facts and description without critical evaluation.

Secondly, in order to inspire EAP into becoming a first line of defence against possible zombification, the questioning of dominant sociological, political and economic influences must be included. This means choosing to build a reading course that includes multiple perspectives on single issues. Students would read, digest and question texts as part of their process of perception, recognition and understandings of the complexity of cultural, economic and political realities. This would integrate the ideas of criticality as first informed by Freire (1970) and followed up by Kincheloe (2000, 2008), Brookfield (2010) and Benesch (2002). Criticality strengthens the antiviral process, allowing students to begin to see that dominant ideas are not necessarily 'natural' or the way the world will always work. Rather, they learn to question these notions as they see historical context as well as consider a range of possible future realities. Students would begin to develop the antibodies they need to survive future attacks.

Finally, to ensure a truly well developed and holistic implementation of criticality, self-reflection must be included. This would be the final inoculation to ensure the antibodies would stand a chance against continual attack by zombies. Lo (2010), Granville and Dison (2005), and Dantas-Whitney (2002) all attempt to do this in their own small-scale inclusions of critical thinking. Students would be asked to consider their own roles and responsibilities in the learning process as well as who they are as independent thinkers. To paraphrase Kincheloe (2008), dialogue with the learning self opens the door for these thinkers to become as important as that which is being thought. To be able to self-reflectively and critically consider oneself and to be conscious of why one thinks and behaves as one does is the antithesis of zombiedom.

In conclusion, the contextual history of EAP, as well as many of its current teaching and learning practices, reveal a field worryingly invested in the encouragement of zombification in young adults aspiring to progress to university study. However, a few EAP teachers have realized that critical thinking offers some hope of helping students to develop immunity against perceived zombification and have explored ways to activate it in their classrooms. These implementations may be small and task-based, but have shown the potential success of criticality to combat the current programme of stultification that promises the stimulus of intellectual activity but simply reinforces lifeless pedagogies. To ensure the relevance of EAP for the future, more animated student cohorts, critical thinking needs to be integrated inside subjects and across the EAP curricula. Then, and only then, will the antibodies against zombification be successfully developed in students before they enter the wider academy.

Acknowledgement

I would like to thank Dr. Ariane Smart for her support in critically reading this chapter. While we agree on the role of critical thinking in higher education, her constant questioning of that role ensured that my own arguments do not fall into the brainless moaning of the zombie hordes.

Zombies in the classroom: education as consumption in two novels by Joyce Carol Oates

Sherry R. Truffin

George Romero's *Dawn of the Dead* (1978) features a 'Gothic mall' (Bishop 2010a: 144) in which survivors of a zombie apocalypse seek shelter, indulge in 'a fantasy of gluttony', and merge 'life with shopping' (146). The living dead, for their part, gravitate to the mall by force of habit or residual memory and in search of living food. The parallel is clear: humans and zombies alike go to the mall to consume. Following Romero's lead, Edgar Wright's satirical *Shaun of the Dead* (2004) suggests that if a zombie contagion were to wreak havoc on a modern urban population, the walking dead might be indistinguishable from most commuters, office workers or cell phone users. Since 9/11, there has been a renaissance in zombie cinema (Bishop 2010a: 11), and enterprising filmmakers wishing to capitalize on the trend might be looking for new spaces in which to explore the theme that humans are already zombies. If so, they would do well to consider a Gothic schoolhouse setting.

Nightmarish schools and menacing teachers already make frequent appearances in literature and film that is Gothic in mood, plot or theme. To review the history of the Gothic as a 'Counter-Enlightenment' discourse (Davenport-Hines 1998: 12) is to see the suitability, if not the inevitability, of the Gothic treatment of education and educators. Schools and schoolteachers are keepers and transmitters of enlightenment, entrusted to transform childish naïveté into confident rationality, replace infantile illusions with hard facts, and initiate students into a life-long quest for knowledge. At the same time, schools and teachers are figures of power. They decide when children work, when they play, when they take trips to the lavatory, and whether they are prodigies or problems. As a result, they can appear to wield an inexhaustible and inscrutable authority. The conflicted mix of promise and terror associated with schools and teachers makes them appropriate subjects for the Gothic, a genre or mode that registers an ambivalence towards post-Enlightenment rationalizations of cultural authority and power similar to what we see in contemporary cultural representations of schools and teachers.

Previously, I have gathered such representations under the designation 'Schoolhouse Gothic' and included under this rubric not only fictional works by writers such as Flannery O'Connor, Toni Morrison, David Mamet, Stephen King and Joyce Carol Oates, but also academic and pedagogical discourse by figures such as Michel Foucault and, it could be added, Henry Giroux (Truffin 2008). Fiction of the Schoolhouse Gothic takes place in a wide variety of settings (primary schools, high schools, universities, and even non-academic settings that are controlled by teachers or academics), but it is united in

*what is a ¿ ?
trope*

portraying Western education, its guardians and its subjects using explicitly Gothic tropes such as the curse, the trap and the monster. The nonfiction variety of Schoolhouse Gothic characterizes the academy using themes suggested by such tropes: the tyranny of history, the terrors of physical or mental confinement, reification and miscreation. In the Schoolhouse Gothic, the academy is haunted or cursed by persistent power inequities (of race, gender, class and age) and, ironically, by the Enlightenment itself, which was to save us from the darkness of the past but which had a dark side of its own. Traps take the form of school buildings, college campuses, classrooms and faculty offices, which are Enlightenment spaces analogous to the claustrophobic family mansions, monasteries and convents of old. According to Chris Baldick, when curse meets trap, the result is paranoia and 'an impression of sickening descent into disintegration' (1992: xix). To these products can be added violence and new, monstrous creation. In the Schoolhouse Gothic, a haunted, incarcerating academy transforms students into zombies, psychopaths and machines. The pervasiveness of the Schoolhouse Gothic implies that our educational institutions are sites of significant cultural anxiety, and the zombie subset of the Schoolhouse Gothic suggests more specifically that schools are places in which teachers and students alike consume and are consumed.

Although Joyce Carol Oates has produced a large and diverse body of work, she is best known for provocative, violent works that examine American culture through the prism of the family (Wesley 1993), appropriate and revise a masculine literary tradition (Daly: 1996), and dramatize the divisions of the self, particularly the female self (Creighton 1992; Daly 1996). She has been described as 'deeply, if somewhat ironically, subscribed to the traditions of American romanticism' and, as the editor of Plume's *American Gothic Tales* (1996), is no stranger to Romanticism's dark sister. Further, Oates has returned throughout her career to the school as a source or scene of alienation, abuse and violence; 'In the region of ice' (1967), for example, is loosely based on her experiences teaching a troubled young Jewish student who eventually planned and executed a public murder/suicide at a synagogue (she revisited this subject in 'Last days', 1985). *Foxfire: Confessions of a Girl Gang* (1993) features a group of high school students who, among other things, conspire to publicly humiliate a high school math teacher who degrades one gang member in class and gropes her breasts in detention. In *Zombie* (1995) and *Beasts* (2002), Oates develops and enhances the Schoolhouse Gothic by comparing schooling to zombification and using consumption as a metaphor for the effects of formal education. Both novels feature hallmarks of the Gothic such as haunted, paranoid protagonists, claustrophobic spaces and monstrous behaviour. These works portray the academy as a cursed, suffocating place in which various forms of mystified authority make monsters both of those who wield its power and those who are subjected to that power. Considered together, they use the trope of the zombie to suggest that schooling does not enlighten young minds and develop their capacity for higher thought but rather enslaves and consumes them, transforming them into mindless servants, amoral shells or savage cannibals. Education becomes a form of consumption in which the line between consumer and consumed disappears.

Both *Zombie* and *Beasts* liken students to the zombies of Caribbean folklore and of 1930s and 1940s cinema, zombies created and controlled by voodoo priests or, in this case, professors. According to Kyle William Bishop (2010a: 12), the zombie is 'a fundamentally *American* creation' (author's emphasis), the 'only canonical movie monster to originate in the New World' (31), and a 'creature born of slavery and hegemony' (37). The American movie zombie originates not in European folklore or literature, as do most monsters of the Gothic, but rather in the complex colonial history of the Americas, especially the Caribbean, as translated into film. The zombie has a 'complicated genealogy' (39): it is a figure from Haitian folklore co-opted into narrative by western observers. The word *zombie*, according to ethnographers Ackermann and Gauthier (1991: 468), is related to African terms for 'corpse' or 'body without a soul' and the zombie is a creature 'deprived of will, memory, and consciousness' (474), as well as speech, by a voodoo priest or sorcerer. The zombie is a slave, a silent worker whose humanity has been consumed and whose existence is a living death. Before George Romero's 1968 movie *Night of the Living Dead* transformed the zombie into the mutilated, decaying, lumbering cannibal so familiar to moviegoers, the source of fear was not the zombie itself, but rather the one who could create a zombie (Bishop 2010a: 53).

The portrayal of teacher as zombie-maker and puppeteer animates Schoolhouse Gothic, especially in Oates's *Zombie* and *Beasts*. The former novel is told from the point of view of the zombie-maker, and the latter from the perspective of the zombie/student who eventually destroys her master/professor. *Zombie* takes place in the mid-1990s and is inspired by the life of Jeffrey Dahmer in general and by Lionel Dahmer's *A Father's Story* (1995) in particular, the latter being a memoir that Oates reviewed favourably. The narrative alternates between first- and third-person perspectives in a style that is busy, loud and juvenile, full of sentence fragments, parenthetical asides, capital letters, dashes and italics, as well as sketches and illustrations. It is divided into two sections: 'Suspended Sentence' describes protagonist Quentin P's family, his past crimes and his life on probation, and 'How Things Play Out' describes, with an exuberance that is jarringly dissonant, the stalking, abduction and murder of a would-be zombie that Quentin names 'Squirrel'. The similarities between Quentin and Dahmer are myriad – the development of alcoholism at a young age, an ability to seem invisible or to project harmlessness, and so on – but among the most significant is the way that Quentin has failed to distinguish himself academically and lives in the shadow of a well-educated, successful father. Jeffrey Dahmer's father held a Ph.D. in analytical chemistry and worked as a chemist with PPG Industries (Davis 1995: 20), while Quentin's father holds dual Ph.D., and dual teaching appointments in physics and philosophy at his university (*Zombie* 1995: 33). When Oates reimagines Dahmer and his crimes in fiction, she makes academia central to the story, more central than it appears to have been in Dahmer's life. Her character Quentin associates school with humiliation, surveillance, judgment and control. It continues to exert a powerful fascination for him well beyond high school graduation, and ultimately becomes the source of his darkest fantasies.

School is omnipresent, and mostly threatening, in Quentin's life. He is a careless, indifferent student at the technical college that his father, who holds a professorial position at a nearby university, regards patronizingly but nevertheless wants him to attend. Quentin serves as caretaker of an apartment that houses university students, and he easily poses as a graduate student himself when he wants formaldehyde (73). His sister is a junior high school principal (135) whose interest in him surges after his molestation arrest; as Quentin sees it, 'having a *sex offender* for a kid brother is a challenge to her, and she is not one to back off from challenges. Like I am one of her problem students' (177, author's emphasis here and following). He gives letter grades to his experiments: 'my first three ZOMBIES—all F's' (56). While stalking a young victim who attends his former high school, Quentin remembers how much he 'hated' the school and how he 'wished' it had 'burnt to the ground. With everybody in it' (106). His therapist is his father's university colleague, and his questions remind Quentin of being 'blank and silent blushing like in school when I could not answer a teacher's question nor even (everyone staring at me) comprehend it' (54). Most of his remarks about school are about being watched, bringing to mind Foucault's description of schools as sites of modern disciplinary control enacted through surveillance strategies and enforced by the figure of the 'teacher-judge' (Foucault 1977: 304). Quentin's father is his model for all teachers, but he is an 'impatient' man, 'always finding fault', as though 'his only son was a student failing a course of his' (74). As an adult, Quentin's compulsive avoidance of his father's judgmental gaze becomes an axiom for life: he continually reminds himself to avoid 'EYE CONTACT' (8, 11, 45, etc.) with anyone for fear that someone will 'slide down into [his] soul' (8). To be looked at is, for Quentin, to be evaluated and found wanting: it is a profound threat to his personhood.

Quentin fears the professorial gaze, but, sensing its power, goes to a large lecture hall at his father's university and attends a class that marks the start of his quest to create a zombie that will be his slave and toy. Quentin does not seem sure of his motives for attending the lecture, but he takes steps to ensure that his lecturer-father does not see (i.e., judge) him. He listens to his father speak about cosmic rays, black holes, '*quantifiable and unquantifiable material*', and mysterious, undetectable parts of the universe disobedient to known physical laws (27). The lesson that he takes from the lecture is the insignificance of human life: 'seeing the Universe like that … you see how fucking futile it is to believe that any galaxy matters let alone … any individual' (29). In the moment, however, Quentin watches students furiously taking notes and decides that 'almost any one of them would be a suitable specimen for a zombie' (27–28). Unlike Quentin, who is thinking about the implications of an unknowable galaxy in which even the laws of physics cannot be taken for granted and finding in his father's words justification for embracing the monster within, the students are mindlessly consuming instruction and information, apparently with no motive beyond pleasing their professor when exam time comes and earning a letter grade that may or may not reflect understanding or engagement. In this, the most important episode in young Quentin's life, teaching is dehumanizing in both form and content. The student is represented as a zombie bowing before its master and devouring facts like meals, and the lesson is that moral laws are meaningless and that humanity is inconsequential. The predatory nature of the academic is further underscored when it comes to light that

Quentin's father's mentor, a famous physicist, had experimented on mentally handicapped children by feeding them radioactive milk (172). The lecture delivered by the father parallels the experiment performed by his own academic father figure: the latter feeds toxic milk to children, while the former feeds psychologically toxic lessons to students. Both children and students are consumed in their acts of consumption.

Beasts portrays education in much the same way as *Zombie* but switches the point of view from victimizer to victim, saying more about the process of academic zombification by which a student is rendered incapable of reason, judgment or discrimination. It also dramatizes the return of the repressed as the slave rebels and the consumed becomes the avenging consumer. The novella opens and closes in 2001, but the bulk recounts four tumultuous months in the mid-1970s, when Gillian, the protagonist, was a student at a women's college in New England. Early on, Gillian learns that her parents are divorcing and reveals her infatuation with a Creative Writing professor named Andre Harrow, a 'verbose, bullying' (36) countercultural figure whose name suggests plunder and pillage. Harrow rhapsodizes about the writings of D.H. Lawrence and the Beats, is rumoured to have been arrested in a Vietnam War protest, and behaves in class like 'the father who withholds his love, with devastating results' (68). Gillian is also fascinated by Harrow's exotic artist-wife Dorcas, who has recently displayed on campus disturbing, controversial sculptures inspired by 'primitive' fertility carvings. As the months proceed, Harrow makes a sexual advance towards Gillian, who pushes him away in confusion. He then claims to have been 'joking', thus supplying 'the narration, the interpretation, for what had happened, as, in his lectures and workshops, he controlled such information' (62). In retaliation, however, Harrow begins to bully and belittle her in class while encouraging her classmates to do the same. Ultimately, Harrow seduces Gillian and draws her into a sexual relationship with himself and his wife. During this time an arsonist begins to victimize the campus, and the suspects include Gillian's poetry workshop classmates and dorm mates, who are also, it is suggested, fellow victims of the professor and his wife.

Oates presents Harrow's teaching as demeaning, exploitative and manipulative, calculated to make students desperate for his approval and keep them emotionally, intellectually and ethically off-balance. After Gillian fails to respond to his 'biting kiss' (62), Harrow stops complimenting her poetry in class and starts patronizing it, prompting other students to join in on the attack. In addition to demeaning Gillian individually, he bullies and insults the class as a whole with voyeuristic assignments and misogynist remarks. He scorns and rejects what he calls 'nice-girl bullshit' (67), instructs the students to write journals in which they scrutinize their 'emotional, physical, sexual lives' as if they were 'anatomical specimens' (68), and teaches them not to violate the 'one cardinal rule' of his class, which is that he not be 'bored shitless' (59). He demands revealing, confessional journals with 'a focus upon childhood, traumatic and demeaning memories' and advises against 'self-censorship', which he refers to as 'self-castration' (68). When Dominique jokingly asks if women can be castrated, he responds, 'Dear girl, women *are* castrated. You must struggle to reverse your pitiable condition,' and Gillian recalls that while the students laughed, Harrow 'wasn't smiling' (68). Harrow teaches them to scorn conventional morality and speaks approvingly of the ancients, whose 'gods were passions, obsessions, appetites' that 'terrified' them (41). The theme that Gillian derives from her study of Ovid is that 'human happiness [is] possible only through metamorphosing into the subhuman', and Harrow appears to concur with what he calls 'Ovid's judgment on the "human"' (41). He also praises D.H. Lawrence, who, according to Harrow, prized 'sensual, sexual, physical love' but detested '"dutiful" love—for parents, family, country, God' (30) because in it he 'saw the "rotted edifice" of bourgeois/capitalist morality' (51). Such statements frighten and excite his students, and Gillian later reflects that 'we, Mr. Harrow's students, had no way of refuting such logic' (51) and reports that 'we believed, or wished to believe, it was true' (51) because 'it was believed that Andre Harrow knew "everything"' (36). Andre Harrow plainly abuses his power in order to strip his students of their defences and render them vulnerable to his advances. At one point, a student says in class, 'if I'm a puppet, I intend to choose who will be my master. *From now on* ... ' (72). As her classmate speaks, Gillian senses her yearning to look at Harrow. The dazzled, needy young women feed Harrow's ego, cater to his sexual desires, and even clean his house.

Harrow's abusive teaching is explicitly compared to 'soul murder' (108). Towards the end of the novel, Gillian and her dorm mate Penelope have a conversation about evil. Gillian takes a morally relativistic position because Harrow would have been 'furious' with her if she did not deride conventional, bourgeois values (107). Penelope suggests that Gillian's relativism is overly facile, and Gillian assumes that her friend is being contrary out of jealousy. Penelope claims, 'there's such a thing as soul murder, ... except you can't see it, the way you see the other' (108). She goes on: 'there are evil people. Cruel people. People who should be punished. If there was anyone to punish them' (108). Within the context of the tale, her remarks only make sense in reference to Harrow and his wife.

'Soul murder' is a psychiatric term defined by Leonard L. Shengold in 1979, and refers to a type of abuse whose effects closely resemble zombification. Shengold picked up the term from Daniel Paul Schreber's nineteenth-century *Memoirs* (1903), themselves the subject of one of Freud's case histories (1911, cited in Shengold 1979). Shengold uses the term to describe a specific set of 'traumatic experiences'; namely, 'instances of repetitive and chronic overstimulation alternating with emotional deprivation ... deliberately brought about by another individual', normally a parent or substitute parent (1979: 534). He argues that alternating periods of abuse and neglect distort 'the primal fantasies that motivate human behaviour' (534) and have a devastating impact on the emotional and intellectual development of the victim, ultimately robbing that victim of an authentic sense of identity. According to Shengold, this kind of abuse ravages the victim's 'individuality, his dignity, his capacity to feel deeply (to feel joy, love, or even hate)' and smothers 'his capacity to think rationally and to test reality' (536). He describes a male patient whose parents, in an effort to toughen him up, had deprived him of warmth and ensured that others did the same. These same parents would 'cultivate the rivalry' between the patient and his siblings (548); they would fight viciously; their fights would often 'end in turbulent and exhibitionist sex' near their 'terrified children'; and they would 'sometimes disappear for weeks' (547). Many such victims become, as Shengold puts it, 'destructive and self-destructive' robots (556). Their humanity is, in short, consumed.

Andre Harrow and his wife can be aptly described as soul murderers, and the negative effects of soul murder are apparent in Gillian and her classmates. The Harrows may not be performing makeshift lobotomies like Quentin P., but they are making zombies out of students nonetheless. The professor and his wife represent substitute parents for Gillian, replacements for biological parents who are cold and negligent. When Gillian visits the Harrows' home, she is plied with drugs and overly rich food, overwhelmed with noise (from the stereo and/or the pet parrot), and sexually exploited. During the visit that leads to the Harrows' deaths, Gillian is sickened by the food Dorcas cooks, and she vomits. Disgusted, Dorcas slaps Gillian's face and pushes her out of the room. The couple proceeds to have sex upstairs, and while she listens to their noises, she thinks, 'they want me to hear, I'm their witness' (129). Sometimes the Harrows withhold their attention or their presence altogether, leaving Gillian to feel neglected and abandoned, as is the case with a 'misunderstanding' (109) about whether or not Gillian would accompany them on a holiday trip to Paris. Such neglect seems intentionally calculated to increase the pliability and vulnerability of the Harrows' victims. When Gillian is able to 'bask' in the glow of attention and approval, she feels 'like a dog that has been kicked but is now being petted, and is grateful' (97). At school, Harrow compounds the emotional torment of his victims by actively cultivating the rivalry for his attentions and approval among Gillian and her classmates, effectively isolating them from one another. This mistreatment takes its toll on Gillian by disrupting her emotional and intellectual development, leaving her 'head filled with static' (129), rendering all classes but Harrow's an undifferentiated 'blur', and causing her to look, act and feel like a 'sleepwalker' (50), a 'doll' (97), a 'puppet' (72) and, of course, a 'zombie' (56).

Abuse and zombification consume Gillian and her classmates, rendering them anonymous and indistinguishable, even to themselves, as is evidenced by Gillian's slippage between first-person singular and first-person plural in her narrative: 'I had no choice' (10), 'we were dazed' (6), 'we felt the sting of his lash' (58). Her facelessness is not, however, simply a matter of her own distorted perception. When Gillian follows Dorcas to the post office at the beginning of the story, Dorcas notices her and demands, 'which of them are *you*?' (20), and her words echo in Gillian's head thereafter, as if to haunt her with fears of her own insignificance. After Gillian and Penelope's conversation about soul murder, Penelope's parents arrive to pick her up for the holiday, and they mistake Gillian for another student and call her 'Sybil' (108). When Gillian investigates a file cabinet of pornographic pictures at the home of her professor, she cannot confidently identify a single classmate, but many of the photos remind her of her peers and of herself. She thinks to herself, 'They'd been drugged, like me. They'd been in love, like me. They would keep these secrets forever. Like me. We are beasts and this is our consolation' (119). Clearly, she has learned the lesson that Andre and Dorcas worked so diligently to teach her. When she was first invited to the Harrows' home, she felt that she was 'blessed' and unique because the couple loved her (92). After she comes upon the pictures, she knows better. She, like the totem to which Dorcas eventually affixes Gillian's severed braid, is only 'minimally human' (1), stripped of anything that distinguishes her as an individual.

Teaching in *Beasts* is enslavement and it is also, of course, consumption. Harrow calls D.H. Lawrence 'the great prophet of the twentieth century', whose 'god was the god of immediate physical sensation, a god to devastate all other gods' (51), and so it is no surprise that Harrow, who relishes the teaching of ancient mythology in which appetites are gods, does not hesitate to satisfy his own cravings. Right before Harrow kisses Gillian the first time, he smiles at her, 'baring his teeth' and leaving her 'shivering as if he'd drawn those teeth over [her]' (57). There is more than a little of the cannibal in this professor, and he and his wife eventually consume his students by helping to create the conditions that result in their anorexia. Throughout the novel, Gillian and her classmates lose alarming amounts of weight and appear increasingly skeletal, as though the process of being emotionally and intellectually consumed is manifesting itself physically.

Much of the literature on anorexia suggests that it represents an attempt by young women who feel powerless to exert some kind of control over their lives and their bodies (Calam and Slade 1994: 102). The need to feel powerful is particularly acute for those who have experienced sexual abuse, especially at the hands of an authority figure or at times 'of other major problems and upheavals in their lives' (Calam and Slade 102–5), such as Gillian's parents' divorce. At least one of Gillian's many doubles also fits the profile of the anorexic; her classmate Marisa is 'painfully thin' (73), perhaps even 'starving herself to death' (20), and she confesses in workshop to having been sexually abused first by a cousin, then by a family friend, and finally by a 'much-beloved grade school teacher' (73). Eventually, Marisa attempts suicide, confesses to setting the fires on campus, recants her confession, and is hospitalized. When Gillian confesses that she cannot 'live without' Harrow, he responds, 'we don't want you to live without us either' (128). Harrow does more than simply use and abuse his students: he devours them – mind, soul and body.

Anorexia has been further linked to 'soul murder', or the reduction of the human to a zombie-like state. Louise Kaplan's *Female Perversions* describes anorexia as 'the outcome of one of those little soul murders of childhood in which, to survive, a child gives up aspects of the self she might have become and instead becomes a mirroring extension of the "all-powerful" parent' (1991: 455). *Female Perversions* challenges the psychoanalytic tradition represented by Freud, Karl Abraham and others that regards perversions as 'pathologies of sexuality' that primarily afflict men; in contrast, Kaplan defines perversions as 'pathologies of gender role identity' that can be found in both men and women (14). She argues that identity formation in both men and women is hindered by 'infantile ideals of sexual prowess demanded of men and sexual innocence demanded of women', and that perversions develop when such 'infantile ideals' are reinforced rather than challenged by 'soul-crippling social gender stereotypes' (16) that 'assign certain narrowly defined characteristics to one sex, and equally narrow but opposite characteristics to the other sex' (15). According to Kaplan, male perversions such as fetishism and masochism both reveal and disguise a man's hatred for his own shameful feminine traits or longings (18). A similar strategy is at work in female perversions, which, according to Kaplan, have been neglected by psychoanalysts both because of the male-normative history of the field but also because the perverse strategies of women are not always explicitly sexual. For Kaplan, various forms of self-mutilation, including anorexia, represent not only a young woman's bid for control but also her attempt at 'forestalling final gender identity and denying that the illusions and hopes and dreams that made life endurable are lost forever' (364). As such, they lend 'expression to forbidden or shameful' masculine desires (367). Anorexia allows the young woman to present 'herself to the world as a sexless child in a caricature of saint-like femininity' that hides 'a most defiant, ambitious, driven, dominating, controlling, virile caricature of masculinity' (457). Anorexia is, in short, an unconscious, compulsive refusal of female identity and sexuality as culturally prescribed.

Kaplan's view of anorexia, the consumption of the physical and sexual self, is clearly evident in *Beasts*. Harrow observes that Gillian 'must weigh eighty-nine pounds', and he refers to her as a 'little girl' immediately before making his first sexual advance (60). In other words, she is far from womanly, and his desire for her has a paedophilic component. Gillian remembers her mother's disappointment at her refusal in high school to try 'to be pretty like the other girls', and she wonders if she 'might have smiled more' and used more lipstick (47); clearly, she has neither embraced feminine stereotypes nor pursued adult sexuality. Nevertheless, remembering Dorcas' adolescent totem with her braid on it causes her to muse on the 'delusion of young-female power', the belief that 'in your beautiful new body, you will be treated with love' (126). Power is linked in her mind not to self-efficacy but rather to attractiveness to and love from others. In some ways, however, despite her frailty and passivity, she imagines herself throughout the novel as quite powerful and aggressive, like a 'hunting dog picking up a scent' while following Dorcas (12), for example. Given her experiences, it is not surprising that Gillian's ambivalence towards her gender, her sexuality and her sense of self is profound. Her anorexia is a sign of that ambivalence.

Gillian's sexual ambivalence is part of her distorted and monstrous self-image, but her monstrosity is an important part of the narrative in its own right. Thus far, the horror of the zombie-makers Quentin and Harrow has been considered, but not the horror of the zombie itself. In *Zombie*, the would-be zombies are pure victims, in part because Quentin is unsuccessful at lobotomizing the young men and ends up murdering them instead. Quentin is the only monster. In *Beasts*, however, the zombies, while victims, are also sources of terror. Harrow robs Gillian and her classmates of the ability to think rationally, which makes them behave throughout the novel either mechanically, 'by instinct' (131), or 'as a child might' (130). Though her mental faculties have been destroyed, she has not, however, lost the 'indomitable will of all life to survive' (125) that she attributes to (or projects onto) the snow-covered evergreens that surround the Harrows' isolated house. Those survival instincts find expression in her murderous act of setting fire to the Harrows' home while the owners enjoy their drunken, post-coital slumber, and it would appear that by the end of the novel, Gillian, like Ovid's Philomela, to whom Harrow has cruelly compared her, refuses to be a 'passive victim' and instead 'takes bloody revenge on her rapist' (46). Of course, Gillian's motives for setting the fire do not seem particularly clear, even to Gillian: if she is out for revenge, then it might be revenge for the abuse and exploitation she suffered at the hands of the Harrows, but then again, it might be revenge for their exclusion of her from the primal scene or for Andre's refusal to leave his wife for her. From the beginning of *Beasts*, there are many suggestions that Gillian is not simply a victim of monstrous abusers but may be something of a monster herself. Throughout the novel she regards herself, perhaps defensively, as having a degree of control that seems ludicrous, considering the power dynamics involved. In any case, she appears to have internalized the amorality that her professor tried to inculcate in her and her classmates, and she feels no remorse about their deaths. Harrow appears to have consumed Gillian's ethical sensibilities along with her intellectual capacities, her sexual identity and her physical body. She says that her story is 'not a confession' because she has 'nothing to confess' (3). She may believe that she had no choice, no other avenue of escape, but then again, she may have come to regard guilt the way that Quentin and Harrow do: as 'superstitious and retro' (*Zombie* 93). Either way, it is safe to say that if zombies represent enslavement, then the possibility of a slave uprising is always around the corner. The consumers are always in danger of being violently consumed.

Zombie and *Beasts* clearly portray formal education as the consumption or zombification of the student. Less fully developed but worth briefly noting are their further suggestions that students are consumed in another sense, which is to say, commodified. Quentin consoles himself for his failure to create a proper student-zombie by taking 'mementos' (85) or 'good-luck charms' (84) from his victims, often items of clothing and sometimes body parts that can be transformed into accessories. He describes these items in detail (including, in some cases, their brand names) and wears them to blend in with other students at his college. In addition, he compulsively fondles them to trigger the sexual excitement he felt in subjugating their former owners. Quentin's dehumanization of his victims, in short, literalizes Marx's concept of 'commodity fetishism' (1959: 71–83). In *Beasts*, the students have been reduced to pornographic images for sale and resale. When Gillian rifles through the Harrows' mysterious file cabinets and locates a cache of pornographic pictures, she inspects the files in a horrified daze, wondering 'would [her] photo turn up in a porn magazine; had that been their intention all along ...?' (114–15). She examines the magazines and guesses that the Harrows have been exploiting young women for at least a decade (114), and when she looks at the pictures, she feels 'as if someone had struck [her] a numbing blow between the shoulder blades' (113). She recognizes that a part of her has been sold, and she is overcome with a desire to destroy the proof of her 'degradation' (115). Like the young women around and before her, Gillian may also have been reduced to a pornographic image endlessly produced, reproduced and circulated. Harrow has exploited both the use and the exchange value of his students. He has consumed them on every level, and he has profited from ensuring that they will continue to be consumed. For her part, Gillian has been schooled in a great many ways, and while the economic dynamics of the education she has received at Harrow's hands have not been the focus of her story, neither have they been completely erased from it.

Critics of the Gothic tend to speak of it in therapeutic terms: both David Punter and Maggie Kilgour, for instance, call the Gothic a form of 'cultural self-analysis' (Punter 1996: 205; Kilgour 1998: 50), and Punter sees the curative powers of the Gothic in its provision of an 'image-language in which to examine … social fears' (117). Some of the most familiar components of this 'image language' are tropes under consideration here: curses, traps and monsters. A curse is a reminder that we are never as free from history as we might think or wish. A trap suggests limitations on our movement, physical and psychic. Monsters manifest evils of all kinds, internal and external. These and other Gothic tropes literalize our fears, forcing us to regard them in their most extreme, grotesque forms. They are psychological caricatures, which is to say, exaggerated portraits from whose broad lines something of the 'real' might nevertheless be inferred. The zombie embodies our fear of enslavement to others, to our own animalistic instincts, or to our daily routines. It represents our fear of being consumed or of consuming others. When the zombie appears in the Schoolhouse Gothic, it manifests a range of cultural anxieties about such things as the role of public education in a modern, pluralistic, secular America and the degree to which the academy both preserves culture and serves a progressive agenda. It raises questions about the nature and meaning of learning and the role of power in the classroom. Most educators will say that far from consuming students, university appears not to interest them in the least, that students should be *more* consumed, more absorbed, more engaged in study. One explanation for the zombie-like appearance and behaviour of so many students is overstimulation from technology, but there are many others, including the impact of the consumer model of higher education, as Richard Arum and Josipa Roksa have recently argued in *Academically Adrift: Limited Learning on College Campuses* (2010). The zombie subset of the Schoolhouse Gothic challenges us to think about education as consumption, an examination that can happen on a local and personal as well as a global level. Many educators want to see their students consumed by study, absorbed by the subject at hand, able to internalize and recreate a body of knowledge. Joyce Carol Oates challenges us to see the fear that lurks behind that ideal and serves as its dark Other: the fear that what educators really want is to feed their egos with their students. Teachers confronting zombified students should consider how they have contributed to their state, or worse, whether they secretly want to keep them that way.

Queer pedagogies in zombie times: parody, neo-liberalism and higher education

Daniel Marshall

Introduction: beware the gay zombies!

Hey Aaron, err, have you noticed, like, an increased amount of homosexuality in the neighbourhood?' So opens the FND Films' sketch, *Gay Zombie* (2008). 'Yeah, I have. You don't think it's contagious do you?' Cue awkward mock laughter. Inevitably, this stagey performance of 'of course not!' immediately gives way to proof otherwise as the dialogue is interrupted by a newsflash:

> *Newsreader:* It appears the dead have risen and are walking among us. These zombies have a certain sexual preference by attacking only men ... officials at the Pentagon are not sure if this is a biological attack or if the zombies are simply doing this by choice. </ext>

Cut to scenes where the sketch's plucky heroes arm themselves with tools from the suburban garden shed and flee the encroaching gay zombie menace: 'He's trying to style my hair' screams one victim as he tries to evade one gay zombie armed with hairdryer and scissors. Another zombie closes in on the camera, with outstretched arms laden with Abercrombie and Fitch bags and the like. One of our heroes gets a hickey from a prancing zombie; anxious, his friend asks:

> Say something manly.
> Um…those shoes are nice?

They both look concerned.

> Those shoes, they complement your outfit?
> You have a lisp dude!
> Oh my God! Oh my God!

Our hero panics in increasingly fey tones as he transmogrifies into the sketch's namesake. Grunting through the transformation, his arrival as gay zombie is made complete by an outstretching of his arms and the limp curling of his hands: 'Your wrist! Your wrist!' cries his friend. And as the groans of transformation give way to a predatory, cruising posture, the newest gay zombie advances towards his friend who duly smashes him with the spade he happens to be holding.

The *Gay Zombie* sketch is a useful place for me to start because it provides a pithy portrait of this chapter's main concern: exploring the conjunction between ideas about male homosexuality, zombification and pedagogy in the contemporary popular imaginary. Providing a potted summary of the sketch's action as I have done here is to understand the sketch in strictly pedagogical terms: the way it sends up popular anxieties about homosexuality is instructive insofar as it subjects those anxieties to ridicule. This chapter's reflections on queer pedagogies starts with the good humour of this parodic moment: staging the contagious, fatal, emasculating and consumerist nature of male homosexuality to lay bare the staged production of the 'natural' itself.

The critical perspective that I mobilize throughout this chapter is situated from the outset in this moment of laughter. As a trope, the zombie embodies a meditation on the fragility of life. The parodic humour of *Gay Zombie* brings into relief the fictional nature of the truths about homosexuality and, for my purposes here, emerges as a pedagogical project similarly invested with a sense of the fragile nature of life, a sense that I reflect upon later through engaging Jasbir Puar's work. As we laugh at the true 'nature' of homosexuality we release ourselves from the authority of these accounts. Unmooring our understandings of the relationship between life and sexuality from codified expressions of homophobia acknowledges both their damage and the limit of their range. This chapter will seek to explore the usefulness of this parodic take on queer pedagogy in the context of an otherwise grim and straight-faced world made sober (if not somber) by the hard 'realities' of economic rationalism and crisis and the earnest identitarian politics of recognition.

Drawing on contemporary queer theories of subjectivity, spatiality, temporality and parody this chapter will theorize ways in which the zombie trope can be used to consider conditions for contemporary queer pedagogy in Australian universities. More precisely, this chapter will offer a 'fresh' take on contemporary critiques of audit cultures and managerialist universities by articulating queer critiques of metrics and normative academic work afforded by an analytical focus on queer pedagogies. In the final section of this chapter, I will draw on queer theories of the parodic and passing to consider how the queer/zombie/pedagogy conjunction might provide something other than a negative critique, but, rather, a theoretical account of working through/against these zombie times.

Elaborating a parodic take on the question of 'living dead pedagogies', this chapter takes up queer pedagogies as an exemplary site for thinking through multiple iterations of this 'living death'. The chapter will consider queer pedagogy as 'undead' in multiple ways: it is the 'undead' of the zombie model of moral panic and contagion, endlessly on the prowl for 'fresh meat' to have its way with and recruit; it is the 'undead' of a homophobic haunting, structured by those pedagogues and pupils cut down by AIDS and phobic historical campaigns against queer instruction; it is the 'undead' of the ritual compliant behaviours that academics participate in which have come to symbolize the zombification of higher education; and, as I shall show in my concluding section, it is the 'undead' of the parodic potential of such compliance – 'undead' as liminally 'living dead', as playing on or performing compliant behaviours to enable life not through death, in that Catholic sense, but to enable life as co-existent with death. We might call to mind Sondheim's 'little deaths', perhaps, with its invocation of *la petite mort*. This camp reference and the interpretive association it allows serves the thrust of my argument handsomely, locating as it does the ebb and flow of life, including the management of life in the academy, within an explicitly sexual schematic.

Fresh meat: the queer hunger for critiquing the turn in higher education

Queer pedagogy is an especially illuminating prism through which we can reflect on the deadening turn towards corporatization and bureaucratization in higher education. Here I want to consider two of the ways in which queer pedagogy is especially illuminating: the first is its exposure of the disciplinary nature of the credentials 'market' and students as 'consumers' and the second is its exposure of the conservatizing nature of bureaucratic modes of work.

First, the marketability of queer pedagogies is a shifting proposition, a volatility that disciplines the good performance of busywork. Through contemporary historical research there is an emerging understanding of the controversies that have attended the teaching of queer curriculum content in Australian universities and schools (Marshall 2005, 2011a). These controversies have routinely sought to challenge the legitimacy of the curricular inclusion of non-heterosexual content and perspectives. Historically, these challenges have been refuted by, among other things, appeals to the responsibilities of the state (as manifest through its various organs, such as legislation and public education systems). As the privatization of education expands in line with a diminution of the role of the state, the history of contests over the legitimate nature of queer pedagogy demonstrates the way in which the concerns and interests of queer pedagogies are especially vulnerable to the vagaries of a monstrous, user-pays, corporatist logic.

In one recent Australian example of this vulnerability, student protests over the inclusion of queer content in an undergraduate curriculum are indicative of the potential influence of student 'market pressures' on such curriculum inclusions. In their article '"The C Words": clitorises, childhood and challenging compulsory heterosexuality discourses with pre-service primary teachers' (2009), Greg Curran, Steph Chiarolli and Maria Pallotta-Chiarolli discuss a controversy that erupted among Curran's students when he introduced a reading by Pallotta-Chiarolli that discussed her daughter's (Steph Chiarolli's) sex education, including her learning about the clitoris. Curran introduces the paper by explaining how even in advance of the experience, which is the subject of the article, he felt an acute awareness as a lecturer 'of the pressure for high course satisfaction ratings from students. Challenging homophobia and advocating for queer youth – as an openly gay male lecturer – posed threats to the popularity of the courses I was teaching in' (155). The article recounts students' complaints to Curran following his discussion of Pallotta-Chiarolli's article: 'Children should be able to be children. They're innocent. They shouldn't be learning about gays and lesbians' (156).

Curran goes on to detail how 'word … spread quickly within the School of Education' with 'a year-level coordinator [informing] me that a complaint [had] been made about me at the Student Representative Council: I was 'pushing' gay and lesbian issues and 'using inappropriate language' in a lecture' (157). Pallotta-Chiarolli describes being 'deeply saddened that Greg has to experience this professional interrogation and emotional disruption in his workplace, a university meant to be a place of learning, dialogue and transgression of unjust and discriminatory norms' (158). Similarly, the 'child' – Chiarolli, Pallotta-Chiarolli's daughter – recounts her feelings of surprise at the students' reactions (159). To address students' complaints, Curran, Pallotta-Chiarolli and Chiarolli decided to present a lecture to the class to respond to the issues raised. The article details how this largely appears to have addressed student concerns. Of particular significance to my argument is the authors' observation that while this intervention appeared to allay student concerns about queer pedagogy, it only did so after such curricula inclusion had been framed by an elaborated justification:

> Why is it important for educators and parents espousing gender and sexual inclusivity and diversity to justify, contextualize and explain their views and positions? Does this not illustrate the pervasiveness of the default Centre position of the 'heterosexualization' of childhood (Butler 1990) and patriarchal constructs of women's bodies and sexualities? Does this not accentuate how they can remain unjustified and unexplained while anything else is the Margin or Other that requires lengthy explanation? (Curran et al. 2009: 163)

Furthermore, the authors also suggest that the queer pedagogy that had been so unacceptable to many students when presented by Curran, a gay man, became acceptable for students when it was advocated by Chiarolli and Pallotta-Chiarolli because, in various ways, they adhered to students' conventional expectations in relation to prevailing codes of 'heteronormalcy and gendernormalcy' in ways that Curran did not (163). Thus, while the crisis instigated by Curran's queer pedagogy was averted, it brings into sharp relief the fragility of the inclusion of such content, with student complaints functioning as an expression of market pressures resulting in the forced disciplinary work of 'justification'. Following the authors' suggestions about the usefulness and problematization of 'being just like them' in legitimizing queer pedagogy, the pressure brought to bear on Curran is also indicative of the homophobia, especially against males, which significantly structures the market pressures applied to queer pedagogical work.

The message sent by these students echoes broader responses to homosexuality: it is increasingly acceptable but only under certain conditions. The prospect of increasing students' 'choice' in a marketplace of higher education, and the corollary reduction of educators to products, raises ominous questions regarding the comparative marketability of gay male educators in the field of queer pedagogy. This reinforcement of well-established anxieties about male homosexuality and pedagogy, most luridly depicted in the common homophobic conflation of homosexuality with paedophilia, raises the ethical and political question of advocating for queer pedagogues who do not conform to prevailing codes of heteronormalcy and gendernormalcy, although such advocacy does not fit into stultifying, stupor-inducing market-based formulations of the provision of higher education.

The second way in which queer pedagogy raises questions about the increasing turn towards corporatization and bureaucratization in higher education is its exposure of the conservatizing nature of bureaucratic modes of work. While there are well-established contemporary critiques of bureaucratization, these accounts do not draw on historical approaches as much as they might, and the example of queer pedagogy demonstrates how historicizing a critique of bureaucratization enables a particular set of reflections on bureaucratization and its effects. A historical reflection on homosexuality and education in Australia demonstrates that since activist efforts around these issues in the 1970s and the ad hoc and sometimes informal banning of gay and lesbian curriculum content in Australia in the 1970s and early 1980s by various governments there has been a gradual incorporation of homosexual content within the bureaucratic frameworks of government policies, programmes and community services (Marshall 2005, 2011b). The fact that queer pedagogy's enjoyment of bureaucratic validation and incorporation (albeit conditional) is only a relatively recent historical development demonstrates that an increased bureaucratization bears criticism not only insofar as it produces the busy work of zombie times, but also because it suggests an asynchronous relationship between queer content and bureaucratic process. While bureaucratic procedures, structures and epistemologies are designed to minimize risk and manage knowledge, the precepts of queer pedagogy (an unstable proposition itself) are inherently risky and challenge the disciplined production of knowledge. In this way the threats to queer pedagogy brought forward by the bureaucratic turn come into focus, further illuminating the conservatizing and disciplining role of bureaucratic labour on higher education in general.

Queer cannot count: audit cultures and queer metrics

As has been made clear by this chapter's historical reflections, questions of queer pedagogy cannot be considered outside of broader analyses of the politics of sexual and gender differences. In particular, the question of the relationship between queer pedagogy and higher education is informed by contemporary debates about the institutional recognition of gay and lesbian people. Most prominently, these public debates centre on the importance of securing the right to marry and (in the United States) the right to join the military. The conservative dimensions of these political campaigns, including the way in which they contribute to the emergence of homonationalist forms of subjectivity and organization, have been scrutinized at length (e.g. Puar 2007). Putting the specifics of those particular debates to one side, these debates demonstrate that in contrast to the 1970s political project of demonstrating that homosexuals were 'real', contemporary political debates in Australia are much more focused on ensuring that gays and lesbians are recognized in ways that are particularly valued. For many people it appears that the heart of the struggle currently lies in contests over how queers 'count'.

However, as has been made clear by a range of critical positions, including anti-homophobic critics of gay marriage, the very measures that non-heterosexual subjects look to in order to be recognized as citizens and as political subjects is currently in flux (Berlant 1997; Halperin and Traub 2010). This indeterminacy, which is reflected by the oscillating assimilation/transformation debate, lies at the heart of contemporary public constitutions of queer experience and knowledge. Alongside these political contests over the epistemological boundaries and forms of queerness itself, Australian universities have witnessed the rise of new practices for measuring research productivity. Such practices, spectacularly represented by the Excellence in Research for Australia (ERA) publication ranking process, reflect a familiar neo-liberal form of governance that atomizes research into assessable units. The indeterminate nature of queerness as an epistemological field necessarily means that the imposition of external audit measures and practices of objective counting and measurement based on pre-established categories either curtails or effaces queer research. Indeed, the predictable bureaucratic review process, which subsequently attended the ERA roll-out, demonstrates how there exists a whole technology of bureaucratization of scholarly work, expressed in part through rolling cycles of process invention and review, which seeks to manage the work done by drawing the energies of the knowledge workers into the endless churn of process design and review.

In February 2011, the Australian Association for Research in Education (AARE) sent a broadcast email to its membership titled 'ERA hides more than it reveals about Education research'. In this message, the AARE argue that educational research is disadvantaged by the ERA because it acknowledges research excellence unevenly across disciplines and because it subsumes educational research within other fields of research (coded as FoRs):

> ERA is not a level playing field in terms of research excellence indicators. In Education, 15.53% of journals are A/A* compared with 19.72% across all disciplines and there are only 60 esteem indicators compared with 372 in Medical and Health Sciences (biomed and clinical) and 471 in Medical and Health Sciences (public and allied health sciences) ... Significant specialist areas of educational research are buried in other FoRs, including Economics (140204); Policy (160506); Sociology (160809); Educational Psychology (170103); Applied Linguistics and Educational Linguistics (200401); History and Philosophy of Education (220202).

The AARE's critique of the ways ERA disadvantages educational research in general points towards the way in which the particular case of queer pedagogy, a small emerging research field within the broader field of education, is even less well-served by audit cultures. However, like debates in relation to gay marriage and military recruitment, there is an incentive for queer pedagogy to 'count' under the prevailing rubric of valued recognition because of the correlation between being counted by the state and being a beneficiary of the state's resources. Performance against the ERA – measured research productivity – carries implications for funding and, at institutional levels, for the allocation of workloads that is also a distributive mechanism for resources although at a more localized level.

Thus, the challenge to count is an important part of the struggle to expand the field of queer pedagogy research insofar as it is related to an expansion in the material conditions for enabling the research, although this is in spite of the antithetical relationship between much queer research and the injunction to be counted. While the attribution of financial incentives to queer research that counts speaks to the material context in which this research occurs, the recognition of 'countable' research also works on a political level where this recognition is connected to a political legitimization. This legitimization plays an important role in the politics of recognition that currently attends the historical illegitimacy of queer pedagogy in the academy, as seen in the earlier discussion of the crisis management by Curran, Chiarolli and Pallotta-Chiarolli (2009).

As with other recognition-based politics, however, arguing for the legitimacy of queer pedagogy is not a straightforward proposition given that much queer research is suspicious of claims to legitimacy. Such scepticism is hardly surprising given the historical application of such terms against people who fail prevailing expectations in relation to sex, gender and sexuality. Critics of gay marriage often critique the way in which this appeal for state recognition is achieved at the expense of making homosexuality intelligible in the terms of heterosexist, patriarchal models of subjectivity and codes of relationship. Replicating the binarized epistemological structures of these models and codes (e.g. man/woman; homo/hetero; married/unmarried), these appeals for recognition also routinely assert a binarized perspective on homosexuality, affirming the 'good' homosexuality that counts for something at the expense of a disavowed 'bad' image of homosexuality parodied by *Gay Zombie*: that homosexuality has a naturalized relationship to contagion and to death. However, these traces of the 'bad' in the discursive constitution of homosexuality in the public imaginary cannot be washed away by the imagination of homosexuals as subjects on whom society can count because they are making contributions in familiar ways. As the parodic moment of *Gay Zombie* and the unease of Greg Curran's students demonstrate, ideas about homosexuality are unstable, informed by historical understandings of the homosexual as bad and synonymous with death as well as by contemporary political affirmations of the good homosexual as the exemplary citizen. The educative value of thinking about homosexuality, then, is how it can open up for analysis the way in which mobile contingent meanings attributed to sexuality, life and death are woven together.

As queerness is performatively constituted through these conflicting notions of life and death, queer pedagogy is necessarily a *living dead* or *undead* pedagogy. As an example of living dead pedagogy, *Gay Zombie* performs its instructive anti-homophobic work by parodically playing with the conflations of homosexuality with death. In the sense that the sketch lampoons the conflation of homosexuality with death, it aspires to be life-giving (a queer pro-life pedagogy, perhaps?) inasmuch as it constructs a position – an audience for the sketch – that exists beyond the disciplinary demands of phobic constructions of homosexuality. Like the gay zombies of the sketch, queer pedagogy calls to mind the slipperiness between the good and bad, and between life and death. In this way, a queer pedagogical text like *Gay Zombie* is educative beyond straightforward questions of sex, gender, sexuality and difference but, more broadly, about the fictionalized accounts of these matters, the work they are called on to perform and how they express anxieties about the fragility of life understood broadly.

In a critique of homonationalist gay and lesbian politics, Jasbir Puar (2007) analyses the 'transition' in contemporary understandings of queer subjects. In Puar's critique, queer subjects achieve departures from associations with death by moving towards 'life' across an axis of normalization/nationalism. Importantly, such transitioning is achieved at the expense of racialized others demonstrating the way in which the good life of the homosexual is often articulated through a process of binarized morality that designates bad others. Puar's analysis shows the importance of learning from the historical moral policing of homosexuality so as to avoid replicating the appeals to problematic sexual moralizing that have historically played such a strong role in histories of homophobia. By calling to mind such historicist reflections, the contested interplay between ideas about sexuality, life and death, the good and the bad, come into focus and it is these reflections that constitute the living dead emphasis of queer pedagogy.

Queer pedagogy is performatively constituted through contested discourses of life, death and sexuality, explaining why its pedagogical work is always tentative, and liminal. This liminality is demonstrated by the routine irresolvable concerns that are articulated through debates over sexuality and education. My discussion here of the way in which queer pedagogy is caught in a conflicted, passionate embrace with audit cultures that simultaneously count and lessen its meaning while also expanding the material basis for its operation is but one such example. Audit cultures like ERA ask of queer work that it finds and assumes a contained space within the recognized metric grid. As the ERA assesses research output over time, the injunction for queer work to take up a position is not only a spatial one but a temporal one as well. It is not only a question of recognizing the type of work but its volume and frequency. However, as queer work is obscured through the ERA process – it is not captured or it is represented otherwise – the normative audit culture cannot be expected to provide a fulsome account of queer research activity. That such activity nevertheless occurs despite its being lost to the ERA suggests that this work requires to be understood through non-normative understandings of time and space. Channeling both life and death, queer pedagogy straddles the enabling life-giving recognitions of the ERA and its material bounty, while also occupying the fatal position of doing work of no value under the prevailing metric.

The queer metrics of the work of the misrecognized and ignored call to mind Judith Halberstam's (2005) queer notions of time and place. Taking up Halberstam's theorizations, queer temporalities and spatialities can help account for queer teaching and research that occurs out of proper place and time. As a normative metric, the ERA only recognizes particular locations and temporal frames for research activity to which value is accorded. The most valued place for research activity is an 'A* journal', with a temporal frame based around a crude 'more is better' logic of articles as interchangeable assessable units. However, queer pedagogy and queer research has its origins not in the academy and so it is little wonder it has a skewed relationship to the disciplinary counting. Emerging, in part, out of political activism, circles of people, 'non-professional' researchers, schools, youth services and other community-based organizations, collections and archives, the history of queer pedagogy and research has been strongly influenced by 'place-making practices' and 'the production of queer counterpublics' that Halberstam discusses in her elaboration of the notion of queer space (2005: 6).

Similarly, for Halberstam, normative models of time are structured around 'the temporal frames of bourgeois reproduction and family, longevity, risk/safety and inheritance' (2005: 6). However, as an emerging, only partially-recognized research field, queer pedagogy research casts doubt upon the very terms of normative temporality. Inherently critical of normative models of reproduction and generation, queer work queries the political and intellectual value (and goals) of simply lifting the production of multiple assessable units ('articles') which are recognized within a normative metric of knowledge. Such an approach clearly consolidates hegemonic epistemological fields. Queer research undermines normative notions of the development of academic fields of research: in its anti-institutional iterations, this work seeks to make radical interventions, repudiating notions of an intellectual inheritance, critiquing the prevailing norms of academic work, while also holding the future up to a sceptical eye, undermining romanticist and utopic narratives. Unshackled from linear, developmental notions of longevity and inheritance, queer pedagogy research instead brings the past and the future into analysis in the current moment, opening up the effects of their performative contemporary interplay.

As that which is (almost) with/out life, (almost) with/out a discipline, (almost) with/out a community of scholars, and (almost) with/out a history, queer pedagogy especially brings into focus disturbances in teleological and essentialized notions of time and place. Through my argument that queer pedagogy, like the zombie, is always-already out of time and out of place, this section of the chapter has provided a queer critique of the way in which normative metrics discipline the way academic work is done, by recourse to dominant expectations in relation to time (when the work is done, the frequency of outputs) and in relation to place (where the work is done, the individualized work space and the league-table-without-end). In these ways, queer pedagogy offers an intellectual and educative space for calling to mind the contemporary conditions for the reproduction of conservative, exclusionary ways of knowing things (for example, the current Australian Field of Research FoR or Socio-Economic Objective SEO codes) and individualized, decontextualized ways of doing knowledge work (e.g. ERA rankings).

Conclusion: queer passing and playing dead

The zombie is a figure that embodies indeterminacy in relation to time (dead/undead) as well as place (do zombies ever have homes?), and the zombie trope enables critical reflection on contemporary queer pedagogy in the Australian academy. This concluding section embraces the history of the zombie's playful and subversive deployment as a parodic figure in order to consider contemporary strategies of resistance. Thinking about the concerns of this chapter through Judith Butler's (1990) work on parody, I want to bring queer work in the academy into focus as a parodic repetition or performance of compliant behaviours, a commingling of 'life' with 'death'. The passionate and conflicted embrace between queer work and audit cultures discussed in the previous section suggests how we can think of this compliance with disciplinary strictures that recognize and ordain legitimate queer research as a form of 'passing'.

Zombies exemplify many of the cultural attributes of passing. Zombies look alive, but they are dead. They do many of the things of the living, but through such performances they manifest the direct opposite: the absence of life. Relatedly, to pass, in a gender and cultural studies sense of the term, is to secure certain benefits, resources and privileges within a system of power on the basis of being (mis)recognized in a particular way. Importantly, passing also refers to the way in which the benefits secured by the (mis)recognized subject as a result of a lucrative (mis)recognition do not account for the subject in the totalizing way that is suggested by the recognition. To pass, then, is also to undermine the authority of such recognitions and the existence of such totalizing identities by showing up their mistake and the limits of their perceptive and analytical registers. By playing along with normative metrics, by being counted under systems like ERA, queer work attracts expanded material support and political legitimacy. The challenge for queer research presented by the accrual of these privileges is to use the expanded resource base to critically engage the dominant logics of neo-liberal (re)productivity that structure the frameworks of resource allocation (e.g. see Edelman 2004). In Butler's terms, this challenge can be thought of as a process of making political the very terms through which the work is recognized and articulated (148). Political work is enmeshed in oppressive terms and conditions so 'trouble is inevitable and the task [is] how best to make it, what best way to be in it' (vii).

Butler's discussion of subversive parody usefully extends my consideration here of the implications of 'passing' in the academy and the parodic repetition/consolidation of normalizing practices of counting and recognition of queer work:

> Parody by itself is not subversive, and there must be a way to understand what makes certain kinds of parodic repetitions effectively disruptive, truly troubling, and which repetitions become domesticated and recirculated as instruments of cultural hegemony. A typology of actions would clearly not suffice, for parodic displacement, indeed, parodic laughter, depends on a context and reception in which subversive confusions can be fostered (1990: 139).

Following Butler's provocations, a key imperative facing queer research as it accrues institutional support is the enactment of research and pedagogy that offers reconsiderations not only of sex, sexuality and gender, but also of the ways in which meanings attributed to these areas of discursive concentration are mobilized to consolidate particular understandings of the 'academy'. The ERA points towards a particular 'life' and future for queer work, and its disciplinary effects are forcefully felt through the translation of normative notions of research spaces and temporalities into professional esteem and workloads. The increasing neo-liberal pressures of these expectations deliberately work against efforts to acknowledge queer spaces and times. Negotiating these pressures collectively is a key challenge. Simultaneously embodying the paradoxical expressions of zombie times – achieving 'life' through ERA by doing the 'death' of compliance, for example – those working within queer pedagogy and research occupy the contested, liminal and undead time and space for doing the academy in different ways. As pedagogue and researcher, the gay zombie scholar works through the material basis provided by the bureaucratized 'busy work' while working against its neo-liberal intentions, demonstrating that such intentions do not foreclose all of the possibilities for the work that actually occurs.

Zombies are us: the living dead as a tool for pedagogical reflection

Shaun Kimber

A cross six zombie films – from *Night of the Living Dead* (1968) to *Survival of the Dead* (2009) – George Romero has employed a range of formal, narrative and thematic strategies to invite audiences to reflect upon contemporary society, deploying the figure of the living dead in distinctive and provocative ways. For example, Romero used the zombie allegorically to contemplate American consumer culture in *Dawn of the Dead* (1978), to critique military and scientific communities in *Day of the Dead* (1985), and to comment upon contemporary global media cultures in *Diary of the Dead* (2007). This chapter borrows a Romero-esque strategy to critically reflect on the state of play for media education in English universities. That is, taking its cue from Romero's insider critiques, the following analysis of higher education is from a surviving English media academic's insider perspective of a discipline perceived to be under attack. Key narrative elements drawn from a range of post-millennial zombie films are also employed to guide this analysis. According to Bishop (2009, 2010a), American zombie films are articulated around a set of plot structures that have stabilized in post 9/11 movies, and which this chapter reads in parallel to the uncertainties of the current era of higher education. These include a post-apocalyptic backdrop, the foregrounding of survivalist fantasies, paranoid suspicion of and between survivors as well as shifting understandings of the role of the zombie and its level of threat.

This chapter aims to harness the narrative elements found in contemporary zombie films to generate new insights into media education within English universities. The specific aims are as follows: to deploy the analogy of the apocalypse to illuminate the current challenges facing media education within English higher education; to examine the relationships between zombies, survivors, and implicated 'experts' found within post-millennial zombie films, and to use these as a lens to consider the relationships between teachers, students and other key stakeholders working within higher education; to consider how shifts in the characterization of the zombie within a sub-set of recent zombie films in many ways mirror how students are differently perceived in English universities and finally to contemplate how subject-level disciplinary challenges faced within media education might be negotiated through a process of collaborative necromancy. Whilst the starting point of this chapter is the specific national and disciplinary context of English media education, its findings apply more generally to the perceived crisis in higher education.

The Romero-esque strategy is built upon some foundational assumptions. There is a general understanding that the zombie has become a key figure in the contemporary cultural landscape. The 1990s saw a zombie renaissance that continues to position the zombie as the pre-eminent monster, whose supernatural presence traverses converging and increasingly hybridized media and film cultures. The zombie has been picked up as an explanatory trope in a number of academic fields, including mathematics (Munz et al. 2009), philosophy (Greene and Mohammad 2010), politics (Drezner 2011), economics (Quiggin 2010), film studies (Balun 2003; Bishop 2010a; Kane 2010; and Newman 2011) and cultural studies (Flint 2009). This chapter's approach is distinguished from these by adopting a more positive and revisionist orientation towards the zombie, and through using zombiedom as a critical tool with which to reflect specifically upon the challenges faced by a particular academic discipline, rather than as an abstract theoretical model for crises located within more generalized political, social or economic spheres.

Another foundational assumption is that the zombie is simply a monstrously reanimated figure of fear. This is an underestimation of the zombie's radical and critical potential. Far from being homogeneous, film representations of the figure of the zombie alert our attention to a wide range of possibilities that can productively be employed as lenses to view individual and group actions in the face of social, political and cultural crises, and can also be usefully focused on the particular reactions of stakeholders of media education. Whilst often maligned as B-grade schlock, appealing to the lowest popular denominator, zombie films can actually offer valuable, complex and contradictory insights into the world around us. Zombie films therefore constitute important cultural texts that actively engage with the desires and fears of the historical period and national context in which they are produced, circulated and consumed. But they do not just act as a barometer; they dynamically and productively work with, and through, the consequences of actions taken in relation to these shifting desires and fears. This reading of the zombie challenges the view expressed by Thrower that zombies are 'unlikely stars', whose decaying flesh lacks glamour and who are 'devoid of any hidden depths' (2006: 250). On the contrary, the zombie can offer valuable insights into the world around us, as well as usefully engage a range of popular media literacies. As Bishop suggests, 'the zombie does its best cultural work not as mere entertainment or cheap thrill but instead as insightful and revelatory allegory' (2010a: 207).

The apocalypse that forms the backdrop of most contemporary zombie film narratives is also a useful starting point to consider the current challenges for teaching of media at universities in the United Kingdom. The resemblances between zombie films and media education are both contextual and textual. The contextual overlap recognizes that the apocalyptic narratives found in many zombie films reflect and refract the fears, anxieties and uncertainties of the times in which they are produced, circulated and consumed. Bishop (2009, 2010a) and Flint (2009) indicate that the recent historical periods within which zombie films have been the most popular tend to be those characterized by the most uncertainty or crisis. Zombie films have therefore become popular over the last decade because of the symptomatic weaving of contemporary fears, uncertainties and crises into their narratives. The movies *28 Days Later* (Boyle 2002), *Land of the Dead* (Romero 2005), *28 Weeks Later* (Fresnadillo 2007), and *Diary of the Dead* (Romero 2007) can all be understood to speak to concerns about national and global finances, conflicts, terrorism, climate change, poverty and the spread of infectious diseases.

This apocalyptic analogy is useful when thinking about the contemporary state of crisis in media education in England, where currently many of the discourses surrounding it are similarly apocalyptic in theme and tone. A review of recent English higher education news stories reveals a wide range of anxieties and potential crises that in combination could signal the serious undermining of media education (see for example Trounsen 2010; UK University 2010; Loveys 2011). The recent flashpoint issue is the English coalition government's austerity policies that advocate the removal of public funding for the social sciences and humanities, which will mean that media programmes will no longer receive government funding and support. Allied to this are real anxieties, especially within the humanities and social sciences, regarding the government's proposed three-fold increase in student tuition fees from £3,200 to £9,000, to take effect in October 2012. This proposed increase in tuition fees has (as at the date of writing) led nationally to an 8.7 per cent, or 44,000, drop in applications to English universities for 2012 (Coughlan 2012). Other major areas of apprehension within the sector are government proposals to restructure the university system to allow for a wider range of private and for-profit providers, increased marketization, pressure on universities to diversify income streams towards research and enterprise, and government scrutiny through instruments like the Key Information Sets (KIS).

The second point of comparison between apocalyptic narratives found in zombie films and media education in English higher education is more textual. A characteristic feature of the post-apocalyptic environment found in recent zombie films is the rapid collapse of social and economic infrastructures and institutions leading to the widespread breakdown of law and order. For example, social bonds start to fragment and then collapse after the apocalyptic event that triggers the narratives in *To Kako/Evil* (Noussias 2005), *The Signal* (Bruckner, Bush and Gentry 2007), *Pontypool* (McDonald 2008) and *La Horde* (Dahan and Rocher 2009). Similarly, the crises, uncertainties and fears underlining contemporary discussions of media education in English higher education arguably mark an impending apocalyptic event: the lesson from many contemporary zombie films is that this situation could trigger the eventual death of the discipline and subsequent fragmentation of institutions and relationships. Couldry and McRobbie (2010) have suggested that the UK student riots in 2010, which gained international media coverage, marked the point when the idea of the university in England received its death warrant. They argue that the recommendations contained in the Browne Review (2010), which were linked to changes in university funding, student fees and the education system, fell hardest upon the humanities and social sciences, and have the potential to precipitate the demise of media education. Moreover, the white paper *Higher Education: Students at the Heart of the System* (BIS 2011a), which outlined how the English coalition government plans to move its higher education agenda forward, has been read by many as a significant step towards the anticipated apocalypse within media education in English higher education. The ongoing daily challenge for educators in this state of crisis is trying to maintain quality learning and teaching experiences for students and staff within an environment of reduced contact time and increased class sizes. These challenges translate into particular concerns for institutions and departments offering media degrees in terms of resources (capital and equipment); staffing (academic, administrative, demonstrator and technical); as well as the perceived value and worth of these degrees for the government, the press and, more broadly, British society. These major political, economic and cultural changes and challenges can be characterized as 'zombifying drives' and have the potential – if unchecked – of further undermining media departments and programmes.

The relationships between survivors and zombies can also be used as a useful mirror to reflect on the relationship between academics and students. According to Bishop (2009, 2010a) an important feature of post 9/11 zombie films is their foregrounding of survivors' fears – of zombies, but also of other survivors. He identifies how recent zombie films increasingly dehumanize survivors by representing them as having the potential to be even more inhuman and monstrous than the zombies themselves. This narrative device is used in Romero's recent *Land of the Dead* (2005), *Diary of the Dead* (2007) and *Survival of the Dead* (2009), as well as in a range of other international zombie films such as *Day of the Dead* (Miner 2008), *Fido* (Currie 2006), *La Horde* (Dahan and Rocher 2009), and *Tormented* (Wright, 2009). The key to understanding this survivalist relationship is the dynamic interplay between media academics' actual and perceived losses during the historic and current periods of uncertainty in British higher education, and a dependency on their perceptions of students for validation of what they feel is right and knowable about higher education, media education and media literacies.

Media academics in England often find themselves trapped in crumbling bunker-like institutions housing the remnants of a collapsing system in terms of spaces, resources, programmes, structures and processes. Like this author, they often perceive themselves as increasingly isolated or hard-pressed in the face of rising teaching and administration loads, unbalanced student-to-staff ratios, and increasingly urgent expectations for research output. Further, media academics are currently contending with redundancies, pay freezes and changes to their working conditions, as evidenced by the rise in short-term and fixed contracts. In England at least there are ongoing industrial actions on the part the Universities and Colleges Union (UCU) and their members over government higher education policy, including proposed changes to academic pension schemes (see for example Ashley 2011; Hunt 2011; Universities and Colleges Union 2011). These professional exigencies are all compounded by the way the complex, dynamic and contradictory processes of media convergence and divergence make mapping the rapidly changing media landscapes within academic curriculum increasingly difficult (Bennett, Kendall and McDougall 2011). For many media academics, their working lives can be perceived as increasingly mirroring the characterization of the clusters of survivors in zombie films who are depicted as bunkering down and either waiting for the resumption of pre-apocalyptic normality or desperately trying to recreate the social order and power structures of their old lives: these recurring characterizations are evident in Romero's seminal *Dawn of the Dead* (1978) and *Day of the Dead* (1985), both of which influenced more recent zombie films including his own

Land of the Dead (2005), as well as *Resident Evil* (Anderson 2002), *Pontypool* (McDonald 2008) and *La Horde* (Dahan and Rocher 2009). Survivors are also often shown trapped in quarantine areas trying to escape from both the zombies and each other, as seen in *28 Days Later* (Boyle 2002), and *[REC] 2* (Balagueró and Plaza 2009). An alternative characterization presents survivors as being so obsessed with their own everyday lives that they are oblivious to the fact that their world is falling apart around them, as in *Shaun of the Dead* (Wright 2004).

In arguably similar conditions, where media academics feel isolated, trapped and embattled, there is a tendency to characterize students in ways that mirror survivalist paranoias. The first draws upon pre-millennial survivor conceptions of the zombie, which frame students as a horde of mindless bodies 'enslaved' by their institutional enrolments and assessment regimes. This largely sympathetic, albeit somewhat patronizing, reading of the student anticipates not only their general passivity, but also the powerlessness of academics to cope with them. In this view, the practices, processes and structures of academic programmes insist on the hypnotizing teacher-centred and didactic or surface approaches to learning, characterized by the foregrounding and rewarding of low order cognitive skills (Ramsden 2003). The media academic's fear is that this kind of student and academic enslavement will lead to disengagement, alienation and possibly even confrontation, such as that of the 2010 riots where students protested the rise in tuition fees (Asthana et al. 2010). These colonialist anxieties mirror similar concerns explored in the early wave of zombie films in the first half the twentieth century – for instance *White Zombie* (Halperin 1932) and *I Walked with a Zombie* (Tourneur 1943) where protagonists feared not infection but the threat of revolt from the horde of slaves who, even before their zombification, had lost their autonomy.

Another familiar way of looking at students draws on more contemporary conceptions of the zombie as 'infected'. This largely unsympathetic and dehumanizing view contends that contemporary learners are compelled by an insatiable consumerist drive to cannibalize new media and treat their education as yet another consumable item. This can be seen to mirror survivalist attitudes towards zombies that react not only to the immediate threat posed by the known-dead, but also the zombie's literal embodiment of their own fears of life after death or the apocalypse. According to this view, media students engage in pragmatic and surface learning activities, informed by summative assessment tasks. Ironically, this is also seen as leading to student expectation and demands for increased levels of supplementary support from academics, support staff, demonstrators and administrators. Media academics, like many other teachers more generally, fear students' undermining of their authority, standards and disciplinary expertise. The anticipated horror is of unstoppable and replicating hordes of students, who would overwhelm the beleaguered academic in e-mails, classes, tutorials – cohort after cohort, term after term, academic year after academic year. The 'othering' discourse that underlies this characterization of students as 'enslaved' or 'infected' is in part a defence mechanism in the face of the escalating uncertainties, challenges and crises in the impending apocalyptic arena of media education. Many media academics, the author included, can simultaneously think of students as collaborative partners, and as 'enslaved' and 'infected' by all that is seen to be ailing media education within contemporary English higher education.

Interesting correspondences can be found in an examination of the relationship in post-millennial zombie films between different groups of survivors. Increasingly, the zombies themselves are less important to the narrative than the relationships between survivors, and this shift mirrors a parallel change in perception of the students as responsible for the rapid decline in media education, to grievances against colleagues and other implicated educational stakeholders. In Romero's original *Night of the Living Dead* (1968), the zombie attack was established as a backdrop to the more character-rich tensions and struggles between survivors trapped in a farmhouse. This narrative device is repeated in a range of subsequent zombie films as rivalries are explored between ordinary survivors and those who were somehow implicated, either in triggering the apocalypse or being aligned to those who attempt to exploit it. A recurring figure is that of the research scientists, often found frantically working in quarantined areas with increasing desperation to identify the source of infection, a cure, or a way of exploiting the zombie outbreak, for example in the *Resident Evil* franchise (2002, 2004, 2007, 2010, 2012) and *28 Weeks Later* (Fresnadillo 2007). A parallel can be found in the rivalries and relationships between academics and institutional agents – such as quality assurance and enhancement units, learning and teaching groups and committees, Faculty/School and institutional senior management teams. In the field of media studies, the relationships between stakeholders is particularly fraught and seeded with suspicion about various parties' agendas for the future of media education, as is evident in the growing tension between media academics and external stakeholders including The Higher Education Academy (HEA), HEA discipline networks such as Art Design Media and Media and Communications), the Sector Skills Council for the creative industries in the United Kingdom (Creative Skillset), disciplinary associations such as the Media, Communications and Cultural Studies Association (MeCCSA), the British Association of Film, TV, Screen Studies (BAFTSS), and research and innovation centres such as The Centre for Excellence in Media Practice (CEMP). In the face of warning signs about the death of the discipline – for instance, as resources, funding and student numbers decline – the power struggles between surviving and competing groups and institutional affiliations have intensified.

Taking this analogy further, the military, corporations, politicians or police are often represented in contemporary zombie films as primarily interested in containment of the outbreak or infection and in processing zombies and survivors for the general benefit and maintenance of the existing capitalist and military systems. This trend can be traced in Romero's recent *Diary of the Dead* (2007) and *Survival of the Dead* (2009), as well as in a range of other zombie movie sequels such as *28 Weeks Later* (Fresnadillo 2007) and *[REC] 2* (Balagueró and Plaza 2009). A central narrative thread is the government or corporate interests' insistence on the maintenance and extension of their pre-apocalypse commercial and political power. It is not hard to trace a correlation between these power hungry or corporate groups in zombie films and the institutional forces that manage education in the United Kingdom, which include the Quality Assurance Agency for Higher Education

(QAA), the Higher Education Funding Council for England (HEFCE), The Department for Business, Innovation and Skill (BIS), the Minister of State for Universities and Science (at the time of writing, David Willetts), and of course the troubled coalition government. It is at times unclear whether the goals of these organizations are to contain, harness, grow or otherwise exploit higher education. Presciently, the relationships between various groups of survivors are often represented in contemporary zombie films as becoming increasingly desperate, dehumanized and monstrous as their ambitions go unmet or are thwarted by other survivors.

On the other hand, the increasingly humanized and sympathetic representations of zombies found within a sub-set of contemporary zombie films can also be used to inform our understanding of media students within English higher education. The equivalences between zombies found in these films and media students have a number of overlapping dimensions. The first is the highlighting of the illusory nature of many of the perceived differences between media academics and their students. In an increasing number of post-millennial zombie films, audiences are invited to relate to zombie characters and even root for them against dehumanized and monstrous survivors. While shifting representations of the zombie are nothing new, for Balun (2003) its antecedents are traceable to Romero in *Day of the Dead* (1985) and other European zombie films of the late 1970s and 1980s. The film scholars Newman (2011), Flint (2009) and Bishop (2010a) have already canvassed the post-millennial intensification of this sympathetic portrayal of the zombie. The recent flood of revisionist zombie films – such as Romero's *Land of the Dead* (2005) and *Survival of the Dead* (2009), as well as *Les Revenents/They Came Back* (Campillo 2004), *American Zombie* (Lee 2007), *Tormented* (Wright 2009) and *Deadheads* (Pierce and Peirce 2011) – all emphasize how survivors and zombies bear uncanny correspondences to each other, and that distinctions made between zombies and survivors have become increasingly fragmented, blurred and illusory. This theme is explored in *Colin* (Price 2008), where the self-titled protagonist is bitten, dies and returns as a zombie wandering through apocalyptic city streets trying to make sense of his past, present and future. These films invite audiences to look closely at the zombie and realize that 'they are us' (Kane 2010: 200). Differences between media academics and students are also largely misconceived, as we are all involved in the same joint project of learning about, participating within, and trying to promote and develop a discipline in which we have shared interests and investments.

The second resemblance between media students and revisionist representations of the zombie is the foregrounding of the zombies' heterogeneous identities, motivations and skills. Within many post-millennial zombie films it is possible to identify not only a diversification of the range of zombies represented but also a foregrounding of more heterodox possibilities. For example, new zombies have a faster pace, agility and dynamism while there is growing survivor recognition that they are increasingly independent, smart and adaptive to changes within their environment. These features have been seen in a range of films including *28 Days Later* (Boyle 2002), *To Kako/Evil* (Noussias 2005), *28 Weeks Later* (Fresnadillo 2007), *Flight of the Living Dead* (Thomas, 2007), *Dance of the Dead* (Bishop, 2008), *Day of the Dead*

(Miner, 2008), and *Devil's Playground* (McQueen 2010). A particularly interesting example in this respect is the mockumentary *American Zombie* (Lee 2007), which follows the daily lives and struggles of the living dead in Los Angeles. This film is unusual in the way that it presents three classifications of zombie: feral zombies (functioning without reason); low functioning zombies (with limited mental capacity but able to care for themselves) and high functioning zombies (with significant proportions of their mental capacity intact so they can pass as human). This taxonomy interrogates not only the heterogeneous nature of the zombie but also the similarities between the struggles of the living and the living dead. A parallel can be traced in English media education, where students have distinct personalities and individual motivations that bring them to the courses they choose. Moreover, like the 'monsters' in *American Zombie,* media students have the potential to be independent, autonomous and self-directed learners, to make their own plans and learn from their mistakes, particularly when provided with the appropriate learning environments, resources and support (Ramsden 2003).

A further likeness between media students and revisionist representations of the zombie lies in the characterization of the rare zombie protagonist. In this sub-set of contemporary zombie films, audiences are invited to view the world from the perspective of a seemingly sentient, sympathetic and humanized zombie. Here the figure of the zombie represents complex and differentiated characteristics and there is a de-emphasizing of them as abject monsters. For example, Romero's treatment of the zombie character 'Big Daddy' in *Land of the Dead* (2005) opens up the possibility of empathy with the 'other', as audiences are invited to see the world through his eyes (Bishop 2010a). Romero draws attention to the inequities that face Big Daddy and his fellow zombies in their position as the underclass within a post-apocalyptic society. A key feature of the revisionist zombie template is the increasingly shared understanding that zombies can, and perhaps should, be a locus for sympathy as they are in turn 'victimized' by survivors. This theme is explored further in films including *Les Revenants/They Came Back* (Campillo 2004), *Fido* (Currie 2006), *American Zombie* (Lee 2007) and *Deadheads* (Pierce and Pierce 2011). Similarly, our sympathies as media academics can be usefully aligned with students through harnessing a more empathetic understanding of their experiences as a means by which to promote student-centred approaches (Martin 1999). This increased empathy towards student experiences would work best when understood and aligned with the changing contexts of media education within English higher education, as well as wider cultural, economic and technological transformations within the sector and media industries.

Media education within English higher education would benefit from stronger collaborative partnerships in learning and teaching between students and academics to maximize their collective strengths, and also offer a unified approach to the some of the key subject, institutional and national challenges facing the discipline. This interaction and participation is referred to here as 'collaborative necromancy' – the collective breathing of life, vitality and deep learning into media education by students and academics. This approach calls for media students and academics to become partners in collaborative modes of learning and teaching that are not only enriching and empowering to each other but also help enhance the quality of media studies. Media academics and students would thereby draw on and discuss their own expectations, interests and expertise.

Such collaborative methods could also inform national debates about not only the future directions of the discipline but also some of the cultural, political and economic challenges facing media education in England. For example, David Gauntlett (2007, 2011) contends that the value and currency of English media education could be enhanced within the academy and wider discourses as a result of a Media Studies 2.0, moving away from traditional approaches to media production, and towards more relevant and contemporaneous approaches. Laughey (2011), on the other hand, contends that the image problems facing media studies in England could be challenged through a re-emphasizing of the core values of Media Studies 1.0. This debate and others like it do not only exist on personal websites and blogs, in national subject association newsletters, mailing lists and forums, academic books and journals; it is interactively and publicly discussed on a variety of media platforms by current students and academics, illustrating how students and teachers could usefully work through their various strengths and weaknesses, convergences and divergences, to enhance their shared teaching and learning experience. Admittedly, collaborative necromantic strategies can only go so far in shaping the future directions of the discipline in terms of teaching, scholarship and research. The threat to higher education more generally needs to be fought at policy level by survivors working higher up within the system. In the meantime, stronger connections fostered between media students and academics through practices inspired by collaborative necromancy can, for example, galvanize protests against policy decisions and put national pressure on the English government to rethink its current plans for higher education that arguably herald its death.

The ambition of this chapter has not been to celebrate zombie/media students and demonize survivor/media academics, but rather to work towards thinking about how their interconnectedness and resemblances, as patterned against some recent zombie films, can be used to advance media studies. Employing the Romero-esque strategy of using the zombie to think allegorically about media education in English universities, this chapter has been framed through an academic's insider account and structured around narrative elements found within post-millennial zombie films. Four overlapping contentions have been presented. First, whilst falling short of an apocalyptic event, the current challenges facing media education, at least in the United Kingdom, can be understood as an allegorical manifestation of the undermining of social institutions, which, if unchecked, could lead to its collapse. Second, the key to understanding the relationship between media studies' teachers and their students is to appreciate the interplay between media academics and other educational stakeholders, and to recognize that the problematic 'othering' of students is a defensive mechanism in the face of departmental, institutional and national uncertainties and power struggles across the discipline. Third, sympathetic representations of the zombie can inform teachers' understanding of students by highlighting the illusory nature of the differences between them and foregrounding their heterogeneous motivations, learning capacities, and existing media literacies and investments in the field, both inside and outside the academy. This in turn could work to promote student-centred approaches to learning and teaching. Finally, media education could benefit from stronger collaborative partnerships in learning and teaching between media students and media academics to maximize their collective strengths, and to offer a unified approach to the discipline, particularly in English universities during a period characterized by crisis and uncertainty.

Escaping the zombie threat by mathematics

Hans Petter Langtangen, Kent-Andre Mardal and Pål Røtnes

Introduction

This chapter presents a mathematical description of the interaction between humans and zombies. In the real world, making mathematical models and combining these with observations have been tremendously successful and constitute the foundation of modern technology and our understanding of nature. Although one gains some understanding of a world with zombies by watching relevant movies and reading books, this understanding is just as partial and incomplete as our understanding of the real world by just observing and experiencing it. With a mathematical model one can gain a deeper understanding of how humans and zombies interact. This understanding combined with computer simulations is here used to investigate if zombie movies are realistic and what will be the best strategies for humans to conquer a zombie threat. The chapter serves as demonstration for students how mathematics and computers are used to explain what we observe and predict the future. The way we apply mathematics and computers to a zombie world herein is in principle similar to the way the same tools are used for building bridges, steering robots or predicting the climate for the next 100 years. We therefore hope to increase the reader's interest in the powerful combination of mathematics and computers.

The strength of mathematical modelling is that we impose a set of rules describing how a world with zombies functions. By the word *model* we mean such a set of rules, expressed as equations. When we then use the model to simulate various human–zombie interaction scenarios, the mathematics ensures that everything that happens in the simulation is consistent with the fundamental rules. Even in a fantasy world of zombies, any scenario is restricted to what can realistically happen according to the rules we have defined.

The rules are based on a set of assumptions and involve a set of parameters that must be estimated from observations. The uncertainty in a mathematical model depends strongly on the validity of the assumptions and the quality and amount of data that are available for parameter estimation. We can easily change assumptions and parameters in a model to see the effect on simulated scenarios and thereby achieve insight about the uncertainty. In the present chapter, we shall describe the assumptions and the parameter estimation procedures we apply in detail so that the reader can judge the quality of the model.

When establishing mathematical rules for human–zombie interaction we must, as usual in the field of mathematical modelling, look at similar problems where mathematics has been successfully applied and try to migrate that well-understood knowledge to the new problem. Although there are no zombies (yet) in the real world, there are zombie-like patterns and processes going on that are similar to what can be seen in the movies. Even taken literally, large-scale zombification is basically a question of how a disease spreads in a population. This latter topic has obviously received much attention from scientists, and mathematics has become key to their research over the last 80 years. More recently, the swine and bird flu epidemics have interested laymen in this field of science known as epidemiology. We shall adopt mathematical ideas and techniques from epidemiology to show how we can understand more about the dynamics of a population threatened by zombification.

The bottom line of the mathematics of zombification is that the number of zombies at time t, denoted by $Z(t)$, can be computed by a quite simple formula that is repeated a lot of times. That is, the formula would be tedious, and in fact impossible, to evaluate by pen and paper, so we need a computer to automate the job and do the calculations with high speed. The idea is that we compute Z at a set of discrete points in time, named $t_0 < t_1 < t_2 \cdots < t_{n-i} < t_n$. We have to know the initial number of zombies at time t_0, but how this number evolves in the future can be computed. Let Z_i represent Z at time t_i, $i = 0, 1,\ldots,n$. The formula takes the form:

$Z_{i+1} = Z_i +$ *other knowe quantities at yime* t_i

That is, we know some quantities at time t_i and then we can evaluate a formula to compute a quantity like Z at some future time t_{i+1}. For such computations to be fairly accurate, the distance $t_{i+1} - t_i$ in time must be quite small. We remark that mathematicians can give precise meaning to the adjectives 'fairly' and 'quite' in this context, and turn such vague qualitative statements into quantitative facts. One aspect that complicates the equation for Z is that that we must solve some similar equations for other quantities, because these quantities are needed in the formula for Z_{i+1}. We shall outline how we reason to construct and solve such equations. You hardly need high school math to understand it, you just need to accept that a certain symbol like Z represents a quantity that changes with time, and that the subscript i, as in Z_i, is a time counter (i may count hours, for instance).

We believe that the way we use mathematics in the present chapter represents a new, attractive way to introduce pupils at schools and students at universities to the fundamental ideas and the craft of modern computation-based science and engineering. Also, the exposition can help to show that mathematics can be useful far beyond the reader's imagination.

Problem definition

In their pioneering paper, Munz et al. (2009) modelled zombie outbreaks mathematically and predicted the extinction of mankind. Although they found doomsday to be nearly inevitable, following a zombie attack, they also found that it could possibly to be prevented if early counter attacks were organized. Their conclusion is supported by most modern zombie movies and stories. In the present chapter, we refine their conclusion by using mathematics, computer simulations, and empirical data culled from some key selected zombie films to question both the validity of the doomsday scenario and the realism of the outbreak patterns in zombie movies.

The zombie archetype that informs this chapter is drawn from *The Night of the Living Dead* (1968) by George A. Romero, a film that has inspired many contemporary zombie movies. In Romero's movie, zombies are flesh-hungry and mindless, and spread their disease by biting living humans. There is no supernatural agency or magic involved in zombie creation, as was more common in the earlier Caribbean or African zombie variants. In Romero's movie, zombies are subject to the nature of the laws of physics and biology, responding like animals infected by rabies. Zombies are not completely dead; they have been infected to become a primitive and ruined form of life. Furthermore, zombies are hard to kill and may survive gunshots that humans would certainly die from. Traditionally, the only effective way of killing a zombie is to destroy its central nervous system, by chopping off its head for instance. Those unfamiliar with the zombie trope in popular culture might suggest that zombies be conquered via fantastical means, for instance by the intervention of new pseudo-scientific, voodoo or unexpected 'magic' effects. This is not relevant: in all virtual worlds, from computer games to internet societies, the environment itself may be fiction, but the accepted behaviour in that environment must be in accordance with existing laws and rules. Using mathematics, we can ensure that the rules of behaviour are followed.

Munz et al. (2009) modelled zombie outbreaks by extending the so-called SIR-type differential equation models, which are well established in epidemiology for representing the spreading of diseases such as flu and HIV. The conclusions in their paper are based on mathematical tools for analysing the stability of nonlinear dynamical systems described by ordinary differential equations. It was shown theoretically that an equilibrium state corresponding to a zombie-free world was unstable. However, humans do combat zombies in movies, with varying success. Munz et al. (2009) incorporated this effect by adding impulsive human attacks on zombies at some distinct points in time.

In the present work we take a different approach. First, we phrase the mathematical model directly as a set of difference equations, incorporating all the effects suggested in Munz et al. (2009). However, since we have excluded magic, we argue that defeated zombies cannot become functioning zombies again, a position that has a fundamental impact on whether the doomsday scenario is likely or not. Second, we propose that the parameters in the model change with time, according to the phases of the human–zombie interaction observed in scenes from a small sample of zombie movies. Third, we put effort into estimating the parameters of the model, based on a single (albeit highly influential) zombie movie, *The Night of the Living Dead* (Romero 1968). We fit the model to this movie so that we can reproduce its scenarios, and thereafter we shall use the model to predict how a zombie outbreak will most likely behave in a bigger community, with some speculative variations to the conditions found in Romero's film.

247

The rest of the chapter is organized as follows: we first list the mathematical model and define the input parameters required by that model. The next section is devoted to estimating parameters from one movie and demonstrating how the model predicts a zombie outbreak. We discuss the limitation of the study in the final section and make some concluding remarks about zombie movies. An appendix presents a brief mathematical explanation of the equations in our model.

The model for human–zombie interaction

Our mathematical model for human–zombie interaction will now be summarized. We have identified four categories of individuals likely to be present during a potential zombie event:

1. S: susceptible humans who can become zombies
2. I: infected humans, being bitten by zombies
3. Z: zombies
4. R: removed individuals, either conquered zombies or dead humans

The mathematical model expresses the temporal transfer of individuals between the four categories: S, I, Z and R. We introduce the number of individuals in each category as functions of time t: $S(t)$, $I(t)$, $Z(t)$ and $R(t)$. (A *function of time*, like $I(t)$, just means that a quantity, here the number of infected (I), varies with time.) These four functions are computed at discrete points in time: $t_1 = i\Delta t, i = 1,2...,n$. The values at time $t_0 = 0$ must be known. Introducing $S^i = S(t_i)$ and a similar short notation for the other three functions, we can write the system of equations governing the temporal evolution of S, I, Z and R as displayed in Figure 1. The parameters Σ, β, δ_s, δ_p, ρ, ζ, α, a, σ and $T_0...T_m$ must be given. We must also know the distribution of individuals initially, i.e., S_0, I_0, Z_0 and R_0.
The interpretations of the parameters are as follows:

Σ: The number of new humans brought into the zombified area per unit time.

β: The probability that a theoretically possible human–zombie pair actually meets physically, during a unit time interval, with the result that the human is infected.

$$S^{i+1} = S^i + \Delta t(\Sigma - \beta S^i Z^i - \delta_S S^i),$$
$$I^{i+1} = I^i + \Delta t(\beta S^i Z^i - \rho I^i - \delta_I I^i),$$
$$Z^{i+1} = Z^i + \Delta t(\rho I^i - (\alpha + \omega(t))S^i Z^i + \zeta R^i),$$
$$\omega(t) = a \sum_{i=0}^{m} \exp\left(\frac{1}{2}\left(\frac{t - T_i}{\sigma}\right)^2\right),$$
$$R^{i+1} = R^i + \Delta t(\delta_S S^i + \delta_I I^i - \zeta R^i + (\alpha + \omega(t))S^i Z^i)$$

Figure 1: The equations in the mathematical model for zombie infection. See the text for explanation of symbols.

δS: The probability that a susceptible human is killed or dies, in a unit time interval.

δI: The probability that an infected human is killed or dies, in a unit time interval.

ρ: The probability that an infected human is turned into a zombie, during a unit time interval.

ζ: The probability that a removed individual turns into a zombie, during a unit time interval.

α: The probability that, during a unit time interval, a theoretically possible human–zombie pair fights and the human kills the zombie.

a: As α, but the probability relates to killing a zombie in an organized and effective war on zombies.

$T_0,\ldots T_m$:   Points in time with strong attacks (war) on zombies.

σ: Length of attacks in the war on zombies (typically, 4σ measures the length and should be much smaller than the time interval $T_i - T_{i-1}$ between attacks).

Note that probabilities per unit time do not necessarily lie in the interval [0,1]. The real probability, lying between 0 and 1, arises after multiplication by the time interval of interest.

The calculation of the S^i, I^i, Z^i and R^i quantities, for the time levels corresponding to $i = 0, 1, 2, \ldots, n$, must be carried out in a computer programme, which is displayed in Figure 2.

Mathematical modelling in epidemiology, which is the scientific discipline laying the foundation for the system of difference equations illustrated in Figure 1's modelling of the zombification process, is very much about systems of *differential equations* (ODEs), not systems of difference equations. However, in the limit $\Delta t \to 0$, the difference equations in Figure 1 approach a system of ODEs. Since some readers may be well educated in differential equations, and find them easier to interpret than difference equations, we list the ODE system corresponding to Figure 1 in Figure 3. We shall not, however, deal more with the equations in Figure 3 in this chapter.

Estimation of parameters

To be able to estimate realistic parameters for our model, we have chosen to divide zombie outbreaks into three different phases:

1. The initial phase
2. The hysterical phase
3. The counter attack

The initial phase is characterized by the way that humans do not know that zombies are devastating man-eating monsters. In this phase, humans typically try to bring infected

```
Sigma = 0
beta = 0.03125
delta_S = 0
delta_I = 0
rho = 1
zeta = 0
alpha = 0.2*beta

a = 10*beta
sigma = 0.5
attacks = [5, 10, 18]
from math import exp
def omega(t, a, sigma, T):
    return a*sum(exp(-0.5*(t-T[i])**2/sigma) for i in range(len(T)))

dt = 0.1                # time step measured in hours
D = 0.7                 # simulation lasts for D days
n = int(D*24/dt)        # corresponding total no of hours

from numpy import zeros
S = zeros(n+1)
I = zeros(n+1)
Z = zeros(n+1)
R = zeros(n+1)

# initial conditions:
S[0] = 50
I[0] = 0
Z[0] = 3
R[0] = 0

# step equations forward in time:
for i in range(n):
    t = i*dt
    omega_t = omega(t, a, sigma, attacks)
    S[i+1] = S[i] + dt*(Sigma - beta*S[i]*Z[i] - delta*S[i])
    I[i+1] = I[i] + dt*(beta*S[i]*Z[i] - rho*I[i] - delta*I[i])
    Z[i+1] = Z[i] + dt*(rho*I[i] - (alpha + omega_t)*S[i]*Z[i] + \
                    zeta*R[i])
    R[i+1] = R[i] + dt*(delta*S[i] - zeta*R[i] + delta*I[i] + \
                    (alpha + omega_t)*S[i]*Z[i])
```

Figure 2: Computer code in the Python programming language for implementing the mathematical model for zombie infection.

patients and/or full blown zombies to hospitals for treatment. The consequence is that the disease spreads fast during this phase and that few zombies are neutralized. The initial phase is usually short. Humans soon realize that helping zombies will likely cause their own death. Needless to say, zombies often have a frightening look and appearance that prevent them from gaining sustained sympathy and rescue attempts, except from immediate family members in denial about their zombie status.

$$S' = \Sigma - \beta SZ - \delta_S S,$$
$$I' = \beta SZ - \rho I - \delta_I I,$$
$$Z' = \rho I - (\alpha + \omega(t))SZ + \zeta R,$$
$$\omega(t) = a \sum_{i=0}^{m} \exp\left(\frac{1}{2}\left(\frac{t - T_i}{\sigma}\right)^2\right),$$
$$R' = \delta_S S + \delta_I I - \zeta R + (\alpha + \omega(t))SZ$$

Figure 3: System of ordinary differential equations corresponding to the difference equation model in Figure 1. The prime denotes the derivative in time.

The second phase is usually characterized by hysteria. Humans, facing a pressing situation, try to hide and only fight back against zombies with the limited tools at their disposal. Often humans barricade themselves in a house and try to communicate with others or gather information through telephones, radio or TV. Zombification does not spread much during this phase.

In the final phase, the surviving humans have fully realized the threat that faces them. They gather weapons and fight back against zombies in an intelligent and strategic manner. However, in this phase zombies often outnumber humans by orders of magnitude, the result of a rapid process of zombification initiated during the first phase.

Example 1: The initial phase in The Night of the Living Dead

The initial phase in *The Night of the Living Dead* movie appears to last for approximately 4 hours. During this time, two humans meet one zombie, and one of the humans gets infected or eaten when trying to help the zombie (the zombie appears to be a human stumbling around). It is, of course, difficult to estimate parameters from such an isolated incidence, but let us try. According to the derivation of the first equation in Figure 1, the term $\Delta t \beta SZ \to 0$ models the increase in the number of infected individuals during a time interval Δt, which is assumed to be small. When applying this formula for a long time interval of 4 hours, we choose to use the value SZ at the beginning of the time interval, when $S = 2$ and $Z = 1$. It is unclear whether the human gets killed or infected, so let us say that there is a 50% chance for survival, resulting in $1/2$ infected, and turned into a zombie. This means that $\beta \cdot 4 \cdot 2 \cdot 1 = 0.5$, implying $\beta = 0.0625$. Furthermore, no zombies are killed in this initial phase, so $\alpha = a = 0$. We assume that infected humans become zombies within one hour with probability 1, giving $\rho = 1$.

These parameters are believed to be representative for the population in this small area of the outbreak. In order to produce as many zombies as appear later in the movie, we must assume that more humans than those represented in the early scenes of the movie are present in the initial phase, say 60. Figure 4 shows the consequence of starting with $S^0 = 60$, $I^0 = 3$ and using the estimated β, ρ and α values. The other parameters, δ_S, δ_I, a and ζ are not considered relevant and hence set to zero. The outbreak is seen to be very

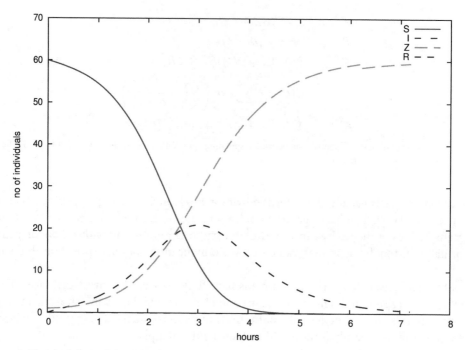

Figure 4: The initial phase of *The Night of the Living Dead*, with $\beta = 0.0625$. Humans are eradicated before the main part of the movie starts.

fast: the humans are eradicated after four hours, that is, during the initial phase of the movie. However, this is not consistent with what we watch later. The problem relates to the large value of β. Therefore, we look more into the sensitivity to β before proceeding with the other two phases.

Example 2: Sensitivity to parameters in the initial phase

The evolution of humans and zombies in the first phase is very sensitive to the value of β. To investigate this sensitivity, we have run a series of simulations where β is varied and where we have measured the number of hours it takes to reduce the human population with 95% compared to the initial value (S^0). Figure 6 shows the sensitivity to β for some choices of initial conditions S^0. Other key parameters for these runs are $\Sigma = \alpha = \delta S = \delta I = a = 0$ and $Z^0 = 1$. We have also computed the sensitivity to β for various values of Z^0. The curves are very similar to the ones in Figure 6 Figure 7. Since we have a logarithmic scale on the axis in Figure 6, the time to eradicate humans behaves as $C_1 \beta^{-C2}$ for positive constants C_1 and C_2. We notice that decreasing the initial amount of humans (S^0), or the initial amount of zombies (Z^0), may help to make the initial phase last longer, but a decrease in S^0 also leaves few humans available for the next phase.

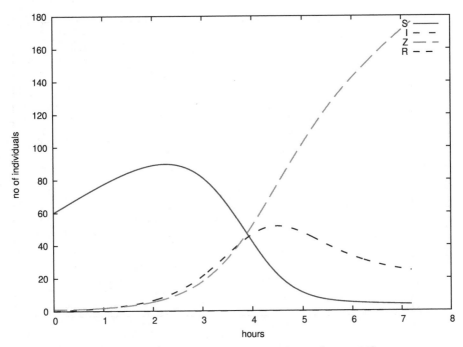

Figure 5: The initial phase of *The Night of the Living Dead* with $\Sigma = 20$, $\beta = 0.0$, $S^0 = 60$ and $Z^0 = 1$.

A different strategy to arrive at a more realistic model for the initial phase is to reduce β to 0.03 and steadily bring in more humans from the outside into the zombified area. Introducing $\Sigma = 20$, so that 20 humans arrive in the zombified area every hour, shifts the $S(t)$ to the right, as depicted in Figure 5. These graphs result in about 10 humans and 100 zombies after five hours, a state that may be compatible with what we see in the next phase of the movie. Another strategy is to reduce β further, e.g., to 0.02 as used later in Figure 12.

It might be of interest to see the sensitivity to β for various Σ values, and Figure 7 provides one example (with S^0 and Z^0 fixed at 60 and 1, respectively). A conclusion is that the estimated $\beta = 0.0625$ is too large to give meaningful results. We either have to decrease β, say to less than 0.02 according to Figure 6, or we have to feed in new humans, say $\Sigma = 20$, and halve the β value.

Example 3: *The hysterical phase in* **The Night of the Living Dead**
Most of the movie concerns the hysterical phase, which seems to last about 24 hours. In this phase the main characters arrive at an isolated house, which they crudely barricade. During this time, six humans get to the house and all but one get infected or killed. Hence we take five to be infected: two of these are eaten (killed) by zombies, while the other three turn into

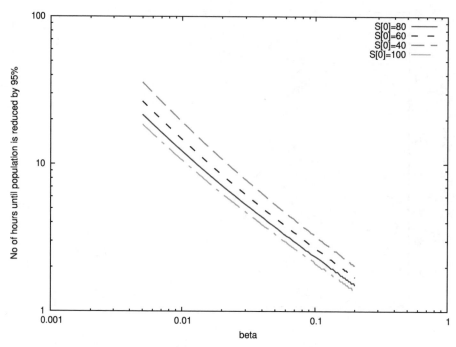

Figure 6: Time to 95% reduction in human population in the initial phase as function of β. Different initial conditions S^0 are varied.

zombies. During the same period seven zombies are killed by the human characters. It appears that around 30 zombies interact with the humans in this phase of the movie. To estimate β and α, we use the terms $\Delta t \beta SZ$ ($= 3 + 5$) and $\Delta t \alpha SZ$ ($= 7$) from the equations, with $\Delta t = 24$ hours, $S = 6$ and $Z = 30$. Hence, $\beta = 3/(6 \cdot 0 \cdot 24) \approx 0.0012$ and $\alpha = 7/(6 \cdot 30 \cdot 4) \approx 0.0016$. We also take the two infected humans that are killed into account in the I equation, giving a contribution $\delta_1 \Delta t S$ equal to 2 in that equation, i.e. $\delta_I = 2/(6 \cdot 24) = 0.014$. With these parameters, there will be some reduction in the human population, but not much. However, starting with 10 humans and 100 zombies – the state after five hours in the initial phase – the number of humans is further reduced, leaving too few for the final phase. We may either assume more humans at the beginning of the hysterical phase, or we may bring in new ones ($\Sigma \neq 0$). Going for the latter strategy and speculating that $\Sigma = 2$, Figure 8 shows the evolution of zombies during the course of 24 hours. In this situation, we see that humans and zombies may coexist for a long time.

***Example 4: The counter attack in* The Night of the Living Dead**
Towards the end of Romero's movie, the humans finally start their counterattack. In this phase, about 30 zombies are killed by about 30 humans in a matter of hours. Here, the

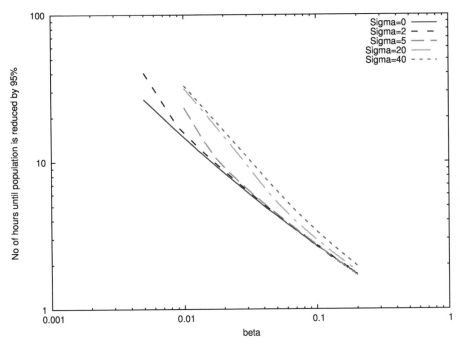

Figure 7: Time 95% reduction in human population in the initial phase as function of β. Different values of Σ (Sigma).

humans act strategically and use weapons to effectively destroy targeted zombies. One sheltered human accidentally gets killed because he was mistaken for a zombie, but otherwise humans destroy the zombies without risking their own lives.

Assuming a time frame of five hours, we can make some estimates: $\alpha \cdot 5 \cdot 30 \cdot 30 = 30$ giving $\alpha = 0.006$; $\beta = 0$ (no humans get infected); $\delta_S \cdot 5 \cdot 30 = 1$, implying $\delta_S = 0.0067$. Figure 9 shows the evolution of humans and zombies during this final phase. We may also put all the three phases together to show the evolution of zombies and humans through the complete movie. Figure 10 combines the phases and shows the evolution over three days. Using the originally estimated $\beta = 0.0625$ and without introducing new humans into the zombified area, we get the evolution as depicted in Figure 11, where doomsday appears to occur before the core of the movie starts. This is obviously unrealistic. A smaller β value 0.02 – as seen in Figure 12 – gives a much more realistic scenario, without any additional transport of humans into the zombified area.

As we have seen in the previous examples, the relation between α and β determines whether mankind faces extinction or not. The parameters are of course very uncertain, even when we base them on specific movies. Furthermore, the $\alpha - \beta$ relation varies a lot within a single movie. In *The Night of the Living Dead*, the zombies are mindless, clumsy and slow, but in *Zombieland* (Fleischer 2009) and *Dead Snow* (Henriksen and Wirkola 2009) they are

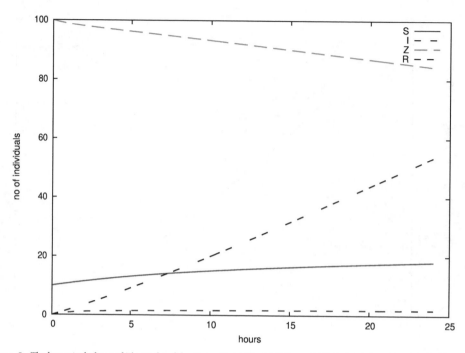

Figure 8: The hysterical phase of *The Night of the Living Dead* ($\beta = 0.0012$, $\alpha = 0.0016$, $\delta_1 = 0.014$, $\Sigma = 2$, with all other parameters set to zero).

considerably faster and may even outrun an average human. However, in all three of these movies it can be assumed that $\alpha \geq \beta$ in phases 2 and 3 because zombies always demonstrate a considerable lack of intelligence. Furthermore, in phase 3, $\alpha \gg \beta$ in all movies, since human response attacks are planned and effective. Hence, the crucial parameters that determine mankind's survival under a zombie outbreak are the duration of the initial phase and the value of the corresponding β. These two parameters are also the most uncertain parameters in typical zombie films since the initial phase is often short, and mostly used to introduce the main characters in the movie. Our sensitivity analysis shows that the time to human extinction has a power-law dependence on β.

Example 5: Allowing the dead zombies to re-enter the action.

So far, we have assumed that dead zombies are out of the game, i.e., $\zeta = 0$, which is in accordance with the non-magic zombie characters depicted in *The Night of the Living Dead*. However, since Munz et al. (2009) allow $\zeta \neq 0$, it is of interest to at least test a scenario where magic allows dead zombies to turn into active zombies again. Obviously, this effect changes the outcome dramatically. Even a small value, $\zeta = 0.05$, leads to a doomsday scenario over eight days, as shown in Figure 13.

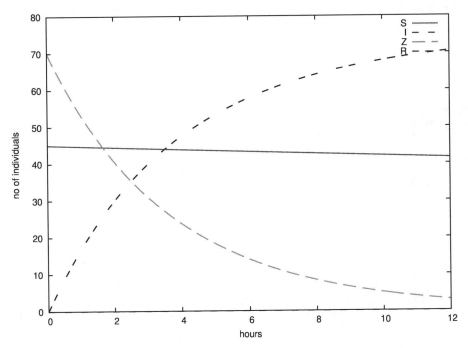

Figure 9: The counterattack in *The Night of the Living Dead*.

Example 6: A theoretical initial counterattack.

We have seen that zombification is rapid in the first phase. A better strategy than depicted in typical zombie movies is to follow the recommendations of Munz et al. (2009) and as soon as possible start with a full-scale war on zombies, containing impulsive attacks. Our $\omega(t)$ function in the mathematical model is exactly designed for this purpose. As a demonstration, we start out with 50 humans and 3 zombies, and $\beta = 0.0625$ as estimated from *The Night of the Living Dead*. These values lead to a rapid zombification. We assume there are some small resistances against zombies from the humans: $\alpha = 0.2\beta$. However, the humans implement three strong attacks, $a = 10\beta$, at 5, 10 and 18 hours after zombification starts. The attacks last for about 2 hours ($\sigma = 0.5$). It appears from Figure 14 that such strategically implemented attacks are sufficient to save mankind.

Conclusion

Zombies are unintelligent, flesh-hungry and clumsy beings. Consequently, once people realize the threat they will need to protect themselves as quickly and as fiercely as possible. In some recent movies like *Dead Snow* (Henriksen and Wirkola 2009) and *Zombieland*

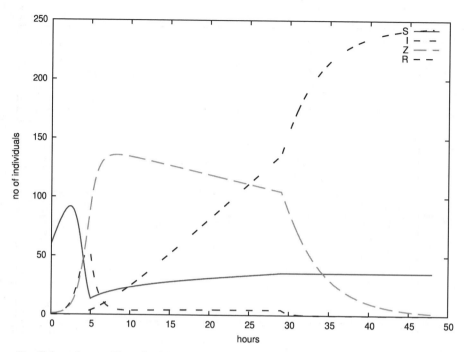

Figure 10: All three phases in *The Night of the Living Dead.*

(Fleischer 2009), the zombies are fast and may even outrun an untrained individual, but they are always un-intelligent. Because of this lack of intelligence, the protagonists in the movies always kill large numbers of zombies. Hence, if the main characters are representative humans, then an average human could kill more zombies than an average zombie could infect. Humans can therefore quickly eradicate zombies as soon as they realize the threat. The key point is that the time it takes to realize this fact must be smaller than the time it takes to infect nearly all humans in the initial phase.

Our estimation of the speed of zombification in the initial phase gave a too-high value, as no disease spreads that fast. The estimation procedure used terms in the difference equations, with time scales much larger than assumed when introducing these terms in the modelling. The data was also based on watching the movie, i.e., what we see is what there is. Claiming that the initial phase of *The Night of the Living Dead* is unrealistic, and that zombification spreads at a significantly lower speed, we could obtain a model that fits the observed evolution of humans and zombies in that movie.

Zombies will never outnumber people if humans recognize their threat quickly enough, and realizing that zombies are monsters is almost inevitable. Zombies will therefore never be a threat to mankind, unless some kind of additional supernatural magic ($\zeta > 0$) is involved.

258

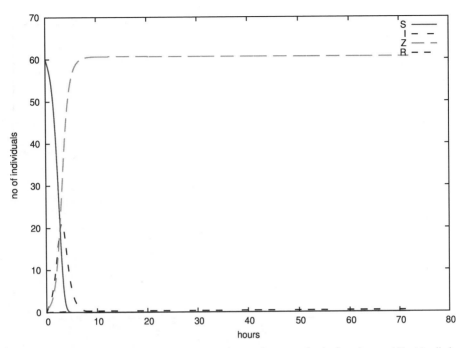

Figure 11: All three phases in *The Night of the Living Dead*, using $\beta = 0.0625$ for the first phase and $\Sigma = 0$ in all phases.

Appendix: modelling zombie infection

We shall here briefly explain the reasoning behind the equations in Figure 1 of our mathematical model. For this purpose, let us start with a quick overview of how zombies behave. Wilson (2009) has described how zombies work:

> Many people credit George A. Romero with setting the standard for modern zombies. In the classic movie *Night of the Living Dead*, Romero portrayed zombies as slow-moving, flesh-eating corpses, reanimated by radiation from a satellite returning from Venus. The radiation affected the recent, unburied dead, and the resulting zombies were invulnerable until someone destroyed their brains or separated their heads from their bodies. In *Night of the Living Dead*, zombies were neither intelligent nor self-aware. They had a very limited use of tools, mostly confined to using blunt objects as cudgels … Many movies and video games have used Romero's concept of zombies. For the most part, zombies are: newly dead corpses reanimated by radiation, chemicals, viruses, sorcery or acts of God; human, although some depictions include zombie animals; very strong, but not very fast or agile; impervious to pain and able to function after sustaining extreme physical damage; invulnerable to injury, except for decapitation or destruction of the brain; relentlessly driven to kill and eat; afraid of fire and bright lights. (Wilson 2009)

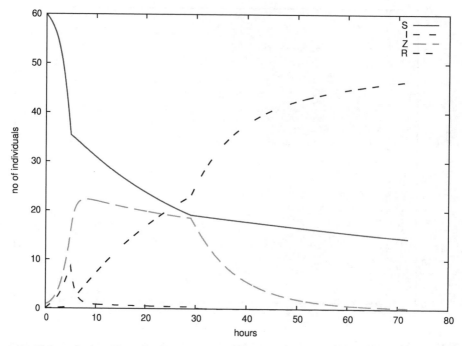

Figure 12: All three phases in *The Night of the Living Dead*, using $\beta = 0.02$ for the first phase and $\Sigma = 0$ in all phases.

Some modern movies introduce intelligent and fast-moving zombies, but these are often claimed to be contradictory to the mythology established by George A. Romero (Pegg 2008).

The basic starting point for the mathematical modelling is that zombification acts like a disease. That is, human susceptibles get infected by zombies. A fraction of the infected are then turned into zombies. On the other hand, humans can overcome individual and groups of zombies. Dead humans and zombies constitute a *removed category*. One particular feature of this category is that some of the dead humans can be turned into zombies.

We introduce four categories: susceptibles (S), infected (I), zombies (Z) and removed (R). The corresponding functions counting how many individuals we have in each category are named $S(t)$, $I(t)$, $Z(t)$ and $R(t)$, respectively.

Now we shall set up all the dynamic features of the human–zombie populations we aim to model. Changes in the S category are due to three effects.

1. Susceptibles are infected by zombies, modelled by a term $-\Delta t \beta S Z$, similar to the S–I interaction in the classical SIR model for epidemic diseases.
2. Susceptibles die naturally and enter the removed category. If the probability that one susceptible dies during a unit time interval is δ_s, the total expected number of deaths in a time interval Δt becomes $\Delta t \delta_s S$.

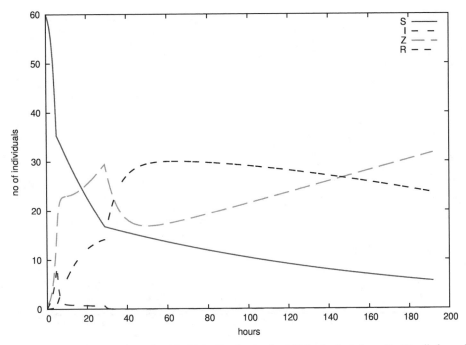

Figure 13: All three phases in *The Night of the Living Dead*, using $\beta = 0.02$ for the first phase, $\Sigma = 0$ in all phases, but $\zeta = 0.05$ to allow dead zombies to re-enter the active zombie category.

3. We also allow new humans to enter the area with zombies, as this effect may be necessary to successfully run a war on zombies (the other two effects alone will solely reduce the number of susceptibles). The number of new individuals in the S category arriving per time unit is denoted by Σ, giving an increase in $S(t)$ by $\Delta t \Sigma$ during a time Δt.

We could also add newborns to the S category, but we have decided to skip this effect since it will only be significant as a threat over time-scales of a decade or more. Our characteristic time in this study is in days rather than decades. The balance equation of susceptibles, incorporating the three mentioned effects, becomes

$$S^{t+1} = S^t + \Delta t(\Sigma - \beta S^t Z^t - \delta_s S^t). \qquad (1)$$

The infected category gets a contribution $-\Delta t \beta S Z$ from the S category, but loses individuals to the Z and R category. That is, some infected are turned into zombies, while others die. Movies reveal that infected may commit suicide or that others (susceptibles) may kill them. Let δ_I be the probability of being killed in a unit time interval. We clearly have that δ_I is much larger than the natural death of humans (δ_s). During time Δt, a total of $\delta_I \Delta t I$ will die and

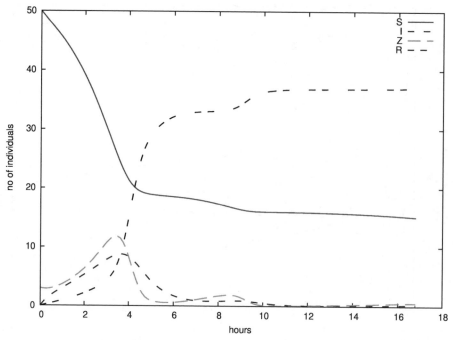

Figure 14: Simulation of a zombie outbreak with β as in the initial phase of *The Night of the Living Dead*, but with an effective war on zombies with strong attacks after 5, 10 and 18 hours ($\delta_S = \delta_I = \zeta = \Sigma = 0, \rho = 1, a = 10\beta, \sigma = 0.5$).

hence be transferred to the removed category. The probability that a single infected is turned into a zombie during a unit time interval is denoted by ρ, so that a total of $\Delta t \rho I$ individuals are lost from the I to the Z category in time Δt. The accounting in the I category becomes

$$I^{t+1} = I^t + \Delta t (\beta S^t Z^t - \rho I^t - \delta_I I^t). \qquad (2)$$

The zombie category gains $-\Delta t \rho I$ individuals from the I category. Following Munz et al. (2009), we also allow a fraction ζ per time unit of the removed category to turn into zombies. During time Δt a total number of $\Delta t \zeta R$ are moved from the R to the Z category. However, we question the relevance of this term, because additional supernatural agencies are needed to turn dead people or zombies back into active zombies. A quotation from Wilson (2009) supports this view: 'In some portrayals, zombism is contagious, and people bitten by zombies become zombies themselves. In others, people die from the bite and are reanimated by the same force that created the other zombies.' The latter case is modelled by β and ρ – it does not matter if the human or infected dies and turns into a zombie after a few minutes or if the death does not occur. The important effect with a $\Delta t \zeta R$ term is that conquered zombies can still be zombies, i.e., there is feedback in the system, and obviously zombies overtake us all. A fundamental feature in zombie movies is that humans can conquer zombies. We introduce two aspects to this feature. First, zombies can be killed in a 'man-to-man' human–zombie fight. This interaction resembles the nature of zombification (or the susceptible–infective interaction in the SIR model) and can be modelled by a loss $-\alpha SZ$ for some parameter α with an interpretation similar to that of β. Second, a war on zombies can be implemented with large-scale effective attacks. A possible model is to increase α by some amount $\omega(t)$, where $\omega(t)$ varies in time to model strong attacks at some distinct points of time $T_1<T_2<\cdots<Tm$. Around these t values we want ω to have a large value, while in between the attacks ω is small. One possible mathematical function with this behaviour is a sum of bell functions:

$$\omega(t) = a\sum_{i=0}^{m} exp\left(1/2\left(t - T_l/\sigma\right)^z\right). \qquad (3)$$

Here a measures the strength of the attacks (the maximum value of $\omega(t)$) and σ measures the length of the attacks, which should be much less than the time between the points of attack: typically, 4σ measures the length of an attack, and we must have $4\sigma<<T_1-T_{l-1}$ to make the length of an attack much smaller than the time between two attacks. We should choose a significantly larger than α to make the attacks in the war on zombies much stronger than the 'man-to-man' killing of zombies. We remark that equation 3) is our continuous way of modelling the discrete impulsive attacks that play a fundamental role in defeating zombies in the work by Munz et al. (2009). Summarizing the loss and gain in the zombie category leads to the following equation for Z:

$$Z^{i+1} = Z^i + \Delta t(\rho I^i-(\alpha + \omega(t))S^iZ^i + \zeta Ri). \qquad (4)$$

The accounting in the R category consists of a gain δS of natural deaths from the S category, a corresponding loss ζR to the Z category (though claimed unrealistic), a gain δI from the I category, and a gain $(\alpha + \omega)SZ$ from defeated zombies:

$$R^{i-1} = R^i + \Delta t(\delta S^i - \zeta R^i + \delta I^i +(\alpha + \omega(t))S^iZ^i). \qquad (5)$$

The mathematical model for zombification involves the four key quantities $S(t)$, $I(t)$, $Z(t)$ and $R(t)$, which can be computed from the equations derived above and listed in Figure 1. The parameters Σ, β, δ_s, δ_p, ρ, ζ, α, a, σ, and $T_0,\ldots T_m$ must be given. We must also know the distribution of individuals initially, i.e., $S(0)$, $I(0)$, $Z(0)$ and $R(0)$ must be given.

Acknowledgement

The authors would like to express their sincere thanks to Karen-Helene Støverud for typesetting the document in Microsoft Office Word, and especially for her never-ending enthusiastic struggle with converting all the beautiful LaTeX mathematics to the world of Word.

Toward a zombie pedagogy: embodied teaching and the student 2.0

Jesse Stommel

A class is also a process, an independent organism with its own goal and dynamics. It is always something more than what even the most imaginative lesson plan can predict.

(Thomas Kasulis 1982: 39)

Students are evolving. The student 2.0 is an altogether different animal from the student 1.0. And our classrooms are ecosystems, an environment all their own, where we as teachers must decide how to engage this new species of student. We teeter at a slowly disintegrating threshold, one foot in a physical world and the other in a virtual one. Our students are no longer just bodies in desks; they are no longer vessels.[1] They have become compilations, amalgams, a concatenation of web sites. They are the people in front of us, but exist simultaneously as their avatars in *World of Warcraft* and the profiles they create on Facebook. They speak with mouths, but also with fingers tapping briskly at the keys of their smart phones. When they want to 'reach out and touch someone', they use Skype and Twitter. They have become more than just ears and eyes and brains to feed. Now, they feed us, and themselves, and each other, with an endless parade of texted and tweeted characters. Should not we, as teachers 2.0, work with and not against the flow of these seemingly errant 1s and 0s? Should not student-centred learning address itself, as fully as possible, to this new breed of student? Should not we understand our students as more than just inert flesh? In fact, flesh is never really inert; an embodied pedagogy recognizes this and demands that we rethink traditional educational paradigms.

The entire educational system is undergoing a swift and certain decay. In 'A file structure for the complex, the changing, and the indeterminate', Ted Nelson writes: 'The physical universe is not all that decays. So do abstractions and categories. Human ideas, science, scholarship, and language are constantly collapsing and unfolding. Any field, and the corpus of all fields is a bundle of relationships subject to all kinds of twists, inversions, involutions, and rearrangement' (1965: 144). Decay is figured here as a process of 'collapsing' and 'unfolding', of twisting, inverting, involuting and rearranging, not a destructive process but a deconstructive one, rebuilding even as it bends and tears and fractures. We generally attribute the word 'decay' to dead things: road kill decays; a fallen tree decays; cadavers decay. Whether living or dead, all human bodies also undergo decay. Our hair decays, our skin decays, the teeth in our mouth decay. All matter in the universe is finite, so the process of decay is, in fact, necessary for the breakdown and eventual replacement of dead matter with new life. So, when an idea decays, it does not die or disappear or become otherwise irrelevant. Rather, it splits, breaks open, and its pieces are set loose. And, for a moment, before they begin to reform into new ideas, philosophies and scholarship, the little idea pieces squirm and flip, tweak and tangle.

The term 'disc rot' describes the tendency of optical discs to deteriorate over time due to oxidation, physical damage, etc. The word 'rot' suggests something far more insidious at work. Certainly, 'going to ruin' is a common definition of the word; however, more often rot connotes decomposition caused by the tireless work of bugs, bacteria and fungus. There is something treacherous about rot, a creeping, compulsive sort of dread. We find ourselves awed by the possibilities it presents and curious, morbidly curious, to discover the various ways it will recontextualize us and our matter. Rot hesitates just between death and rebirth, a teetering deconstructive moment. Emerson writes in *The Poet*, 'So when the soul of the poet has come to ripeness of thought, she detaches and sends away from it its poems or songs, – a fearless, sleepless, deathless progeny, which is not exposed to the accidents of the weary kingdom of time; a fearless, vivacious offspring, clad with wings' (1844: 253). For Emerson, the deconstructive moment gives way to the monstrous birth, a chimera-like creature, born of ideas but with a life of its own, a progeny of words that weave through the world and into the 'hearts of men'. Rapid advances in technology are just now allowing for exactly this kind of moment, a moment of play, a (de)evolution, in which we mourn the death of books and films and composition (as we once knew them or thought we knew them) even as we fiddle gleefully with the haptic interfaces of our mobile devices.

Digital texts invite us to do other things with our eyes, brains and bodies as we experience them. My own pedagogy juxtaposes digital media, literature and film, because this is exactly what our apparatuses for media-consumption are doing: now, we watch Ridley Scott's *Alien* in a window on our laptop screens alongside Twitter and Facebook. Film no longer exists as a medium distinct from these other media. The same is true of new modes of reading. As I write this, I have nine windows open on my computer, each vying for my attention. Some of these windows have several frames in further competition: advertisements, e-mail, documents, widgets, social-networking tools, chat interfaces and more. Each affects how I engage the digital text, but I do not experience a *decreased* attention; rather, the digital text demands a different *sort* of attention. Even as my direct engagement is challenged, my brain is offered more fuel for making connections and associative leaps. A proactive approach to digital pedagogy asks us to put these associative leaps to work. So, Twitter and Facebook may be a distraction, but that distraction can be harnessed for good pedagogy.

Embodied pedagogies

In this chapter, I utilize the figure of the zombie to examine current pedagogical practice and to propose a new, and more fully embodied, brand of postmodern pedagogy. I work with the zombie as a theoretical tool while also discussing my own experiments with teaching zombie texts in film, literature, and composition courses. Much work has focused on the zombie as an allegorical figure symptomatic of cultural problems, a representation of the human at its most tedious and banal. My own work is about re-reading and reclaiming the zombie, about exploring its liberatory potential. The zombie body is all meat, textured, dangling, hideous meat. It is both *dead*, ecstatic decaying flesh, and *in pieces*, with missing bits and outer layers worn away to reveal its viscera. The zombie body is lively, in many ways more lively than our own, which have become overrun by iPods, holstered cell phones and other digital prostheses. We find ourselves increasingly drawn to zombie narratives, because zombies embody a part of ourselves we have lost touch with, because they represent a physicality that is turning more and more virtual in the technological age. We want zombies in our lives, because they offer something we cannot get from representations, avatars and emoticons. We want zombies in our lives, because they have matter we can cling to, because they are after (*hungry for*) exactly what we are afraid we have lost, the matter left in us.

For many teachers, the increasing disembodiment of ourselves and our students leads to a pedagogy that is even more fundamentally disembodied. In the classroom 1.0, the teacher all too often lectures to a roomful of mute brains and eyeballs, the students' physicality relegated to a waggling hand, a mere medium between the drone of the expert and the scrawl in their notebooks. Should we forget these bodies altogether, and turn instead to their virtual doubles? No – I would argue that, in the classroom 2.0, we must turn simultaneously in two directions. As teachers, we must engage our students at the level of 1s and 0s but also at the level of flesh. Even as the classroom moves more and more into digital space, we must find ways to make learning ecstatic. In our land-based classes, we might embrace the convenience of technology by eliminating paper syllabi and accepting all of our students' assignments online, but we must also remind ourselves and our students that their work has (and will always have) a distinctly physical character. Even though the Kindle and iPad offer compelling alternatives, the material object of a book or film will never be fully lost. A book has an odour, a certain weight in our hands, a tactile pleasure at the turn of a page. The film strip has an audible clack as it moves through the projector, and the emulsion dissolves sweetly before our eyes. Even if these media are rendered mostly intangible, books and films will always have a physical impact on us, causing us to recoil, sigh, bristle and scream.

And student work has the potential for all these same qualities. It has heft and gravity, meaning and substance. The best academic and creative work is rooted in experience – the experience of a world, a book, a film, a self. Analysis and critical thinking are like eating, they are lively and voracious, things that drip and reel. They are not (and cannot be) purely digital. And yet, paradoxically, in the classroom 2.0, we must find a way for this kind of analysis and critical thinking to happen online, even as we also find ways to reengage our students in the physical work of the face-to-face classroom. The so-called 'live classroom' can be neither here nor there. It has to be *both* simultaneously. We must bring our subjects to life for our students and their digital counterparts. Learning must fire every neuron, it must touch students at the highest levels of consciousness and at the cellular level. No matter where it happens, whether online or in a classroom, this is what learning must do. It must evolve – and revolt.

The dead and the undead

In 'The Dead and the Undead', a multimodal composition course I began teaching in the Spring of 2011 at Georgia Tech, USA, I focus on the figure of the zombie to help students consider the material and immaterial nature of composition and media.[2] On the opening page of the syllabus, I ask the following sorts of questions: 'What constitutes the flesh of an essay? Does a word have flesh? Does film have flesh? Do interactive texts have flesh? And to what extent do these media engage us at the level of flesh?' During the semester, the students examine a multimedia array of texts that explore zombies and their literary and figurative precursors including Mary Shelley's *Frankenstein* (1823), Mary Roach's *Stiff: The Curious Lives of Human Cadavers* (2003), George Romero's *Night of the Living Dead* (1968), Cormac McCarthy's *The Road* (2007), and Robert Kirkman's comic book series *The Walking Dead* (2003–present).

The major project for the course has all 25 students collaborating for the entire semester to produce one film. Early in the semester, they are subdivided into departments: production, screenwriting, filmmaking, postproduction and marketing. In addition to 20-minute films, they produce treatments, a screenplay, storyboards, market research, a legal brief, a press release, posters, previews, a blog, a website, and more. They also offer pitches with visual aids, conduct peer reviews of their own contributions, and work closely with campus organizations and the surrounding business community on marketing and production tasks. Throughout the process, the students carefully reflect on their own roles, while also researching topics related to the subject of their film. They work together in a classroom, but the course also expands their digital literacy by having much of their collaboration happen online using tools like *Google Docs* and a course blog.

The best teachers, in my mind, are willing to take risks. I frequently tell students, somewhat cheekily, 'if you are going to fail, it's best to make it a *spectacular* failure.' I go on to explain that the best projects are often the most ambitious, the ones that ask us to work outside our comfort zones, the ones that make mediocrity impossible. I ask students to be ambitious and to risk failure, and I ask the same of myself. When I first taught this particular course, I considered the project an *experiment*, a labyrinthine (and seemingly impossible) task. I told the students we should be less worried about the end-results, given that none of them were professional filmmakers, and more concerned with the process itself. The students, though, rose to the challenges of the course in ways I never would have expected, and I rose to the challenge as well, juggling three film productions (one for each section I was teaching), while also remaining attentive to the rhetorical and research-based objectives of the course.

My goal is not to teach students to become zombie experts, filmmakers, professional writers/rhetoricians or supreme commanders of web-based media. My goal is to have them thinking critically – about media, about horror, about the filmmaking process, about collaboration, about the many audiences for their work, and about themselves as readers, viewers, thinkers and content-producers. The students create something meaningful and entertaining, which has a rhetorical effect on its audience. But more importantly, they engage in a focused process that challenges them to rethink how they look at and approach composition, as well as their own educations. The zombie film project is itself a bit of a conceit, its content being somewhat arbitrary; however, it is my argument here that the content of this course is only somewhat and not entirely arbitrary. Many of the methods I use in this course are not peculiar to courses I teach about zombies. They have worked equally well in courses focused on other topics, in other disciplines, in classrooms, online and at several universities. Nonetheless, the zombie as a figure functions in a very specific way in this course, serving as both subject-matter *and* as a model for the pedagogical practices I employ.

The zombie as pedagogical model

In my previous work on the zombie as a literary icon, I have argued that we are at a point in our evolution as a species where we have become not quite living not quite dead (Stommel 2007). With the advent of virtual bodies (in video games, chat rooms, online profiles, etc.), cloning, cyborg technology and even the cell phone, we are seeing ourselves become more and more disembodied (Stommel 2007, 2009). As our flesh erodes, who we are is reconstituted in the 1s and 0s of our Facebook profiles and Twitter feeds. This feeling of disembodiment is why we have become so obsessed in our entertainment media with bodies, dead and otherwise – with cadavers, crime scenes, bodily mutilation and torture – with television shows like *Six Feet Under* (2001–2005) and *CSI* (2000–present), films like *Hostel* (2005) and *Saw* (2004), video games like *Manhunt 2* (2007) and *Resident Evil* (2002), and novels like McCarthy's *The Road* (2007). This is, by no means, a newfound fascination, reflecting a far more universal fear, a fear Shakespeare explores in *Hamlet*, which begins with the ominous words 'Who's there?'; a fear Mary Shelley explores in *Frankenstein*, wondering about identity and physicality from the first phrase, 'I am by birth': and a fear Herman Melville explores in 'The Tartarus of maids', where he describes 'blank-looking girls' (1855: 69) working in a paper factory, slaves to a new-fangled machine. Each text wonders what constitutes a self, of what sort of matter are we made, what is it to be a body, to be human.

We crave, and are nostalgic for, a truly visceral experience of the body – of bodies torn apart and reassembled, bodies breathing and being stopped of breath, bodies scrutinized post-mortem, and bodies (no matter how gruesome) as aesthetically viable objects. The zombie is part and parcel of this cultural obsession, but it is also the antidote. The zombie threatens to deconstruct us (to eat us) in an altogether different way from the machine. Whereas a machine devours our flesh, turning us all into automata, the zombie just chews, turning us into zombies, which are the epitome of flesh. Machines take our flesh away. Zombies proffer it back. Put simply, zombies cannot do their messy work if their victim is just data.

Whether we want them to or not, zombies remind us that we have bodies, that we are flesh. The final thesis of Jeffrey Jerome Cohen's essay 'Monster culture (seven theses)' proposes that 'the Monster Stands at the Threshold of Becoming' (1996: 20). Monsters exist, for Cohen, not because we want them to but because we need them to, because they not only reflect who we are but influence who we will become. So, at a moment when the very fabric (the very flesh) of who we are is being redefined by the machines with which we have put ourselves in such close, intimate proximity, we turn to monsters. In the postmodern, technological age, our bodies have become 'bodies-in-process', in the words of Judith Halberstam, 'virtual bodies: in unvisualizable amniotic indeterminacy, and unfazed by the hype of their always premature and redundant annunciation, posthuman bodies thrive in the mutual deformations of totem and taxonomy' (1995: 19). At exactly this moment, when the human gives way to the posthuman, when the body is made virtual and flesh becomes an anachronism, we turn (in)to monsters, monsters that plod and reel, monsters that ooze and drip, monsters that grab and chew, feeding on flesh, feeding us our own flesh, monsters that are just matter, monsters that matter.

Embodiment and the classroom 2.0

Technology certainly changes the way we live our lives, the shape of our days, how we read, and how we learn, but there has been a good deal of recent work that suggests we are being changed in a far more profound way. In *iBrain: Surviving the Technological Alteration of the Modern Mind*, Gary Small writes,

> The current explosion of digital technology not only is changing the way we live and communicate but is rapidly and profoundly altering our brains. Daily exposure to high technology – computers, smart phones, video games, search engines like Google and Yahoo – stimulates brain cell alteration and neurotransmitter release, gradually strengthening new neural pathways in our brains while weakening old ones. Because of the current technological revolution, our brains are evolving right now – at a speed like never before. (2008: 1)

According to Small and others, the neurons in our brains are literally rewiring themselves to create pathways to accommodate our increasing interaction with computers and digital technology.[3] I myself did not grow up with the internet. I did not have a network connection until my first year in college. I recognize the ways that my brain is being rewired by the internet; however, many of my students have had internet access in their homes as long as they can remember, so their brains were wired (not rewired) by the internet.

How, then, should we reimagine or adapt our teaching strategies to reach these students? If newer generations of students learn differently, if their brains *function* differently, must we also teach differently? Students now hold an encyclopedic wealth of information literally in their hands, available to them at the press of a button or the swipe of a finger across a touchscreen. The teacher is no longer just a depository and depositor of knowledge. Our job has become altogether more complex. The teacher 2.0 must shift the focus from individual learners to the community of learners, drawing new boundaries that reflect a much larger hybrid classroom. Now, our work in the world must be done also (and simultaneously) online.

On the front page of the syllabus for every course I teach, I include the quotation from Thomas Kasulis (1982: 39) that serves as the epigraph to this chapter. Kasulis captures the dynamic nature of the contemporary classroom, suggesting each of our courses will necessarily have a life of its own no matter how certain we are in advance of the parameters. As teachers, how do we contend with the sort of organism Kasulis describes? How does an embodied pedagogy, a zombie pedagogy, manifest itself in the classroom? What literal and figurative shapes or configurations does it take?

To begin an answer, I set forth a series of provisional tenets. In the classroom 2.0:

Flesh is connected: Emerson writes, 'When the mind is braced by labor and invention, the page of whatever book we read becomes luminous with manifold allusion. Every sentence is doubly significant, and the sense of our author is as broad as the world' (1837: 58). I find Emerson's use of the word 'allusion' particularly meaningful here, because it suggests the importance of the sorts of connections we make when reading, when writing, when viewing a film. A text is, for all intents and purposes, meaningless without these connections. A classroom offers a physical place that encourages these connections, a room with many experts in all manner of things. In digital space, where information is networked, the possibilities for these connections increase exponentially.

Collaboration is viral: I never consider myself the primary audience for student work. Instead, I have students work collaboratively, interacting as both readers and writers, learning as much from each other as they do from me. Students in the zombie class, for example, function as a hive mind. They have individual bodies, but the course project emphasizes the capacities of many bodies working in concert. Digital space allows students the opportunity to collaborate not only with each other and me but with a much broader digital community.

Authority centres decay: When I walk into most classrooms, the desks are in neat and tidy rows, all facing forward so that students stare through the back of each other's heads and towards the teacher's lectern at the front. My first act upon entering these rooms is to remove the lectern, because there is no front of the room in my classroom. This can be a literal or figurative gesture. In an online or hybrid class, this might be achieved by moving outside the closed space of the LMS and into the open space of the web. I have increasing difficulty with the phrase Learning Management System, because I believe learning is not something that can or should be strictly managed. Students in my classes come to realize that they and their work are the primary texts. I bring my own ideas, but they are part and parcel with the rest. My job as the teacher is to inspire, to listen, to question, to marvel. And the Learning Management System is just a portal.

Tools for dismantling conventional classroom dynamics are built into the learning space itself: In the classroom 2.0, the space of the classroom is itself recognized as a sort of body, a container with a marked influence on its contents. Within weeks of the start of each new semester, my students are fully aware that I'm obsessed with rearranging our classroom: small circular clusters of four and five desks dotting a large room, one large circle of desks around the perimeter, a u-shape facing a projected image. We move frequently between these arrangements and others, often several times in a single class session. I'm also quite fond of the chaotic jumble of bodies and desks that forms when I ask a classroom of students in small groups to abruptly turn their desks to the centre of the room. Oddly wonderful things happen when students find themselves in a mass of jumbled desks. It is a profoundly egalitarian configuration.

Participants chew but do not swallow: Emerson writes, 'Books are the best of things, well used; abused, among the worst' (1837: 56). Books have instrumental, not just intrinsic, value. I encourage students to take full possession of their books, to treat them roughly and without excessive reverence. I'm less interested in the books themselves and more interested in what my students do with them, more interested in the carnage they spill upon them. The same is true of the films we study. Films have value because they provoke us, because they scare us, because they instruct us, each in their own way. But their greatest value is brought out when we engage them, substantially and meaningfully. The best films, the best books, speak to us only when we speak to them. Content becomes even more democratic in digital space, where student work appears right alongside the other works we study.

Technologically-mediated interactions are haptic: A colleague of mine recently tweeted: 'what a drag responding 2 e-mails only breeds yet more e-mails – I remember the days when it was thrilling 2 send/receive these cursed messages.' I find her use of the word 'breeds' particularly interesting, suggesting that an e-mail can at least figuratively copulate and reproduce – that e-mail has a life of its own. We think of e-mailing as a disembodied mode of communication, but it is becoming increasingly embodied. When my phone is in my pocket, an incoming message tickles my leg, as though a critter is climbing into (or out of) my phone. And the touch screen allows me to interact tactilely with e-mail, flicking messages back and forth in a flurry of text. Technologically-mediated interactions now have an intimacy, a real human connection, that goes beyond the code that constructs it. Digital pedagogy should, as much as possible, take advantage of this evolution, moving off the computer screen and into the hands (and pockets) of students.

Participants embrace chaos and self-cannibalism: An attachment to outcomes discourages experimentation. The work of participants in classroom 2.0 is playful and messy. In *Deep Play*, Diane Ackerman writes, 'Play is far older than humans. It's so familiar to us, so deeply ingrained in the matrix of our childhood, that we take it for granted … We may think of play as optional, a casual activity. But play is fundamental to evolution. Without play, humans and many other animals would perish' (1999: 3–4). George Dennison offers a similar account of play in *The Lives of Children*. He describes 'children's natural play' as 'expansive and diverse, alternately intense and gay', whereas more formal play (games with umpires, rules, etc.) becomes 'strained and silent', 'serious', and 'uncomfortable' (1969: 195–96). There is no learned self, only learning as a present participle. In my classroom, play functions not as a methodological approach towards a set of outcomes but as the outcome in and of itself.

Participants use hands, limbs, and mouths to compose: I design courses that ask students to look closer and to dig. None of the class activities are done merely as exercises. The purpose of a literature, film or writing course, is to encourage students to engage more thoughtfully with their world and the things in it. I'm less interested in the results of this exploration and more interested in the process. In *Schooling the Postmodern Body: Critical Pedagogy and the Politics of Enfleshment*, Peter McLaren (1995: 61) describes the various ways that 'bodily knowledge, the memory our body has about how our muscles should move, our arms should swing, and our legs should stride', is connected to other forms of knowledge. For McLaren, learning is an embodied practice.[4] We learn best by doing, feeling, experiencing and interacting.

All learning is necessarily hybrid: No matter what or where we teach, it is important to engage both the physical and digital selves of students. With digital pedagogy, our challenge is not to merely *replace* (or offer substitutes for) face-to-face instruction, but to find new and innovative ways to engage students in the practice of learning. We must look back even as we look forward, considering what learning has become while simultaneously examining the hows and whys of its becoming. We must consider the interface between digital and analogue culture, between the pixels of our computer screens and the printed text of bound books. What we *do* online has little meaning if it is not linked (literally or figuratively) to embodied practice. What we *are* online only exists insofar as it is connected to what we are in the flesh.

Conclusion

Rather than simply reversing the hierarchy of the technology/flesh binary, I would advocate a more thorough dismantling in which we recognize technology as a *tool* for building new worlds and *not* as a world in and of itself.[5] At the various institutions where I have taught, I have found myself talking more with colleagues about technological tools than about students or the subjects we are teaching. The same is true of many educational technology conferences, where participants talk more about learning management than about learning. And when our digital tools fail us, as they so often do, our impulse is to become even more preoccupied with them. For me, this feels like sitting down to write an essay with pencil and paper and becoming distracted by ruminations about the nature of No. 2 pencils and loose-leaf paper. Even as I incorporate more and more technology into my pedagogical arsenal, I work to keep the bells and whistles of new-fangled tools from dictating my pedagogy, which should instead rise organically out of a critical interrogation of those tools and the subjects and students of a particular course.

The title of this chapter advocates only moving *towards* a zombie pedagogy, in part because there is no one pedagogical strategy that works for all students/teachers or in all situations. The space of the classroom is shifting and dynamic. As a pedagogical beast, the zombie advances slowly and deliberately. It does not consume or devour its victims but chews without digesting, creating an increasingly large throng of zombies in its wake. Unlike clones, pod people, replicants or automata, each zombie is not a mere duplicate of another. Zombies move in packs and attack in mobs, but they maintain their individuality all the while, each with its own idiosyncratic gait and dressed in its own random spattering of gore. They limp, stumble, moan and clamour as they surge forth, all in imperfect unison, a cacophony of sounds, always walking, always reaching.

Notes

1   Nor were they ever. This idea has been explored extensively by numerous writers that are worth mentioning here. Paulo Freire argues against the 'banking' model of education in *Pedagogy of the Oppressed*. Freire writes, 'The teacher is no longer merely the-one-who-teaches, but one who is himself taught in dialogue with the students, who in turn while being taught also teach' (1970: 61). David Bartholomae begins his essay 'Inventing the University' with the lines, 'Every time a student sits down to write for us, he has to invent the university for the occasion' (1965: 273).

2   The syllabus for the course is available online at http://www.zombieclass.com. There is also a link to the course blog at this address, which is housed at http://zombieclass.wordpress.com. The majority of the entries on this blog were written by the students to explore their thinking about course topics and to reflect further on work they completed during the semester.

3   There are quite a few other recent books on this subject, such as Nicholas Carr's *The Shallows* (2010) or Cathy N. Davidson's *Now You See It* (2011). Carr published an essay in *The Atlantic* in 2008 that formed the basis for his book. According to Carr, the internet is changing how we learn and how our brains function. He argues that Google (computers, the internet, etc.) are not making us think *less*; rather, they are changing the *way* we think. Likewise, I would argue that students do not learn *less* than they once did; they learn *differently*.

4   McLaren writes, 'Our bodies are now regulated by a fascist economy of signs, precisely because they are now so fully detached from the body's service. The body in this process has become reduced to a sign of itself. The body has been abandoned for a better version of itself. The body is now just another idea for commodity logic to terrorize' (1995: 56).

5   This sort of pedagogical work does not valorize or hinge on access to advanced technology. The viral video 'A Vision of Students Today' (2007) produced by Michael Wesch in collaboration with 200 students at Kansas State University, argues just the opposite – that a technology as simple and readily available as the chalkboard can be used as a (more immediate and physically dynamic) tool for world-generation.

SECTION 4

The post-apocalyptic terrain

'Sois mort et tais toi': zombie mobs and student protests

Sarah Juliet Lauro

Being president of the University of California is like being manager of a cemetery: there are many people under you and no one is listening.

(Mark Yudof, UC President, cited in Solomon 2009)

Introduction

In October of 2003, a young woman from Toronto, Canada named Thea Faulds (aka Thea Munster) put up flyers asking people to meet downtown dressed up like zombies; it was at this moment that she unwittingly invented the non-promotional 'Zombie Walk', and she organized the first of what would become an annual occurrence in Toronto (Thea Faulds, personal communication).[1] Unlike previous events that orchestrated public displays of zombies for promotional purposes, Munster's event was novel because it was entirely devoid of any purpose, commercial enterprise or social agenda – besides, of course, that of the disruption of the everyday. Munster's Zombie Walk engendered a new kind of zombie narrative, one that was nonetheless in step with the larger mythology: particularly, in light of the event's deliberate divorce from consumer capitalism, the zombie's longstanding associations with slavery and resistance were staged in a new form.

The goal of Munster's Toronto Zombie Walk was not to raise money, make money or even to raise awareness. A few years later, events of the kind were held in Vancouver, San Francisco and other major cities in North America: the Zombie Walk bug began to spread. As of the writing of this chapter there are registered zombie walk forums in 20 countries worldwide and 49 of the United States – with only Delaware apparently staying zombie-free, according to the original *Zombie Walk* forum, which has a geographically searchable archive. More events are continually being planned, with organizers using social network websites such as Facebook, Twitter, Craiglist and Plancast, or posting to newer forums such as *Zombie Hub*, *All Things Zombie* or *Crawl of the Dead*. Still other organizers have their own websites, for instance *Eat Brains*, the zombie mob forum for San Francisco, California; *Eye Heart Brains*, for Denver, Colorado; *NYC Zombie Crawl* for New York and *Philly Zombie Crawl* for Philadelphia.

Though there have been many types of zombie events in the past few years, my interest is solely in the non-promotional zombie mob, precisely *because* such events blur the line between social protest and performance art. In a previous study, I concluded that such zombie mob gatherings amounted to the *form* but not the substance of insurrection, allowing people the freedom to coordinate via new technologies, disrupt traffic and congregate *en masse* in public spaces, but that they removed from themselves the burden of having to wave a particular banner, support a cause, or say anything definitive about their motives for participating (see Lauro 2011b, do Vale 2009 and Peake 2010). If such events seem mute demonstrations of the citizenry's ability to demonstrate, what happens in a political climate with social protest on the rise? Does the zombie mob gathering continue to perform its valuable (non)function?

The zombie mob phenomenon was inaugurated in Canada in 2003, but its popularity really began to rise in the United States in 2005, during a period of relative calm but pervasive social dissatisfaction. Demonstrations against the US invasion of Iraq had had no impact on an administration determined to go to war in 2003; the type of citizens participating in zombie mobs likely felt voiceless, but were cut off from immediate connection to the war, especially by the Bush administration's restriction of media images, which prohibited even the publication of images of the coffins of US casualties in 2006. Perhaps, on the level of the collective unconscious, the contemporary zombie mobs becoming ever more popular were making visible the corpses that could not be shown; or perhaps these events were an expression of a particular demographic's inability to express itself politically. As yet there has not been a study of the demographics of zombie mobs, but from my own observations as both a witness and studying documentary evidence, I would estimate that this population is made up largely of urban men and women of European descent (aged 18-45), from affluent suburbs and towns.

The assessment broadly espoused was that the current generation of students was apathetic and that as long as they were not directly affected by the war, they would not be interested in protesting. An article from the student paper of Bowling Green University on the lack of student social interest on the campus quotes Mike Zickar, a professor who recalls 'during the Iraq war, myself and some other students were protesting and students walking by would come up to me and say "why are you protesting? It's a waste of time"' (James 2010). This anecdote suggests that perhaps the relative inaction of student populations did not signify apathy so much as jaded frustration. Protesting indeed may have seemed like a 'waste of time' to a group of people who doubted that the government, which clearly had been unmoved by the massive demonstrations held worldwide in February 2003 before the Iraq invasion, could or would be swayed by popular opinion. However, during the same time that the article quoted above reports the political lifelessness of the student body, the very same campus of Bowling Green was beginning to be besieged by zombies, first in the form of week-long games of 'zombies vs. humans' tag, played annually at Bowling Green since at least 2006, and later, by zombie walks occurring in the community.[2]

I wondered what would happen to the zombie mob phenomenon in a time of widespread social upheaval. My impression – gleaned from evidence like that above regarding zombies and a lack of political interest at Bowling Green and my own ethnographic research of zombie mobbers in general – was that although students might not feel it was worth their time to overtly demonstrate their disaffection with the system, these zombie events were nonetheless productive of a kind of inchoate catharsis for the participants that was directly related to the urge to protest. Too often people merely associate the zombie with the slave, but its early associations with the Haitian working in the cane fields – the very same cane fields that were burned during the slave revolt that became the Haitian Revolution – make clear that it should be equally theorized as a figure of rebellion. Ultimately, however, I think that it resists easy categorization as either an icon of successful revolt or of morbid failure (Lauro and Embry 2008).

Because the dialecticality of the living dead resists any attempt to make the zombie into a legitimate symbol of rebellion (though it has sometime tended that way) – for the zombie is not a resurrected being triumphantly reclaiming agency, but an animate corpse with a singular mission (most often, in contemporary film, to eat the living) – and because the zombie mob phenomenon likely arose as a means of expressing political disempowerment and cultural ennui, my theory was simply this: surely one does not need zombies as much when one has a real-life social issue to protest. Or, in short: in a period of time in which the demographic that most actively participates in zombie mobs is occupied by active political demonstrations, the popularity of the zombie in popular culture and particularly of the phenomenon of the zombie mob must decrease. This is the *hypothesis* from which this exploration departs.

As I witnessed firsthand, fee hikes were implemented at the end of 2009 in public institutions in California (where I reside), across the United States and elsewhere in the world, allegedly due to the weakened global economy. Student protests over increases in administrative spending and tuition hikes were prevalent throughout the scholastic year 2009–10 in 52 countries. There were major student protests that involved the occupation of public buildings, many of which lasted for days at a time. The demographic that had been organizing zombie pageants and zombie pub crawls was now using the same social media to organize the occupation of public buildings on their college campuses; a hasty tweet about a spontaneous zombie mob had, I felt sure, paved the way for an urgent one proclaiming the formation of an actual mob determined to make their discontent visible to university administrators and government bureaucrats. I set out to discover whether the statistics would bear out my theory that zombies and student protesters existed in inverse proportion, and that the rise of student demonstrations was related to a decrease in zombie mob gatherings.

Methods and materials

Zooming out to a macro view of the zombie mob phenomenon that operates diachronically and synchronically, I compared the frequency and attendance of zombie events to student protests in specific locales, in order to highlight what I suspected was their polar relationship. To determine attendance, I relied on various resources, but especially, the figures submitted to me personally by event organizers, newspapers' reports of events, and, where applicable, certified numbers from outside sources (such as *Guinness World Records*). To determine how often events were planned, I made use of a variety of social media and online forums.

I began by researching which cities had major student protests last year, what the attendance numbers of these events were, and when they took place. In these same cities, I then looked at how much of a zombie mob phenomenon existed in the vicinity before and after the period of student protest activity. How many events were scheduled in previous years as compared to last year? How many 'zombies' attended in previous years (such as 2007 and 2008), as opposed to in the same year as political events (2009 and 2010)? Finally, how close (geographically and temporally) were the zombie events scheduled to the protests?

Data and results

To give a preliminary idea of the rise of the popularity of the zombie walk and other types of zombie events (such as zombie tag, zombie pub crawls, zombie skates, zombie subway rides, zombie proms), I conducted searches for newspaper articles and charted the frequency with which certain terms appeared in the body or in the titles of articles. Tracking the frequency of events rather than their individual attendance seemed an efficacious way to gauge the popularity of the movement, but finding articles proved difficult in and of itself since this type of event may be called diverse things. Picking 2004 as the starting point – since Thea Munster's inaugural event took place in October of 2003 – I conducted searches on the WorldNews database, for the terms 'zombie walk' ('zombie mob' not yielding very many hits), for the terms 'zombie' and 'protest' occurring in the lead-in paragraph, and for the phrase 'dressed as zombies'. The results are displayed in the figure below.

In order to contrast these results, I searched also for the phrase 'zombie tag' and 'zombie prom'[3] (see Figure 2 below). These charts can hardly be thought of as providing exact measurements, but following the arcs of the graphs should give a rough idea of the

Figure 1: Frequency of appearance of terms in newspapers worldwide.

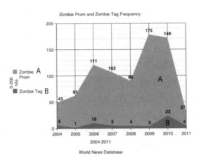

Figure 2: Frequency of specific events chronicled in newspapers.

popularity of zombie gatherings. The low numbers in 2011, of course, are impacted by the fact that this data was compiled in early May; most zombie events occur in May, which has been declared 'Zombie Awareness Month' by the Zombie Research Society and at the end of October, close to Halloween.

Narrowing my focus to the years in which we saw marked social protest, I sought next to chart how many zombie events were planned, or at least were suggested and began to be organized (whether or not they were actually carried out), by plotting the statistics of forum posts in 2009 and 2010, as opposed to previous years. The first thing I noticed as I did preliminary research immediately contradicted my suspicions: the zombie mob phenomenon had only begun to garner interest in France in October 2009, directly around the time of the student protests. In France at least, zombie mobs had not, as I had previously imagined, sprung up in a time of absent student activity and waned in the face of student demonstrations; rather, France's first large-scale zombie events were planned in online forums in 2009. Seeing this, I immediately reformulated a preliminary trio of questions:

1. Were fewer zombie events planned and carried out in times and places where student protests were occurring (taking into consideration both flashmobs and annual events)?
2. Were there fewer attendees of those zombie events that were held in 2009 and 2010 than in previous years?
3. Was the same result equally true of Europe, the United States, and other geographic regions that have a zombie walk presence?

I soon discovered, however, that France proved not to be the exception to the rule, but rather indicative of a trend: unilaterally, zombie events had become more frequent, and had drawn larger crowds in the same time and place as student protests. To the questions posed above, I was obliged to reply as follows:

1. No; zombie flashmobs maintain an equivalent frequency to previous years, or indeed, in certain places (such as the United Kingdom), seem to become more prevalent directly

around the time and spaces of student protests; annually scheduled zombie events follow a similar pattern of growth to the trajectory established over previous years, suggesting that the student protests have no diminishing effect on their popularity.[4]

2. No; on the contrary, new records for zombie event attendance were set worldwide in 2009, and various cities competed for the *Guinness Book of World Records* title.[5] The student protests overall do not seem to have had an effect upon the popularity of such large-scale zombie gatherings, though that is not to say that certain zombie walks may not have had diminished numbers, or saw attendance numbers that did not match the expectations of organizers given the steady curve of growth to which these events had become accustomed.[6]

3. On the whole, yes, zombie events worldwide are not impacted by the presence of student events, which in 2009, took place in 52 countries, far more countries, of course, than are active participants in the zombie walk tradition. However, there is one exception: Germany.

Indeed, Germany is the only place in which my findings mirrored my initial expectations. There are posts advertising or querying zombie events for the following dates: 26 September 2006; 26 June 2007; 5 July 2007; 7 July 2007; 11 July 2007; 14 September 2007 and then nothing until 6 February 2011 and 31 March 2011: the zombie chatter diminishes around the time of political protests. This is precisely the type of arc that I would have expected to see in those countries that often hold zombie events. Instead, zombie events fall about the middle of the range for popularity in the United Kingdom and are the high water mark for France at the time of the student protests. Ironically, France only seems to have become interested in the zombie walk at the same time that student protests were heating up in the United States.[7] But to get an entire picture of the zombie walk phenomenon, particularly in Europe, one should not rely solely on the forums: as I have said before, there are a diverse number of ways that people can get the word out about zombie events, many of which, such as leaflet dropping, leave no digital footprint. Though the data provided above (in reference to Germany, the United Kingdom and France) is culled only from a single forum website (zombiewalk.com) and is intended to serve merely as a sample to map the larger trend, the following statistics, and my conclusions in general, have been calculated by checking various forums, as well as newspaper databases for reports of zombie events. It is certain that these figures are, nonetheless, incomplete, but they should give us some sense of the movement's ebbs and flows insofar as we may compare them to the frequency of student demonstrations. For the sake of comparison, I created the chart immediately below from the 2009 overview of education protests worldwide produced by the International Student Movement (2009).

I juxtapose the graph charting the frequency of protests held in 52 countries with this meagre foray into zombie statistics. To give the reader an idea of whether or not zombie events were diminished in the presence of student protests, I picked a sample of five geographic regions that had pre-existing zombie activity and that saw student protests at

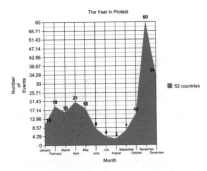

Figure 3: Worldwide student protests in 2009.

various points during the 2009 year: California, New York, the greater Washington D.C. area (which includes surrounding suburbs in both the states of Virginia and Maryland), Texas, and the United Kingdom.

As can be plainly seen, student protests actually overlap with the height of the zombie season (the September-October-November months, the period surrounding Halloween). What one cannot see as readily from this chart, but which I assert, is that we do not seem to find a diminution in the popularity of zombie events in this year as compared to other years. Further, zombie events occurred in the same geographic locale as other zombie events, at about the same time. Despite the limitations of the data presented here, this preliminary study helps to create a picture of the way that zombie events coexist with (and perhaps respond to) social protests.

Of course, some factors should be taken into consideration when the data I have assembled is examined: September 2009 saw many zombie events inspired by or even tied to the release of the film *Zombieland*; this may skew the number of zombie events. Michael Jackson's death on 25 June 2009 may also have had an impact, as zombie events often incorporated or were structured around live stagings of 'Thriller' (Agence France-Presse 2009b). Indeed, several of these events were held in France, and a particularly successful one in Breton in October 2009 (Agence France-Presse 2009a).

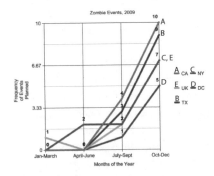

Figure 4: Zombie events in 2009 in key areas.

Results and conclusions

If we do not find that zombie events fade away in times of increased social protest, then, what do we find? Surprisingly, zombies were actually included in a significant number of student protests, to the point that we must revisit the message proclaimed by this mythic figure and question whether these events provide a way for us to consider the zombie walk events that had been sanctified by mainstream co-optation (and thus, desalinated) as being reconstituted, re-energized with a revolutionary power.

In an article titled '2010, the year an army of zombies came for our brains', Johann Hari (2010) writes that 'this stinking creature has risen with a groan and a shriek from our collective unconscious. From Brisbane to Chicago to Rome, there has been a surge of zombie walks – flashmobs of up to 8,000 people at a time dressed as zombies.' I am sceptical of the notion that 2010 exhibited a 'surge' in zombie walks – according to my numbers, 2007 was the watershed year – and I feel that any claims about the popularity of the trend would have to differentiate between flashmobs and scheduled walks, which are lumped in together in Hari's estimation. Hari only makes this broad claim in order to ask the question, 'Why now? Why would a global recession be matched by the global procession of zombies?'

The association between the worldwide economy and the popularity of zombies is an important question, but one that seems to have been dispelled by an article in *Wired Magazine*, which finds no direct correlation between the 'popularity' of the zombie in popular culture, judged by means of its appearance in films and television shows, and the Dow Index (Edwards 2010). Hari's flirtations with the subject here are straightforward: 'As disaster occurs all around us – economic, ecological, political – who hasn't felt that their own little life of shopping and eating and consuming isn't a little zombie-like?' (2010). The tradition of associating zombies with the mindless consumer stretches back to Romero's *Dawn of the Dead* (1978). Newitz (2006) and Williams (2010) offer new spins to the correlation between capitalism and the living dead.

Nonetheless, Hari does hit upon what I think is a crucial difference between the association of the economy with the overall popularity of the zombie, and the zombie walk's allure: the act of playing dead in zombie events enables people to protest their own inability to protest, or their sense that they are not being heard. Therefore, regardless of the Dow's fluctuations, one finds the zombie the most prevalent when the general public feels disempowered or disenfranchised.

At times, the use of zombies in protest is rather cutesy: in Oakland, California, for examples, zombie-drag was recently donned by concerned citizens in order to protest the defunding of public libraries. Protestors purportedly groaned, 'Zombies need brains, keep libraries open!' (Jones 2011b). Elsewhere, the use of zombies may be playfully oblique, but suggestive of more serious issues. Zombies protested at San Francisco's City Hall, ostensibly demonstrating the need for equal rights for the living dead. Occurring in a state that has recently been embroiled in the debate over the legality of gay marriage, however, the subtext becomes clear: one protester's sign read: 'It's not necrophilia if we're both dead' (Quevado 2009).

The appropriateness of using the undead in protest has been questioned, and the imagery needs to be handled with care; for example, students dressed as zombies turned up to protest cuts in education in Wisconsin, at a speech given by Governor Scott Walker. Unfortunately, however, the governor's talk was devoted to the Special Olympics, leading some to cry foul, claiming that the protesters' representations of themselves as zombies was a defamation of the disabled (Jones 2011a). A similar critique was levelled, perhaps more fairly, at a charity event organized in New Zealand, where a zombie walk was held to raise money for the victims of brain injury (Agence France-Presse 2010).

If any reader yet doubts that the presence of unwanted zombies in the public exudes a whiff of threat, consider the following case. On the day of the royal wedding, several girls dressed as zombies were arrested and held by London police:

> Hannah Eiseman-Renyard and four friends were sitting in a West End coffee shop in zombie fancy dress when they were arrested for 'potential breach of the peace' and taken to a nearby police station … 'We asked under what grounds, they said "Section 60" … they had reason to suspect we were going to disturb the peace'. (Parsons 2011)

The journalist goes on to suggest, however, that the 25-year-old Eliseman-Renyard was not arrested just for 'being dressed as a zombie', as she had asserted. And though she has promised to file a suit because 'Being detained for nearly four hours is not an acceptable or legal consequence of wearing some fake blood', her arrest may also have been influenced by her involvement in a protest earlier in the day 'in Oxford Square over the impact of government cuts on HIV clinics, hate crime prevention, and other services'. In a similar case in Minneapolis, Minnesota in 2006, seven people hoping to demonstrate their 'anti-consumerist' philosophy were arrested for being dressed as zombies and carrying 'probable weapons'. They were eventually awarded $165,000 in a free speech lawsuit (O'Reilly 2010).

These zombies were not like those innocuous ones from Bristol participating in 'Infest', who can join a large scale game of 'Zombie tick' (equivalent to Zombie tag), for the purchase of a £10 ticket (Bristol Evening Post 2010); or those descending upon Liverpool, urging people to give blood (Miller 2009); or those congregating to advertise the opening of a new film and digital media centre (Nottingham Evening Post 2009a); or those in Glasgow, Scotland to advertise 'Glas-goals' a health and fitness campaign (Fotheringham 2010); or in Manchester to raise money for the Christie Hospital and the Manchester Carers' Centre (Welsh 2010); nor of course, any of the various participants of zombie pub crawls (Coyle 2010), or film and music festivals (Leicester Mercury 2010), or numerous 'Thriller' stagings, such as that in Nottingham (Nottingham Evening Post 2009b), which raised money for the NSPCC, a children's charity. One crucial difference between a zombie and a vampire is that a zombie can show up even where it hasn't been invited, although as Hannah Eiseman-Renyard and her friends learned, there may be consequences to playing dead without a permit.

There was also an event called 'Parliament of the Living Dead' (30 October 2009) that was self-described as both a 'Zombie Walk' and a 'protest'. In reality, however, this was a publicity stunt organized by video-game manufacturer Capcom Entertainment to publicize its latest game, *Dead Rising 2* (Hussain 2010). Staging this event during the time of the student protests also served to co-opt the excitement and momentum of that movement and redirect it towards the purchase of video games. Looking at this and the list above of more laudable charity events, one might assume that the zombie mob phenomenon has been completely taken over, anesthetized by those who see opportunities to make money. However, even these more clearly commercial events that incorporate iconography of the undead protests reveal that there is still power to this protest that remains true to the auspices under which Thea Munster first dreamed of the Zombie Walk. For example, in London, zombie protesters calling themselves 'The Government of the Dead' burned an effigy of a banker with a clear message: 'We are witnessing the economy's zombie remains destroying the lives of ordinary people in the form of rising unemployment and home repossession' (Moore-Bridger 2009). Zombies also ran through a crowded shopping centre in Bristol unannounced, genuinely disrupting commerce as a part of Co-Mutiny's week of action, titled the 'Bristol Anarchist Games' (Bristol Evening Post 2009). One should neither overlook the use of zombie flashmobs as a direct mode of critique, nor the zombie's ability to insert itself effectively into overt social protests.

Finally, I want to turn my attention to specifically academic zombies: to the appearance of zombies in protests that demonstrate against the defunding of education or other related issues. In March of 2011, students and staff from Stow College in Edinburgh, Scotland, 'dressed as zombies and held a mock funeral procession for higher education as part of a campaign against plans to transfer courses to Glasgow College' (Cassidy 2011). In October of 2009, a similar event was staged at the University of California at Santa Barbara, where participants wore shirts that said 'Zombies United – Free UC!'(Magnoli 2009).

Such invocations of the dead clearly point to the staff members' and students' sense that they are not being listened to, but they also warn that public education is dying, being murdered by corporate interest and government cuts. The zombie myth, more broadly, has been at various points in its history representative of social disempowerment in such a way that it becomes an icon of the kind of social death experienced by prisoners, slaves, and others who are visibly excluded from the system. In most cases, it is easy to map the use of the zombie in student protests onto a similar commentary; however, in one performance protest staged by students in California, the zombie's historical associations (stemming from its Haitian origins) with both the slave and slave rebellion are played upon in a way that dramatizes the living dead's undecidability as either powerful or powerless.

On June 1, 2010, at the University of California at Davis, the same campus where 52 students and teachers were arrested for a building occupation on a single day earlier that school year, performance art students staged an event that crossed the boundaries of student protest and zombie event. Playing off the quotation cited at this article's opening – extracted from an interview with university president Mark Yudof in *The New York Times*, in which he compared himself to the keeper of a cemetery – students performed their own version of *Michael Jackson's Thriller*, which has become a common favourite among zombie event planners, especially since the artist's death. Prior to this performance, during the height of the political actions on University of California campuses, postcards had been circulated that featured a picture of the UC president and his infamous line comparing himself to a cemetery manager (see epigraph). The back of the card reads, 'Will public education survive the drive for profits? That depends on us. See your dean, e-mail your chancellor, mail this to your local or state government official … Don't be a corpse and act up!' At the time of the performance, some months after Yudof's interview, this quotation would have been familiar to students. The flyer that advertised the performance included an illustration that remixes an iconographic Mai '68 student protest poster with the head of the president of the university.

The performance, which was directed by student Christina Noble and involved the participation of a dozen others, was titled *Mark Yudof's Thriller*, and it combined the students' sense that they were being quieted with Yudof's infamous depiction of himself as the keeper of a graveyard. It was held on the concrete plaza in front of the campus's central green area at the Memorial Union, where many students go to buy lunch, and began with a student dressed as Yudof, sitting on a picnic blanket in a high traffic area, drinking what appeared to be champagne, and casually answering the questions of an interviewer. The performers' parts were pre-recorded and played over a loudspeaker; and the lines of dialogue were pulled from the real substance of Yudof's *New York Times* interview (Soloman 2009).

Figure 5: Flyer anonymously posted on UC Davis campus, 2009.

After 'Yudof' delivered the line about being a manager of a cemetery, the musical interlude to *Thriller* began to play, and a group of zombies lumbered up behind the picnicking gentleman. At the same time, the campus bells ominously chimed the noon hour, thus incorporating the campus setting into the performance. The overlay of bells with the intro music may remind the viewer of the beginning of another Michael Jackson song, 'Beat it', where synthesized sounds emulate a bell tolling in the first measures of the song, helping to foster the kind of disorientation between levels of fiction and reality for which flashmobs and other interventionist art pieces, or guerrilla performance art, often aim.

At first, Yudof looks about as if concerned, but then he dons the signature red leather jacket worn by Michael Jackson in the video, and begins a choreographed dance along with the zombies. The chorus of *Thriller* emphasizes the position of the human victim threatened by external violence as in a horror film, which is the frame of the 1983 video: a young couple leave a scary movie, only to encounter a living nightmare that could be real or imagined. However, in this UC student performance, the undead are to be pitied (see Mercer 1986). It is in the performance's rewriting of Jackson's song lyrics, in its revision of the classic dance moves, and in the dualism of the zombie as both rebel and slave, powerful and powerless, that one finds the most inventive critique of Yudof's position, as king of the mausoleum that is the UC system. Obviously, the sense of threat that the original song expresses, of being under siege, is appropriate to the students' positions, especially at a publicly funded school system like the University of California, where many worry that with the rapidly rising costs of tuition, higher education will no longer be an option for those in a certain economic bracket.

The altered lyrics read, in part:

Start of the quarter, something evil's lurking in the dark, Inside your inbox; your billing statement almost stopped your heart. You start to scream, but you're not loud enough to reach the board of Regents. You start to freeze. McDonald's isn't hiring right now: You're marginalized. You know it's Yudof, Mark Yudof. You're fighting for your rights while your fees go up, go up, go up.[8]

Aside from the clever revision of the song, what should we make of the fact that the students here are invited to identify with disempowered zombies? One thing that this performance harks back to is the longer history of the zombie myth: the original zombie was not a flesh hungry ghoul, but the victim of Voodoo sorcery, made to do the bidding of its master. Indeed, in this performance, the zombies are very clearly abused, and the only threats of violence come from Yudof himself. Some of the best parts of the performance include the re-appropriation of Jackson's classic dance moves: the Yudof impersonator replaces Jackson's crotch grabs by rubbing cash stolen from the zombies in that area. In addition to repeatedly pantomiming kicking the zombies when they are down, Yudof also walks on the backs of zombies, striking the same pose as Jackson does atop a car, another of his iconic moves.

Since the essential nature of the Haitian zombie is that it is an individual that has been altered, repossessed by a Voodoo master and made to work for his own benefit (as an obvious allegory for the slave), such repurposing of Jackson's original song seems apt. Because the zombie myth originates in Haiti, the site of what is arguably the only successful slave rebellion in history, it carries with it all of the associations of slave rebellion and revolution that the former French colony calls to mind.

Ultimately, it was the appearance of some zombies in an Occupy Wall Street demonstration in early October of 2011, and the critique this prompted, that helped me to refine my understanding of the kind of cultural work that the zombie achieves when it is incorporated in protest. Occupy Wall Street participants were encouraged to 'come dressed as a corporate zombie!' in a missive from headquarters. Organizers wrote: 'This means jacket and tie if possible, white face, fake blood, eating monopoly money, and doing a slow march, so when people come to work on Monday in this neighborhood they see us reflecting the metaphor of their actions.' This demonstration prompted a critique from a political blogger titled 'Hey Occupy Wall Street, dressing like zombies is dumb!' (Apple 2011). The blog argues that zombies have been so co-opted by the mainstream as to be an ineffectual symbol of rebellion; I would argue that because of its associations with colonial slavery, it never could have been otherwise.

The zombie can make visible the populace's sense of its own inability to protest; it can also serve as a protest icon to lament the fact that their voices are not being heard. But because of the dual nature of the zombie, and its ultimately ambivalent representation of slave/slave rebellion: we can follow this as a guideline in the future: if there is a zombie there, then it isn't a real revolution.[9]

Further notes

Although, as the form of this article may suggest, I see the value in a project that would produce a completely scientific, statistical history of the zombie walk phenomenon, I acknowledge that it was never my intention to carry that out here. I hope that someone may see this as a first step in that direction, and take up the journey herself. However, there are several obstacles to the creation of such a project at this time, not the least of which is a problem of definition.

Because the zombie forums allow posters to advertise for all manner of zombie events, one has to start by deciding what comprises a 'zombie walk', and the setting of such parameters subjectively delimits the zombie event as one doing a particular kind of cultural work. As I have said, I would feel compelled to exclude any zombie event where money is made or even raised, because of the origins of the zombie walk in an anticapitalist framework that is central to the mythology. As a necessity, then, I would have to exclude pub crawls and any event that charged an entrance fee, even for charitable purposes. I would equally disbar some of the biggest annual zombie events, which are specifically fund-raisers for charity.

Even as I write this, however, an annual zombie event is probably taking on corporate sponsorship or adopting a charitable cause that will validate it in the eyes of the community. The effect of these philanthropic and corporate adoptions, of course, is an anesthetization of the zombie walk that makes it palatable to mainstream society and divorces the event from its revolutionary resonance.

The volume of data available from disparate sources poses another difficulty, and particularly those sources that may be amended over time, such as Facebook and MySpace websites and other social media. Though it would be useful to have a sense of what kinds of numbers events have drawn over the years, statistics are hard to come by, for one should not be reliant solely on the estimates of organizers, who may have a vested interest in the shape of the numbers they provide to the public, particularly if they are trying to draw sponsorship. Local papers rarely publish attendance figures, though they have increasingly started to publicize the annually scheduled events beforehand – in part so that people are not startled by the appearance of the living dead in the city centre, and also presumably to draw a crowd of spectators (as well as participants) who would otherwise be uninformed of the event. The tolerance of such events by city officials is likely connected to its benefits for local businesses, and this cooperation begins to look like co-option. Because the annual zombie walks are advertised in this manner, newspapers rarely write them up afterwards – unless, for example, a world record is secured – and one often has to wait an entire year before finding out what the 'official' tally of the event was, when journalists begin to hype the next one; even then, newspapers most often just quote the organizers' estimates.

For all of these reasons, an in-depth statistical analysis of the zombie walk phenomenon has not yet been produced. In the face of the corporate and capitalistic takeover of the zombie walk, the zombie flashmob becomes all the more important, as it is much more in keeping with the original aspirations of the movement – a display of the presence of the masses, unbidden, in the public square – than funded and fund-raising events. Zombie flashmobs mirror the spontaneity of protests and their viral spread through social network devices, such as were seen during the 2009 student demonstrations and more recently in the London riots. Zombie mobs may also be a kind of dress rehearsal, or a harbinger: recently, flashmobs have been organized for the sole purpose of robbing stores. In his recent article 'Flashmob violence raises weighty questions', John Timpane (2011) writes: 'From Minneapolis, Chicago, and Cleveland to Washington and New York, people have used social media to organize robberies, fights, and mayhem. Such media are suspected in group violence in Center City and in areas such as Upper Darby, where a mob rampaged through the Sears store on June 21.' In Timpane's argument the London riots are lumped in together with flashmob robberies, like those described by Jouvenal and Morse (2011).

Whether or not groups participating in zombie events also partake in other kinds of social protests, the prevalence of zombies in a given geographic area may serve as a kind of canary in the coalmine, indicating that a darker tide is turning on the powers that be, and that the dead are no longer willing to take it lying down.

Notes

1   Where I have signalled that a piece of evidence comes from personal communication, it is likely derived from an interview, piece of email correspondence, or first-hand encounter with an informally published document such as a web-posting or flyer collected in the course of writing my dissertation about 'zombie walks' or 'zombie mobs' (Lauro 2011a).

2   The Humans vs. Zombies version of tag was invented around the same time that the zombie walk was rising in popularity. According to the Humans vs. Zombies website, it was created at Goucher College in 2005. Like the zombie mob, too, its inventors claim to have an interest in its protection from corporate takeover. Its creators write: 'Humans vs. Zombies is (and always will be) free to play. This is in our company's charter, and it is our core belief. The rules are available under a Creative Commons copyright, and we offer a free game hosting service called HvZ SOURCE that helps people organize their games. Gnarwhal Studios makes money from Humans vs. Zombies by selling our own merchandise and by partnering with affiliates who buy a license to use the Humans vs. Zombies name. Any money we make from Humans vs. Zombies goes back into the company, and we use it to keep the game freely available.' Whether or not this is convincing, the pretence that the game is free from profit motives is at least in line with the founding ideals of the zombie mob (Humans vs. Zombies 2012).

3   'Zombie Prom' is also the name of a musical made into a movie in 2006; this likely accounts for the spike of numbers in that year. While the frequency of this play's production still bears relevance in regard to the zombie's overall popularity, it is impossible to tell by looking at these statistics which are theatre performances, and which are the type of communal 'zombie prom' performances already described.

4   Posters organized zombie events in Manchester for 1 November 2009, and although October and September had been relatively quiet months for student protests in the United Kingdom, November would be explosive, with student occupations, protests and strikes occurring in London from the 9th to the 12th, in Birmingham (11th); Hull (17th); Bradford (18th); Dublin (24th and 28th) and Newcastle (24th).

5   Asbury Park, New Jersey currently holds the Guinness World Record for largest gathering of zombies, 'achieved by 4,093 participants at the New Jersey Zombie Walk at the Asbury Park Boardwalk in Asbury Park, New Jersey, USA, on 30 October 2010,' (Guinness World Records 2011). Louisville, Kentucky hoped its annual 'Zombie Attack' might break the Guinness World Record in 2010, and purportedly had certifiers on hand for the event (Lord 2010). The previous Guinness World Record holder, with 3,894 participants in the 'Red White and Dead Zombie Party' event organized by Fremont Outdoor Movies in Seattle, Washington, USA, on 3 July 2009 attempted to regain the title from Asbury Park in July 2011. Events had not yet been certified at the time of writing.

6   The organizer of the Atlanta event, for example, told me that his numbers have increased by 200 people every year; the Toronto event saw annual numbers double until recently. It is very difficult to account, however, for all of the various factors that should be taken into consideration when looking at attendance, which is why I have preferred to concentrate on frequency. For example, in 2010, Toronto saw severely reduced attendance – from 5,500

in 2009 to 3,500 in 2010 – but the organizer blames this on inclement weather, rather than zombie fatigue. At the same time, Pittsburgh's annual Zombie Walk had to change its location from the Monroeville Mall (site of Romero's classic film *Dawn of the Dead*, 1978) to Market Square to accommodate the growing number of participants (Dezayas 2010).

7   Listings are posted on Zombie Walk for France, under the archives section, only for the following dates: 18 October 2009 (Toulouse); 31 October 2009 (Paris); the Toulouse event was repeated the following October (on the 10th). There were no reported student protests occurring in France at precisely these times (as there were in the Netherlands, Austria and Poland), although protests in France were held in January, February, April, May and November of 2009.

8   Quoted with permission of Christina Noble, director of *Mark Yudof's Thriller*.

9   Recent events on my own campus would seem to bear this out. UC Davis was catapulted to international fame when police forces pepper sprayed students who were peacefully demonstrating on campus on Friday, 18 November 2011. I have seen no zombies present at any of the events leading up to or following this event.

Living-dead man's shoes? Teaching and researching glossy topics in a harsh social and cultural context

David Beer

We have been travelling through some times of change in higher education. Fee structures are altering, research money is being cut or reallocated, and there are vast new systems of measurement and metricization that capture what is done within universities. It has been suggested that this swirl of transformations undermines the confidence of academics and plays out through a series of bodily and emotional affects (Burrows 2012). What is certain is that these emergent and intricate infrastructures of measurement are being used to compare individuals, departments and universities by allocating numeric values to our teaching and research that then feed into various league tables and the like. We already know that such metrics have material consequences for people, and even where these metrics are misleading or misguided they maintain the potential to shape our reality (Lash 2007; Hayles 2009; Amoore 2011). These systems and cultures of measurement have come to foster something close to neo-liberal market-based competition in the sector (see Gane 2013). The inevitable result is that value is placed in certain types of academic activity; these are the things that are easily measured or that have a tendency to produce positive outcomes within this competitive environment. It is not too much of a stretch to begin to assume that these changes are likely to alter what is valued in academic work, that is to say that they may come to actively reshape the formation of knowledge and to push us towards certain forms of knowledge that provide insights into certain types of issues (for an early set of observations on this, see the chapter on the 'bureaucratic ethos' in Mills 1959).

Indeed, more generally, it has already been widely observed that what might be thought of as the 'audit culture' is having a negative impact upon higher education; this has become something of a leitmotif of our times. It has also been noted that this 'audit culture' is having a disproportionate impact upon different disciplines and fields of work (Holmwood 2010; and for information on the particular vulnerability of certain disciplines, see Stinchcombe 1994). It is clear in the political (and often public) rhetoric that some subject areas are perceived to have more innate value than others (materially played out in some cases with ring-fenced funding). In this instance I want to focus upon a category of research and teaching topics that are already finding the going to be quite tough. As I write this chapter, a new undergraduate fee regime is being implemented in the United Kingdom. This has been designed to fill the gap left by a large-scale removal of public funding from university teaching. This is a transformation that has caused a great deal of debate and unrest. This though is not just a national issue; the reduction in higher education spending is clearly something of a global issue that is in many instances a direct consequence of the economic downturn. The severity of the fiscal policies will no doubt vary between national contexts, but this is not just about finance, we might also point towards the associated questions that arise about the value of particular disciplines and topics as a consequence of these broader social issues and cultural expectations. It is to this challenge that I would like to focus this chapter. Here I focus upon a particular category of topics, which I describe as *glossy topics* that are likely to, or have already been experiencing, attacks on the basis of their perceived value within our teaching and research agendas. As I describe in greater detail below, *glossy topics* are those subjects deemed to be frivolous, unimportant or perhaps even a luxury that cannot be afforded in more 'austere' times. These are times within which competition is heightened and the systems of measurement of academic worth become more pronounced, with material consequences.

As I have implied, one of the outcomes is likely to be an increasing questioning of the value of particular forms of knowledge. We might find that lots of topics that previously seemed established university staples are suddenly considered to be 'glossy' and therefore extraneous, or that we will become cautious about integrating new types of topics and issues into academic research. With this in mind the underlying concern of this piece is that some important subjects and topics, damned by their lack of prominence in systems of measurement and therefore lacking in innate value, will be lost from the analytical spectrum. They will inevitably be replaced by what are understood to be *safe topics* and thus we will lose the vitality and variation that is central to a vibrant social sciences and humanities. As such, it might be that choosing to research and teach *glossy topics*, to borrow the expression from the old Wild West films (and the recent British film of the same name directed by Shane Meadows), could be seen as the equivalent of choosing to wear 'dead man's shoes' (please forgive the gendered nature of this expression, I am afraid that it is a consequence of its origins, I hope you will bear with me). I am not sure though that this expression is entirely accurate in this instance, these topics and subjects are unlikely to die out completely, but are far more likely to carry on in some withered, directionless and maybe zombie-like form on the margins of the academy. We might, to import an analogy fitting to this collection, think back to the classic 1960s zombie horror film *Night of the Living Dead* (Romero 1968). In this seminal film, the classic set piece is established: the living survivors are trapped in the farmhouse surrounded by the living-dead zombies, who are desperate to gain entry to the building. Those on the inside form makeshift barricades to fortify the house and the zombies outside are unable, due to the lack of ability to foster collaborative effort or to think creatively, to enter the house. So, it is perhaps more accurate, and more fitting given the framing of this book, to be concerned that choosing to study or teach glossy topics might be understood to be choosing to wear *living-dead man's shoes*. That is to say that it might be seen to be to choosing to be outside of the safety of the house and amongst the hopeless wandering zombies. The problem, as I see it, is that there is a real danger in the current, often hostile climate, that we might abandon those topics deemed to be glossy, whatever they might turn out to be, and we might instead gravitate only to those topics perceived to provide us with safe analytical territory (for fear of our zombification). This would be to let the system dominate our efforts, and it would also be to choose a much narrower and less vital remit of teaching and research possibilities. Let me elaborate on this further by first explaining the concept of glossy topics.

Glossy topics?

The concept of glossy topics is intended as a sensitizing concept that enables us to consider how the perception of particular topics might impact upon their presence and profile in research and teaching. As you might expect, glossy topics are those things that are at risk of being understood to be frivolous, insignificant and unimportant. Glossy topics, to put it crudely, are topics that are largely found to be of *public interest* but are perhaps not considered to be of *public value*. That is to say that people find them of interest in general terms but do not necessarily think that there is any value in the academic study and teaching of such subjects. To give an example, a colleague recently built an undergraduate module around the TV show *The Wire* (see Penfold-Mounce et al. 2011); this generated a significant amount of press coverage including one article that caused a vast online debate around the 'dumbing down' of higher education. The module was actually about local economies, urban issues, segregation and inequality, and other social problems around drugs and the like, but the centring of the TV show within the module led to its demarcation as a glossy topic, of interest but not necessarily seen to be of public value. This particular example is useful in illustrating the power of glossy topics to demarcate value in higher education (for a further account of the reception of glossy topics see the opening editorial for the journal *Celebrity Studies*: Holmes and Redmond 2010). Glossy topics can be found mapped out in the heuristic diagram in Figure 1.

The original notion of glossy topics derived from a coauthored article that attempted to track the trajectory of the academic study of celebrity (Beer and Penfold-Mounce 2010). Celebrity, we suggested, can be thought of as the archetypal glossy topic: it has mass appeal but is largely seen as a frivolous and insignificant part of everyday cultural life. In this article we tracked the number of academic journal article publications on the topic of celebrity using the *ISI Web of Knowledge database*. In our analysis of the articles published between 1958 and 2008 we found a dramatic increase in the number of outputs on this topic over recent years, with more than half of the total recorded publications being published between 2006 and 2008 (when we stopped the measure). This trajectory has continued in the last 2 years, although it has levelled out a little. Our concern is that as glossy topics are challenged by the more hostile social conditions, and the presumptions to value created by measurement and competition, so this type of trajectory will continue to level off and may even drop back substantially. Some readers may be thinking that this might be a good thing, and indeed it might, but let us not be too hasty in reaching such conclusions. We suggested in the original article that glossy topics

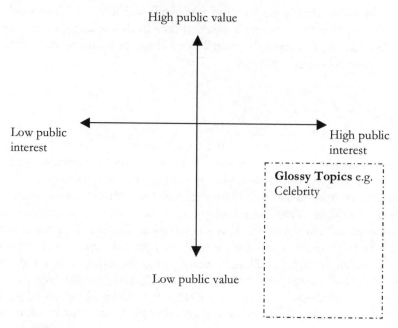

High public value

Low public
interest

High public
interest

Glossy Topics e.g.
Celebrity

Low public value

Figure 1: Mapping out glossy topics.

like celebrity (we might also include such things as film, television, media, gaming, music, popular culture, amongst many others) are going to be tough to research in an economic downturn because of the types of questions that will inevitably be raised about the worth of certain subjects for research and teaching. Further to this, my concern given the developments over the last 3 years or so is that we might find that more and more topics become categorized as glossy and are thus disincentivized for researchers and lecturers. In other words, what is considered to be glossy is changeable and might shift to cover large parts or, in an extreme case, even all of the social sciences and humanities (or even beyond). Given the context in which we are operating, what we need is teaching and research that shows exactly why glossy topics matter. This will help us to avoid academic, organizational and public withdrawal from such areas of research *and* teaching, which would be to leave vast and highly significant swathes of the social and cultural sphere uncovered by academic work. This would be a real problem. If we think again of celebrity, just imagine how important this is in people's lives and in shaping their world-views. This is too important to be left alone. And this is not to mention the limitations of academic endeavour that will occur if we always choose to play safe and adhere to the motivating principles of the system – a bit of undirected zombie wandering work can be a good thing, certainly compared to playing it too safe.

Some thoughts on making glossy topics matter

In response to the above we can reflect briefly on why glossy topics matter, and some of the ways in which we might emphasize their importance. In this instance, I am going to take a relatively narrow view of what glossy topics are, focusing upon the study of popular culture, but many of these points are applicable to glossy topics in the broader sense – this will hopefully be useful to readers who are worried that rising instrumentalism may lead to their areas of interest being swamped by negative sentiment or demarcated as a no-go area.

I am eager to avoid the return to previous debates about the academic legitimacy of non-high-brow culture that have raged since the 'cultural turn' of the 1970s. These struggles for legitimacy can be found in the defensive and combative aspects of the foundational writings of important figures like Stuart Hall and Dick Hebdige – forcing their way into the farmhouse perhaps. There is a clear desire by these writers, because of the context in which they were writing, to show that culture and particularly working class and popular culture were legitimate academic topics. These battles, to a moderate extent, were won and things have changed. The expansion of the higher education sector in many national contexts and the rise of particular disciplines attuned to the study of culture allowed this recalibration of legitimate topics to occur (see Savage 2010a, 2010b). The challenges I am pointing towards in this chapter are seemingly new and are the product, as I have already indicated, of external forces resultant from the global economic downturn, changes to funding and the value judgments made about our expanded and more public higher education sector, and the types of measurement and competition typical of neo-liberal capitalism (again, see Gane 2013).

The underlying premise of this article is that glossy topics are actually highly significant and need to be preserved within our analytical agendas. At the same time as they face externally manifest challenges, we might also note some important transformations in culture that are making glossy topics increasingly socially important. Paradoxically, the moment that they face a hostile climate is just the moment when glossy topics seem to matter the most. Let us consider just a few selected examples that demonstrate the importance of some of the most obvious glossy topics. Recently *The Guardian* newspaper reported on a survey entitled *The Lonely Society*, which indicated that 53% of 18- to 34-year-olds have felt depressed because of loneliness. This was connected in the report to the use of social networking sites, a negative outcome perhaps of what internet researchers have described as 'networked individualism' (Wellman and Haythornthwaite 2002). This runs alongside the social networking site Facebook reaching over 600 million members (with projections that this figure might reach over 1 billion by the time that this book is due to be published). Apple has sold over 220 million iPods worldwide. Celebrity gossip magazines like *Heat* and *Closer* have audited weekly sales of over half a million copies a week in the United Kingdom alone. In the United Kingdom more than 19 million people watched the 2010 final of the TV singing talent show *The X Factor*. Amazon's sales of Kindle e-books are now higher than hardbacks. The *Call of Duty* video game has surpassed $3 billion in sales. There are nearly 3.5 million user-generated articles on Wikipedia. And so on.

These examples map on to a range of public anxieties and concerns about the direction in which we are going culturally. There is a clear sense of public unrest about the darker side of glossy topics. These public concerns include: the decline of critical cultural forms due to a rise in commercial interests and the fragmentation of media content across digital and on-demand services (this includes the implications of the cutting of funding to public broadcasters like the BBC); the impact of the types of lifestyles and body images and narratives consumed by young people; the 'dumbing down' of culture and the perceived erosion of rich and educational cultural resources; the moral and ethical decline of cultural content, including the sexualization of media content; the loss of skills and craft in cultural production; the collapse of social interaction due to mobile and web-based technologies. I could continue. This is not an exhaustive list but it does include some of the more prominent public concerns that are currently apparent in relation to the themes of glossy topics. The question is simply this, are we able to find a means for tapping into such public concerns in order to show why it is that glossy topics matter? Can we also use such public concerns to find a route to wider public engagement in order to satisfy the pressing need for a demonstration of 'impact' and 'value'? If so, then it might be possible to set out our own research and teaching agenda whilst at the same time using such public concerns as pathways to communication with a wider audience.

So far though this only suggests that glossy topics are significant in people's lives and that they are responsible for exacerbating public concerns, which in turn might be used as vehicles for demonstrating relative importance and value. What this does not do is suggest how we should approach glossy topics in the first place. To return for assistance to the *Night of the Living Dead*, how is it that we can stay outside the farmhouse without becoming directionless and ostracized zombies? The answer, in my view, is to approach glossy topics with the clear ambition of making them matter. The aim will be to generate grounded insights into the workings of glossy topics, and to avoid any lightweight commentary on these topics that might simply become a part of the glossy topics themselves (such lightweight commentary would be choosing living-death). There are clearly a number of ways of making glossy topics matter. As a point for discussion, we might suggest four focal points as intersections that enable us to see their social and cultural significance. First, we may develop an engagement with the spatiality of glossy topics; in particular, given geo-demographic trends and the increasing populations living in cities, we should focus upon intersections of glossy topics with urban spaces and urban issues. This area of focus will give glossy topics a material territory and show the sites of conflicts, tensions and difficulties. Second, we might wish to focus upon intersections with new media and forms of technological development so that we might clearly see the implicated transformations and continuities of culture and everyday life. Glossy topics, as highly popular forms of culture, provide really helpful focal points for understanding the appropriation of new media in people's lives. Third, and related to this, we might wish to explore how glossy topics are implicated in large scale contemporary developments in capitalism and how they contribute to the ways in which by-product data about people and populations are generated, mined and used in predictive analytics (for more on by-product data, see Savage and Burrows 2007; Ruppert and Savage 2012; Abbott 2000). This approach would use glossy topics in order to gain a greater understanding of what Savage et al refer to as 'transactional actors', in that they bring to realization the data generated by digital devices and thus afford 'post-individualist, non-humanist accounts of the social, where it is the play of transactions that can be studied in all their fluidity and dynamism' (2010: 11). Finally, we might focus upon the way in which glossy topics perpetuate or even 'make' social divisions and inequality (Skeggs 2005). We need to think creatively about what part they play in social ordering, in creating and maintaining difference, in keeping some people on the inside and others on the outside – Georg Simmel's work on fashion as a site of class conflict and realization provides a really instructive example of this kind of work (see Frisby and Featherstone 1997: 187). These are just some of the areas of focus we might use to provide a framework for making glossy topics matter. There are sure to be other possibilities and I hope that this initial framework will stimulate some response from readers who either research and/or teach glossy topics, or perhaps from those readers whose research and teaching areas might be at risk of becoming glossy in the changing social climate. These are suggestions for avoiding zombification without retreat to the overtly safe ground of the farmhouse.

Concluding thoughts

What I have presented in this chapter is not so much a set of concrete facts about what is happening in higher education, but rather a set of concerns about the direction in which we might head as the conditions in which we work are altered. In the late 1970s, Jean-François Lyotard made some famous observations on the formulation and transformation of knowledge. He developed a relatively complex argument that is not appropriate to unpick in detail here, but there are some central tenets to his position that are worth reflecting on. Lyotard identified the importance of the rise of new database technologies for the future of knowledge. He anticipated that such databases would far transcend the knowledge of the individual, and would thus draw into question the status of the expert. Alongside this technological shift, Lyotard identified a more general cultural shift towards relativism and a rising scepticism towards the expert. The problem, for Lyotard, was that knowledge was also changing, as was the means for making that knowledge legitimate. Lyotard argued that the legitimation of knowledge through proof and evidential fact had become a problem, hence his comment that this was 'sounding the knell of the age of the professor' (Lyotard 1979: 53) – or to place it within the themes of this book, perhaps sounding the knell of the living-dead professor. In this context, Lyotard predicted two things: (1) the rising commodification of knowledge and, (2) the rise of new forms of legitimacy based not on authority but on efficiency. It is not too much of a stretch of the imagination to see that these predictions have now become central to the contemporary academy; they have become the challenges we now face. Further to this, we see in Lyotard's work a concern that the socio-technological conditions of the time shape what knowledge is and what questions shape its formation. This has myriad consequences for our day-to-day routines, some of which are very difficult to see and can emerge in unpredictable and strange forms (we might only be able to conceive of these emergent consequences in years to come). Following Lyotard's lead, we may need to reflect again on how transformations in the technological and cultural setting are coming to implicate what knowledge is, how it is formed, and what topics it includes.

The important thing will be to make sure that choosing topics that are perceived as glossy is not tantamount to choosing to wear those *living-dead man's shoes* that I mentioned earlier. Let us not migrate away from these topics as we will be encouraged to do by the structures within which we will be operating; instead let us respond by integrating such topics into our repertoire and by showing to a range of audiences why exactly it is that they matter and why they have wider significance. We should take advantage of our position in a still relatively critical space within higher education to provide considered engagement with these things rather than choosing to *play it safe*. They can then be defended and used to address the new expectations placed upon us to be 'public' and to have 'impact'.

In very broad terms, there are a number of ways in which we might respond: by showing why these things are not glossy at all, by completely removing the gloss and revealing the harmful properties of consumption and the often even more harmful production and working practices behind the scenes. We might respond by allowing these topics to remain glossy, but then explain exactly why it is that these glossy topics matter. This will require us to demonstrate social and cultural significance and to elaborate what might be thought of as the *politics of glossy topics*. The four intersections I set out earlier in this piece are intended for this purpose.

To close, I would like to emphasize that we should not let the structures in which we work discourage an engagement with important glossy topics and we should not turn our back upon them for the safer territories mapped out by regulatory, technological and policy-based structures – we should not automatically select the safety of the farmhouse because of the fear of finding ourselves in the *living-dead man's shoes* of zombification. At the same time though, we should not anticipate that we are going to be allowed to retreat into a space that removes the need for wider engagement, where addressing the questions of value or purpose is not necessary. As I have argued elsewhere with Rowland Atkinson, what is needed is something like an 'ivorine tower', a synthetic space that affords both long-term and slow consideration, as well as quick and short-term engagement (Atkinson and Beer 2010). The balance is being able to respond without being reactionary, to take time and space when necessary but also to be ready to get involved as things happen. This is not as easy as it might seem: it will be a real challenge that will require us to pick our battles and to carve and reshape what it is that we do in our research and teaching. There are aspects of our conditions that we know that we have little control or influence over; we might need to go with this flow at times to satisfy the demands on us. My argument here though is that we must not abandon glossy topics for apparently safer options. This would be to lose vitality and vibrancy. Further to this, it would also be to ignore some of the topics central to the contemporary condition. Glossy topics matter, the challenge is to show why they matter as we build them into our reshaped teaching and research in what is likely to be a challenging and maybe even hostile social and cultural context. As the global economic crisis and its consequences continue to unfold, more of us are likely to find our teaching and research territory challenged in various ways, we need to anticipate these challenges and position our work so as to respond in very explicit and accessible terms. The way to avoid the scramble for the farmhouse, or the life of the marginal zombie, is to elaborate an agenda that shows why these things matter. I hope that the initial provocations provided in this brief chapter will make a small contribution towards just such a response.

Feverish homeless cannibal

George Pfau

Body Before Zombie

In the film *Zombieland*, a scene flashes back to a moment before the term 'zombie' had entered into the characters' vocabularies. A frantic woman bursts into her neighbour's apartment, struggling to describe an uncategorized attacker. The narration that follows declares that a 'feverish homeless cannibal' had chased and bitten her. It becomes apparent that this attacker was in fact, a zombie. When intermingled with 'zombie', the phrase 'feverish, homeless, cannibal' takes on complex new meanings and associations. This essay examines several occurrences of feverish, homeless or cannibalistic zombies in film, television and videogames, highlighting instances when social stigmas are reinforced. Subsequently, further unpacking of 'zombie' will provide a new lens into these often negated states of being.

Zombie narratives often teach prejudice towards people who embody negative-sounding traits, such as contagion, illness, strangeness, otherness or savagery. The word zombie has become slur-like, relegating beings to a zone that is dangerous, cursed or subhuman. When 'zombie' is aligned with the phrase 'feverish homeless cannibal', are all beings represented, fictional or real, to be equated with a class of dangerous people unworthy of the rights granted to the label 'human'?

It is possible for 'zombie' to be exonerated from the common negative framework, and to come to represent the complexities of in-betweenness. It provides a useful space for conversations about mortality, visibility, recognition and rights in regards to illness, homelessness and cannibalism. One can begin by viewing zombie' through philosopher, Mikhail Bakhtin's idea of the image of the grotesque body:

> The grotesque body, as we have often stressed, is a body in the act of becoming. It is never finished, never completed; it is continually built, created, and builds and creates another body ... The grotesque image displays not only the outward but also the inner features of the body: blood, bowels, heart and other organs. The outward and inward features are often merged into one. (1984: 317–18)

The grotesque image of the zombie can effectively exemplify the in-flux parameters of the human body, its ephemerality and its relationship with other bodies. Defined by liminality, the zombie is a tangible body that appears in a state between several countervailing pairs: alive and dead, person and thing, human and animal, individual and group, the pronouns 'he/she' and 'it'. In many cases, it provides us with a way of looking simultaneously at both the inside and the outside of the body.

While at first glance the association between zombie and 'feverish homeless cannibal' may seem reciprocally disparaging, the notion of the grotesque, liminal zombie can offer empowering correlations. My hope is that this reframing of the word zombie can resist the promotion of deeply entrenched social stigmas and provide an investigation of the physicality and parameters of the self.

Feverish

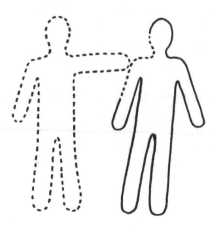

In *Zombieland*, the first descriptive word attributed to a zombie is 'feverish'. This is one example of many in which fever is a symptom of a rapidly spreading, infectious epidemic. Many current undead narratives, such as the film *28 Days Later*, and the *Left 4 Dead* videogame series, refer to zombies as 'the infected'. In these cases, fans and journalists then later apply the word zombie. This is similar to how the 'ghouls' of George Romero's *Night of the Living Dead* took on the label of 'zombie'.

In an era of SARS, Swine Flu, HIV and other potent diseases, the association between zombie and infected/feverish taps into the societal fears of contagion and terminal illness. While the zombie disease is typically spread though biting or blood transfusion, its real-life counterparts are transmissible through a range of means, from airborne inhalation, to mosquito bites, to sexual intercourse. The zombie virus, or 'Rage virus' as it is called in *28 Days Later*, resembles rabies in that it agitates its host and can be transmissible via saliva into a wound caused by biting. Most narratives promote the idea that while similar to a real-life disorder, the disease is beyond a cure and that the infected must be destroyed.

There is a scene in the film *Planet Terror* that exemplifies this fear of contagion, in which a hospital transforms from a site of healing to the centre of an outbreak. A doctor catches the attention of a recently infected zombie holding a surgical saw, which is plugged in to the wall. The only thing that separates them is a door-sized piece of plastic sheeting. The zombie lurches towards the doctor, slicing the semitransparent plastic in two. The saw lashes out at the doctor's face, cutting through his black-rimmed glasses; however, he is momentarily saved when the electrical cord pops out of the socket, causing the blade to stop. In the scene's finale, the zombie grasps a bulging, pus-filled welt from his own cheek and smears its bloody, contagious goo across the doctor's face.

From the plastic sheet to the grotesque pus, from one penetrated membrane to the next, the notion that there is danger in boundary crossing is heavily emphasized. This scene not only conjures up fear surrounding surgical tools, it also associates contagion and life-ending terror with the uncontrolled interior of the body. Bodies that are somehow transparent, turned inside-out or appear dead are shown as not only disgusting but threatening.

A body out of control can be a scary thing. So often the human body betrays its owner's hopes and gives in to their fears. A diseased body is a vulnerable body. It becomes a place that is examined, manipulated, drugged or surgically pried open. In the case of most zombies, when a person becomes 'feverish' or 'infected', their sense of self either shifts drastically, or is lost. Bodies serve as hosts, or empty shells inhabited by a parasitic virus. Their body, willpower and thinking are under the control of the virus. Zombie narratives frequently depict medical experts desperately seeking a way to control or 'cure' the zombie plague. However, the search for the cure can become a way to avoid thinking about the reality of death and the loss of the self.

Fear of fever and illness are closely linked to fear of death. While fever indicates a body at a high temperature, real-life 'zombie' scenarios are unfolding at low temperatures. In his book *Cheating Death*, neurosurgeon Sanjay Gupta discusses the success of induced hypothermia as a last effort to keep a person alive even when they have gone into shock and their vital signs appear to be gone. He suggests that procedures like this can hold bodies in a 'gray zone – a faint no-man's-land where you are neither truly dead nor actually alive', long enough to transport a person to a place where they can get additional care (2009: xi). Subsequently, there are now practices that involve using liquid nitrogen and tightly sealed body-sized tanks to preserve newly dead bodies in a state of cryostasis. This process operates within the assumption that these bodies are to be kept 'frozen' until the technology is developed to reconstruct and reanimate them. The Cryonics Institute is an organization that offers this service for 'legally dead' and 'deanimated' people. Their website states: 'A person held in such a state is said to be a "cryopreserved patient", because we do not regard the cryopreserved person as being really "dead"' (The Cryonics Institute 2011). While these examples come from the desire to 'cheat' death, they can also be used to complicate the life and death binary, creating a non-threatening space for entities like zombies.

While the raw body of the zombie in *Planet Terror* is oozing into its environment in a cartoonish manner, the image can be interpreted as an exaggeration of the organic impermanence of human life. Healthy, living bodies are also profoundly grotesque: seething with bacteria, sweating, salivating, ejaculating, defecating, and constantly shedding hair, skin, pus and mucous. Further acknowledgement of this can allow humans to accept their in-flux, zombie-like qualities by resisting the shame, violence or prejudice attached to them by pop-cultural stereotypes.

Homeless

As in *Zombieland*, many satirical depictions of the uncanny zombie both expose and reinforce common negative stereotypes of homeless people. Both zombies and homeless people are portrayed as mentally volatile, unclean and even repulsive. They destabilize various modes of civilized life, and are thus promoted as discomforting or dangerous. In an episode of the TV series *South Park* entitled 'Night of the Living Homeless', the town of South Park is overrun by a growing mass of ragged, cup-rattling homeless people who shamble around moaning 'chaaange' rather than 'braaaiins' (as in *Return of the Living Dead*). In the film *Shaun of the Dead*, the main character, Shaun, passes a homeless beggar on his daily walk to his job at an electronics store. Once the zombie outbreak has begun, this homeless man turns into a zombie. Shaun does not notice and brushes by him, mumbling that he does not have any change today. In the first case the homeless zombies are a hostile homogeneous mass, and in the second, a walking obstacle, with status equivalent to that of a parking meter.

Zombieland actually portrays both the living and the undead as unsheltered or homeless. Once the zombie apocalypse is in full swing the idea of home is shifted. Houses have mostly been destroyed or proven unsafe, and territorial borders strictly delineated by governmental entities have now been rendered trivial. The main characters, now transients, have all exchanged their birth names for the names of their hometowns. The four characters go by 'Columbus', 'Tallahassee', 'Wichita' and 'Little Rock'. Homes are now a nostalgic memory, as this foursome goes from place to place on a road trip across the former United States, referred to as 'Zombieland'. Despite the common nomadic status of the living and the un-living, the film's protagonists show no sympathy for the zombies, destroying them at will.

Stereotypical depictions of homeless people portray bodies that are out of control. Their voices, thoughts, clothes, odours and defecations are all somehow untethered. They represent the opposite of homeowners, and thus fail to live up to societal standards. In many cases homelessness is intertwined with mental illness such as post-traumatic stress disorder, chronic depression or schizophrenia. Quite often, these conditions are identified by the ways in which they disrupt the perception of a normal, stable self. These portrayals of the homeless, like those of zombies, display precarious bodies that are simultaneously linked to and decoupled from a sense of comfort and normality. Both zombies and homelessness exemplify Sigmund Freud's concept of the *unheimlich*, a hazy zone where the strange encroaches upon the familiar. While *unheimlich* is usually translated from German to the English word 'uncanny', it is etymologically and morphologically 'unhomely', stressing the link between body and home (McClintock 2003: lxiii).

Philosopher and political scientist Achille Mbembe aligns the 'living dead' with those who are pushed to the margins, forced to cross geographic borders, and shunned by governments. Their sense of home is in transition. The artist Gean Moreno highlights Mbembe's discussion of the in-betweenness of people who are persecuted by their own countries to the point where they must flee and take on refugee status. Like zombies, these deterritorialized people are censored, quarantined and lacking rights. They are politically uncategorized, existing outside the boundary of legal recognition. Moreno writes:

> Surveying the deathscapes that the political instrumentalization of the massacre has created on the African continent (as well as in the Middle East, the Balkans, and Latin America), Achille Mbembe has spoken of those that 'survive' the event and go on to live in refugee camps or those who have not yet encountered it but are destined to, those who live unprotected from the whims and strategies of State power and private armies, who can be killed with impunity, as the living dead ... Those that live politically unsheltered lives, pushed beyond the protection of the social order and the space of legality, are the new zombies. (Moreno 2006: 30)

These living-dead survivors are unfixed from homes delineated by architectural structures or cartographic borders. The body (one's skin, clothes and fixed identity) can be perceived as a new sense of 'home'. When ownership and control over one's geographic surroundings is undone, the body becomes the site where these ideas take place. Films like *Michael Jackson's Thriller* or *Night of the Living Dead* present vivid images of homes (houses) acting as the primary boundary separating the living and the undead. The windows, doors and walls act as almost skin-like, permeable membranes, eventually allowing zombies to pass through.

Bruce LaBruce's recent film *L.A. Zombie* (2010) provides a surreal alternative to the stereotypical homeless zombies. He portrays a homeless schizophrenic zombie who wields the power to resurrect the dead through sex acts. In some cases the dead are often men who have been violently murdered, and the homosexual, necrophilic act is not only a reanimation, but a redemption. Instead of the stereotypical societal menace, LaBruce's homeless zombie is a grotesque nomad who heals through sexual boundary crossing acts, while moving freely through the world uncontrolled by the parameters of a home.

Cannibal

A basic trope of the contemporary zombie is the desire to eat the flesh of human beings by literally biting into their living bodies. Popularized by *Night of the Living Dead*, this cannibalism complicates the idea of the individual as distinctly separate from other bodies. As skin tears away, so do recognizable features, at times creating homogeneous, unidentified bodies. Also, when a bite is occurring an exchange happens. Flesh is traded for zombiedom and subhuman status. As in the previous categories, bodily boundary crossing is a cause for alarm.

Bakhtin explores the sense of mortality encapsulated within this permeable bodily borderline:

The events of the grotesque sphere are always developed on the boundary dividing one body from the other and, as it were, at their points of intersection. One body offers its death, the other its birth, but they are merged in a two-bodied image. (1984: 322)

Bakhtin reminds the reader of the birth that is intertwined with this boundary crossing, thus resisting the stereotypical feelings of negativity and danger. This grotesque zone is complex, as is the exchange between zombie and living human. The consumed body not only filters into the body of the zombie, it splatters and oozes onto the outer surface of the zombie and the living. Categorical labels are then shifted, causing life and death (or undeath) to become confusing. A cannibal is typically one who consumes or eats one of their own: a human who eats a human, a dog who eats a dog. However, when zombies eat living humans in a fictionalized world in which 'zombie' is a subhuman category, does the term cannibal still apply?

The term 'cannibal' has often been in close proximity to the notion of the zombie, even before flesh eating became visible in films. The 1932 film, *White Zombie* promoted negative stereotypes associated with the idea that cannibalistic practice would ensue in Haiti if a breakdown in white governmental control were to occur. Film historian Chera Kee suggests that in this narrative, '[B]lack Voodoo was no match for white reason. Thus *White Zombie* and much of the zombie fiction that would follow implicitly asserted the need to reimpose control over Haitians and the rest of the colonies' (Kee 2011: 12–13).

Historically, cannibalism tends to bring about associations with uncontrolled savagery. The term 'Caníbales' is derived from the sixteenth-century Spanish colonialist label for the Carib people indigenous to the West Indies. The Spanish created propaganda about these people, which promoted the notion that they regularly consumed human flesh, portraying this practice as an uneducated, barbaric act. This legitimized their task to either civilize these Caribbean people or kill them, while exploiting their labour and natural resources.

The zombie genre has at times provided a platform for the reinforcement of stereotypes and the justification and glorification of quasi-colonial acts of extreme violence. The game

317

Resident Evil 5 presents a zombie-esque outbreak as the horrific side effect of a bioterrorist attack in a vulnerable part of 'Kijuju', a fictional region in West Africa (Capcom 2009). The gamer controls the Caucasian main character and his British-accented sidekick, who have been sent to restore stability in the region. It is determined that a necessary step for dealing with this plague is the violent extermination of the infected, uncivilized people. As one explores the ramshackle village, gunning down mobs of brown skinned, machete wielding 'Majini' (zombies), ammunition supplies often run dry. There also happen to be random pieces of gold jewellery lying around that can be picked up (pillaged) and exchanged for more ammunition. Even the uncontaminated Africans in this game seem to act with hostile intentions, which further enforce a long history of negative depictions.

In videogames like this, acts of violence towards zombies are merciless and casual. One might infer that the zombie has often been appropriated because it is no longer acceptable or politically correct to promote images of violence towards people of 'inferior' race or class. In order for humans to inflict guilt-free violence upon other humans, a categorical boundary must differentiate between killer and killed.

In the film *Land of the Dead*, the supposedly primitive zombies get the last laugh. United by their hunger for flesh, zombies of different races wearing working class uniforms rise up against the elite living class. They become a cooperative group, moving as a unit across a large body of water, and then breaking through layers of fencing to overtake the wealthy, white overlord.

'Zombie'

The word 'zombie' is entrenched in the pop-cultural lexicon, and is quite often taken for granted. The meaning of 'zombie' can be stretched to give a topic more pop-appeal. In other cases the pop-culture itself declares that 'zombie' can be applied to 'the infected', the African Majini, or even the ghouls of *Night of the Living Dead*, all of which dance around the usage of the Z-word.

When used to discuss topics such as illness, homelessness and cannibalism in a way that does not promote negative stereotypes, the word zombie must undergo extensive clarification to be shed of its negative implications. Bakhtin's notion of the grotesque or Mbembe's writing about the living dead serve as reminders that the term 'zombie' can be applied to in-between bodies other than those of the negated and stereotyped.

The meaning of 'zombie' is elusive and fixed at the same time. From one film to the next, audiences observe zombies operating under stringent sets of rules, which are then broken by the next writer or filmmaker. They are contradictory at their core. Therein lies their power to promote the complexity of the liminal zones between life and death, healthy and sick, home and homeless, individual and group, other and self.

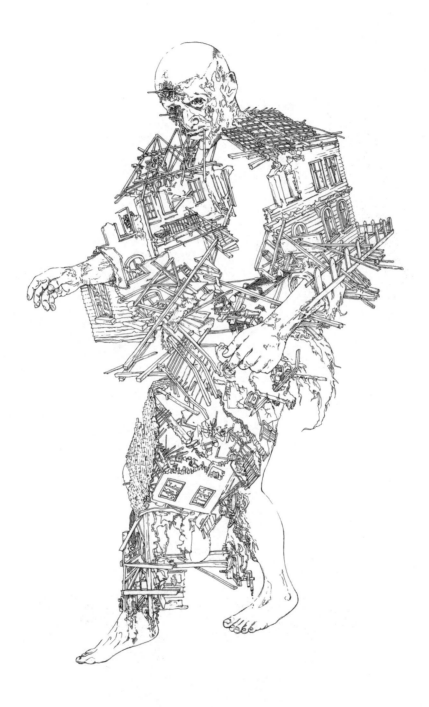

A report on the global Viral-Z outbreak and its impact on higher education

Howard M. Gregory II and Annie Jeffery

The case study

Conditions before the Viral-Z outbreak are well documented in the copious amounts of information contained in the now obsolete electronic archives, which are only superficially tapped as yet. The period is also recorded in a plethora of popular cultural artefacts of the twenty-first century, such as television, film and fiction, where it was often romanticized as a golden age of rapid social, technological and scientific advancement. These popular media representations tend to gloss over the less glamorous aspects of the era, including what are now recognized as prescient concerns about global warming, terrorism, financial crises and the insidious corporatization of public institutions, including, most notably for this report, higher education. The Viral-Z outbreak, now commonly referred to as the 'Zombie apocalypse' (see Zombiepedia 2025), reshaped the world of education in unforeseen ways. Although the origins of the Viral-Z outbreak are unknown, written evidence in the form of eyewitness accounts of an event in Houston, Texas in January 2010 coincided with the first reported cases and mention 'strange lights in the sky', 'an enormous crater, really huge and it had burns marks around it', and that 'there were strange men in black suits and sunglasses everywhere' (Fraser 2010).

According to one of the earliest testimonies of a survivor, Jim Pike (Anderson and Stall 2010), this viral infection appeared to animate the recently deceased bodies of humans who would consequently wander aimlessly until they detected the presence of an uninfected human, whom they would then bite and either cannibalize or infect. All known human victims were introduced to the *virus intelligent iuguolo*, or intelligent killer virus, through this process. Pike speculated that amongst these 'zombies', as he termed them, the mere presence of an uninfected individual acted as a trigger for an instinctive feeding behaviour. If the zombies were in a group the victim was most likely overwhelmed and eaten. Individual zombies on the other hand were notably weak and uncoordinated, so victims had a chance of escape, although there was some risk of infection. The bite victim who escaped to 'safety' could subsequently succumb – Pike observed that the process of zombification varied from mere seconds to over an hour. Continual vigilance was considered vital to group survival because failure to detect infection in friends, neighbours, relatives and emergency medical technicians resulted in widespread infection throughout the areas demarcated as 'safe' zones.

When the outbreak spread, local, federal and international government organizations collapsed as institutional processes were inadequate to deal with the demands of the cataclysmic epidemic. Many who lived during this episode anticipated a breakdown of all cultural, political and economic structures, and would lead to the complete disintegration of the social order. However, the rise in the epidemic marked the parallel development of global research centres and data collectives that worked together in 'the cloud' (a term that referred to early twenty-first-century social, collaborative computing networks). These research centres' primary brief was to research, learn and teach survival strategies. The successful dissemination of both findings and recommendations to local and international population clusters has been credited as responsible for the continuing survival of the human race (Kowalski 2021).

It is ironic that the unwitting contributions of the zombie sufferers themselves led to the endorsement of what had already been established as a universally participative mode of communication and, ultimately, to the development of an antidote. A near-universal symptom of the virus was the marked predisposition to obsessively maintain routine behavioural patterns, found subsequently to be caused by decomposition of the left inferior frontal gyrus (LIFG) area of the brain. This mental deterioration was soon accompanied by more obvious physical symptoms of tissue necrosis and hyper-metabolic regeneration of vital structures at the expense of less short-term critical tissue maintenance, which ultimately generated the appearance of the 'typical' zombie. Learned actions – which had become reflexive and psychosomatically instinctual – were retained because they were more closely linked to the vital motor cortex. In practice, this meant that zombies who in life had been trained to play football could be found roaming sports fields, and were observed compulsively engaging in a myotatic reflex, or kicking action, in the vicinity of circular objects. It was not until 2 years after the epidemic died down that the final train full of undead commuters was neutralized and removed from the London Underground system some 6 months after the network was put back in operation by the general public. These zombie commuters had been endlessly travelling round the Circle Line. Tragically, in the immediate outbreak of Viral Z many innocents were attacked by paranoid survivors after being observed compulsively checking their iPhones and Blackberries for network signal strength. However, it was a significant finding that zombies who had in their pre-infected state made heavy use of social media websites, continued to do so. In the early stages of postmortem infection, when considerable brain function was still in progress, a number of zombies were found to have attempted to place video diaries of their predicament on YouTube. Indeed, the term 'hungryyyyy' became a common 'status' setting on Facebook.

The critical breakthrough came when research scientists, despairing of a risk-free way to physically analyse an intact zombie specimen, realized that they could maintain contact-at-a-distance and virtual communication with newly infected sufferers as they continued to blog while succumbing to the zombification process, albeit with fast-deteriorating coherency. It was now possible to behaviourally analyse the zombie mindset to a frighteningly detailed degree.

Literature review

While there is already a number of detailed reviews of the academic literature on the outbreak of the Viral-Z outbreak (see Vecchio 2019; Zuko 2020), what is yet to be completed is a survey of the electronic database archives, remnants of social media content from the time as well as historical fiction that itself drew heavily on first-hand accounts of the events by eyewitnesses. It is our contention that historical fiction acts as a lens for those who wish to study the period, turning myth into facts and temples into museums (Campbell 1949). Van Maanen advocated an approach that allowed 'a fieldworker to use the culture of the setting (the socially acquired and shared knowledge available to the participants or members of the setting) to account for the observed patterns of human activity' (1979: 539).

For instance, Anderson and Stalls' novel, *Night of the Living Trekkies* (2010), based on survivor interviews and diaries, has proved to be an invaluable resource for a complete understanding of the early stages of the Viral-Z outbreak. The book drives home the urgency of the events and their overwhelming impact on individuals and institutions. This novel provides insight into motivations behind the Houston, Texas bombing, further illustrated by the millions of crisis entries mapped on Ushahidi (an early twenty-first-century crowdsource crisis information platform). Similarly, Madeleine Roux's novel, *Allison Hewitt Is Trapped* (2011) clearly shows how social media was used to share knowledge, offer support and to encourage isolated groups of survivors to continue the fight for survival.

Methodologies for survival

As has been well recorded (see the Zombiepedia page 'Viral-Z outbreak'), the global governmental, corporate, military and religious organizations found themselves overwhelmed and overrun within the first 3 months of the Viral-Z epidemic. Because churches, government buildings and military bases were quickly destroyed, alternative locations had to be selected as sites for surviving population clusters to regroup. Large secondary schools and universities were quickly determined to be the most suitable, and in North America the infestation led to the creation of a number of regional rescue centres on these campuses, with a goal to save as many healthy individuals as possible while simultaneously neutralizing infected hordes. Within these rescue centres, academic leaders quickly leveraged a core population of young, healthy, technologically savvy and educated citizens into the survival movement.

Several factors proved essential to the rescue centres' ability to create a population more capable of adapting to the continuously dangerous and rapidly evolving environment. It is clear from the accounts of contemporary scholars that Emergency Order 152 (issued from the North American united emergency capital in Ottawa hours before it fell silent), allowed for the formation of the North American University Rescue Centre Alliance (NAURCA). Order 152 placed all remaining military units under academic rescue centre control and consequently saved hundreds of thousands of individuals from certain death during a period of the chaos, which is commonly referred to as the Dead Ages (Williams and Walsh 2025a).

We argue that by this time, existing military tactics and traditional educational strategies were clearly failing to support the survivalist movement. An examination of contextual factors will help obtain a deeper understanding of why some rescue centres survived while others did not.

Hypothesis: social media pedagogies as antidote

Our initial research revealed that the adoption of pedagogies of participatory learning (New Learning), as well as open source software and knowledge shared via social media, proved essential to human survival. The most successful rescue centres were those that were maintained by renewable energy sources. It was the adoption of collaborative 'green' approaches in North American Rescue Centres (NARCs) and other citizen-led organizations around the world that enabled populations to adapt to volatile environmental and social conditions. NARCs also harnessed early twenty-first-century media platforms and skills in the fight against Viral-Z, which proved their worth as they filled the gap left by the disintegration of reactive response procedures. Other participatory groups instrumental to the survival effort included the Cricket Clubs of England, the Geisha Communities of Japan, the Drug Cartels of Mexico and Doctor Who Societies worldwide. But without doubt, it is the Web 3.0 Student survival groups who should be credited with disseminating vital zombie-specific knowledge. These informal communities not only stepped unexpectedly into the foreground after the fall of local governments, but also collaborated with NARCs to employ New Learning techniques and ultimately served to aid the surviving generation to eradicate the remaining zombies.

Emergence of the new communities

Events in the early twenty-first century created opportunities to develop what Howe (2008) described as 'a new kind of quickly formulated, potentially powerful community – the ad-hoc crisis community'. Howe observed that these communities were most effective when they were generated by the kinds of social media that supported crowd sourcing. Crowd sourcing radically reorganized patterns of economic exchange that proved particularly effective during the Global Financial Crisis (GFC), a largely forgotten but important precursor to the Viral-Z outbreak. Social media was seen to 'provide the means of creating new communities and for re-energizing old communities'

(Williams and Walsh 2025a: 427), and unfortunate subsequent events proved this claim to be singularly prescient.

Early traces of these new communities occur in the surviving archives of software like Ushahidi (Swahili for 'witness or testimony'), which was an open source software for information collection, visualization and interactive mapping for specific date ranges. It was possible for any agency or group, no matter how small, to adopt and utilize the software themselves. Ushahidi had previously been used in response to the Haiti earthquake in 2010, and the H1N1 flu pandemics in 2015.

Survivors and nongovernmental organizations used Ushahidi extensively during the Viral-Z outbreak, particularly during major confrontations. Each message marked a position on the map and a numbered circle increased in size as related reports poured in. Rescue teams were able to access vital location reports, photos and videos by clicking this numbered circle. The images and videos retrieved from the Ushahidi archive that depict the Houston bombing, the evacuation of Toronto as well as the collapse of Harvard University are now regarded as iconic. Previous generations of research scholars had faced the arduous task of finding scraps of information that could be considered part of the historical record so that they could discuss and analyse the past. In contrast, by the start of the Viral-Z outbreak, 'every world citizen had created a vast wealth of information' (Beck and Pele 2010). In Sweden, groups of statistical code-warriors formed a Gapminder movement to analyse and disseminate the most effective strategies against zombie infestation (Totmann 2027). Indeed, as Tom Scheinfeldt (cited in Beck and Pele 2010) was among the first to attest during the outbreak, 'Everyone is producing history, everyone has access to history and everyone [has to become] a historian.'

Previous historians have overlooked one important factor in their analysis of rescue centre effectiveness in the post-outbreak period (Williams and Walsh 2025a). We have identified this factor as early twenty-first-century investment in renewable energy. Our initial research powerfully demonstrates that universities were among the first large entities to embrace green initiatives and alternative power supplies (Williams and Walsh 2025a). Statistical data demonstrates that successful centres were equipped with alternative energy sources when traditional power plants stopped working. Rooftop windmills provided power not only to buildings but also to ensure that water pumps continued to make available essentials such as plumbing and drinking water, lights, heat, electronics, electric cooking and food storage. In other areas, solar panels replaced roofing tiles. Significantly, these alternative sources of electricity powered the computers, networks, software and satellite uplinks needed to supply power for participatory media and technologies essential to the fight against Viral-Z. Unsurprisingly, given the location of power sources, rescue centres focused on the preservation and use of the social media platforms that surviving participants – largely clusters of students and academics – were most familiar with. Social media was the key component of the New Learning that proved to be the antidote to the devastating effects of the Viral-Z outbreak.

The 'New Learning'

The New Learning was foreshadowed by major events such as the 2010 Haiti Earthquake, during which open source knowledge and social media were deployed as part of the disaster management strategy. During the outbreak, NAURCA developed Zombiepedia and Zombr, which were instrumental in the fight against contagion. Zombr, as a social news service, provided user-generated maps, sightings, battle strategies, whilst Zombiepedia's typology linked directly to the Zombr news and maps service.

Online communities around the world worked with NARCs to update information and share knowledge. Initially, Open Street Maps was used to locate and share areas of high infestation and this later became key to rescue centre survival itself. However, some rescue centres failed due to an over reliance on proprietary software services, run by commercial organizations unable to continue support services after they were overrun. Anecdotal accounts from surviving staff (Williams and Walsh 2025b) support the theory that while Silicon Valley developers had the means to protect themselves, they proved unwilling to cooperate within a joint defence pact with their commercial competitors. The copyright protected software was therefore the first to succumb to the anarchy following the outbreak and subsequently a great number of knowledge networks were destroyed. This is perhaps a loss to subsequent generations but the inordinate number of widgets and hardware designed with planned obsolescence prior to the outbreak will not be missed. It has been argued that these developers would have better spent their time developing widgets that benefited the global community for the common good rather than to generate income for the corporate shareholders (Manjoo 2011). This is an issue that will be discussed in a follow-up publication. In summary, however, it was quickly apparent that the loss of corporate IPR, copyrights and firewalls were not considered a serious blow as they effectively inhibited social growth.

Open learning networks support zombie defence and protection training

Prior to the development of NARC and NAURCA, the majority of 'serious' academic learning and teaching was restricted to a select few within formal institutions that were heavily invested in replicating what was thought by a number of dead, but still powerful, scholars. The ivory (fire)walls of educational institutions proved to be a factor to this strangely zombified process, with a few North American exceptions found in projects such as MIT's Open Courseware, the OpenCourseWare Consortium, OpenYale, Open Learn and Smart History. Notably, iTunes U content survived through the network of mp3 downloads distributed around the world. However, by 2011 Udemy.com's 'Academy of You' had begun to gain ground as a centralized service for zombie prevention, containment and eradication studies. Udemy's (2011) aim to 'disrupt and democratize the world of education by enabling anyone to teach and learn online' provided fertile ground for collaborative course development. This eventually led to a sister service 'Zomcademy', a free and dedicated zombie studies network. Zomcademy itself led to the development of the Global New Learning Centres (GloNeC), which were formed from the most active Zomcademy authors and curators remaining at the end of the Viral-Z outbreak (Williams and Walsh 2025a).

The above genealogy shows how traditional universities were already vulnerable long before the outbreak, as they had already been forced by the marketization of higher education to provide online delivery of teaching and learning. This 'flexible' delivery flourished in the post-outbreak era where leaving rescue centres and gathering in groups remained hazardous. The rapid decline in the numbers of teaching faculty due to either (1) cannibalism by or (2) infection and conversion to zombies ultimately forced the development of self-paced asynchronous learning reliant on crowd-sourcing and practical application as assessment. On entry to the programme, students were generally graded by their relative state of inevitable zombification, such as the number of their remaining limbs and their ability to remain focused and self aware. Repetitive, mindless activities, such as a predilection for rote learning, were viewed as highly suspicious indicators of impending zombification. Unfortunately, much of the existing online learning modelled on Ramsden's (2003) and Biggs and Tang's (2007) theories of 'deep learning', a commonly accepted antidote to the zombification of both students and delivery platforms, was lost with the downfall of the traditional university system. The once abundant Open CourseWare sites of Yale, MIT and the Open University in the United Kingdom were lost forever in the sustained campus zombie attacks in the later stages of the outbreak.

Social media technologies such as smartphones, tablets and ebook readers allowed learners to not only crowdgrade assignments but to form dispersed project teams, to collaborate on projects as well as to provide distance mentoring. The activity of learning itself became increasingly distributed across a vast and converging network of social groups, technologies and media, each forming an essential component in the system providing information and feedback needed by the system (Hutchins 1995). The development of globally distributed cognition ensured that learning remained within the social and technology networks and was no longer vulnerable through dependency on a single individual.

Online games provided another avenue for sharing knowledge of defensive survival strategies. Video games provided a fertile training ground, because they offered a degree of control over their environment; games shift, change and adapt to gameplay whilst the gamer monitors their interactions and adapts their strategy accordingly. Games such as Zombie FarmVille were created as hybrid entertainment and learning aids for pre-teens while considerably more technically sophisticated games were developed as dedicated training games for adults actively engaged in combating Viral-Z. The companies that had originally created these games in Silicon Valley were decimated during Viral-Z, so the code was quickly renamed and reclassified as 'open source'.

Gameplay acted as both a motivator and teacher for younger zombie-fighting squads. Very small children and older members of the public learned vicariously through the many zombie movies shared on OpenCulture or TeacherTube. For instance, Virtual Explorer, originally a virtual reality (VR) model of immunology, was designed as an immersive, highly interactive environment that provided an engaging, playful, enjoyable way to experience science (Dean et al 2000). The original Virtual Explorer had survived unharmed in a janitor's cupboard in a basement of a well-known university now defunct due to lack of resources provided by its alumni. (We are prevented from naming this institution since a few of its alumni who are still alive refuse to admit that almost 90% of its revenue was not generated from its fees prior to the Viral-Z outbreak. Our lawyers have advised us to refrain from also indicating the physical location of said institution. It appears that these alumni would like to gain control of said software for future profitable purposes.) The rich game-like experience of Virtual Explorer involved two interactive missions designed for students raised on video games. The first of these missions was repurposed by NAURCA as an orientation to zombie studies while the second was a carefully designed audio-visual training experience delivered by a high quality dedicated sound system. A replica virtual reality installation was reconstructed from disused engineering experiments, media studio components and volunteer labour. Once the project had been successfully reconstructed, the software and instructions were freely distributed to other training centres. Other NAURCA centres began to create and share VR tutorials, which proved instrumental in the success of the project.

These new anti-zombie networks and media were characterized by the awareness that they were no longer situated either in a single institution or individual but the networks as a whole. Each component of the network was considered active participants from games to movies to collaborative maps. It has been argued that this distributed cognition was essential to the fight for survival, as success depended on the contributions of each member and the ability for knowledge networks to survive the loss of individual members (Bell and Winn 2000; Hutchins 2005).

Resistance to social media

A recurring question asks what it was that prevented governmental agencies from rapidly adopting these social medial tools in the fight against the Viral-Z contagion? The remnants of blogs written by both recently infected zombies and survivors of the outbreak reveal how these technologies had caused considerable alarm in many corporatized government organizations in the decade immediately before the Viral-Z outbreak. Goolsby (2010) had pointed out that these tools were seen as potential gateways for security threats such as viruses and Trojans, and so even preceding the outbreak, provoked anxiety about maintaining pristine information environments and unease about the potential spread of inaccurate, unsourced and questionable information.

The academy in particular looked upon social media with suspicion: one survivor's testimony bitterly recalls her professor saying 'My dog can upload entries to Wikipedia, why would I let you cite it as a source for this assignment?' The result is that agencies (academic, governmental and military such as the United States Marine Corp) banned social media entirely. Goolsby (2010) recounts how in 2009 police went so far as to arrest activists for tweeting about police activities during a G20 protest in North America. The police considered that 'assisting lawbreakers was punishable by law' and it did not matter what medium was used; early evidence that new technologies were both changing the rules and the laws that policed them.

Conclusion

It is clear that public experience with existing social media and games enabled the transition of learning, knowledge and collaboration to the new NAURCA. The NAURCA networks and Zomcademy have themselves transitioned into the Global New Learning Centres (GloLeC) of today. After the outbreak of Viral-Z, knowledge proved too precious a commodity to be located in any one location or institution, and was consequently distributed throughout the globe. As the prescient book *The Wisdom of Crowds* pointed out:

> What allows this strange blend of collaboration and competition to flourish is the scientific ethos that demands open access to information. This ethos dates back to the origins of the scientific revolution in the seventeenth century … If anything, in fact, the more a piece of knowledge becomes available, the more valuable it potentially becomes, because of the wider array of possible uses for it. (Surowiecki 2004: 116)

This pre-outbreak comment supports our argument that the 'fight' for the common good, without regard for the excessive intellectual property legislation of the twenty-first century, enabled the creation of continent-wide cooperation between rescue centres through the remnants of the open source knowledge networks, alternative energy and remaining satellite communication networks. History has made manifest that teamwork is a necessary precondition for survival. Indeed collaboration is what allowed for the success of the NAURCA and the other academic rescue centres, leading to the eventual creation of the global alliance we enjoy today.

Bibliography

Abbott, A. (2000), 'Reflections on the future of sociology', *Contemporary Sociology*, 29: 2, pp. 296–300.

Ackerman, D. (1999), *Deep Play*, New York: Vintage.

Ackermann, H.W. and Gauthier, J. (1991), 'The ways and nature of the zombi', *Journal of American Folkore*, 104: 414, pp. 466–494.

Adelaide Advertiser (2002), 'Universities in pay rise push', *Adelaide Advertiser*, October 7, p. 13.

Agence France-Presse (2006), 'Iraq war as unpopular as Vietnam', March 23, http://www.commondreams.org/headlines06/0323-13.htm. Accessed 11 February 2012.

——— (2009a), 'French village joins "Thriller" zombie tribute to Michael Jackson', October 25, http://iw.newsbank.com. Accessed 8 February 2012.

——— (2009b), 'From Canada to Argentina, Jackson fans shake to "Thriller"', October 25, http://iw.newsbank.com. Accessed 8 February 2012.

——— (2010), 'N. Zealand brain injury charity defends "zombie walk"', October 14, http://iw.newsbank.com. Accessed 8 February 2012.

Alexander, J., Eyerman, R., Giesen, B., Smelser, N.J., and Sztompka, P. (2004), *Cultural Trauma and Collective Identity*, Berkeley, CA: University of California Press.

Altbach, P., Reisber, L. and Rumbley, L. (2009), 'Executive summary', *Trends in Global Higher Education: Tracking an Academic Revolution, a Report Prepared for the UNESCO 2009 World Conference on Higher Education*, Paris: United Nations Educational, Scientific and Cultural Organization, pp. iii–xxi.

Amoore, L. (2011), 'Data derivatives: on the emergence of a security risk calculus for our times', *Theory, Culture and Society*, 28: 6, pp. 24–43.

Anderson, K.D. and Stall, S. (2010), *Night of the Living Trekkies*, Philadelphia, PA: Quirk Books.

Anderson, P. (2002), *Resident Evil*, USA/Germany: Constantin Film.

——— (2010), *Resident Evil: Afterlife*, USA/Germany: Constantin Film.

——— (2012), *Resident Evil: Retribution*, USA/Germany: Constantin Film.

Apple, Lauri (2011), 'Hey, Occupy Wall Street! Dressing like zombies is dumb!' *Gawker*, October 3, http://gawker.com/5846013/hey-occupy-wall-street-dressing-up-like-zombies-is-dumb. Accessed 8 February 2012.

Arum, R. and Roksa, J. (2010) *Academically Adrift: Limited Learning on College Campuses*, Chicago, IL: University of Chicago Press.

Ashley, D. (2011), '63 universities to be hit with strike action this month as UCU announces strike dates', *Universities and Colleges Union (UCU)*, March 8, http://www.ucu.org.uk/index.cfm?articleid=5371. Accessed 25 February 2012.

Asthana, A., Dyer, E. and Helm, T. (2010), 'Riots, fire, anger at tuition fees protest and a defining political moment', *The Guardian*, September 12, http://www.guardian.co.uk/education/2010/dec/12/riots-fire-anger-defining-political-moment. Accessed 22 February 2012.

Atkinson, R. and Beer, D. (2010), 'The ivorine tower in the city: engaging urban studies after *The Wire*', *City*, 14: 5, pp. 529–544.

Austin, H. (1912), 'The worship of the snake: Voodooism in Haiti today', *New England Magazine*, vol. 57, pp. 170–182.

Austin, J. (2010), *So Now You're a Zombie: A Handbook for the Newly Undead*, Chicago, IL: Chicago Review Press.

Australian Association for Research in Education (2011), 'ERA hides more than it reveals about Education research', *Australian Association for Research in Education*, http://www.aare.edu.au/live/index.php?option=com_contentandview=articleandid=178andItemid=1. Accessed 21 February 2012.

Australian Research Council (2009), *The Excellence in Research for Australia (ERA) Initiative*, www.arc.gov.au/era/. Accessed 21 February 2012.

Australian Vice-Chancellors' Committee (2006), *AVCC Action Plan for Women Employed in Australian Universities*. Canberra: AVCC.

Bakhtin, M. (1984), *Rabelais and His World*, Bloomington, IN: Indiana University Press.

Balagueró, J. and Plaza, P. (2009), *[REC] 2*, Spain: Castelao Producciones.

Baldick, C. (1987), *In Frankenstein's Shadow: Myth, Monstrosity, and Nineteenth-Century Writing*, Oxford: Clarendon.

—— (1992), *The Oxford Book of Gothic Tales*, Oxford: Oxford University Press.

BALEAP (2008), 'Competency framework for teachers of English for Academic Purposes', *British Association of Lecturers in English for Academic Purposes*, http://www.baleap.org.uk/teap/teap-competency-framework.pdf. Accessed 20 June 2011.

—— (2011), 'EAP course guide', *British Association of Lecturers in English for Academic Purposes*, http://www.baleap.org.uk/course_guide/index.aspx. Accessed 11 March 2011.

Ball, A. (2001–05), *Six Feet Under*, USA: Home Box Office.

Ball, S. (2001), 'Performativities and fabrications in the education economy: towards the performative society', in D. Gleeson and C. Husbands (eds), *The Performing School: Managing Teaching and Learning in a Performance Culture*, London: RoutledgeFalmer, pp. 210–226.

Balun, C. (2003), *Beyond Horror Holocaust: A Deeper shade of Red*, Key West, FL: Fantasm Books.

Banks, D. (1986), *Doctor Who Cybermen*, London: Virgin.

Barry, M. (1967a), *The Moonbase*, February 11–March 4, London: BBC.

—— (1967b), *Tomb of the Cybermen*, September 2–23, London: BBC.

Barthes, R. (1988), 'The death of the author', in *Image, Music, Text*, trans. and ed. S. Heath, London: Fontana Press, pp. 142–148.

Bartholomae, D. (1985), 'Inventing the university', in M. Rowe (ed.), *When a Writer Can't Write: Studies in Writer's Block and Other Composing Process Problems*, New York: Guilford, pp. 273–285.

Bataille, G. (1957), *Erotism: Death and Sensuality*, trans. M. Dalwood, San Fransisco: City Lights Books.

Bayne, S. (2008), 'Higher education as a visual practice: seeing through the virtual learning environment', *Teaching in Higher Education*, 13: 4, pp. 395–410.

Beck, K. and Pele, C. (2010), 'Why everyone has to be a historian in the digital age', BBC World News: America, http://news.bbc.co.uk/2/hi/programmes/world_news_america/8999128.stm. Accessed 23 February 2012.

Beck, U. (2000), 'The cosmopolitan perspective: sociology of the second age of modernity', *British Journal of Sociology*, 51: 1, pp. 79–105.

Beck, U. (2002), 'The terrorist threat: world risk society revisited', *Theory, Culture and Society*, 19: 4, pp. 39–55.

—— (2003), 'Toward a new critical theory with a cosmopolitan intent', *Constellations*, 10: 4, pp. 453–468.

—— and Beck-Gernsheim, E. (2002), 'Zombie categories: conversations with Ulrich Beck', in *Individualization: Institutionalised Individualism and its Social and Political Consequences*. London: Sage, pp. 202–205.

Beer, D. and Penfold-Mounce, R. (2010), 'Researching glossy topics: the case of the academic study of celebrity', *Celebrity Studies*, 1: 3, pp. 361–366.

Bell, P. and Winn, W. (2000), 'Distributed cognitions: by nature and by design', in D.H. Jonassen and S.M. Land (eds), *Theoretical Foundations of Learning Environments*, Mahwah, NJ: J.L. Erlbaum Associates, pp. 123–145.

Benesch, S. (2002), *Critical English for Academic Purposes: Theory, Politics, and Practice*, Mahwah, NJ: Lawrence Erlbaum.

—— (2009), 'Theorizing and practicing critical English for Academic Purposes', *Journal of English for Academic Purposes*, 8: 2, pp. 81–85.

Benjamin, W. (1917/1996), 'On paintings, signs and marks', in M. Bullock and M. Jennings (eds), *Walter Benjamin: Selected Writings*, vol. 1, 1913–26, Cambridge, MA: Harvard University Press, pp. 83–86.

—— (1928/2008), 'One way street', in *One Way Street and Other Writings*, trans. J.A. Underwood, London: Penguin, pp. 46–115.

Bennett, P., Kendall, A. and McDougall, J. (2011), *After The Media: Culture and Identity in the 21st Century*, London: Routledge.

Benstock, S. (1983), 'At the margins of discourse: footnotes in the fictional text', *PMLA*, 98: 2, pp. 204–225.

Bentham, J. (1821), *The Elements of the Art of Packing, as applied to Special Juries, particularly in Cases of Libel Law*, London: Effingham Wilson.

—— (1827), *Rationale of Judicial Evidence: Specially Applied to English Practice*, vol. 4, London: Hunt and Clarke.

—— (1843), *The Works of Jeremy Bentham*, vol. 8 (Chrestomathia, Essays on Logic and Grammar, Tracts on Poor Laws, Tracts on Spanish Affairs), Edinburgh: William Tait.

—— (1983), *Deontology, Together with a Table of the Springs of Action, and the Article on Utilitarianism*, Oxford: Clarendon Press.

—— (2000), *An Introduction to the Principles of Morals and Legislation*, Kitchener: Batoche Books.

—— (2001), *The Works of Jeremy Bentham*, vol. 10, New York: Elibron Classics.

Berg, M. and Timmermans, S. (2000), 'Orders and their others: on the constitution of universalities in medical work', *Configurations*, 8: 1, pp. 31–61.

Berlant, L. (1997), *The Queen of America Goes to Washington City: Essays on Sex and Citizenship*, Durham, DC: Duke University Press.

Berman, M. (1983), *All That is Solid Melts into Air: The Experience of Modernity*, London: Verso.

Bernstein, B. (2003), *Class, Codes and Control*, New York: Routledge.

Bersani, L. (1990), *The Culture of Redemption*, Cambridge, MA: Harvard University Press.

Bexley, E., James, R. and Arkoudis, S. (2011), *The Australian Academic Profession in Transition: Addressing the Challenge of Reconceptualising Academic Work and Regenerating the Academic Workforce*, Centre for the Study of Higher Education, Melbourne: University of Melbourne.

Biggs, J.B. and Tang, C.S.K. (2007), *Teaching for Quality Learning at University: What the Student Does*, Maidenhead: McGraw-Hill/Society for Research into Higher Education and Open University Press.

Biletzki, A. and Matar, A. (2011), 'Ludwig Wittgenstein', in E. Zalta (ed.), *The Stanford Encyclopedia of Philosophy* (Summer 2011 Edition), http://plato.stanford.edu/archives/sum2011/entries/wittgenstein/. Accessed 5 March 2012.

BIS (2011a) *Higher Education: Students at the Heart of the System*, White paper for the Department for Business, Innovation and Skills, London, http://discuss.bis.gov.uk/hereform/white-paper/. Accessed 29 June 2011.

——— (2011b), *Participation Rates in Higher Education: Academic Years 2006/2007–2009/2010*, London: Department for Business, Innovation and Skills.

Bishop, G. (2008), *Dance of the Dead*, USA: Compound B.

Bishop, J. (2006), 'Using *Turn It In* at UCLA', Office of Instructional Development, University of California, Los Angeles, http://www.scribd.com/doc/21467023/Using-Turn-It-in-at-UCLA-Jack-Bishop-Ph-D-UCLA. Accessed 18 February 2012.

Bishop, K. (2009), 'Dead man still walking: explaining the zombie renaissance', *Journal of Popular Film and Television*, 37: 1, pp. 17–25.

——— (2010a), *American Zombie Gothic: The Rise and Fall (and Rise) of the Walking Dead in Popular Culture*, Jefferson, NC: McFarland.

——— (2010b), 'The idle proletariat: *Dawn of the Dead*, consumer ideology, and the loss of productive labor', *The Journal of Popular Culture*, 43: 2, pp. 234–248.

Blackwell, A. (2012), 'Casual work hurting sector, inquiry told', *Campus Review*, February 13, http://www.campusreview.com.au/blog/news/casual-work-hurting-sector-inquiry-told/. Accessed 15 February 2012.

Blake, J. (2010), 'The "zombie theology" behind the walking dead', *CNN Belief Blog*, http://religion.blogs.cnn.com/2010/12/20/the-zombie-theology-behind-the-walking-dead. Accessed 20 December 2011.

Blamires, C. (2008), *The French Revolution and the Creation of Benthamism*, New York: Palgrave Macmillan.

Bloom, H. (1973), *The Anxiety of Influence: A Theory of Poetry*, New York and Oxford: Oxford University Press.

Boden, R. and Epstein, D. (2011), 'A flat earth society? Imagining academic freedom', *The Sociological Review*, 59: 3, pp. 476–495.

Boluk, S. and Lenz, W. (2010), 'Infection, media, and capitalism: from early modern plagues to postmodern zombies', *The Journal For Early Modern Cultural Studies*, 10: 2, pp. 126–147.

Boon, M. (2010), *In Praise of Copying: Concerning Contemporary Cultures of the Copy*, Boston, MA: Harvard University Press.

Bosc, H. and Harnad, S. (2005), 'In a paperless world a new role for academic libraries: providing open access', *Learned Publishing*, 18: 2, pp. 95–100.

Bourdieu, P. and Passeron J.C. (1977), *Reproductions in Education, Society and Culture*, trans. R. Nice, London: Sage.

Bourdieu, P., Passeron, J. and de Saint Martin, M. (1994), *Academic Discourse: Linguistic Misunderstanding and Professorial Power*, trans. R. Teese, Stanford: Stanford University Press.

Bowman, V. (ed.) (2004), *The Plagiarism Plague: A Resource Guide and CD-ROM Tutorial for Educators and Librarians*, New York: Neal-Schuman Publishers.

Bowrey, G. and Smark, C.J. (2010), 'The influence of Jeremy Bentham on recent public sector financial reforms', *Journal of New Business Ideas and Trends*, 8: 1, pp. 1–34.

Boyer, D. (2010), 'What is driving university reform in the age of globalization?', *Social Anthropology/Anthropologie Sociale*, 18: 1, pp. 74–82.

Boyer, E.L. (1990), *Scholarship Reconsidered: Priorities of the Professoriate*, Princeton, NJ: Carnegie Foundation for the Advancement of Teaching.

Boyle, D. (2002), *28 Days Later*, UK: DNA Films and UK Film Council.

Bozovic, M. (2004), 'Of "farther uses of the dead to the living": Hitchcock and Bentham', in R. Allen and S. Ishii-Gonzáles (eds), *Hitchcock: Past and Future*, London: Routledge, pp. 243–256.

Brabazon, T. (2011), 'Dealing with digital incontinence', *Times Higher Education Supplement*, February 23, http://www.timeshighereducation.co.uk/story.asp?c=2&sectioncode=26&story code=415266. Accessed 16 June 2011.

Bradley, D., Noonan, P., Nugent, H. and Scales, B. (2008), *Review of Australian Higher Education Final Report*, Canberra: Department of Education, Employment and Workplace Relations, Commonwealth of Australia, http://www.deewr.gov.au/HigherEducation/Review/Documents/PDF/Higher%20Education%20Review_one%20document_02.pdf. Accessed 7 July 2011.

Braithwaite, R. (2003), 'The "pubstro" phenomenon: Robin Hoods of the Internet', *ACIS 2003 Proceedings*, http://aisel.aisnet.org/acis2003/104. Accessed 13 December 2010.

Bretag, T. and Mahmud, S. (2009), 'Self-plagiarism or appropriate textual re-use?', *Journal of Academic Ethics*, 7: 1, pp. 93–205.

Briant, M. (1975), *Revenge of the Cybermen*, April 19–May 10, London: BBC.

Brigs, N. (2006), *Cyberman*, Maidenhead: Big Finish.

Bristol Evening Post (2009), 'More care needed in the co-mutiny', *Bristol Evening Post*, September 18, http://iw.newsbank.com. Accessed 8 February 2012.

Britain, S. and Liber, O. (2004), *A Framework for the Pedagogical Evaluation of eLearning Environments*, JISC Technology Applications Programme, Report No. 41, http://halshs.archives-ouvertes.fr/docs/00/69/62/34/PDF/Liber-2004.pdf. Accessed 28 October 2012.

Britton, P.D. (2011), *TARDISbound: Navigating the Universes of Doctor Who*, London: I.B. Tauris.

Bronner, S. (2011), *A Very Short Introduction to Critical Theory*, New York: Oxford University Press.

Brookfield, S. (2010), *Radicalizing Learning: Adult Education for a Just World*, New York: Jossey.

Brooks, M. (2003), *The Zombie Survival Guide: Complete Protection from the Living Dead*, New York: Three Rivers Press.

Brown, P. and Lauder, H. (2010), 'Economic globalisation, skills formation and the consequences for higher education', in M. Apple, S. Ball, and L. Gandin (eds), *The Routledge International Handbook of Sociology of Education*, New York: Routledge, pp. 229–240.

Brown, P., Lauder, H., and Ashton, D. (2011), *The Global Auction: The Broken Promises of Education, Jobs, and Incomes*, Oxford: Oxford University Press.

Brown, R. (2009), 'Australia approaching academia anaemia: Australia set for academia exodus', *Australian Broadcasting Corporation (ABC)* Transcripts, October 2, http://www.abc.net.au/worldtoday/content/2009/s2703097.htm. Accessed 7 July 2011.

Browne, J. (2010), 'An independent review of higher education funding and student finance', *The Browne Report,* Department for Business, Innovation and Skills, http://www.bis.gov.uk/news/topstories/2010/Oct/Browne-Report-published. Accessed 20 June 2011.

Browne, T., Hewitt, R., Jenkins, M., Voce, J., Walker, R. and Yip, H. (2010), 'Plotting the sea-change: a longitudinal survey between 2001 and 2010 of technology-enhanced learning in UK higher education', *ALT-C 2010 Into Something Rich and Strange – Making Sense of the Sea-Change*, Nottingham: Association of Learning Technologists.

Browne, T., Jenkins, M. and Walker, R. (2006), 'A longitudinal perspective regarding the use of VLEs by higher education institutions in the United Kingdom', *Interactive Learning Environments*, 14: 2, pp. 177–192.

Bruckner, D., Bush, D. and Gentry, J. (2007), *The Signal*, USA: POP Films.

Bruno, I. and Newfield, C. (2010), 'Can the cognitariat speak?', *e-flux*, 14, http://www.e-flux.com/journal/can-the-cognitariat-speak/. Accessed 13 December 2011.

Buckell, J. (2003), 'New deal pending for a casual future', *The Australian*, March 5, p. 21.

Burrows, R. (2012), 'Living with the H-Index? Metrics, markets and affect in the contemporary academy', *Sociological Review*, 60: 2, pp. 355–372.

Butler, J. (1990), *Gender Trouble: Feminism and the Subversion of Identity*, New York: Routledge.
——— (1993), *Bodies That Matter: On the Discursive Limits of Sex*, New York: Routledge.

Caffentzis, G. and Federici, S. (2009), 'Notes on the Edu-factory and cognitive capitalism', in The Edu-factory Collective (ed.), *Toward a Global Autonomous University*, New York: Autonomedia, pp. 125–131.

Calam, R. and Slade, P. (1994), 'Eating patterns and unwanted sexual experiences', in B. Dolan and I. Gitzinger (eds), *Why Women? Gender Issues and Eating Disorders*, London: The Athlone Press, pp. 101–109.

Cameron, M. (2007), 'Whose e-learning is it anyway? A case study exploring the boundaries between student-owned social networks and institutional VLEs', *Beyond Control*, Nottingham: UK Association of Learning Technologists.

Camfield, D. (1968), *Invasion*, November 2–21 December, London: BBC.

Campbell, D. (2009), 'The plagiarism plague: in the internet era, cheating has become an epidemic on college campuses', *Crosstalk: The National Centre For Public Policy And Higher Education,* http://www.highereducation.org/crosstalk/ct0106/news0106-plagiarism.shtml. Accessed 12 January 2012.

Campbell, J. (1949), *The Hero with a Thousand Faces*, MJF Books: New York.

Campillo, R. (2004), *Les Revenants/They Came Back*, France: Haute et Court.

Cantamessa, C. (2007), *Manhunt 2*, USA: Rockstar Games.

Capcom (2009), *Resident Evil 5* [Xbox 360], Japan: Capcom Co. Ltd.

Carr, N. (2008), 'Is Google making us stupid? What the internet is doing to our brains', *The Atlantic*, http://www.theatlantic.com/magazine/archive/2008/07/is-google-making-us-stupid/6868/. Accessed 1 March 2012.

Carr, N. (2010), *The Shallows: What the Internet is Doing to Our Brains*, New York: Norton.

Cassidy, F. (2011), 'Academics stage protest over pensions changes', *Aberdeen Press and Journal*, March 18, http://www.pressandjournal.co.uk/Article.aspx/2184108. Accessed 8 February 2012.

Castro, D. (2011), 'PIPA/SOPA: responding to critics and finding a path forward', *Information Technology and Innovation Foundation*, http://www.itif.org/publications/pipasopa-responding-critics-and-finding-path-forward. Accessed 10 February 2012.

Chan, L. et al. (2002), 'Budapest Open Access Initiative', Open Society Foundations, http://www.soros.org/openaccess/read.shtml. Accessed 18 February 2011.

Cholodenko, A. (2007), *The Illusion of Life II: More Essays on Animation*, London: Power Publications.

Christie, D. and Lauro, S.J. (eds) (2011), *Better Off Dead: The Evolution of the Zombie as Post-Human*, New York: Fordham University Press.

Clarke, P. and Frijters, P. (2010), 'Invert the funding pyramid', *The Australian*, December 8, http://www.theaustralian.com.au/higher-education/opinion/invert-the-funding-pyramid/story-e6frgcko-1225967182801. Accessed 14 December 2011.

Clements, S. (2011), *The Vampire Defanged: How the Embodiment of Evil Became a Romantic Hero*, Grand Rapids MI: Brazos Press.

Cohen, J. (1996), 'Monster culture (seven theses)', in J. Cohen (ed.), *Monster Theory: Reading Culture*, Minneapolis: University of Minnesota Press, pp. 3–25.

Collings, D. (2000), 'Bentham's auto-icon: Utilitarianism and the evisceration of the common body', *Prose Studies*, 23: 3, pp. 95–127.

—— (2009), *Monstrous Society: Reciprocity, Discipline, and the Political Uncanny, c. 1780–1848*, Lewisburg, PA: Bucknell University Press.

Collini, S. (2012), *What are Universities For?*, London: Penguin.

Collins, H. (1985), 'Political ideology in Australia: the distinctiveness of a Benthamite society', in S. Graubard (ed.), *Australia, the Daedalus Symposium*, North Ryde, N.S.W.: Angus and Robertson, pp.147–170.

Comaroff, J., and Comaroff, J. (2002), 'Alien nation: zombies, immigrants, and millennial capitalism', *South Atlantic Quarterly*, 101: 4, pp. 779–805.

Conversations With Enemies (2009), *Nowhere, OK*, Digital CD album: USA.

Cook, T. (2012), 'The meate was mine': Donne's *Satyre II* and the prehistory of proprietary authorship', *Studies in Philology*, 109: 1, pp. 103–131.

Cooke, E., Jahanian, F. and McPherson, D. (2005), 'The zombie roundup: understanding, detecting, and disrupting botnets', *Proceedings of the USE- NIX Workshop Steps to Reducing Unwanted Traffic on the Internet (SRUTI '05)*.

Cooper, S. and Poletti, A. (2011), 'The new ERA of journal ranking: the consequences of Australia's fraught encounter with "quality"', *Australian Universities' Review*, 53: 1, pp. 57–65.

Coughlan, S. (2012), 'UK university applications down as fees rise', *BBC News*, http://www.bbc.co.uk/news/education-16787948. Accessed 9 February 2011.

Couldry, N. and McRobbie, A. (2010), 'The death of the university, English style', *Culture Machine*, http://www.culturemachine.net/index.php/cm/article/view/417/429. Accessed 30 June 2011.

Council of Australian Postgraduates (2009), *10 Things Sessional Staff Want*, http://www.capa.edu.au/article/2010/10-things-sessional-staff-want. Accessed 21 June 2011.

Coyle, H. (2010), 'Bouncers ban racist zombies', *Daily Star* (Sheffield), November 11, http://www.dailystar.co.uk/news/view/162396/Bouncers-ban-racist-zombies. Accessed 8 February 2012.

Crampton, J. (2009), 'Cartography: Maps 2.0', *Progress in Human Geography*, 33: 1, pp. 91–100.

Craven, W. (1988), *The Serpent and the Rainbow*, USA: Universal Pictures.

Creighton, J.V. (1992), *Joyce Carol Oates: Novels of the Middle Years*, New York: Twayne Publishers.

Crutcher, M. and Zook, M. (2009), 'Placemarks and waterlines: racialized cyberscapes in post-Katrina Google Earth', *Geoforum*, 40: 4, pp. 523–534.

Cryonics Institute (2011), *Cryonics: A Basic Introduction*, http://www.cryonics.org/prod.html. Accessed 8 December 2011.

Curran, G., Chiarolli, S. and Pallotta-Chiarolli, M. (2009), '"The C words": clitorises, childhood and challenging compulsory heterosexuality discourses with pre-service primary teachers', *Sex Education: Sexuality, Society and Learning*, 9: 2, pp. 155–168.

Currie, A. (2006), *Fido*, Canada: Lions Gate Films.

Dahan, Y. and Rocher, B. (2009), *La Horde/The Horde*, France: Capture The Flag Films.

Dahmer, L (1995), *A Father's Story*, New York: Avon Books.

Dallmeier-Tiessen, S., Darby, R., Goerner, B., Hyppoelae, J., Igo-Kemenes, P., Kahn, D., Lambert, S., Lengenfelder, A., Leonard, C., Mele, S., Nowicka, M., Polydoratou, P., Ross, D., Ruiz-Perez, S., Schimmer, R., Swaisland, M., and van der Stelt, W. (2011), 'Highlights from the SOAP project survey. What scientists think about open access publishing', *Study of Open Access Publishing Project*, http://arxiv.org/abs/1101.5260. Accessed 10 February 2011.

Daly, B. (1996), *Lavish Self-Divisions: The Novels of Joyce Carol Oates*, Jackson, MS: University Press of Mississippi.

Dann, C. (2010), 'From where I sit logos do not deliver popularity', *The Times Higher Education Supplement*, September 23, http://www.timeshighereducation.co.uk/story.asp?storyCode=413586&sectioncode=26. Accessed 7 July 2011.

Dantas-Whitney, M. (2002), 'Critical reflection in the second language classroom through audiotaped journals', *Systems*, 30: 4, pp. 543–555.

Darabont, F. (2010), *The Walking Dead*, USA: American Movie Classics.

Davenport-Hines, R. (1998), *Gothic: Four Hundred Years of Excess, Horror, Evil, and Ruin*, New York: North Point Press.

Davidson, C. (2011), *Now You See It: How the Brain Science of Attention Will Transform the Way We Live, Work, and Learn*, New York: Penguin.

Davis, D. (1995), *The Jeffrey Dahmer Story: An American Nightmare*, New York: St. Martin's Paperbacks.

Davis, W. (1985), *The Serpent and the Rainbow*, New York: Simon and Shuster.

Davis, W. (1988), *Passage of Darkness: the Ethnobiology of the Haitian Zombie*, Chapel Hill, NC: University of North Carolina Press.

Davison, N. (2002), 'FED – non-academic staff are working for nothing', *AAP*, March 8.

Dawkins, J. (1987), *The Challenge for Higher Education in Australia*, Canberra: Australian Government Publishing Service.

Dawkins, R. (2006), *The Selfish Gene*, New York: Oxford University Press.

Dayan, J. (1997), 'Vodoun, or the voice of the gods', in M. Fernandez Olmos and L. Paravisini-Gebert (eds), *Sacred Possessions: Vodou, Santeria, Obeah, and the Caribbean*, New Brunswick: Rutgers University Press, pp. 13–36.

de Vere, S. (1872), *Americanisms: The English of the New World*, New York: Charles Scribner.

Dean, K.L., Asay-Davis, X.S., Finn, E.M., Foley, T., Friesner, J.A., Imai, Y., Naylor, B.J., Wustner, S.R., Fisher, S.S. and Wilson, K.R., (2000), 'Virtual explorer: interactive virtual environment for education', *Presence: Teleoperators and Virtual Environments*, 9: 6, pp. 505–523.

DEEWR (2011), *Aboriginal and Torres Strait Islander Education Action Plan 2010-2014*, Canberra: Department of Education, Employment and Workplace Relations, Commonwealth of Australia, http://www.deewr.gov.au/Indigenous/HigherEducation/Pages/default.aspx. Accessed 21 June 2011.

Deleuze G. and Guattari F. (1972/2004), *Anti-Oedipus*, trans. R. Hurley, M. Seem and H. Lane, New York: Continuum.

Deleuze, G. (1992), 'Postscript on the societies of control', *October*, 59: Winter, pp. 3–7.

Deller-Evans, K., Evans, S. and Gannaway, D. (2003). 'Collaborative efforts to resist fraudulent educational practice', paper presented at the *Educational Integrity: Plagiarism and Other Perplexities Conference*, Adelaide, South Australia, November 21–22.

Dendle, P. (2007), 'The zombie as barometer of cultural anxiety', in N. Scott (ed.), *Monsters and the Monstrous: Myths and Metaphors of Enduring Evil*, Amsterdam: Rodpi, pp. 45–59.

Dennison, G. (1969), *The Lives of Children: The Story of the First Street School*, New York: Random House.

Deresiewicz, W. (2011), 'Faulty towers: the crisis in higher education', *The Nation*, May 4, http://www.thenation.com/article/160410/faulty-towers-crisis-higher-education. Accessed 16 June 2011.

Derrida, J. (1982) *The Ear of the Other: Otobiography, Text, Transference*, New York: Shocken Books.

—— (1991), 'This is not an oral footnote', in S. Barney (ed.), *Annotation and its Texts*, New York and Oxford: Oxford University Press, pp. 192–205.

—— (2002), 'Le Parjure: perhaps, storytelling and lying', in P. Kamuf (ed.), *Without Alibi*, Stanford: Stanford University Press, pp. 161–201.

Derrida, J. and Stiegler, B. (2002), *Echographies of Television: Filmed Interviews*, trans. J. Bajorek, Cambridge: Polity.

DeVere, C. (1968), *Wheel in Space*, April 27–June 1, London: BBC.

DeVito, J.A. (1968), 'The teacher as behavioural engineer', *Today's Speech*, 16: 1, pp. 2–5.

—— (1971), *Communication: Concepts and Processes*, New York: Prentice-Hall.

—— (1978), *Communicology: An Introduction to the Study of Communication*, 1st ed., New York: Harper and Row; 2nd ed., 1982.

—— (1985), *Human Communication: The Basic Course*, 3rd ed., New York: Harper and Row; 4th ed., 1988; 5th ed., 1991; 6th ed., 1994.

—— (1986), *The Communication Handbook: A Dictionary*, New York: Harper and Row.

——— (1995), *The Interpersonal Communication Book*, 7th ed., New York: Harper Collins.

——— (1997). *Human Communication: The Basic Course*, 7th ed., New York: Addison Wesley Longman; 8th ed., 2000.

——— (2003), *Human Communication: The Basic Course*, 9th ed., Boston: Pearson, 10th ed., 2006; 11th ed., 2009.

Dezayas, H. (2010), 'Annual zombie walk shuffles to Market Square', *Pittsburgh Tribune-Review*, September 16, http://www.pittsburghlive.com/x/pittsburghtrib/ae/s_699877.html#ixzz1PxC3AeCt. Accessed 8 February 2012.

do Vale, S. (2009), 'Trash mob: zombie walk and the positivity of monsters in western popular culture', in S. Hill and S. Smith (eds), *There be Dragons out There: Confronting Fear, Horror, and Terror*, Oxford: Inter-Disciplinary Press, pp. 131–137.

Docherty, T. (2011), 'The unseen academy', *Times Higher Education*, November 10, http://www.timeshighereducation.co.uk/story.asp?sectioncode=26&storycode=418076&c=1. Accessed 15 December 2011.

Doctorow, C. (2011), *The Coming War on General Computation*, http://www.youtube.com/watch?v=HUEvRyemKSg . Accessed 10 February 2012.

Donne, J. (1593-1600/1967), *Satyre II*, in *John Donne: The Satires, Epigrams and Verse Letters*, Oxford: Oxford University Press.

Donoghue, F. (2008), *The Last Professors: The Twilight of the Humanities in the Corporate University*, New York: Fordham University Press.

Drezner, D. (2011), *Theories of International Politics and Zombies*, Princeton, NJ: Princeton University Press.

du Gay, P. (1994), 'Making up managers: bureaucracy, enterprise and the liberal art of separation', *British Journal of Sociology*, 45: 4, pp. 655–674.

du Gay, P. (2000), *In Praise of Bureaucracy*, London: Sage.

Dworkin, C. (2005), 'Textual prostheses', *Comparative Literature*, 57: 1, pp. 1–24.

Dyens, O. (2001), *Metal and Flesh: The Evolution of Man, Technology Takes Over*, Cambridge, MA: MIT Press.

Dyer-Witheford, N. (2005), 'Cognitive capitalism and the contested campus', *European Journal of Higher Arts Education*, 2, pp. 71–93.

Edelman, L. (2004), *No Future: Queer Theory and the Death Drive*, Durham DC: Duke University Press.

Edensor, T. and Holloway, J. (2008), 'Rhythmanalysing the coach tour: the ring of Kerry, Ireland', *Transactions of the Institute of British Geographers*, 33: 4, pp. 483–501.

Edwards, G. (2010), 'When will the great zombie bubble burst?', *Wired Magazine*, September 27, http://www.wired.com/magazine/2010/09/pl_zombietv/. Accessed 8 February 2012.

Eisner, C. and Vicinus, M. (2008), *Originality, Imitation and Plagiarism: Teaching Writing in the Digital Age*, Ann Arbor, MI: University of Michigan.

Ellaway, R., Begg, M., Dewhurst, D. and MacLeod, H. (2006). 'In a glass darkly: identity, agency and the role of the learning technologist in shaping the learning environment', *E-Learning*, 3: 1, pp. 75–87.

Emerson, R.W. (1837/1981), 'The American scholar', in C. Bode and M. Cowley (eds), *The Portable Emerson*, New York: Viking Penguin Inc, pp. 51–71.

———— (1844/1981), 'The poet', in C. Bode and M. Cowley (eds), *The Portable Emerson*, New York: Viking Penguin Inc, pp. 241–265.

Enders, J. (2000), 'Academic staff in Europe: Changing employment and working conditions', in M. Tight (ed.), *Academic Work and Life: What it is to be an Academic, and How this is Changing (International Perspectives on Higher Education Research, Volume 1)*, London: Elsevier Science, pp. 7–32.

Ennis, R. (1987), 'A taxonomy of critical thinking dispositions and abilities', in J. Baron and R. Sternberg (eds), *Teaching Thinking Skills: Theory and Practice*, New York: W. H. Freeman.

———— (1991), 'Critical thinking: a streamlined conception', *Teaching Philosophy*, 41: 1, pp. 5–25.

Entman, R. (1993), 'Framing: toward clarification of a fractured paradigm', *Journal of Communication*, 43: 4, pp. 51–58.

———— (2003), 'Cascading activation: contesting the White House's frame after 9/11', *Political Communication*, 20: 4, pp. 415–432.

Entman, R. (2004), *Projections of Power: Framing News, Public Opinion, and U. S. Foreign Policy*, Chicago, IL: University of Chicago Press.

Evans, M. (2004), *Killing Thinking: The Death of the Universities*, London: Continuum.

Eyerman, R. (2001), *Slavery and the Formation of African American Identity*, Cambridge: Cambridge University Press.

Fair Work Australia (2009), *Swan Services and LHMU Clean Start Union Collective Agreement*, Sydney: Fair Work Australia, http://www.fwa.gov.au/documents/agreements/fwa/AE874900.pdf. Accessed 21 June 2011.

Fasano, S. (2009), *Woke Up Dead*, USA: Crackle, Sony Pictures Entertainment.

Fauconnier, G. (1994), *Mental Spaces: Aspects of Meaning Construction in Natural Language*, Cambridge: Cambridge University Press.

Ferguson, M. (1966), *War Machines*, June 25–July 16, London: BBC.

Fisher, M. (2009), *Capitalist Realism: Is There No Alternative?* Winchester: Zero Books.

Fleischer, R. (2009) *Zombieland*, USA: Columbia Pictures.

Flint, D. (2009), *Zombie Holocaust: How The Living Dead Devoured Pop Culture*, London: Plexus.

Floud, R. (2002), 'Age of wisdom: the academic workforce is getting old', *Guardian Higher Education*, October 1, p. 10.

FND Films (2008), *Gay Zombie*, http://www.youtube.com/watch?v=1ZuK_wYrqp8. Accessed 15 December 2010.

Foot, P. (1985), 'Utilitarianism and the virtues', *Mind*, 94: 374, pp. 196–209.

Ford, H. and Ford, J. (2010), *The Dead*, UK: Indelible Productions.

Forster, M. (2012), *World War Z*, USA: Plan B Entertainment.

Fotheringham, A. (2010), 'Zombie and Zumba fun as city gears up for scary Halloween', *Evening Times* (Glasgow), October 28, http://www.eveningtimes.co.uk/news/zombie-and-zumba-fun-as-city-gears-up-for-scary-hallowe-en-1.1064439. Accessed 8 February 2012.

Foucault, M. (1977), *Discipline and Punish: The Birth of the Prison*, trans A. Sheridan, New York: Vintage.

———— (1980), 'Body/power', in C. Gordon (ed.), *Power/Knowledge: Selected Interviews and Other Writings 1972-1977*, Brighton: Harvester Press, pp. 55–62.

——— (2003), '14 January 1976' (trans. D. Macey), in M. Bertani and A. Fontana (eds), *'Society Must Be Defended': Lectures at the Collège de France, 1975-1976*, London: The Penguin Press, pp. 23–41.

Frankel, B. (2004), *Zombies, Lilliputians and Sadists: The Power of the Living Dead and the Future of Australia*, Fremantle, WA: Fremantle Arts Centre Press.

Fraser, B. (2010), 'What I saw: the day the outbreak started', in P. Williams (ed.), *Death and Dying in the Dead Ages*, New York: Joenes and Daughters, pp. 1–12.

Free Software Foundation (2010), 'The free software definition', *Free Software Foundation*, http://www.gnu.org/philosophy/free-sw.html. Accessed 18 February 2011.

Freeman, D. and Garety, P. (2004), *Paranoia: The Psychology of Persecutory Delusions*, Hove: Psychology Press.

Freire, P. (1970), *Pedagogy of the Oppressed*, New York: Continuum Press.

Fresnadillo, J. (2007), *28 Weeks Later*, UK/Spain: Fox Atomic.

Freud, S. (1913), 'The case of Schreber', *The Standard Edition of the Complete Psychological Works of Sigmund Freud: Volume XII*, trans. and ed. J. Strachey et al., London: Hogarth Press, pp. 9–80.

Frisby, D. and Featherstone, M. (1997), *Simmel on Culture*, London: Sage.

Gallagher, C. (2006), *The Body Economic: Life, Death and Sensation in Political Economy and the Victorian Novel*, Princeton, NJ: Princeton University Press.

Gallhofer, S. and Haslam, J. (1996), 'Analysis of Bentham's *Chrestomathia*: or, towards a critique of accounting education', *Critical Perspectives on Accounting*, 7: 1/2, pp. 13–31.

——— (2003), *Accounting and Emancipation: Some Critical Interventions*, London: Routledge.

Gane, N. (2013 forthcoming) 'Surveillance and neoliberalism', *Sociological Review*.

Garber, M. (2003), *Quotation Marks*, London and New York: Routledge.

Garfield, E. (1994), 'The Thomson Reuters impact factor', *Thomson Reuters* http://thomsonreuters.com/products_services/science/free/essays/impact_factor/. Accessed 18 February 2011.

Gauntlett, D. (2007), 'Media Studies 2.0', http://www.theory.org.uk/mediastudies2.htm. Accessed 20 June 2011.

——— (2011), *Media Studies 2.0 and Other Battles Around the Future of Media Research*, London: Kindle Edition.

Giddens, A. (1991), *Consequences of Modernity*, Stanford, CA: Stanford University Press.

Giglia, E. (2010), 'The Impact Factor of open access journals: data and trends', at *Publishing in the Networked World: Transforming the Nature of Communication, 14th International Conference on Electronic Publishing*, June 16-18, Helsinki, Hanken.

Gill, R. (2009). 'Breaking the silence: the hidden injuries of neo-liberal academia', in R. Flood and R. Gill (eds), *Secrecy and Silence in the Research Process: Feminist Reflections*, London: Routledge, http://www.kcl.ac.uk/artshums/depts/cmci/people/papers/gill/silence.pdf. Accessed 15 December 2011.

Gilling, J. (1966), *Plague of Zombies*, UK: Hammer Film Productions.

Gilmore, B. (2008), *Plagiarism: Why it Happens and How to Prevent It*, Portsmouth, NH: Heinemann.

Gilmore, H. (2009), 'Not enough academics to fulfil uni plan', *The Sydney Morning Herald*, February 28, http://www.smh.com.au/news/national/not-enough-academics-to-fulfil-uni-plan/2009/02/27/1235237919958.html. Accessed 7 July 2011.

—— (2010), 'Cream of academe as vice-chancellors near $1m pay', *Sydney Morning Herald*, June 5, p. 9.

Giroux, H. (2005), *Bordercrossings: Cultural Workers and the Politics of Education*, New York: Routledge.

—— (2009), 'Democracy's nemesis: the rise of the corporate university', *Cultural Studies/ Critical Methodologies*, 9: 5, pp. 669–695.

—— (2011), *Zombie Politics and Culture in the Age of Casino Capitalism*, New York: Peter Lang Publishing.

Glaeser, E.L. (2011), *Triumph of the City: How Our Greatest Invention Makes Us Richer, Smarter, Greener, Healthier and Happier*, New York: Penguin Press.

Goodchild, M. and Glennon, A. (2010), 'Crowdsourcing geographic information for disaster response: a research frontier', *International Journal of Digital Earth*, 3: 3, pp. 231–241.

Goolsby, R. (2010), 'Social media as crisis platform: the future of community maps/crisis maps', *Transactions on Intelligent Systems and Technology*, 1: 1, http://portal.acm.org/citation. cfm?doid=1858948.1858955. Accessed 19 February 2012.

Gora, J. and Whelan, A. (2010), 'Invasion of the aca-zombies', *The Australian*, November 3, 2010, http://www.theaustralian.com.au/higher-education/opinion-analysis/invasion-of-aca-zombies/story-e6frgcko-1225946869706. Accessed 16 June 2011.

Gould, T. (2009), 'The future of academic publishing: application of the long-tail theory', *Publishing Research Quarterly*, 25: 4, pp. 232–245.

Graham, G. (2002), *Universities: The Recovery of an Idea*, Charlottesville: Imprint Academic.

Graham, M. (2010), 'Neogeography and the palimpsests of place: Web 2.0 and the construction of a virtual earth', *Tijdschrift Voor Economische en Sociale Geografie*, 101: 4, pp. 422–436.

—— (2011a), 'Time machines and virtual portals: the spatialities of the digital divide', *Progress in Development Studies*, 11:3, pp. 211–227.

—— (2011b), 'Wiki space: palimpsests and the politics of exclusion', in G. Lovink and N. Tkacz (eds), *Critical Point of View: A Wikipedia Reader*, Amsterdam: Institute of Network Cultures, pp. 269–282.

Graham, M., and Zook, M. (2011), 'Visualizing global cyberscapes: mapping user-generated placemarks', *Journal of Urban Technology*, 18: 1, pp. 115–132.

—— (2013 in press). 'Augmented realities and uneven geographies: exploring the geo-linguistic contours of the web'. *Environment and Planning A*.

—— and Boulton, A. (2012 in press) 'Augmented reality in the urban environment'. *Transactions of the Institute of British Geographers*.

Granville, S and Dison, L. (2005), 'Thinking about thinking: integrating self-reflection into an academic literacy course, *Journal of English for Academic Purposes*, 4: 2, pp. 99–118.

Graupp, R. (1914), 'The scientific significance of the case of Ernst Wagner', in S. Hirsch and M. Shepherd (eds), *Themes and Variations in European Psychiatry*, Charlottesville, VA: University of Virginia Press, pp. 121–133.

Graves, N., Barnett, A. and Clarke, P. (2011), 'Funding grant proposals for scientific research: retrospective analysis of scores by members of grant review panel', *British Medical Journal*, 343: d4797.

Gray, C. (1995), *The Cyborg Handbook*, New York: Routledge.

Greene, R. and Mohammad, S. (2010), *Zombies, Vampires and Philosophy: New Life For The Undead*, Chicago, IL: Open Court Publishing.

Gregg, M. (2009), 'Why academia is no longer a smart choice', *New Matilda*, November 24, http://newmatilda.com/2009/11/24/academia-no-longer-smart-choice. Accessed 16 June 2011.

—— (2011), *Work's Intimacy*, Cambridge, UK: Polity.

Griffin, E. (2006), *A First Look at Communication Theory*, 6th ed., Boston, MA: McGraw Hill.

Grimwade, P. (1982), 'Earthshock', *Dr Who* Season 19, March 8–16, London: BBC.

Grobman L. (2009), 'The student scholar: (re)negotiating authorship and authority', *College Composition and Communication,* 61: 1, pp. 175–196.

Gross, D. (2009), 'Why we love those rotting, hungry, putrid zombies', *CNN*, http://www.cnn.com/2009/SHOWBIZ/10/02/zombie.love/index.html. Accessed 2 October 2011.

Guinness World Records (2011), 'Largest gathering of zombies', *Guinness World Records*, http://www.guinnessworldrecords.com/records-5000/largest-gathering-of-zombies. Accessed 8 February 2012

Gunn, J. and Treat, S. (2005), 'Zombie trouble: a propaedeutic on ideological subjectification and the unconscious', *Quarterly Journal of Speech*, 91: 2, pp. 144–174.

Gupta, S. (2010), *Cheating Death*, New York: Grand Central Publishing.

Habermas, J. (1987), *The Theory of Communicative Action: Volume 2: Lifeworld and System,* Boston, MA: Beacon Press.

Haklay, M., Singleton, A. and Parker, C. (2008), 'Web mapping 2.0: the neogeography of the GeoWeb. *Geography Compass*, 2: 6, pp. 2011–2039.

Halberstam, J. (2005), *In a Queer Time and Place: Transgender Bodies, Subcultural Lives*, New York: New York University Press.

Halberstam, J. and Ira, L. (eds) (1995), *Posthuman Bodies*, Bloomington, IN: Indiana University Press.

Hall, G. (2009), 'Pirate philosophy version 1.0: open access, open editing, free content, free/libre/open media', *Culture Machine*, 10, http://www.mininova.org/tor/2620411. Accessed 22 June 2009.

Halperin, D. and Traub, V. (eds) (2010), *Gay Shame*, Chicago, IL: University of Chicago Press.

Halperin, V. (1932), *White Zombie*, USA: Edward and Victor Halperin Productions.

Haraway, D. (1991a), 'A cyborg manifesto: science, technology, and socialist-feminism in the late twentieth century', in D. Haraway (ed.), *Simians, Cyborgs and Women: The Reinvention of Nature*, New York: Routledge, pp. 149–181.

—— (1991b), 'Cyborgs at large: interview with Donna Haraway' in C. Penley and A. Ross (eds), *Technoculture*, Minneapolis: University of Minnesota Press, pp. 21–26.

Haraway, D. (2003), *The Companion Species Manifesto*, Chicago, IL: Prickly Paradigm Press.

Hardt, M. and Negri, N. (2000), *Empire*, Cambridge, MA: Harvard University Press.

Hari, J. (2010), 'The year an army of zombies came for our brains', *London Independent*, December 3, http://www.independent.co.uk/opinion/commentators/johann-hari/johann-hari-2010-ndash-the-year-a-zombie-army-came-for-our-brains-2149697.html. Accessed 8 February 2012.

Harman, C. (2009), *Zombie Capitalism: Global Crisis and the Relevance of Marx*, Chicago, IL: Haymarket Books.

Harper, G. (2006a), 'Rise of the Cybermen', *Dr Who* Series 2, May 13, BBC Wales.

—— (2006b), 'Age of Steel', *Dr Who* Series 2, May 20, BBC Wales.

—— (2006c), 'Doomsday', *Dr Who* Series 2, July 8, BBC Wales.

Harper, S. (2002), 'Zombies, malls, and the consumerism debate: George Romero's *Dawn of the Dead*', *Americana: The Journal of American Popular Culture (1900-present)*, 1: 2, http://www.americanpopularculture.com/journal/articles/fall_2002/harper.htm. Accessed 2 February 2012.

Harrington, D. (2011), '(Moral) hazards of scanning for plagiarists: evidence from shoplifting', *David Harrington Blog*, http://davideharrington.com/?p=594. Accessed 18 February 2012.

Hart, H. (1982), *Essays on Bentham: Studies in Jurisprudence and Political Theory*, Oxford: Clarendon Press.

Harvie, D. (2004), 'Commons and communities in the university: some notes and some examples', *The Commoner*, 8, pp. 1–10. http://hdl.handle.net/2381/3288. Accessed 16 June 2011.

Haviland, B. (1997), 'Passing from paranoia to plagiarism: the abject authorship of Nella Larsen', *Modern Fiction Studies*, 43: 2, pp. 295–318.

Hayles, N.K. (2009) 'RFID: Human agency and meaning in information-intensive environments', *Theory, Culture and Society*, 26: 2–3, pp. 47–72.

Hearn, L. (1890), *Two Years in the French West Indies*, New York: Harper.

Heidegger, M. (2001), *Phenomenological Interpretations of Aristotle: Initiation into Phenomenological Research*, trans. R. Rojcewicz, Bloomington, IN: Indiana University Press.

Henriksen, S.F. and Wirkola, T. (2009), *Dead Snow*, Norway: Storm Studios.

Hertz, G. and Parikka, J. (2011), *Zombie Media Talk: Circuit Bending Media Archaeology into Art*, transmediale 2011, http://vimeo.com/20473856. Accessed 18 February 2012.

Hertz, N. (1985), *The End of the Line: Essays on Psychoanalysis and the Sublime*, New York: Columbia University Press.

Highmore, B. (2009), *A Passion for Cultural Studies*, Basingstoke: Palgrave Macmillan.

Holmes, S. and Redmond, S. (2010), 'Editorial: a journal in celebrity studies', *Celebrity Studies*, 1: 1, pp. 1–10.

Holmwood, J. (2010), 'Sociology's misfortune: disciplines, interdisciplinarity and the impact of audit culture', *British Journal of Sociology*, 61: 4, pp. 639–658.

hooks, b. (1994), *Teaching to Transgress: Education as the Practice of Freedom*, New York: Routledge.

Horkheimer, M. (1937/1972), 'Tradition and critical theory', in *Critical Theory: Selected Essays*, New York: Continuum Press, pp. 188–243.

Horkheimer, M. and Adorno, T. (2002), *Dialectic of Enlightenment: Philosophical Fragments*, ed. G. Schmid Noerr, trans. E. Jephcott, Stanford, CA: Stanford University Press.

Hoskin, K. (1996), 'The "awful idea of accountability": inscribing people into the measurement of objects', in R. Munro and J. Mouritson (eds), *Accountability, Power, Ethos and the Technologies of Managing*, London: International Thomson Business Press, pp. 265–282.

Houghton, J.W. (2011), 'The costs and potential benefits of alternative scholarly publishing models', *Information Research*, 16: 1, http://informationr.net/ir/16-1/paper469.html. Accessed 26 February 2011

Howard, R. (1995), 'Plagiarisms, authorship, and the academic death penalty', *College English*, 57: 7, pp. 788–806.

—— (1998), 'The literary production of power: citation practices among students and authors' *Technorhetoric*, www.technorhetoric.net/3.1/coverweb/ipc/practcite.htm. Accessed 12 January 2012.

—— (1999), *Standing in the Shadow of Giants: Plagiarists, Authors, Collaborators,* Stamford, CT: Ablex.

—— (2000), 'Sexuality, textuality: the cultural work of plagiarism', *College English,* 62: 4, pp. 473–491.

Howard, R. and Robillard, A. (eds) (2008), *Pluralising Plagiarism: Identities, Contexts, Pedagogies,* Portsmith, NH: Boynton/Cook.

Howe, J. (2008), *Crowdsourcing: How the Power of the Crowd is Driving Business,* Kindle Edition.

Hughes, J. (2004), *Cyborg Citizen: Why Democratic Societies Must Respond to the Redesigned Human of the Future,* Cambridge: Westview.

Hugo, G. (2007), *The Demography of Australia's Academic Workforce: Patterns, Problems and Policy Implications,* University of Adelaide, http://www.atn.edu.au/docs/demography_australias_academic_workforce.pdf. Accessed 21 June 2011.

Humans vs. Zombies (2012), 'About', *Humans vs. Zombies,* http://humansvszombies.org/about. Accessed 8 February 2012.

Hume, D. (1888), *A Treatise of Human Nature,* Oxford: Clarendon Press.

Hume, L. (1981), *Bentham and Bureaucracy,* Sydney: Cambridge University Press.

Hunt, S. (2011), 'Why the UCU is right to strike', *New Statesman,* June 13. http://www.newstatesman.com/blogs/the-staggers/2011/06/government-strike-teachers. Accessed 25 February 2012.

Hussain, T. (2010), 'Capcom plans parliament zombie stunt', *Computer and Video Games,* August 16, http://www.computerandvideogames.com/259994/capcom-plans-parliament-zombie-stunt. Accessed 8 February 2012.

Hutchins, E. (1995), *Cognition in the Wild,* Cambridge, MA: MIT Press.

—— (2005), 'Material anchors for conceptual blends', *Journal of Pragmatics,* 37: 10, pp. 1555–1577.

Illing, D. (2002), 'Standards are slipping', *The Australian,* October 23, p. 24.

Institute of International Education (2011),'International student enrolments rose modestly in 2009/10, led by strong increase in students from China', *Institute of International Education,* http://www.iie.org/Who-We-Are/News-and-Events/Press-Center/Press-Releases/2010/2010-11-15-Open-Doors-International-Students-In-The-US. Accessed 12 February 2012.

InTech (2011), 'Open access author survey', *InTech,* http://www.intechweb.org/public_files/Intech_OA_Apr11.pdf. Accessed 26 May 2011.

International Student Movement (2009), 'Overview of Education Protests 2009', *International Student Movement,* http://www.emancipating-education-for-all.org/content/overview-education-protests-2009. Accessed 8 February 2012.

Jackson, C. (2002), 'Nelson reform would cut campus red tape', *The Canberra Times,* August 15, p. 2.

James, C.L.R. and Walvinm J. (2001), *The Black Jacobins: Toussaint L'Ouverture and the San Domingo Revolution*, London: Penguin.

James, J. (2010), 'University sees decline in student protests, demonstrations on campus,' *Bowling Green News*, April 28, http://bgnews.com/campus-university-sees-decline-in-student-protests-demonstrations-on-campus. Accessed 6 July 2011.

Jenkins, M., Browne, T. and Armitage, S. (2001), *Management and Implementation of Virtual Learning Environments: A UCISA Funded Survey*, Universities and Colleges Information Systems Association (UCISA), http://www.immagic.com/eLibrary/ARCHIVES/GENERAL/UCISA_UK/U030627J.pdf. Accessed 28 October 2012.

Jonas, T. (2009), 'The crisis in education isn't looming, it's here,' *New Matilda*, December 16, http://newmatilda.com/2009/12/16/crisis-education-isnt-looming-its-here. Accessed 16 June 2011.

Jones, B. (2011a), 'Zombie protest spurring debate: students protest budget at Special Olympics event,' *Associated Press*, June 9, http://www.fox11online.com/dpp/news/zombie-protest-spurring-debate. Accessed 8 February 2012.

Jones, N. (2011b), 'Zombies lurch down Telegraph to support public libraries,' *Oakland North*, May 23, http://oaklandnorth.net/2011/05/23/zombies-lurch-down-telegraph-to-support-libraries-brains. Accessed 8 February 2012.

Jouvenal, J. and Morse, D. (2011), 'Police probe Germantown flashmob thefts,' *Washington Post*, August 15, http://www.washingtonpost.com/blogs/crime-scene/post/possible-flash-mob-robbery-in-germantown/2011/08/15/gIQAmZFvGJ_blog.html. Accessed 8 February 2012.

Kamola, I. and Meyerhoff, E. (2009), 'Creating commons: divided governance, participatory management, and struggles against enclosure in the university,' *Polygraph*, 21, pp. 5–27.

Kane, J. (2010), *Night of the Living Dead*, London: Aurum Press Ltd.

Kanuka, H. (2008), 'Understanding e-learning technologies-in-practice through philosophies-in-practice,' T. Anderson (ed.), *The Theory and Practice of Online Learning*, Athabasca: Athabasca University, pp. 91–120.

Kaplan, L. (1991), *Female Perversions: The Temptations of Emma Bovary*, New Jersey: Jason Aronson, Inc.

Kasulis, T.P. (1982), 'Questioning,' in M. Gullette (ed.), *The Art and Craft of Teaching*, Harvard: Harvard-Danforth Center for Teaching and Learning.

Kaufman, P. (1978), *Invasion of the Body Snatchers*, USA: MGM.

Kay, G. (2008), *Zombie Movies: The Ultimate Guide*, Chicago, IL: Chicago Review Press.

Kee, C. (2011), 'They are not men ... they are dead bodies!: From cannibal to zombie and back again,' in D. Christie and S.J. Lauro (eds), *Better Off Dead: The Evolution of the Zombie as Post-Human*, New York: Fordham University Press, pp. 9–23.

Khan, A.S. (2011), 'Preparedness 101: zombie apocalypse,' *Center for Disease Control*, http://blogs.cdc.gov/publichealthmatters/2011/05/preparedness-101-zombie-apocalypse/. Accessed 1 February 2012.

Kiely, R. (2004), 'Learning to critique in EAP,' *Journal of English for Academic Purposes*, 3: 3, pp. 211–227.

Kilgour, M. (1998), 'Dr. Frankenstein meets Dr. Freud,' in R. Martin and E. Savoy (eds), *American Gothic: New Interventions in a National Narrative*, Iowa City: University of Iowa Press, pp. 40–53.

Kincheloe, J. (2000), 'Making critical thinking critical', in D. Weil and H. Anderson (eds), *Perspectives in Critical Thinking: Essays by Teachers in Theory and Practice*, New York: Peter Lang, pp. 211–220.

—— (2008), *Knowledge and Critical Pedagogy: An Introduction*, Montreal: Springer.

King, S. et al. (2006), 'SubVirt: implementing malware with virtual machines', *Proceedings of the 2006 IEEE Symposium on Security and Privacy*, http://ix.cs.uoregon.edu/~butler/teaching/10F/cis607/papers/king2006.pdf. Accessed 28 October 2012.

Kirkman, R. (2005), *Marvel Zombies*, New York: Marvel Comics.

—— (2011–12), *The Walking Dead*, USA: Image Comics.

Kitalong, K. (1998), 'A web of symbolic violence', *Computers and Composition*, 15: 2, pp. 253–264.

Kochhar-Lindgren, G. (2009), 'The haunting of the university: phantomenology and the house of learning', *Pedagogy: Critical Approaches to Teaching Literature, Language, Composition, and Culture*, 9: 1, pp. 3–12.

Kowalski, R. (2021), 'Research centres as key to human survival' in P. Williams (ed.), *Death and Dying in the Dead Ages*, New York: Joenes and Daughters, pp. 110–131.

Kristeva, J. (1982), *Powers of Horror: An Essay on Abjection*, trans. L. Roudiez, New York: Columbia University Press.

LaBruce, B. (2010) *L.A. Zombie*, USA/Germany: PPV Networks.

LaCapra, D. (2001), *Writing History, Writing Trauma*, Baltimore, MD: Johns Hopkins University Press.

Lachapelle, T. and Kuchera, D. (2011), 'Blackboard shareholders seen losing 50% gain with private equity: Real M&A', June 17, *Bloomberg News*, http://www.bloomberg.com/news/2011-06-17/blackboard-shareholders-seen-losing-50-gain-with-private-equity-real-m-a.html. Accessed 1 February 2012.

Land, R. and Bayne, S. (2005), 'Screen or monitor? Issues of surveillance and disciplinary power in online learning environments', R. Land and S. Bayne (eds), *Education in Cyberspace*, London: Routeledge, pp. 165–178.

Landis, J. (1983), *Michael Jackson's Thriller*, USA: Optimum Productions.

Langacker, R. (2002), *Foundations of Cognitive Grammar*, Stanford, CA: Stanford University Press.

Larsen, L. (2010), 'Zombies of immaterial labor: the modern monster and the death of death', *e-flux*, 15 http://www.e-flux.com/journal/view/131. Accessed 16 June 2011.

Lash, S. (2007) 'Power after hegemony: cultural studies in mutation', *Theory, Culture and Society*, 24: 3, pp. 55–78.

Lather, P. (2006), 'Paradigm proliferation as a good thing to think with: teaching research in education as a wild profusion', *International Journal of Qualitative Studies in Education*, 19: 1, pp. 35–57.

Latour, B. (2004), 'How to talk about the body. The normative dimensions of science studies', *Body and Society*, 10: 2–3, pp. 205–229.

Laughey, D. (2011), 'Media studies 1.0: back to basics', *Three:d: The Newsletter of MeCCSA*, 16, pp. 14–16.

Lauro S. (2011a) *The Modern Zombie: Living Death in the Technological Age*, Ph.D. thesis, Davis, CA: University of California.

——— (2011b), 'Playing dead: zombies invade performance art, and your neighborhood', in D. Christie and S. Lauro (eds), *Better Off Dead: The Evolution of the Zombie as Posthuman*, New York: Fordham UP, pp. 205–230.

Lauro, S. and Embry, K (2008), 'A zombie manifesto: the nonhuman condition in the era of advanced capitalism', *boundary 2*, 35:1 pp. 85–108.

Le Bon, G. (1896/1901), *The Psychology of the Crowd*, London: T. Fisher Unwin.

Lee, D (2001), *Cognitive Linguistics: An Introduction*, Oxford: Oxford University Press.

Lee, G. (2007), *American Zombie*, USA/South Korea: Lee Lee Fims.

Lefebvre, H. (2010), *Rhythmanalysis: Space, Time and Everyday Life*, trans. S. Elden and G. Moore, London: Continuum.

Leicester Mercury (2010), 'Scary movies at zombie festival', *Leicester Mercury*, November 15, http://iw.newsbank.com. Accessed 8 February 2012.

Lenon, I. (2009), 'Zombies: the only pandemic that can really get us', *The Telegraph*, August 19, http://www.telegraph.co.uk/comment/personal-view/6055263/Zombies-the-only-pandemic-that-can-really-get-us.html. Accessed 24 November 2010.

Levy, M. (2007), 'Culture, culture learning and new technologies: towards a pedagogical framework', *Language Learning and Technology*, 11: 2, pp. 104–127.

Librero, L. (2011), 'Plagiarism: an intellectual leprosy', paper from the *11th Talakayan Series for Environment and Development* (TSED) conference, January 13, 2011, www.upou.edu.ph/papers/flibrero2011/PlagiarismFL.pdf. Accessed 23 February 2012.

Lindsay, B. (2007), 'Govt dances about its problems', *Geelong Advertiser*, May 12, p. 33.

Liu, A. (2004), *Laws of Cool: Knowledge Work and the Culture of Information*, Chicago, IL: University of Chicago Press.

Lo, Y. (2010), 'Implementing reflective portfolios for promoting autonomous learning among EFL college students in Taiwan', *Language Teaching Research*, 14: 1, pp. 77–95.

Long, S. (2003), 'Casualisation of workforce a myth: labour market scholar', *Australian Broadcasting Corporation Transcripts*, December 22, http://www.abc.net.au/am/content/2003/s1014534.htm. Accessed 7 July 2011.

Lord, J. (2010), 'I walk with the zombies', *Louisville Metromix*, August 24, http://louisville.metromix.com/bars-and-clubs/article/i-walk-with-the/2147416/content. Accessed 8 February 2012.

Loveys, K. (2011), 'Students face degree crisis: troubled universities may axe courses before they're completed', *Daily Mail*, June 8. http://www.dailymail.co.uk/news/article-2000621/Students-face-degree-crisis-Troubled-universities-axe-courses-theyre-completed.html#ixzz1nIw6aMBW. Accessed 23 February 2012.

Lucy, N. (2004), *A Derrida Dictionary*, Oxford: Blackwell.

Lunsford, A. and West, S. (1996), 'Intellectual property and composition studies', *College Composition and Communication*, 47: 3, pp. 383–411.

Lyotard, J. (1979), *The Postmodern Condition: A Report on Knowledge*, Manchester: Manchester University Press.

Macherey, P. (2006), *A Theory of Literary Production*, trans. G. Wall, London: Routledge.

Mack, M. (1968), 'Jeremy Bentham', *International Encyclopaedia of the Social Sciences, Volume 2*, New York: MacMillan Company and The Free Press, pp. 55–57.

Magnoli, G. (2009), 'UCSB the first stop as UC Commission looks to future', *Noozhawk*, October 22, http://www.noozhawk.com/article/102209_ucsb_the_first_stop_as_uc_commission_looks_to_the_future. Accessed 8 February 2012.

Malinowski, B. (1926), *Myth in Primitive Psychology*, New York: W.W. Norton.

Mallon, T. (2001), *Stolen Words: The Classic Book on Plagiarism*, Bristol: Marina Books.

Manjoo, F. (2011), 'The great tech war of 2012', *Fast Company Magazine*, October 19 http://www.fastcompany.com/magazine/160/tech-wars-2012-amazon-apple-google-facebook. Accessed 23 February 2012.

Mann, P. (1995), 'Stupid undergrounds', *Postmodern Culture*, 5: 3, http://pmc.iath.virginia.edu/text-only/issue.595/mann.595. Accessed 12 January 2011.

Marmoy, C. (1958), 'The "Auto-Icon" of Jeremy Bentham at University College, London', *Medical History*, 2: 2, pp. 77–86.

Marsh, B (2007), *Plagiarism: Alchemy and Remedy in Higher Education*, Albany: SUNY Press.

Marshall, D. (2005), 'Young, gay and proud in retrospect: sexual politics, community activism and pedagogical intervention', *Traffic*, 6, pp.161–187.

Marshall, D. (2011a), 'The queer archive: teaching and learning sexualities in Australia', *Transformations: The Journal of Inclusive Scholarship and Pedagogy*, 21: 2, pp. 36–46.

—— (2011b), 'Young gays: towards a history of youth, queer sexualities and education in Australia', *La Trobe Journal*, 87, pp. 60–73.

Marshall, J.P. (2009), *Depth Psychology, Disorder and Climate Change*, Sydney: JungDowunder Books.

Marshall, R. (2011), *Pirates of the Caribbean: On Stranger Tides*, USA: Walt Disney Pictures.

Martin, B. (1994), 'Plagiarism: a misplaced emphasis', *Journal of Information Ethics*, 3: 2, pp. 36–47.

Martin, E. (1999), *Changing Academic Work: Developing the Learning University*, Buckingham: The Society for Research in HE and Open University Press.

Martin, L. (1997), 'Jeremy Bentham: Utilitarianism, public policy and the administrative state', *Journal of Management History*, 3: 3, pp. 272–282.

Martinus, D. (1966), 'Tenth Planet', *Dr Who* 4, October 8–29, London: BBC.

Marx, K. (1959), *Capital: A Critique of Political Economy, Volume 1*, ed. F. Engels, trans. S. Moore and E. Aveling, Moscow: Foreign Languages Publishing House.

Mason, G. (2010), 'Violence against Indian students in Australia: a question of dignity', *Current Issues in Criminal Justice*, 21: 3, pp. 461–466.

Matchett, S. (2008), 'Bradley sets terms of unis debate', *The Australian*, June 11, http://www.theaustralian.com.au/bradley-sets-terms-of-unis-debate/story-fna7dq6e-1111116595529. Accessed 7 July 2011.

May, J. (2010), 'Zombie geographies and the undead city', *Social and Cultural Geography*, 11: 3, pp. 285–298.

Mbembe, A. (2003), 'Necropolitics', *Public Culture* 15: 1, pp. 11–40.

McCabe, D. and Stephens, J. (2006), 'Epidemic as opportunity: internet plagiarism as a lever for cultural change', *Teachers College Record*, http://www.tcrecord.org/content.asp?contentid=12860. Accessed 12 December 2011.

McCarthy, C (2007), *The Road*, New York: Alfred A. Knopf.

McClintock, D. (2003), 'Translator's preface', in S. Freud (ed.), *The Uncanny*, London: Penguin Classics, pp. i–lxiii.

McCulloch, G. (2003), 'Academe Under the Jackboot', *The Australian*, October 16, p. 13.

McDonald, B. (2008), *Pontypool*, Canada: Ponty Up Pictures.

McGuigan, G. and Russell, R. (2008), 'The business of academic publishing: a strategic analysis of the academic journal publishing industry and its impact on the future of scholarly publishing', *Electronic Journal of Academic and Special Librarianship*, 9: 3, http://southernlibrarianship. icaap.org/content/v09n03/mcguigan_g01.html. Accessed 9 February 2012.

McLaren, P. (1995), 'Schooling the postmodern body: critical pedagogy and the politics of enfleshment', *Journal of Education*, 170: 3, pp. 53–83.

McPeck, J. (1981), *Critical Thinking and Education*, New York: Palgrave Mcmillan.

McQueen, M. (2010), *Devil's Playground*, UK: Intandem Films.

Meltzer, F. (1994), *Hot Property: The Stakes and Claims of Literary Originality*. Chicago, IL: University of Chicago Press.

Melville, H. (1855), 'The paradise of bachelors and the tartarus of maids', *The Harpers New Monthly Magazine*, 59, pp. 670–678.

Mercer, K. (1986), 'Monster metaphors: notes on *Michael Jackson's Thriller*', *Screen*, 27: 1, pp. 26–43.

Meyers, K. (2011), 'Dawn of the grad: rules for surviving the zombie apocalypse and your first year at grad school', *The Chronicle of Higher Education*, http://chronicle.com/blogs/profhacker/ dawn-of-the-grad-rules-for-surviving-the-zombie-apocalypse-and-your-first-year-at-grad-school/31694. Accessed 2 February 2012.

Midgley, M. (2003), *The Myths We Live By*, New York: Routledge.

Mikami, S. (2002), *Resident Evil*, Japan: Capcom.

Mill, J.S. (2003), *Utilitarianism and On Liberty Including Mill's 'Essay on Bentham' and Selections from the Writings of Jeremy Bentham and John Austin*, Oxford: Blackwell Publishing.

Miller, D. (2011), 'ESL reading textbooks vs. university textbooks: are we giving our students the input they may need?', *Journal of English for Academic Purposes*, 10: 11, pp. 32–46.

Miller, K. (2009), 'Zombies descend on Liverpool shopping centres to convince people to give blood', *Liverpool Echo*, October 29, http://www.liverpoolecho.co.uk/liverpool-news/local-news/2009/10/29/zombies-descend-on-liverpool-shopping-centres-to-convince-people-to-give-blood-100252-25039827. Accessed 8 February 2012.

Mills, C.W. (1959) *The Sociological Imagination*. Oxford: Oxford University Press.

Milne, E. (2010), *Letters, Postcards, Email: Technologies of Presence*, New York: Routledge.

Miner, S. (2008), *Day of the Dead*, USA: Millennium Films.

Minsky, M. (1975), 'A framework for representing knowledge', in P. Winston (ed.), *The Psychology of Computer Vision*, New York: McGraw Hill, pp. 211–277.

Moffatt, P. (1983), 'Five Doctors', *Dr Who* Special, November 23, London: BBC.

Molesworth, M., Nixon, E. and Scullion, R. (2009), 'Having, being and higher education: the marketisation of the university and the transformation of the student into consumer', *Teaching in Higher Education*, 14: 3, pp. 277–287.

Moodie, G. (2003), 'Navigating the maze of party proposals', *The Australian*, July 30, p. 25.

Mooney, S. (2001), 'Challenges to scholarly publishing', *Publishing Research Quarterly*, 17: 3, pp. 26–28.

Moore-Bridger, B. (2009), 'Dead angry protesters hang effigy of a banker in zombie demo', *London Evening Standard*, February 25, http://www.thisislondon.co.uk/standard/article-23652255-protestors-hang-effigy-of-banker-from-marble-arch.do. Accessed 8 February 2012.

Moore, T. and Morton, J. (2005), 'Dimensions of difference: a comparison of university writing and IELTS writing', *Journal of English for Academic Purposes*, 4: 1, pp. 43–66.

Moreno, G. (2006), 'The new zombie: Tupac-n-Biggie in Clichy-sous-Bois', *ArtUS*, issue 12, pp. 28–30.

Moretti, F. (1982), 'The dialectic of fear', *New Left Review*, 136, pp. 67–85.

Morris, M. (2000), 'Losing our minds', *The Australian*, July 22, p. 19.

Moten, F. and Harney, S. (2004), 'The university and the undercommons', *Social Text*, 22: 2, pp. 101–115.

Munro, R. and Mouritson, J. (eds) (1996), *Accountability, Power, Ethos and the Technologies of Managing*, London: International Thomson Business Press.

Munz, P., Hudea, I., Imad, I. and Smith, R.J. (2009), 'When zombies attack!: Mathematical modelling of an outbreak of zombie infection', in J. Tchuenche and C. Chiyaka (eds) *Infectious Disease Modelling Research Progress*, Hauppauge, NY: Nova Science Publishers, pp.133–150.

Murphy, E. 'Plagiarism software WriteCheck troubles some educators' *USA Today*, http://www.usatoday.com/news/education/story/2011-09-09/college-cheating-plagiarism/50338736/1. Accessed 20 February 2012.

Murray, J. (2009), 'The wider social benefits of higher education: what do we know about them?' *Australian Journal of Education*, 53: 3, pp. 230–244.

Myers, B. and Rowe, D. (2011) 'Interview with Henry Giroux', *The Critical Lede* podcast, May 2011. http://www.thecriticallede.com/The_Critical_Lede/The_Critical_Lede_Podcast/Entrie s/2011/5/4_055__Interview_with_Dr._Henry_Giroux.html. Accessed 4 February 2011.

Naidoo, R. and Jamieson, I. (2005), 'Empowering participants or corroding learning? Towards a research agenda on the impact of student consumerism in higher education', *Journal of Education Policy*, 20: 3, pp. 267–281.

National Tertiary Education Union (2009), *Our Universities Matter*, NTEU, http://www.ouruniversitiesmatter.com.au/. Accessed 16 June 2011.

Neilson, B. (2010), 'Are we all cultural workers now? Getting by in precarious times', *Cultural Economy and Globalisation*, Sydney: Centre for Cultural Research, University of Western Sydney, http://ccr.uws.edu.au/2010/11/30/are-we-all-cultural-workers-now-getting-by-in-precarious-times/. Accessed 21 June 2011.

Nelson, T.H. (1965), 'A file structure for the complex, the changing, and the indeterminate', in N. Wardrip-Fruin and N. Montfort (eds), *The New Media Reader*, Cambridge, MA: The MIT Press, pp. 84–100.

Newfield C. (2008), *Unmaking the Public University: The Forty-Year Assault on the Middle Class*, Cambridge, MA.: Harvard University Press.

Newitz, A. (2006), *Pretend We're Dead: Capitalist Monsters in American Pop-Culture,* Durham, NC: Duke University Press.

Newman, K. (2011), *Nightmare Movies*, 2nd ed., London: Bloomsbury.

Ngain, S. (2005), *Ugly Feelings*, Cambridge, MA: Harvard University Press.

Nicoll, K. and Fejes, A. (2008), 'Mobilizing Foucault in studies of lifelong learning', in A. Fejes and K. Nicoll (eds), *Foucault and Lifelong Learning: Governing the Subject*, London: Routledge, pp. 1–18.

Nordau, M. (1993), *Degeneration*, Lincoln, Nebraska: University of Nebraska Press.

Nottingham Evening Post (2009a), 'Bloody good fun in the city of the dead', *Nottingham Evening Post*, October 26, http://iw.newsbank.com. Accessed 8 February 2012.

Nottingham Evening Post (2009b), 'Zombies sought for charity fun', *Nottingham Evening Post*, September 17, http://iw.newsbank.com. Accessed 8 February 2012.

Noussias, Y. (2005), *To Kako/Evil*, Greece: Ekso Productions.

NTEU (2001), 'Don't squeeze, it hurts', *The Australian*, May 16, p. 34.

Nusche D (2008), 'Assessment of learning outcomes in higher education: a comparative review of selected practices' *OECD Working Paper No 15*, www.oecd.org/dataoecd/13/25/40256023.pdf. Accessed 12 February 2012.

Nussbaum, M. (2010), *Not For Profit: Why Democracy Needs The Humanities*, Oxford: Princeton University Press.

O'Bannon, D. (1985), *The Return of the Living Dead*, USA: Herndale Film.

O'Reilly, S. (2010), 'Minneapolis to pay protestors dressed as zombies $165,000 to settle free speech lawsuit', *Scripps Media*, August 28, http://www.abcactionnews.com/dpp/news/national/minneapolis-to-pay-protestors-dressed-as-zombies-$165,000-to-settle-free-speech-lawsuit. Accessed February 8, 2012.

Oates, J.C. (1995), *Zombie*, New York: Ecco.

————— (1996), *American Gothic Tales*, New York: Plume/Penguin.

————— (2002), *Beasts*, New York: Carroll and Graf Publishers.

Ogden, C. (2001), *Bentham's Theory of Fictions*, London: Routledge.

OpenCourseWare (2011), 'Unlocking knowledge, empowering minds', *Free Online Course Materials MIT*, http://ocw.mit.edu/index.htm. Accessed 19 February 2012.

OpenCulture (2012), *The Best Free Cultural and Educational Media on the Web 2006-2012* http://www.openculture.com/faq. Accessed 19 February 2012.

Osborne, D. (2011), 'Fungus turns Amazonian ants into zombies', *ABC News*, March 3, http://www.abc.net.au/news/stories/2011/03/03/3154387.htm. Accessed 7 March 2011.

Paffenroth, K. (2006), *Gospel of the Living Dead: George Romero's Vision of Hell on Earth*, Waco: Baylor University Press.

Pagano, D. (2008), 'The space of apocalypse in zombie cinema', in S. McIntosh and M. Leverette (eds), *Zombie Culture: Autopsies of the Living Dead*, Toronto: Scarecrow Press, pp. 71–86.

Park, C. (2003), 'In other (people's) words: plagiarism by university students, literature and lessons', *Assessment and Evaluation in Higher Education*, 28: 5, pp. 471–488.

Park, Y. (2011), 'Using news articles to build a literacy classroom in an EFL setting', *TESOL Journal*, 2: 1, pp. 24–51.

Parker, T. (2008), *South Park, Season 11, Episode 7: Night of the Living Homeless*, USA: Comedy Central.

Parkinson, C.N. (1958), *Parkinson's Law: or the Pursuit of Progress*, London: John Murray.

Parsons, R. (2011), 'Zombies held in police swoop', *The Evening Standard (London)*, May 20, http://www.thisislondon.co.uk/standard/article-23951992-zombies-held-in-police-swoop-protesters-spend-four-hours-in-cells-on-day-of-royal-wedding.do. Accessed 8 February 2012.

Peake, B. (2010), 'He is dead, and he is continuing to die: a feminist psycho-semiotic reflection on men's embodiment of metaphor in a Toronto zombie walk', *Journal of Contemporary Anthropology*, 1: 1, pp. 48–71.

Pearce, N. and Tan, E. (2011), 'Open education videos in the classroom: exploring the opportunities and barriers to the use of YouTube in teaching introductory sociology', *International Conference on Education and New Learning Technologies*, Barcelona, Spain. http://library.iated.org/view/PEARCE2011OPE. Accessed 8 July 2012.

Pearce, N., Weller, M., Scanlon, E. and Kinsley, S. (2010), 'Digital scholarship considered: how new technologies could transform academic work', *In Education*, 16: 1, http://ineducation.ca/article/digital-scholarship-considered-how-new-technologies-could-transform-academic-work. Accessed 28 February 2012.

Peck, J. (2010), 'Zombie neoliberalism and the ambidextrous state', *Theoretical Criminology*, 14: 1, pp. 104–110.

Pecorari, D. (2008), *Academic Writing and Plagiarism: A Linguistic Analysis*, London and New York: Continuum.

Pedler, K. (1979), 'Forward: what's in a name? In science fiction everything' in *Dan Dare Pilot of the Future in The Man from Nowhere*, Henrik-ido-Ambacht: Dragon's Dream.

Pegg, S. (2008), 'The dead and the quick', *The Guardian*, http://www.guardian.co.uk/media/2008/nov/04/television-simon-pegg-dead-se. Accessed 29 February 2012.

Penfold-Mounce, R., Beer, D. and Burrows, R. (2011), '*The Wire* as Social Science Fiction?', *Sociology*, 45: 1, pp. 152–167.

Percy, A. (2011), 'A new age in higher education or just a little bit of history repeating? Linking the past, present and future of ALL in Australia', *Journal of Academic Language and Learning*, 5: 2, pp. 131–144.

Perkins, M. (2009), 'Unis too casual on staff', *The Age*, October 5, http://www.theage.com.au/national/unis-too-casual-on-staff-20091004-ghwp.html. Accessed 7 July 2011.

Phillipson, R. (1992), *Linguistic Imperialism*, New York: Oxford University Press.

Pierce, B. and Pierce, D. (2011), *DeadHeads*, USA: FroBro films.

Pippin, T. (2010), '"Behold, I stand at the door and knock": the living dead and apocalyptic dystopia', *The Bible and Critical Theory*, 6: 3, pp. 40.1–40.15.

Popper, K. (1957), *The Poverty of Historicism*, Boston, MA: The Beacon Press.

Possami, A. (2007), '"Secularisation" and "religion" as zombie categories? A review essay', *ARSR*, 20: 2, pp. 233–242.

Postema, G. (1986) *Bentham and the Common Law Tradition*, Oxford: Clarendon Press.

Potter, A.E. (2009), 'Voodoo, zombies and mermaids: U.S. newspaper coverage of Haiti'. *The Geographical Review*, 99: 2, pp. 208–230.

Power, M. (1996), 'Making things auditable', *Accounting, Organizations and Society*, 21: 2/3, pp. 289–315.

—— (1997), *The Audit Society: Rituals of Verification*, Oxford: Oxford University Press.

Price, M. (2008), *Colin*, UK: Nowhere Fast Productions.

Priest, A. (2009), '"I have understanding as well as you": supporting the language and learning needs of students from low socio-economic status backgrounds', *Journal of Academic Language and Learning*, 3: 2, pp. 1–12.

Puar, J. (2007), *Terrorist Assemblages: Homonationalism in Queer Times*, Durham, DC: Duke University Press.

Punter, D. (1996), *The Literature of Terror, Volume 2*, London: Longman.

Purdy, J. (2005), 'Calling off the hounds: technology and the visibility of plagiarism', *Pedagogy*, 5: 2, pp. 275–296.

Pynchon, T. (1995), *Gravity's Rainbow*, London: Vintage.

Quevado, H. (2009) 'Photographs', *SF Weekly*, July 12, http://www.sfweekly.com/slideshow/zombie-rights-protest-at-city-hall-27992306. Accessed 8 February 2012.

Quiggin, J. (2010), *Zombie Economics: How Dead Ideas Still Walk Among Us*, Princeton, NJ: Princeton University Press.

Ramsden, P. (2003), *Learning to Teach in Higher Education*, 2nd ed., London: Routledge.

Rasmussen, A. (2006), 'Interaction in virtual learning environments: an ethical perspective', *Networked Learning Conference*, Lancaster, UK.

Rea, J. (2011), 'Crisis of confidence in universities', *Campus Review*, November 28, http://www.campusreview.com.au/blog/analysis/crisis-of-confidence-in-universities/. Accessed 15 February 2012.

Readings, B. (1996), *The University in Ruins*, Cambridge, MA: Harvard University Press.

Redden, G. (2008), 'From RAE to ERA: research evaluation at work in the corporate university', *Australian Humanities Review*, 45, http://www.australianhumanitiesreview.org/archive/Issue-November-2008/redden.html. Accessed 30 June 2011.

Redmond, S. (2004), 'Liquid metal: the cyborg in science fiction', in S. Redmond (ed.), *Liquid Metal: the Science Fiction Film Reader*, London: Wallflower, pp. 156–157.

Reid, I. (2009), 'Auditors of the managerial university: neo-liberal business advisers or paternal controllers?' *Globalisation, Societies and Education*, 7: 3, pp. 337–355.

Reynolds, N. (2006) *Geographies of Writing: Inhabiting Places and Encountering Difference*. Carbondale, IL: Southern Illinois University Press.

Richardson, R. (1987), *Death, Dissection, and the Destitute*, London: Routledge.

Ritzer, G. (1998), *The McDonaldization Thesis*, London: Sage.

Roach, M. (2003), *Stiff: The Curious Lives of Human Cadavers*, New York: W.W. Norton and Company.

Roazen, P. (1969), *Brother Animal: The Story of Freud and Tausk*. New York: New York University Press.

Robb, B. (2009), *Timeless Adventures: How Doctor Who Conquered TV*, Harpenden: Kamera Books.

Roberts, P. (1977), *Face of Evil*, January 1–22, London: BBC.

Robinson, M. (1985), *Attack of the Cybermen*, January 5–12, London: BBC.

Rodriguez, R. (2007), *Grindhouse Presents: Planet Terror*, USA: Dimension Home Entertainment.

Romero, G. (1968), *The Night of the Living Dead*, USA: Image Ten.

—— (1978), *Dawn of the Dead*, Italy/USA: Laurel Group.

—— (1985), *Day of the Dead*, USA: Dead Film Inc.

—— (2004), *Night of the Living Dead*, USA: Rajon Vision.

—— (2005), *Land of the Dead*, Canada/France/USA: Universal Pictures.

—— (2007), *Diary of the Dead*, USA: Artfire Films.

—— (2009), *Survival of the Dead*, USA/Canada: Blank of the Dead Productions.

Ross, A. (2003), *No-Collar: The Humane Workplace*, Philadelphia, PA: Temple University Press.

—— (2008), 'Beyond the siege mentality', *American Association of University Professors*, http://www.aaup.org/AAUP/pubsres/academe/2008/SO/Feat/ross.htm. Accessed 16 June 2011.

Roth, E. (2005), *Hostel*, USA: Lion Gate Films.

Roux, M. (2011), *Allison Hewitt Is Trapped: A Zombie Novel*, New York City: St. Martin's Griffin.

Rowbotham, J. (2010), 'Casual number blow out', *The Australian*, December 8, http://www.theaustralian.com.au/higher-education/casual-numbers-blow-out/story-e6frgcjx-1225967201826. Accessed 7 July 2011.

Royle, N. (2003), *The Uncanny*, New York: Routledge.

Ruppert, E. and Savage, M. (2012), 'Transactional politics', in L. Adkins and C. Lury (eds), *Measure and Value*, London: Wiley-Blackwell, pp. 73–92.

Russel, G. (2002), *Spare Parts*, July, Maidenhead: Big Finish.

Russell, J. (2005), *Book of the Dead: The Complete History of Zombie Cinema*, Godalming, Surrey: FAB press.

Rutkowska, J. (2006), 'Introducing blue pill', *Invisible Things Lab's Blog*, http://theinvisiblethings.blogspot.com/2006/06/introducing-blue-pill.html. Accessed 4 April 2011.

Ryan, M. and Kellner, D. (2004), 'Technophobia/dystopia' in S. Redmond (ed.), *Liquid Metal: the Science Fiction Film Reader*, London: Wallflower, pp. 48–56.

Sage, V. (1988), *Horror Fiction in the Protestant Tradition*, London: Macmillan Press.

Sahasrabudhey, S. (2009), 'Management of knowledge vs. production of knowledge', in The Edu-Factory Collective (ed.), *Toward a Global Autonomous University*, New York: Autonomedia, pp. 42–44.

Salmi, J. (2009), *The Challenge of Establishing World-Class Universities*, Washington, DC: The World Bank.

Saltmarsh, S., Sutherland-Smith, W. and Randell-Moon, H. (2011a), 'Best foot forward, watching your step, jumping in with both feet, or sticking your foot in it? The politics of researching academic viewpoints', *Qualitative Research Journal*, 11: 2, pp. 17–30.

—— (2011b), '"Inspired and assisted", or "berated and destroyed"? Research leadership, management and performativity in troubled times', *Ethics and Education*, 6: 3, pp. 293–306.

Santiago, P., Tremblay, K. Basri, E. and Arnal, E. (2008), *Tertiary Education for the Knowledge Society, Volume 2. Special features: Equity, Innovation, Labour Market, Internationalisation*, Paris: OECD, http://www.oecd.org/dataoecd/17/23/41266759.pdf. Accessed 11 July 2012

Saravanamuthu, K. (2002), 'Information technology and ideology', *Journal of Information Technology*, 17: 2, pp. 79–87.

Saunders, R. (2007), *Lamentation and Modernity in Literature, Philosophy, and Culture*, New York: Palgrave Macmillan.

Savage, M. (2010a), *Identities and Social Change in Britain Since 1940: The Politics of Method*, Oxford: Oxford University Press.

—— (2010b), 'Unpicking sociology's misfortunes', *British Journal of Sociology*, 61: 4, pp. 659–665.

Savage, M. and Burrows, R. (2007), 'The coming crisis of empirical sociology', *Sociology*, 41: 5, pp. 885–900.

Savage, M., Ruppert, E. and Law, J. (2010), 'Digital devices: Nine theses', Center for Research on Sociological Change (CRESC) and The Open University, Working Paper Series, 86.

Schiesel, S. (2009), 'There's no time to rest until the last zombie in Africa is toast', *The New York Times*, March 15, http://www.nytimes.com/2009/03/16/arts/16evil.html. Accessed 8 December 2011.

Schiffrin, D., Tannen, D. and Ehernberger, H. (eds) (2003), *The Handbook of Discourse Analysis*, Hoboken, NJ: Wiley-Blackwell.

Schlozman, S. (2011), *The Zombie Autopsies: Secret Notebooks from the Apocalypse*, New York: Grand Central Publishing.

Schmidtlein, F. (2004), 'Assumptions commonly underlying government quality assessment practices', *Tertiary Education and Management*, 10, pp. 263–285.

Schofield, P. (2006), *Utility and Democracy: The Political Thought of Jeremy Bentham*, Oxford: Oxford University Press.

Schramm, W. (1954), 'How communication works', in W. Schramm (ed.), *Communication: Concepts and Processes,* Urbana: University of Illinois, pp. 12–21.

Schreber, P. (1903/1955), *Memoirs of My Nervous Illness*, I. MacAlpine and R. Hunter (eds), London: Dawson.

Scott, P. (1998), 'Massification, internationalization and globalization', in P. Scott (ed.), *The Globalisation of Higher Education*, Buckingham: Open University Press, pp. 108–129.

Seabrook, W. (1929), *The Magic Island*, London: George Harrap.

Seager, S. (2009), *Street Crazy: America's Mental Health Tragedy*, California: Westcom Press.

Sennett, R. (2006), *The Culture of the New Capitalism*, London: Yale University Press.

Seropian, A. (2006), *Stubbs the Zombie: Rebel Without a Pulse*, USA: Wideload.

Shakespeare W. (1603), *Hamlet, Norton Shakepeare Anthology*, New York: W.W. Norton and Company.

Shannon, C. and Weaver, W. (1949), *The Mathematical Theory of Communication*, Urbana: University of Illinois.

Sharpe, M. (2009), 'University reform: yes – but what is it for?', *Crikey*, October 14, http://www.crikey.com.au/2009/10/14/university-reform-yes-but-what-is-it-for/. Accessed 7 July 2011.

Shaviro, S. (2002) 'Capitalist monsters', *Historical Materialism*, 10: 4, pp. 281–290.

Shaw, R. (2012), 'Use of Turnitin software does not deter cheating, study finds', *Times Higher Education*, January 19, http://www.timeshighereducation.co.uk/story.asp?sectioncode=26andstorycode=418740. Accessed 2 February 2012.

Shelley, M. (1823), *Frankenstein, or, the Modern Prometheus*, Indianapolis: Bobs-Merrill.

Shelton, T., Matthew, Z. and Graham, M. (forthcoming), 'The technology of religion: mapping religious cyberscapes', *The Professional Geographer*, 65: 1.

Shengold, L. (1979), 'Child abuse and deprivation: soul murder', *Journal of the American Psychological Association*, 27: 3, pp. 533–559.

Sherman, C. (2012), 'What Wikipedia won't tell you', *The New York Times*, http://www.nytimes.com/2012/02/08/opinion/what-wikipedia-wont-tell-you.html?_r=1, Accessed 24 February 2012.

Shore, C. (2008), 'Audit culture and illiberal governance: universities and the politics of accountability', *Anthropological Theory*, 8: 3, pp. 278–298.

—— (2010), 'Beyond the multiversity: neoliberalism and the rise of the schizophrenic university', *Social Anthropology/Anthropologie Sociale*, 18: 1, pp. 15–29.

Shore, C. and Wright, S. (1999), 'Audit culture and anthropology: neo-liberalism in British higher education', *Journal of the Royal Anthropological Institute*, 5: 4, pp. 557–575.

Shore, C. and Wright, S. (2000), 'Coercive accountability: the rise of audit culture in higher education', in M. Strathern (ed.), *Audit Cultures: Anthropological Studies in Accountability, Ethics and the Academy*, London: Routledge, pp. 57–89.

Shubber, K. (2011), 'RLUK vs. publishers', *Felix*, February 11, http://www.felixonline.co.uk/?article=808. Accessed 29 March 2011.

Sidgwick, H. (2002), *Methods of Ethics*, London: Macmillan, http://www.laits.utexas.edu/poltheory/sidgwick/me/me.b04.c05.s03.html. Accessed 13 December 2011.

Siegel, D. (1956), *Invasion of the Body Snatchers*, USA: Allied Artists Pictures.

Sievers, B. (2008), 'The psychotic university', *ephemera*, 8: 3, pp. 238–257, http://ephemeraweb.org/journal/8-3/8-3sievers.pdf. Accessed 17 February 2012.

Sil, N. (1986), 'Bentham's jurisprudence revisited', *Modern Age*, 30: 3–4, pp. 245–250.

Sirota, D. (2009), 'Zombie zeitgeist: why undead corpses are dominating at the box office, *Alternet*, http://www.alternet.org/media/143179/zombie_zeitgeist%3A_why_undead_corpses_are_dominating_at_the_box_office/. Accessed 12 February 2012.

Skeggs, B. (2005), 'The making of class and gender through visualizing moral subject formation', *Sociology*, 39: 5, pp. 965–982.

Slaughter, S. and Leslie, L. (1997), *Academic Capitalism: Politics, Policies, and the Entrepreneurial University*, Baltimore, MD: Johns Hopkins University Press.

Small, G. (2008), *iBrain: Surviving the Technological Alteration of the Modern Mind*, New York: Harper Collins.

Smith, R. (2009), 'A report on the zombie outbreak of 2009: how mathematics can save us (no, really). *Canadian Medical Association Journal*, 181: 12, pp. E297–E300.

Snyder, Z. (2004), *Dawn of the Dead*, USA/Canada/Japan/France: Strike Entertainment.

Soloman, D. (2009), 'Big man on campus: interview with Mark Yudof', *New York Times*, September 24, http://www.nytimes.com/2009/09/27/magazine/27fob-q4-t.html. Accessed 8 February 2012.

Sondheim, S. (1973), 'Every day a little death', *A Little Night Music*, http://www.sondheimguide.com/nightrecs.html. Accessed 21 February 2012.

Sousa, C., de Nijs, W. and Hendriks, P. (2010), 'Secrets of the beehive: performance management in university research organizations', *Human Relations*, 63: 9, pp. 1439–1460.

Southey, R. (1819), *History of Brazil. Part the Third*, London: Longman, Hurst, Rees, and Orme.

Sparkes, A. (2007), 'Embodiment, academics, and the audit culture: a story seeking consideration', *Qualitative Research*, 7: 4, pp. 521–550.

Spengler, O. (1932), *The Decline of the West*, New York: Modern Library.

Spitzer, A.N. (2011), *Derrida, Myth and the Impossibility of Philosophy*, London: Continuum.

Steintrager, J. (2004), *Bentham*, London: Routledge.

Stewart, N. (1978), *The Power of Kroll Norman*, December 23, 1978–January 13, 1979, London: BBC

Stewart, S. (1991), *Crime of Writing: Problems in the Containment of Representation*, New York and Toronto: Oxford University Press.

—— (1993), *On Longing: Narratives Of The Miniature, The Gigantic, The Souvenir, The Collection*, Durham and London: Duke University Press.

Stinchcombe, A. (1994), 'Disintegrated disciplines and the future of sociology', *Sociological Forum*, 9: 2, pp. 279–291.

Stommel, J. (2007), '"Pity poor flesh": terrible bodies in the films of Carpenter, Cronenberg, and Romero', *Bright Lights Film Journal*, 56, http://www.brightlightsfilm.com/56/. Accessed 29 February 2012.

—— (2009), 'The dead things we already are: pod people, body snatching, and the horrors of business as usual', *Bright Lights Film Journal*, 66, http://www.brightlightsfilm.com/66/66deadthings.php. Accessed 2 March 2012.

Storey, J. (2001), *Cultural Theory and Popular Culture: An Introduction*, 3rd ed., Harlow, UK: Prentice Hall.

Strathern, M. (2000), 'The tyranny of transparency', *British Educational Research Journal*, 26: 3, pp. 309–321.

Stratton, J. (2011a), 'The trouble with zombies: bare life, *Muselmänner* and displaced people', *Somatechnics*, 1, pp. 188–208.

—— (2011b), 'Zombie trouble: zombie texts, bare life and displaced people', *European Journal of Cultural Studies*, 14: 3, pp. 265–281.

Suber, P. (2008), *SPARC Open Access Newsletter*, 124, http://legacy.earlham.edu/~peters/fos/newsletter/08-02-08.htm#gratis-libre. Accessed 18 February 2011.

Surowiecki, J. (2004), *The Wisdom of Crowds: Why the Many are Smarter than the Few and How Collective Wisdom Shapes Business, Economies, Societies, and Nations*, New York: Doubleday.

Sutherland-Smith, W., Saltmarsh, S. and Randell-Moon, H. (2011), 'Research mentoring on the edge: early career researchers and academic fringe-dwelling', *Higher Education Research and Development Society of Australasia (HERDSA) – 'Higher Education on the Edge'*, Gold Coast, Australia, July 4–7, Refereed Conference Proceedings.

Suttle, W. (1971), 'African religious survivals as factors in American slave revolts', *Journal of Negro History*, 56: 2, pp. 97–104.

Taussig, M. (1980), *The Devil and Commodity Fetishism in South America*, Chapel Hill: University of North Carolina Press.

Taylor, R. (2002), 'Fed – Gov't higher ed paper would deal a blow to uni education', *Australian Associated Press General News*, August 16.

TeacherTube (2007), *TeacherTube*, http://www1.teachertube.com/. Accessed 23 February 2012.

Telegraph, The (2010), 'University offers class on zombies', *The Telegraph*, September 7, http://www.telegraph.co.uk/news/worldnews/northamerica/usa/7988114/University-offers-class-on-zombies.html. Accessed 20 November 2010.

Terranova, T. (2004), *Network Culture: Politics for the Information Age*, London: Pluto Press.

Thacker, E. (2010), *After Life*, Chicago, IL: University of Chicago Press.

Thomas, M. (2011), 'Jeremy Bentham misread: an examination of Utilitarianism', *Summer Institute for the History of Economic Thought*, Jepson School of Leadership Studies, University of Richmond, Virginia, June 27, 2011, http://jepson.richmond.edu/conferences/adam-smith/paper11thomas.pdf. Accessed 12 December 2011.

Thomas, S. (2007), *Flight of the Living Dead*, USA: Imageworks Entertainment International.

Thompson, J.B. (2005), 'Survival strategies for academic publishing', *Publishing Research Quarterly*, 21: 4, pp. 3–10.

Thorkelson E. (2012), 'Research', *Decasia: Critique of Academic Culture*, http://decasia.org/research.html. Accessed 24 February 2012.

Thrower, S. (2006), 'Zombies', in J. Marriott and K. Newman (eds), *Horror: The Definitive Guide to the Cinema of Fear*, London: Andre Deutsch.

Timpane, J. (2011), 'Flashmob violence raises weighty questions', *Philadelphia Inquirer*, August 14, http://articles.philly.com/2011-08-14/news/29886718_1_social-media-flash-mob-facebook-and-other-services. Accessed 8 February 2012.

Tomkins, S. (1963), *Affect. Imagery. Consciousness*, vol. 2, New York: Springer Publishing Co.

Totmann, E.N. (2027), 'Zombies analyses and dissemination', *Gapminder Studies: Unveiling the Beauty of Statistics for a Fact Based World View*, 1: 3, pp. 33–46.

Tourneur, J. (1943), *I Walked With a Zombie*, USA: RKO Radio Pictures.

Trotter, D. (2001), *Paranoid Modernism: Literary Experiment, Psychosis, and the Professionalization of English Society*, New York: Oxford University Press.

Trounsen, A, (2010), 'UK crisis sounds a warning to sector', *The Australian*, December 15, http://www.theaustralian.com.au/higher-education/uk-crisis-sounds-a-warning-to-sector/story-e6frgcjx-1225971175557. Accessed 15 February 2012.

Trounson, A. (2009), 'Union in $223m bid for uni jobs', *The Australian*, January 21, http://www.theaustralian.com.au/higher-education/union-in-223m-bid-for-uni-jobs/story-e6frgcjx-1111118616783. Accessed 7 July 2011.

Truffin, S. (2008), *Schoolhouse Gothic: Haunted Hallways and Predatory Pedagogues in Late Twentieth-Century American Literature and Scholarship*, Newcastle upon Tyne: Cambridge Scholars Publishing.

Tudor, A. (1989), *Monsters and Mad Scientists: A Cultural History of the Horror Movie*, Oxford: Blackwell Publishing.

TvFix (2011), 'Golden Globes 2011: TV nominations and predictions', http://www.yourtv.com.au/mobile/blog.aspx?blogentryid=760841&showcomments=true. Accessed 1 January 2010.

Twohy, M. (2008), *From Voodoo to Viruses: The Evolution of the Zombie in Twentieth Century Popular Culture*, Dublin: Trinity College.

Udemy (2011) 'Academy of you', http://www.udemy.com/. Accessed 23 February 2012.

Universities and Colleges Union (2011), '30 November: Defend public sector pensions', http://www.ucu.org.uk/30nov2011. Accessed 25 February 2012.

Universities UK (2010), 'Preventing a funding crisis in higher education', *Universities UK*, http://www.universitiesuk.ac.uk/PolicyAndResearch/PolicyAreas/Funding-and-Management/Pages/Preventingafundingcrisis.aspx. Accessed 20 February 2012.

University of Melbourne (2010), 'Collective agreement', *University of Melbourne*, http://www.hr.unimelb.edu.au/__data/assets/pdf_file/0015/321144/University_of_Melbourne_Collective_Agreement_2010_incl_signatures.pdf. Accessed 21 June 2011.

University of Sydney (2009), 'Enterprise agreement 2009–2012', *University of Sydney*, http://sydney.edu.au/staff/enterprise_agreement/documents/University_of_Sydney_Enterprise_Agreement_2009-2012_FINAL.pdf. Accessed 21 June 2011.

Valentino, S. (2010), *How to be a Zombie: The Essential Guide for Anyone Who Craves Brains*, New York: Random House.

Valve. (2008). *Left 4 Dead*. Xbox 360. USA: Valve Corp.

Van Maanen, J. (1979), 'The fact of fiction in organizational ethnography', *Administrative Science Quarterly*, 24: 4, pp. 539–550.

Vandermensbrugghe, J. (2004), 'The unbearable vagueness of critical thinking in the context of the Anglo-Saxonisation of education', *International Education Journal*, 5: 3, pp. 417–422.

Vecchio, R. (2019), 'Viral Z outbreak: reviewing the ethnographic literature', *New Anthropological Quarterly*, 5: 3, pp. 21–40.

Vidovich, L. and Currie, J. (2011), 'Governance and trust in higher education', *Studies in Higher Education*, 36: 1, pp. 43–56.

Voyce, M. (2006), 'Shopping malls in Australia: the end of public space and the rise of "consumerist citizenship"', *Journal of Sociology*, 42: 3, pp. 269–289.

Wacquant, L. (2004), 'Critical thought as solvent of doxa', *Constellations*, 11: 1, pp. 97–101.

Walker, S. (1995), *Jung and the Jungians on Myth: An Introduction*, New York: Garland.

Walters, W.H. (2007), 'Institutional journal costs in an open access environment', *Journal of the American Society for Information Science and Technology*, 58:1, pp. 108–120.

Wan, J. (2004), *Saw*, USA: Evolution Entertainment and Twisted Pictures.

Warwick, K. (2004), *I Cyborg*, Champaign, IL: University of Illinois Press.

Webb, J. and Byrnand, S. (2008), 'Some kind of virus: the zombie as body and as trope', *Body and Society*, 14: 2, pp. 83–98.

Weber, M. (1968), *Economy and Society: An Outline of Interpretive Sociology, Three volumes*, New York: Bedminster.

Weed, C. (2009), *The Zombie Manifesto: The Marxist Revolutions in George A. Romero's Land of the Dead*, M.A. thesis, Waco, TX: Baylor University.

Weller, M. (2007), *Virtual Learning Environments: Using, Choosing and Developing Your VLE*, London: Routledge.

Wellman, B. and Haythornthwaite, C. (eds) (2002), *The Internet in Everyday Life*, Oxford: Blackwell.

Welsh, P. (2010), 'Video and pictures: 1,000 zombies take to the streets', *Manchester Evening News*, November 1, http://menmedia.co.uk/manchestereveningnews/news/s/1361295_video_and_pictures_1000_zombies_take_to_the_streets. Accessed 8 February 2012.

Wesch, M. (2007), 'A vision of students today', *Kansas State University*, http://www.youtube.com/watch?v=dGCJ46vyR9o. Accessed 1 March 2012.

Wesley, M. (1993), *Refusal and Transgression in Joyce Carol Oates' Fiction*, Westport, CT: Greenwood Press.

West, E.G. (1992), 'The Benthamites as educational engineers: the reputation and the record', *History of Political Economy*, 24: 3, pp. 595–621.

Wharton, S. (2010), 'Critical text analysis: linking language and cultural studies', *ELT Journal*, 68: 1, pp. 1–9.

Widdicombe, L. (2012), 'The plagiarist's tale', *The New Yorker*, February 13–20, pp. 52–59.

Williams, A. and Walsh, S. (2025a), 'The decline and fall of the Silicon Valley', in P. Williams (ed.), *Death and Dying in the Dead Ages*, New, New York: Joenes and Daughters, pp. 402–432.

────── (2025b), 'The North American rescue centres and the green power movement,' in P. Williams (ed.), *Death and Dying in the Dead Ages*, New York: Joenes and Daughters, pp. 256–271.

Williams, E. (2010), *Combined and Uneven Apocalypse,* Winchester: Zero Books.

Wilson, T.V. (2009), 'How zombies work', *How Stuff Works,* http://science.howstuffworks.com/zombie.htm. Accessed 29 February 2012.

Winter, R. (1995), 'The University of Life plc: the "industrialisation" of higher education', in J. Smyth (ed.), *Academic Work: The Changing Labour Process in Higher Education*, Buckingham: Society for Research into Higher Education and Open University Press, pp. 129–143.

Witt, A. (2004), *Resident Evil: Apocalypse,* Germany/France/UK/Canada: Constantin Film Produktion.

Wittgenstein, L. (2001), *Tractatus Logico-Philosophicus*, London: Routledge.

────── (2009), *Philosophical Investigations,* trans. G. Anscombe, P. Hacker and J. Schulte, Oxford: Blackwell.

Wood, F. (2010), 'Occult innovations in higher education: corporate magic and the mysteries of managerialism', *Prometheus*, 28: 3, pp. 227–244

Wright, E. (2004), *Shaun of the Dead*, UK/France/USA: Universal Pictures.

Wright, J. (2009), *Tormented*, UK: BBC Films.

Wylie, T. (1964), 'Ro–Langs: The Tibetan zombie', *History of Religions*, 4: 1, pp. 69–80.

Yale University (2012) 'Open Yale courses', http://oyc.yale.edu/about. Accessed 23 February 2012.

Yeatman, A. (1990), *Bureaucrats, Technocrats, Femocrats: Essays on the Contemporary Australian State*, Sydney: Allen and Unwin.

Young, V. (2004), 'Your average nigga', *College Composition and Communication,* 55: 4, pp. 693–715.

Zangrando, R. (1991), 'Historians' procedures for handling plagiarism', *Publishing Research Quarterly*, 7: 4, pp. 57–64.

Zombiepedia (2025), 'Viral Z and the zombie apocalypse', http://en.zombiepedia/wiki/zombie apocalypse. Accessed 12 February 2028.

Zook, M. and Graham, M. (2007), 'Mapping DigiPlace: geocoded internet data and the representation of place', *Environment and Planning B: Planning and Design*, 34: 3, pp. 466–482.

────── (2010), 'Featured graphic: the virtual 'bible belt', *Environment and Planning A*, 42:.4, pp. 763–764.

Zook, M., Graham, M., Shelton, T. and Gorman, S. (2010), 'Volunteered geographic information and crowdsourcing disaster relief: a case study of the Haitian earthquake', *World Medical and Health Policy*, 2: 2, pp. 7–33.

Zuiker A. (2000–2012), *CSI: Crime Scene Investigation,* USA: Jerry Bruckheimer Television.

Zuko, F. (2020), 'Who said that: a literature review', *Journal of International Zombie Studies*, 4: 16, pp. 1003–2001.

List of contributors

Kristian Adamson, University of Sydney, Australia.
Kristian is a full-time member of general staff and a postgraduate research student at the University of Sydney. His research centres on gendered divisions of creative labour in Hollywood.

David Beer, University of York, United Kingdom.
David's research focuses upon popular culture, particularly in relation to new media and sound. His publications include *New Media: The Key Concepts* (2008, coauthored with Nick Gane), and recent articles in the journals *Mobilities*, *Sociology*, *Cultural Sociology*, *Sociological Research Online*, *New Media and Society*, *City*, and the *International Journal of Urban and Regional Research*.

Gordon S. Carlson, Society for Conceptual Logistics in Communication Research, United States.
Gordon has taught in the areas of persuasive, organizational and technological communication for universities in Oregon, Chicago, Hawaii and Kansas, with recent work in mass media and media literacy. While working in the Electronic Visualization Lab at the University of Illinois at Chicago, Gordon was a member of the National Science Foundation funded Project Lifelike, where he worked with a team to develop realistic avatars that can function as intelligent interfaces for complex computer systems. This work was highlighted in popular media outlets including the PBS program *NOVA scienceNOW*, the Discovery Channel's *PopSci's Future Of: Immortal Avatars*, and the book *Infinite Reality*. His work with the Society for Conceptual Logistics in Communication Research focuses on leveraging social and web technologies so that students and faculty can work together on 'conceptual logistics' – the use of terminology in the trans-disciplinary study of human communication.

Ann Deslandes, Sydney, Australia.
Ann is a researcher, writer and community services worker in Sydney. She has a Ph.D. in Gender and Cultural Studies from the University of Sydney and has worked variously as a casual administrator, research assistant, tutor and lecturer at five Australian universities. Other publications include 'Giving way at the intersection: Anticolonial feminist ethics of solidarity in the global justice movement' in *Australian Feminist Studies* (2009).

Martin Paul Eve, University of Sussex, United Kingdom.
Martin is an associate tutor and lecturer in English Literature at the University of Sussex. His research interests span from the novels of Thomas Pynchon, Don DeLillo and David Foster Wallace, through to the philosophy of Ludwig Wittgenstein and Michel Foucault, the critical theory of the Frankfurt school, critical university studies, and open access technology. Martin is the founding editor of the open access journal *Orbit: Writing Around Pynchon*, and has worked extensively on the interdisciplinary-studies journal *Excursions*, at Sussex. Martin regularly writes online for the *Guardian Higher Education* network and on his own blog, at https://www.martineve.com.

Sara Felix, University College London, Kazakhstan.
Sara is a doctoral candidate at the University of Sussex, where she is studying international education. She is also a Teaching Fellow in English for Academic Purposes for University College, London's Centre for Preparatory Studies in Astana, Kazakhstan, where she aids in the design and teaching of a research course for pre-university students focused on encouraging critical thinking, argumentation and learner autonomy. Her other research interests include the use of online course management systems and their impacts on non-native speakers' learning in university courses. Sara has worked previously at Istanbul Bilgi University and National-Louis University's Poland campus.

Mark Graham, Oxford Internet Institute, United Kingdom.
Mark is a Research Fellow at the Oxford Internet Institute. His research focuses on Internet and information geographies, and the overlaps between ICTs and economic development. Mark's work on the geographies of the Internet examines how people and places are ever more defined by, and made visible through, not only their traditional physical locations and properties, but also their virtual attributes and digital shadows. His writing has been featured in media outlets including *The Guardian*, *The New York Times* and *Wired*; his most recent work can be accessed on his website (geospace.co.uk) and blogs (zerogeography.net and floatingsheep.org).

Howard M. Gregory II, Western Reserve University, United States.
Howard holds an undergraduate degree in Computer Information Systems and completed a Master of Science degree in Knowledge Management via the Kent State University IAKM program. A case study on social network learning and international collaboration in virtual worlds he coauthored was published in *Teaching Arts & Science With the New Social Media* (2011). He is currently a Standardized Patient Trainer/Coordinator for the Mount Sinai Skills and Simulation Center of Case Western Reserve University School of Medicine in Cleveland, Ohio. Howard's ultimate goal is to begin working towards an Ed.D. with a focus in educational technology.

Rowena Harper, University of Canberra, Australia.
Rowena is the Director of the Academic Skills Centre at the University of Canberra, and Vice President of the Association for Academic Language and Learning (AALL). She has taught in a range of university contexts, from enabling programmes to staff development courses, but her area of interest lies in embedding skills and literacies into the curriculum. Her early research focused on first year and scaffolding academic literacy skills during transition. More recently, she has published on English language policy and worked on cross-institutional research examining the integration into the curriculum of research skill development.

Annie Jeffrey, Boise State University, United States.
Annie is an experienced educational technologist and social media and virtual worlds educator. She is currently studying for her doctorate at Boise State University. She holds a Bachelor and Master of Arts in Archaeology and a Master of Science in Interactive Multimedia Production. Her other interests include the senses in learning, pedagogy of sound and virtual museums. She recently coauthored a case study on social network learning and international collaboration in virtual worlds in Charles Wankel's *Teaching Arts and Science with the New Social Media*.

Shaun Kimber, Bournemouth University, United Kingdom.
Shaun is a Senior Lecturer in media theory in the Media School at Bournemouth University. His main research interests include film violence and censorship, audience research and film cultures, and media and film pedagogies. His book *Henry: Portrait of a Serial Killer* (2011) was one of the launch titles for a new series, 'Controversies', published by Palgrave Macmillan. Other recent publications include 'Valuing Violent Films: an investigation into the inclusion of film violence within the undergraduate programme', in *Valuing Film: Shifting Perceptions of Worth* (2011); and 'Controlling Passions: the regulation, censorship and classification of *The Passion of the Christ* within the British context' in *Holy Terror: Understanding Religion and Violence in Popular Culture* (2010). Shaun's current research activities include a journal article exploring the possibilities for and limits upon transgression within *Srpski Film/A Serbian Film*; a project examining the relationship between theory and practice in the writing of horror screenplays; an investigation into food and eating within the contemporary horror film; and a book project exploring fictional representations of snuff within world cinema.

Hans Petter Langtangen, Simula Research Laboratory and University of Oslo, Norway.
Hans Petter is director of the Centre for Biomedical Computing, a Norwegian Centre of Excellence doing inter-disciplinary research in the intersection of mathematics, physics, computer science, geoscience and medicine. He is on 80% leave from a position as Professor of Computer Science at the University of Oslo. His scientific speciality is mathematical modelling. Hans is deeply passionate about describing the world by mathematics and

conquering equations on the computer to create realistic, virtual worlds. Although he has not yet watched a complete zombie movie, he is very confident about the mathematics of zombie behaviour.

Sarah Juliet Lauro, University of California at Davis, United States.
Sarah is the coauthor of 'A Zombie Manifesto: The Nonhuman Condition in the Era of Advanced Capitalism', published in the journal *boundary 2* in 2008, coeditor of *Better Off Dead: The Evolution of the Zombie as Posthuman*, published by Fordham Uuniversity Press in 2011, and recently completed her doctorate, an intellectual history of the zombie myth, at the University of California at Davis, where she currently serves as a postdoctoral lecturer in the English department.

Kent-Andre Mardal, Simula Research Laboratory and University of Oslo, Norway.
Kent-Andre is a Senior Research Scientist at Simula Research Laboratory and an adjunct Associate Professor of Computer Science at the University of Oslo, studying computational methods for differential equations with particular focus on the mechanics of the human brain. Recently, his research has concerned some biomedical applications of blood flow in the brain and its association with the development and rupture of aneurysms. Kent-Andre is also an enthusiastic consumer of science fiction and horror books and movies, with a special taste for zombies.

Daniel Marshall, Deakin University, Australia.
Daniel is a Senior Lecturer in the School of Education, Faculty of Arts and Education at Deakin University, Melbourne, Australia. Daniel conducts research focused on sexualities, publishing in the fields of queer studies, cultural studies, history, education and social policy. He has a doctorate in Cultural Studies from the University of Melbourne, is President of the Australian Lesbian and Gay Archives and Associate Editor of *Critical Studies in Education*.

Jonathan Paul Marshall, University of Technology Sydney, Australia.
Jonathan is an ARC funded QEII fellow at the University of Technology Sydney. He is an anthropologist currently working on the disorder caused by, and entering into, the making of software. This project has branched out into looking at the importance of disorder in society generally, and how systems of ordering create the disorder which either subverts them or is used to justify them. His book, *Living on Cybermind*, is an ethnography of life on the internet mailing list Cybermind between 1994 and 2007. Another ARC research grant supported investigation of gender online and resulted in the 'Cybermind Gender Project', a special issue of the *Transforming Cultures E-journal*. He has also written about the psychology of climate change, edited *Depth Psychology, Disorder and Climate Change*, and studied the history of alchemy in the UK. He also tries to write novels and is a failed avant-rock musician, who has been watching *Dr Who* since it started and would love to have found a Tardis.

Holly Randell-Moon, Macquarie University, Australia.
Holly teaches cultural studies at Macquarie University, Australia. She has published on race, religion and secularism in the journals *Critical Race and Whiteness Studies*, *borderlands*, and *Social Semiotics*, and in the edited book collections *Religion, Spirituality and the Social Sciences* (2008), and *Mediating Faiths* (2010). Her publications on popular culture, gender and sexuality have appeared in the edited book collection *Common Sense: Intelligence as Presented on Popular Television* (2008) and the journals *Topic: The Washington & Jefferson College Review* and *Feminist Media Studies*.

Christopher Moore, Deakin University, Australia.
Christopher is a Lecturer in Media and Communication at Deakin University, Melbourne Australia. He has previously published research on intellectual property and copyright, e-waste, video games digital distribution, machinima and academic integrity. His current research explores the role of affect in military FPS games, the construction of online personae across multiple social and digital media networks, and looks to the role of online personae in the indie and independent cultures of video game production. Most recently, he has published on issues of the 'mobility of play' in *Convergence: The International Journal of Research into New Media Technologies*. He has an obsession for virtual hats and zombie survival games.

Christian McCrea, RMIT University, Australia.
Christian is an essayist who publishes on videogames, animation, film, philosophy and digital culture. His work also includes design and scriptwriting for videogames. He works in RMIT University's games design research environment, and can be contacted at christian@christianmccrea.net.

Nick Pearce, Durham University, United Kingdom.
Nick is a social sciences teaching fellow at Durham University, teaching classes in anthropology and sociology. His research interests lie in critically examining the uptake and use of new technologies by academics, and the effects of this on scholarship practice. He is also interested in the use of critical theory to examine and critique technological determinism. As well as being interested in new technologies, he is also interested in resurrecting old technologies, such as his C64 and Nintendo Game Boy, and finding contemporary uses for these zombie machines.

George Pfau, www.georgepfau.com.
George is an artist working in a variety of media with the notion of the zombie as his central focus. He grew up in San Francisco, received a BA from New York University, and in 2010, an MFA from California College of the Arts. George is currently Instructor of Art at San Francisco University High School, and Mentor at California College of the Arts. George's essay for *Zombies in the Academy* stems from his MFA thesis, and is the basis of a slideshow performance/lecture entitled 'Zombies, identified'. Various iterations of this slideshow have

been presented at Observatory (New York), Unspeakable Projects (San Francisco), The Wassaic Project (New York), Macarthur B Arthur (Oakland), Broward College (Florida), Cal Arts and at California College of the Arts. He is currently embroiled in several new zombie art projects that will stagger into the world sometime soon.

Pål Røtnes, Simula Research Laboratory, Norway.
Pål is educated in computer science and information technology, and when not contributing to scientific papers on zombies he works in the ITC division of Simula Research Laboratory. He has a deep interest in and extensive knowledge of both classical and modern zombie lore.

Sue Saltmarsh, Australian Catholic University, Australia.
Sue is Associate Professor of Educational Studies at the Australian Catholic University in Sydney, Australia. Her research in higher education concerns the intersection of policy contexts, economic discourse, institutional cultures and subjectivities. Recent publications in *Cultural Studies Review* and *Ethics and Education* consider how economic discourse, research leadership and policy implementation shape subjectivities, academic work and university cultures. She is Reviews Editor for the *Australian Educational Researcher*, and founding coeditor of *Global Studies of Childhood*.

Taylor Shelton, University of Kentucky, United States.
Taylor is a Ph.D. student in the Graduate School of Geography at Clark University in Worcester, MA. Prior to coming to Clark, Taylor earned BA and MA degrees in geography from the University of Kentucky. His research interests lie primarily in the socio-spatial dimensions of technology, with particular attention to internet geographies and emerging forms of user-generated geographic information.

David Slattery, National College of Art and Design, Ireland.
David is a social anthropologist and author. His anthropological writings embrace a wide range of contemporary topics from weddings to public transport. He wrote *How To Be Irish: Uncovering the Curiosities of Irish Behaviour* (2011), and is currently working on a popular history of lesser known Irish men and women. He has an MA in the Philosophy of Science from University College Cork. His doctorate, from the University of St. Andrews in Scotland, examines the application of Foucault's archaeology to classic social anthropological method. David provides Quality Assurance and Course Design consultancy to the tertiary education sector in Ireland.

James J. Sosnoski, University of Illinois at Chicago, United States.
James is the author of *Token Professionals and Master Critics* and *Modern Skeletons in Postmodern Closets*, and coeditor of *Configuring History: Teaching the Harlem Renaissance through VR Cityscapes* as well as various essays on instructional technology, computer-assisted pedagogy and online collaboration. With David Downing, he coedited 'The Geography

of Cyberspace', 'Conversations in Honor of James Berlin' and 'The TicToc Conversations' – special issues of *Works and Days*. He has been a member of the MLA's Delegate Assembly, Ethics Committee and Emerging Technologies Committee. He coordinated the Virtual Harlem project (98-2004), an instructional technology project using virtual reality scenarios. His current research focus is on conceptual logistics – the study of the uses of research concepts. He is the President of the Society for Conceptual Logistics in Communication Studies (SCLCR).

Jesse Stommel, Marylhurst University, United States.
Jesse's work runs the gamut from Shakespeare to postmodernism to horror film. His scholarship focuses on film theory, body horror, new media and digital pedagogy. He received his doctorate in 2010 from the English Department at the University of Colorado at Boulder. He is currently Assistant Professor of English and Digital Humanities at Marylhurst University in Portland, OR, and Director of the English and Digital Humanities online degree program at Marylhurst, which is pioneering approaches to student interaction in digital space. His professional web site, with links to his curriculum vitae and current classes can be found at www.jessestommel.com. He is coeditor of *Hybrid Pedagogy: A Digital Journal of Teaching & Technology*, online at www.hybridpedagogy.com.

Wendy Sutherland-Smith, Deakin University, Australia.
Wendy is a Senior Lecturer at the Institute of Teaching and Learning, Deakin University, Australia. Although her background is in Law, she has been actively researching the concept of embodied justice in higher education for over a decade, particularly in issues of academic integrity, higher education policy and practice, technologies in teaching, and ethical relationships in higher education between staff /students and institutions/academic community. In the area of academic integrity, she has published a book, *Plagiarism, the Internet and Student Learning: Improving Academic Integrity* (2008), and more recently papers in the journals *Semiotica* (2011), and the *Journal of Higher Education Policy and Management* (2010). Wendy's recent work in higher education policy and practice has appeared in the *Qualitative Review Journal* (2011), *Social Alternatives* (2011) and in special issues of *Ethics and Education* (2011) and the *London Review of Education* (2010).

Elaine Tan, Durham University, United Kingdom.
Elaine is a learning technologist in the Computing and Information Service of Durham University. She is completing a doctorate in technology enhanced learning at Lancaster University, and her research interests surround the adoption of technology to support teaching practice by early career staff.

Sherry R. Truffin, Campbell University, North Carolina, United States.
Sherry is an Associate Professor of English at Campbell University in Buies Creek, North Carolina, where she teaches courses in American Literature, Rhetoric and Composition and

Modern/Contemporary Fiction. Her first monograph, *Schoolhouse Gothic: Haunted Hallways and Predatory Pedagogues in Late Twentieth-Century American Literature and Scholarship,* was published in 2008. In addition, she has published essays on the television series *The X-Files,* and on James Baldwin, Stephen King and Chuck Palahniuk. She has also presented papers at both national and regional conferences on works by Toni Morrison, Alice Walker, Flannery O'Connor, Bret Easton Ellis and Lydia Davis. Upcoming essays on Gothic metafiction and on Edgar Allan Poe are scheduled for publication, and she and coeditor James Rovira are at work on an anthology of essays that historicize the writings of key figures in literary interpretation and theory.

Ruth Walker, University of Wollongong, Australia.
Ruth teaches academic writing in the Faculty of Creative Arts and the Sydney Business School at the University of Wollongong. She has previously coedited the books *Masochism* (1999) and *Anatomies of Violence* (2001). Ruth is currently co-chair of the Asia Pacific Forum of Educational Integrity (APFEI), and is working on an Australian Learning and Teaching Council (ALTC/OLT) Priority Project on 'Academic Integrity: Aligning Policy and Practice in Australian Higher Education' (2010–12). For APFEI, she coordinated the student video competition 'zombies and plagiarism': www.apfei.edu.au/activities/competition/2011. html. She is currently working on her monograph *Remix Australia: Plagiarism, Appropriation and Cultural Citation.*

Andrew Whelan, University of Wollongong, Australia.
Andrew teaches in the sociology program at the University of Wollongong. He has research interests in subculture, popular music, computer-mediated communication, social interaction and organization and social theory. He is the author of *Breakcore: Identity and Interaction on Peer-to-Peer* (2008), and has contributions in the edited collections *Being Cultural* (2011), *Cybersounds* (2006) and *Dichotonies* (2009).

Rowan Wilken, Swinburne University of Technology, Australia.
Rowan is a Lecturer in Media and Communications at Swinburne University of Technology. His present research interests include domestic technology use, digital technologies and culture, mobile and locative media, old and new media and theories and practices of everyday life. He is the author of *Teletechnologies, Place, and Community* (2011), and is coeditor of the *Mobile Technology and Place* collection (2012). He can be contacted at rwilken@swin.edu.au.

Matthew Zook, University of Kentucky, United States.
Matthew is an Associate Professor in Geography at the University of Kentucky. His interests centre on the impact of technology and innovation on human geography, including geographies of e-commerce, software-created spaces, Internet geographies, networks of global air travel and user-generated information about places. He has published in the

Annals of the Association of American Geographers, Journal of Economic Geography, GeoForum, Environment and Planning A, Journal of Transportation Geography, and *International Journal of Urban and Regional Research.* His first book, *The Geography of the Internet Industry: Venture Capital, Dot-coms and Local Knowledge,* was published in 2005. More information is available at www.zook.info (website) and www.floatingsheep.org (blog). His preferred anti-zombie tool is the machete, but he is actively exploring novel uses of flamethrowers as well.

Index

H

Habermas, Jurgen 194, 201
habitus 71, 72, 95
Haiti 136, 141, 142, 293, 317, 327, 328
Haitian 57, 95, 123, 141, 142, 207, 283, 290, 293, 317
Halberstam, Judith 226, 227, 272
Halloween 153, 285, 287
happiness 13, 16–19, 21, 25, 50, 83, 127, 145, 210
Haraway, Donna 124, 126–130
Hardt, Michael 127
Harman, Chris 56, 150, 192
headless 23, 177
Hearn, Lafcadio 122, 123
heteronormalcy 222, 223
Holloway, Julian 50
homeless 8, 126, 309–319
homophobia 220–222, 226
homosexuality 219, 220, 222, 223, 225, 226
Horkheimer, Max 34, 194, 201
horror 8, 29, 30, 34, 93–97, 159, 164, 178, 213, 237, 270, 292, 300
human 18, 20, 22, 36, 46, 50, 56, 57, 64, 70, 77, 97, 98, 102, 103, 123–132, 135, 136, 140, 142, 156, 159, 164, 169, 178, 192, 205, 208, 210, 212, 240, 245, 247–263, 267, 269, 270–272, 274, 282, 292, 295, 311, 312–314, 316–318, 323–326
humanities 42, 44, 51 70, 74, 112, 235, 300, 302
hybrid 121, 126, 127, 134, 135, 150, 234, 273, 275, 329
hyper-citation 7, 183, 184

I

I Walked With a Zombie (Tourneur, 1943) 145, 237
ideology 29, 31, 35, 36, 44, 45, 47, 49, 69, 76, 95, 98, 107, 109, 122, 194, 198
illusion of life 48, 50
immaterial 4, 7, 74, 96, 98–101, 103, 270

Impact Factor 107, 110
Internet Relay Chat (IRC) 113
'In the region of ice' (Oates, 1967) 206
individualization 98
infected 56, 65, 76, 103, 165, 192, 193, 200, 237, 238, 247–255, 260–262, 313, 318, 324, 325, 330
infrastructure 113, 114, 235, 299
instrumentalization 17, 19, 20, 24, 63, 316
integrity 103, 177, 178, 179, 180
intellectual property 97, 99–103, 183

J

Jackson, Michael 287, 292–293
job security 62, 75, 76
Jung, Carl 122, 136, 182

K

Kaplan, Louise 212, 213
Kirkman, Robert 103, 156, 270
knowledge work 42, 97, 224, 227
Kristeva, Julia 30, 34, 35, 95

L

labour 4, 16, 20, 36, 41, 42, 44–48, 52, 55, 57–60, 62, 70, 72, 74–76, 94, 98, 99, 100, 101, 102, 103, 133–135, 140, 191, 193, 195, 196, 223, 317, 330
LaCapra, Dominick 47
Land of the Dead (Romero, 2005) 36, 70, 71, 234, 236, 237, 239, 240
Larsen, Lars Bang 34, 37, 74, 75, 76, 96, 99, 100
'Last days' (Oates, 1985) 206
Lather, Patti 35, 38
laughter 219, 220, 228
Lauro, Sarah Juliet 7, 29, 34, 74, 95, 96, 141, 279, 282, 283
Lawrence, D.H. 209, 210, 212
learning 3, 7, 8, 31, 34, 36, 57, 61, 94, 97, 103, 137, 139–145, 149, 159, 164, 165, 166, 170, 177, 183, 192, 195–202, 215, 221,